Understanding and Using

Microsoft® Word

for Windows® 95

Emily M. Ketcham
Hankamer School of Business
Baylor University

WEST PUBLISHING COMPANY
Minneapolis/St. Paul • New York
Los Angeles • San Francisco

WEST'S COMMITMENT TO THE ENVIRONMENT

In 1906, West Publishing Company began recycling materials left over from the production of books. This began a tradition of efficient and responsible use of resources. Today, 100% of our legal bound volumes are printed on acid-free, recycled paper consisting of 50% new paper pulp and 50% paper that has undergone a de-inking process. We also use vegetable-based inks to print all of our books. West recycles nearly 27,700,000 pounds of scrap paper annually—the equivalent of 229,300 trees. Since the 1960s, West has devised ways to capture and recycle waste inks, solvents, oils, and vapors created in the printing process. We also recycle plastics of all kinds, wood, glass, corrugated cardboard, and batteries, and have eliminated the use of polystyrene book packaging. We at West are proud of the longevity and the scope of our commitment to the environment.

West pocket parts and advance sheets are printed on recyclable paper and can be collected and recycled with newspapers. Staples do not have to be removed. Bound volumes can be recycled after removing the cover.

Production, Prepress, Printing, and Binding by West Publishing Company
Project Management by Labrecque Publishing Services

 Text Is Printed on 10% Post Consumer Recycled Paper

Microsoft®, MS-DOS®, and Windows® are registered trademarks of Microsoft Corporation. Macintosh and TrueType are trademarks for Apple Computer, Inc. Arial and Times New Roman are registered trademarks of The Monotype Corporation PLC. Helvetica and Palatino are registered trademarks of Linotype AB and its subsidiaries. IBM is a registered trademark of International Business Machines Corporation. PostScript is a registered trademark of Adobe Systems Incorporated. TIFF is a trademark of Aldus Corporation. Harvard Graphics is a registered trademark of Software Publishing Corporation. Avery is a registered trademark of Avery Denison Corporation.

Copyright ©1996 by WEST PUBLISHING COMPANY
610 Opperman Drive
P.O. Box 64526
St. Paul, MN 55164-0526

Library of Congress Cataloging-in-Publication Data

Ketcham, Emily
    Understanding and using Microsoft Word for Windows 95
        p.   cm.
    Includes index.
    ISBN 0-314-07235-7 (soft : alk. paper)
    1. Microsoft Word for Windows. 2. Word processing.
Z52.5.M523K483   1996
652.5'536—dc20   95-46586
                                                              CIP

British Library Cataloguing-in-Publication Data. A catalogue record for this book is available from the British Library.

Contents

Preface, xiii
Publisher's Note, xvii
About the Author, xxiv

Word Processing Basics   1

INTRODUCTION TO WINDOWS   2

Learning Objectives   2
Important Commands   3
What Is Windows 95?   3
Windows 95 Interface   3
    Working with the Mouse   4
Guided Activity 1: Starting Windows 95   5
    The Windows Desktop   6
Guided Activity 2: Mousing Around   7
    Components of a Window   9
Guided Activity 3: Manipulating a Window   11
Multitasking   15
    Starting Programs   15
Guided Activity 4: Starting Programs   17
    Using the Keyboard   18
Sharing Data   18
Guided Activity 5: Copying and Moving   19
Doing Difficult Things Easily   21
    Customizing Windows Properties   22
Guided Activity 6: Customizing the Mouse   22
    Customizing the Desktop   25
Guided Activity 7: Customizing Desktop Properties   25
    Shortcuts   28
Guided Activity 8: Creating Shortcuts on the Desktop   28
Exiting Windows   30
Guided Activity 9: Exiting Windows   30
Summary   30
Exercise 1: A Day in the Life of a College Student   31
Exercise 2: Serious Business   32
Review Questions   34
Key Terms   36

UNIT 1 / RUNNING START   38

Learning Objectives   38
Using Microsoft Word   38

Guided Activity 1.1: Setting Up the Word Screen 40
Guided Activity 1.2: Entering Text 41
Guided Activity 1.3: Formatting the Business Card 43
Guided Activity 1.4: Enhancing the Design 44
Guided Activity 1.5: Changing Text 47
    Executing Commands from the Keyboard 47
Guided Activity 1.6: Executing Commands Using the Keyboard 48
Guided Activity 1.7: Getting Help 48
Summary 52
Review Questions 52
Key Terms 53

UNIT 2 / ENTERING AND EDITING TEXT **54**
Learning Objectives 54
Important Commands 55
Entering Text 55
Guided Activity 2.1: Entering Text 56
Reviewing the Document 58
Guided Activity 2.2: Moving Within a Document Using the Keyboard 59
Guided Activity 2.3: Moving Within a Document Using the Mouse 61
Editing Text 61
Guided Activity 2.4: Using Overtype and Insert 62
Selecting Text 63
Guided Activity 2.5: Selecting Text Using the Keyboard 63
Guided Activity 2.6: Selecting Text Using the Mouse 64
Delete and Undo 66
Guided Activity 2.7: Deleting and Undeleting 67
Saving the Document 67
Guided Activity 2.8: Saving Files 68
Summary 69
Exercises 69
Exercise 2.1: A Day in the Life of a College Student 70
Exercise 2.2: Crusty's Pizza 71
Exercise 2.3: The Internet 72
Exercise 2.4: Thrill Seeker Tours 73
Review Questions 74
Key Terms 75

APPLICATION A / CREATING A NAME TENT **76**

UNIT 3 / DOCUMENTS AND DISKS **77**
Learning Objectives 77
Important Commands 78
Disks and File Names 78
    Types of Disks 79

Preparing Disks for Use   80
Guided Activity 3.1: Formatting a Disk   81
Files and File Names   82
The File Menu   83
File | New   83
Guided Activity 3.2: Creating New Files   85
File | Close   87
Guided Activity 3.3: Closing Files   88
File | Open   88
Guided Activity 3.4: Opening Files   90
Searching for Files   92
Guided Activity 3.5: Searching for a File   93
Cut, Copy, and Paste   93
Guided Activity 3.6: Copying and Moving Text   95
File | Save As   97
The Automatic Save Feature   97
Backing Up Files and Disks   98
Guided Activity 3.7: Making a Backup Copy of a Single File   100
Guided Activity 3.8: Making a Backup Copy of a Floppy Disk   100
Summary   101
Exercise 3.1: Using the File Commands   102
Exercise 3.2: Using Cut, Copy, and Paste   103
Exercise 3.3: Backing Up a Single Document and a Floppy Disk   103
Review Questions   104
Key Terms   105

UNIT 4 / PROOFING TOOLS   106
Learning Objectives   106
Important Commands   107
Spell Checking   107
Automatic Spell Checking   107
Guided Activity 4.1: Turning on Automatic Spell Checking   108
Guided Activity 4.2: Working with Automatic Spell Checking   109
AutoCorrect   110
Guided Activity 4.3: Watching AutoCorrect Work   110
Guided Activity 4.4: Customizing the AutoCorrect Tool   111
Checking Spelling All at Once   112
Guided Activity 4.5: Checking Spelling All at Once   113
Limitations   115
Grammar Checking   116
Guided Activity 4.6: Using the Grammar Checker   117
Readability Statistics   118
The Thesaurus   118
Guided Activity 4.7: Using the Thesaurus   119
Search and Replace   120
Guided Activity 4.8: Replacing Text   120

Counting Words   121
Summary   121
Exercise 4.1: A Day in the Life of a College Student   122
Exercise 4.2: Crusty's Pizza   122
Exercise 4.3: The Internet   123
Exercise 4.4: Thrill Seeker Tours   123
Review Questions   124
Key Terms   125

UNIT 5 / PRINTERS AND PRINTING   **126**
Learning Objectives   126
Important Commands   127
Types of Printers   127
Computer Connections   128
Guided Activity 5.1: Setting Up Printers in Windows   129
Print Commands   131
Guided Activity 5.2: Preparing the Printer   132
Guided Activity 5.3: Previewing a Document   132
Printing   134
Guided Activity 5.4: Printing   136
Printing Envelopes   137
Summary   137
Exercises   138
Review Questions   138
Key Terms   139

APPLICATION B / CREATING A MEMO   **140**

Formatting   *141*

UNIT 6 / FORMATTING CHARACTERS   **142**
Learning Objectives   142
Important Commands   143
Formatting Characters   143
    Font and Point Size   143
Guided Activity 6.1: Changing Font and Size   146
    Bold, Italics, and Underline   149
Guided Activity 6.2: Applying Bold, Italics, and Underline   150
    Commands in the Font Dialog Box   151
    Character Spacing   152
    Changing from Capital to Lowercase Letters   152
Guided Activity 6.3: Changing the Case of Text   153
Copying Formats with Format Painter   155
Guided Activity 6.4: Using the Format Painter   155

Inserting Special Characters   155
Guided Activity 6.5: Inserting Special Characters   156
    The Highlighter   157
Summary   157
Exercise 6.1: A Day in the Life of a College Student   158
Exercise 6.2: Crusty's Pizza   158
Exercise 6.3: The Internet   159
Exercise 6.4: Thrill Seeker Tours   160
Review Questions   160
Key Terms   162

UNIT 7 / FORMATTING PARAGRAPHS   **163**
Learning Objectives   163
Important Commands   163
Formatting Paragraphs   164
    Alignment   165
Guided Activity 7.1: Aligning Paragraphs   165
    Line Spacing   166
Guided Activity 7.2: Setting Line Spacing   167
    Tabs   168
Guided Activity 7.3: Creating Tabs   170
    Paragraph Indents   172
Guided Activity 7.4: Indenting Paragraphs   174
    Text Flow   175
    Borders and Shading   177
Guided Activity 7.5: Adding Borders and Shading   178
    Placing Numbers and Bullets on Paragraphs   178
Guided Activity 7.6: Adding Numbers and Bullets to Paragraphs   180
    Checking and Copying Formats   181
    Style   182
Guided Activity 7.7: Defining and Applying Styles   182
Summary   183
Exercise 7.1: A Day in the Life of a College Student   183
Exercise 7.2: Crusty's Pizza   184
Exercise 7.3: The Internet   185
Exercise 7.4: Thrill Seeker Tours   186
Review Questions   186
Key Terms   188

UNIT 8 / FORMATTING DOCUMENTS   **189**
Learning Objectives   189
Important Commands   189
Formatting Documents   190
    Margins   190
Guided Activity 8.1: Setting Margins Using Page Setup   191

Paper Size and Orientation | 192
Guided Activity 8.2: Changing Paper Size and Orientation | 193
Paper Source | 194
Numbering Pages | 194
Guided Activity 8.3: Inserting Numbers on Pages | 195
Working in Other Views | 195
Guided Activity 8.4: Changing the Margins with the Ruler | 196
Guided Activity 8.5: Using Other Views of a Document | 198
Summary | 199
Exercise 8.1: Printing Pages for Two-Sided Bound Documents | 200
Exercise 8.2: Using Manual Feed | 201
Exercise 8.3: Printing Sideways | 201
Review Questions | 201
Key Terms | 202

APPLICATION C / CREATING A FLYER | **203**

Advanced Word Processing | **205**

UNIT 9 / TABLES | **206**
Learning Objectives | 206
Important Commands | 207
Purpose of Tables | 207
Creating Tables | 208
Creating an Empty Table | 208
Guided Activity 9.1: Creating a Table | 209
Guided Activity 9.2: Entering Text into a Table | 210
Modifying Tables | 211
Adding and Deleting Rows and Columns | 212
Guided Activity 9.3: Adding and Deleting Rows and Columns | 213
Formatting Tables | 215
Column Width | 215
Guided Activity 9.4: Changing Column Widths | 216
Column Alignment and Tabs Within a Table | 217
Guided Activity 9.5: Changing Column Alignment | 218
Row Height and Alignment | 219
Guided Activity 9.6: Setting Row Height and Alignment | 219
Borders, Shading, and AutoFormat | 220
Guided Activity 9.7: Using Cell Borders | 221
Sorting and Calculating | 222
Guided Activity 9.8: Sorting and Calculating | 223
Merging Cells in a Table | 224
Guided Activity 9.9: Merging Cells | 224
Summary | 226
Exercise 9.1: A Daily Schedule in the Life of a College Student | 226

Exercise 9.2: Work Schedule for Crusty's Pizza   227
Exercise 9.3: The Internet: Comparing Internet Access Providers   228
Exercise 9.4: Thrill Seeker Tours   228
Review Questions   230
Key Terms   231

APPLICATION D / USING TABLES TO CREATE A RÉSUMÉ   **232**

UNIT 10 / DESKTOP PUBLISHING   **233**
Learning Objectives   234
Important Commands   234
Columns   234
    Creating Columns   235
    Changing Column Widths   235
Guided Activity 10.1: Creating Columns   236
Separating Sections   239
    Changing the Columns in One Section   239
Guided Activity 10.2: Creating an Article with a Headline   240
Pictures   241
    Inserting Word Clip Art   242
Guided Activity 10.3: Inserting Clip Art into Text   243
    Modifying Pictures   244
Guided Activity 10.4: Scaling, Cropping, and Deleting a Picture   245
Positioning Pictures   246
Guided Activity 10.5: Positioning Pictures   247
    Creating Pictures from Text   248
Guided Activity 10.6: Using WordArt and Drop Caps   250
Summary   251
Exercise 10.1: A Day in the Life of a College Student   251
Exercise 10.2: Crusty's Pizza   253
Exercise 10.3: The Internet   254
Exercise 10.4: Thrill Seeker Tours   255
Review Questions   256
Key Terms   258

APPLICATION E / CREATING A NEWSLETTER   **259**

APPLICATION F / CREATING A BROCHURE   **260**

UNIT 11 / CHART AND DRAW   **261**
Learning Objectives   261
Important Commands   261
Adding Charts to Documents   262
    Entering Data in the Datasheet   263

Guided Activity 11.1: Using the Datasheet   264
    Selecting the Chart Type   265
Guided Activity 11.2: Chart Types   266
    Enhancing the Chart   268
Guided Activity 11.3: Modifying Charts   269
    Formatting the Chart   270
Guided Activity 11.4: Formatting Charts   271
Draw   272
Guided Activity 11.5: Using the Drawing Tools   274
Guided Activity 11.6: Using Text Boxes   276
    Editing Graphics   277
Guided Activity 11.7: Editing Clip Art   277
Summary   279
Exercise 11.1: Charting   279
Exercise 11.2: Editing Clip Art   280
Exercise 11.3: Using Text Boxes   280
Review Questions   281
Key Terms   282

APPLICATION G / COMBINING A CHART WITH A DOCUMENT   **283**

APPLICATION H / PLACING A WATERMARK ON A PAGE   **284**

UNIT 12 / HEADERS AND FOOTERS   **285**
Learning Objectives   285
Important Commands   286
Headers and Footers   286
Inserting Headers and Footers on Every Page   286
Guided Activity 12.1: Creating and Deleting Headers   289
Creating a Unique Header and Footer for the First Page   290
Guided Activity 12.2: Creating First-Page Headers and Footers   290
Creating Headers and Footers for Odd and Even Pages   292
Guided Activity 12.3: Creating Odd-Page and Even-Page Headers and Footers   292
Headers and Footers in Different Sections   293
Summary   295
Exercise 12.1: Headers and Footers the Same on All Pages   295
Exercise 12.2: Different Page Headers and Footers   296
Exercise 12.3: Different Section Headers and Footers   296
Review Questions   297
Exercise 12.4: Key Terms   298

UNIT 13 / MAIL MERGE   **299**
Learning Objectives   299
Important Commands   300

Requirements for Mail Merge   300
  The Data Source Document   301
Guided Activity 13.1: Creating a Data Source   302
  The Main Document   304
Guided Activity 13.2: Creating a Main Document   304
Merging the Two Documents   306
Guided Activity 13.3: Merging   308
  Using IF Fields with Conditional Text   309
Guided Activity 13.4: Using an IF Merge Field   310
  Creating Catalogs of Information   311
Guided Activity 13.5: Creating a Catalog   311
  Merging Mailing Labels and Envelopes   313
Summary   315
Exercise 13.1: A Day in the Life of a College Student   315
Exercise 13.2: Crusty's Pizza   317
Exercise 13.3: The Internet   318
Exercise 13.4: Thrill Seeker Tours   319
Review Questions   320
Key Terms   322

APPLICATION I / USING MAIL MERGE TO APPLY FOR JOBS   323

UNIT 14 / WORKING WITH LONG DOCUMENTS   325
Learning Objectives   326
Important Commands   326
Outlines   326
  Creating an Outline   327
Guided Activity 14.1: Creating an Outline   329
  Modifying and Adding Text to an Outline   332
Guided Activity 14.2: Adding Text and Moving Headings   332
  Formatting Outline Headings   335
Using Master Document View   336
Guided Activity 14.3: Sampling Master Document View   337
Footnotes   338
  Creating Footnotes   339
Guided Activity 14.4: Inserting Footnote Reference Marks   340
  Editing Footnotes   341
Guided Activity 14.5: Editing and Deleting Footnotes   342
  Moving Footnotes   342
Guided Activity 14.6: Moving Footnotes   342
Adding an Index   344
Guided Activity 14.7: Creating an Index   345
Creating a Table of Contents   346
Guided Activity 14.8: Creating a Table of Contents   347
Summary   348

Exercise 14.1: Outline View 349
Exercise 14.2: Master Document View 349
Exercise 14.3: Footnotes 350
Exercise 14.4: Index 350
Exercise 14.5: Table of Contents 351
Review Questions 351
Key Terms 353

UNIT 15 / MACROS AND CUSTOMIZING **354**
Learning Objectives 354
Important Commands 355
Recording Macros 355
Guided Activity 15.1: Recording a Macro 356
Executing and Editing Macros 357
Guided Activity 15.2: Executing a Macro 357
Customizing the Toolbars 358
    Rearranging Toolbars 358
Guided Activity 15.3: Rearranging Toolbars 359
    Assigning Macros and Other Commands to a Toolbar 360
Guided Activity 15.4: Creating a Toolbar and Buttons 361
Customizing the Keyboard 362
Guided Activity 15.5: Customizing the Keyboard 363
Customizing Menus 363
Guided Activity 15.6: Customizing a Menu 364
Summary 365
Exercise 15.1: Creating a Macro 366
Exercise 15.2: Customizing a Menu 366
Exercise 15.3: Customizing a Toolbar 367
Review Questions 367
Key Terms 368

APPENDIX A / ANSWERS TO REVIEW QUESTIONS **369**

APPENDIX B / USING WORD WITH OTHER APPLICATIONS ... **379**
Using Word with Excel 380
    Embedding an Excel Worksheet or Chart 380
    Linking Word to Excel 382
Using Word with Access and Schedule+ 383
Using Word with PowerPoint 383

INDEX **385**

Remember those old Atari and Nintendo games we used to play? Just when we could race through one level, we advanced to the next level and faced all the unknown obstacles on the *new* screen. Each new release of Microsoft Word reminds me of that. At the stage when we've learned how to use most of the features efficiently, along comes a *new* release bringing even greater challenges. Software evolves so rapidly that we must be continuous, lifelong learners, welcoming progress and adapting quickly as changes occur.

In many ways, technology has dramatically altered the way we communicate. Only a few years ago, professional documents could only be created by professional printers or typesetters. Now, a laser printer with a Macintosh or an IBM-compatible personal computer (PC) running Windows software can create sophisticated documents using a variety of typefaces, pictures, charts, and graphs.

Documents no longer mean words on paper sent through the mail. Now we send messages and pictures (as well as sound and video) *instantly* around the world. We view the information on people and companies in distant places with a click of the mouse, and often download it in a few moments for future use in our own computer system.

Microsoft Word has kept pace with these innovations. This release of Word includes two features that were unheard of when the previous version of Word came out only a few years ago: (1) Word can be used to prepare and read electronic mail, and (2) Word can be used to create HTML (hypertext markup language) documents for the World Wide Web.

The challenge to us is to use Word and other computer programs to help us get our work done in the most efficient, most professional manner. A related challenge—one that requires constant vigilance—is to make our computer work for *us*, not us for *it*. Whether you are a beginner or an experienced user, this text gives you what you need to know to create your documents.

FOUNDATIONAL KNOWLEDGE COVERED THOROUGHLY From the foundations of the Windows 95 operating system, the text builds step by step, giving beginners the frame of reference they need for more advanced techniques. No previous computer knowledge is necessary, as you are instructed in proper mouse and keyboard techniques and offered definitions for terms such as *cursor*.

ADVANCED TOPICS INCLUDED These units offer the foundational techniques and theory first, and then build to advanced skills. Once the basic skills of opening and saving files, editing text, copying text and pictures, and spell checking are mastered, the book moves on to more advanced subjects. These include using the amazing tools available through desktop publishing, making attractive and instantly comprehensible charts, preparing multiple documents with the mail merge feature, working with an academic thesis or other long documents, and mastering macros for even greater speed and efficiency in all your computing work.

PRACTICAL CONSIDERATIONS OFFERED Students are given more than just the "how-to" for using the multitude of features in Microsoft Word. Rather, this book's strength lies in its instructing students when and how each feature is best used.

Throughout the book, boxes offering practical tips lead students into thinking in a new way about the ultimate goal of the document. For instance, what size and types of fonts are best used in a brochure or in business correspondence? Or how should a newsletter be designed with columns and pictures to invite the reader to come in and browse? Why should you use Outline view for long, complex documents? Or what type of chart represents most effectively the increased sales of a product? These types of questions are answered in every unit, often amplified and illustrated in screen shots.

THRILL SEEKER TOURS Many of the Exercises and Applications build on the activities and operations of Thrill Seeker Tours, a fictitious travel agency specializing in adventures and fantasy vacations. Using Thrill Seeker Tours, you can apply your knowledge in word processing and using Word to creating real-life documents typical of a business enterprise. Use your imagination to design an adventure for your clients and create these documents:

- Your business card
- A memorandum about the tour
- An advertising flyer
- A brochure to send to potential customers
- An agenda or itinerary to pique more interest
- A personalized mass mailing to efficiently communicate essential information to clients taking your tour

The Exercises based on Thrill Seeker Tours appeal to you as students, encouraging you to branch out and apply the knowledge gained in previous units. Besides, you can have a lot of fun and really get creative with these projects.

Other series of Exercises include the very practical Day in the Life of a College Student, where students apply the features of Word to practical uses in their daily lives; Crusty's Pizza, another type of business popular with both young and old; plus the Internet, a fast-evolving hot topic.

Best Features of the U&U Series Retained

Which is worse: a text book with long, dull explanations, or a text book with pages of computer busywork? This book creates a lively and functional alternative. The name *Understanding and Using* means that fundamental knowledge is covered in a complete and organized way. Only after that are students led step by step through the process.

Understanding comes through the way each unit is structured. Good pedagogy includes a preview of what will be covered, presents the material in detail, and then summarizes the key points. The *Using* portion comes in the form of hands-on Guided

Activities, structured Exercises, and open-ended Applications—because many students learn best by *doing*.

Each unit contains these key features that enhance learning:

LEARNING OBJECTIVES   list the skills and knowledge contained in the unit. This gives a framework for students to preview the unit as well as to skim what topics are covered in it.

IMPORTANT COMMANDS   list the menu commands used in the procedures covered.

THOROUGH DISCUSSION   included in each unit serves the purpose of increasing *understanding*. Because theory, techniques, guidelines, and practical considerations are discussed completely before diving into computer work, the book may be used for introduction as well as reference.

GUIDED ACTIVITIES   give step-by-step instructions in performing the new techniques. Often, the Guided Activities give students several ways to accomplish the same task, allowing them to develop flexibility and experience, rather than using a rigid, "cookbook" approach (in which you *must* have all the ingredients or the soufflé falls).

SCREEN PICTURES   presented throughout the units offer a frame of reference to the student reading the material for the first time—or reviewing it away from the computer. The screens place the various commands, buttons, and dialog boxes in the proper context.

EXERCISES AND APPLICATIONS   present additional opportunities for hands-on practice of the skills and knowledge gained in each unit. Structured Exercises found at the end of every unit are based on business and individual applications that students can use immediately. They require more independence than the Guided Activities, since they do not spell out every single step. Open-ended Applications require students to customize and apply their knowledge to a given case.

REVIEW QUESTIONS   focus students' attention on important concepts and also reinforce knowledge of word processing procedures. Students gain from answering both open-ended short essay questions and multiple-choice questions, both of which typically appear in tests and quizzes. The answers to selected questions are given in Appendix A.

KEY TERMS   are listed at the end of each unit, allowing the student to review and self-test.

HELPFUL HINTS   are sprinkled throughout the text in a boxed format, to present useful tips on concepts, practical considerations, do's and don'ts, and specific Microsoft Word techniques.

QUICK REFERENCE   gathers all the buttons, toolbars, and shortcut keys at the back of the book where students can easily refer to them.

Complete Instructional Package

A complete support package provides instructors and students with everything they need to teach and learn in order to use Microsoft Word proficiently for business applications. The textbook is accompanied by a traditional Instructor's Manual and

Test Bank, as well as West's Product Library CD-ROM, which contains the following features:

WESTTEST COMPUTERIZED TESTING   In this updated version of West's computerized testing, instructors can copy questions individually, sequentially, or randomly—and then arrange them automatically by type, randomly, or directly on-screen using the drag-and-drop feature. Users can even control the font and style, spacing, and margins. WESTEST also allows you to view exam summaries or test bank chapters, preview test pages, and import or export graphics.

CLASSROOM MANAGER   is an application that allows instructors to store and keep track of student data, assignments, scores, overall grades, and ranking. Statistics are automatically updated as class scores are entered or changed.

CLASSROOM-READY POWERPOINT PRESENTATIONS   are offered, in unit-by-unit sequence, to give students an overview of the capability of Word. Also included are presentations to engage students with the fictitious travel agency Thrill Seeker Tours, which is featured in the book's Applications and Exercises. The presentations are designed to be used either as visual aids for an introductory lecture in the classroom, or as individual computer-based instruction for students. Each comes with a script for an accompanying lecture. Since they are created in PowerPoint, instructors can easily customize them to fit the individual needs of their classroom.

INSTRUCTOR'S MANUAL   includes general teaching suggestions, sample syllabi, methods for testing and grading, and information about the student data files. Answers to Review Questions, Exercises, and Applications are also provided.

STUDENT DATA FILES   that are required for completion of the Guided Activities, Exercises, or Applications are included. These files may be copied individually for students, or installed on a lab network.

Acknowledgments

The tremendous advantage of having bright, able people working with me keeps this book going.

My thanks go to Developmental Editor Sara Schroeder of West Publishing Company. Her style and management skill keep these projects on track to completion.

Karen Young, my colleague at Baylor University, dreamed up Thrill Seeker Tours, and I am dependent on her for many great teaching ideas.

I am also grateful for those at Labrecque Publishing Company who made this book a physical reality: Lisa Auer, who performed the crucial accuracy check and who coordinated the process; copyeditor Mark Woodworth, who made excellent suggestions to enhance clarity of the material; and the production crew—Curtis Philips and Andrea Fox—who created an attractive and readable book.

This book is dedicated to my sisters Susan, Jane, and Rebecca, whom I admire for their many achievements.

Emily Ketcham
Baylor University
March 1996

This book is part of THE MICROCOMPUTING SERIES. This popular series provides the most comprehensive list of books dealing with microcomputer applications software. We have expanded the number of software topics and provided a flexible set of instructional materials for all courses. This unique series includes five different types of books.

1. *West's Microcomputing Custom Editions* give instructors the power to create a spiral-bound microcomputer applications book especially for their course. Instructors can select the applications they want to teach and the amount of material they want to cover for each application—essentials or intermediate length. The following titles are a sample of what is available for the 1996 Microcomputing Series custom editions program:

Understanding Information Systems	*PageMaker 4.0*
Management, Information, and Systems: An Introduction to Information Systems	*PageMaker 5.0*
	Lotus 1-2-3 for Windows Release 4
Understanding Networks	*Lotus 1-2-3 for Windows Release 5*
NetWare 3.x	*Microsoft Excel 4*
DOS (3.x) and System	*Microsoft Excel 5*
DOS 5 and System	*Microsoft Excel for Windows 95*
DOS 6 and System	*Quattro Pro 5.0 for Windows*
Microsoft Windows 3.1	*Quattro Pro 6.0 for Windows*
Microsoft Windows 95	*dBASE IV Version 1.0/1.1/1.5*
WordPerfect 6.0	*dBASE IV Version 2.0*
WordPerfect 6.0 for Windows	*Paradox 3.5*
WordPerfect 6.1 for Windows	*Paradox 4.5 for Windows*
Microsoft PowerPoint 4.0	*Microsoft Access 2.0*
Microsoft PowerPoint for Windows 95	*Microsoft Access for Windows 95*
Microsoft Word for Windows 6.0	*QBasic*
Microsoft Word for Windows 95	*Microsoft Visual Basic*

For more information about *West's Microcomputing Custom Editions*, please contact your local West Representative, or call West Publishing Company at (512) 327-3175.

2. General concepts books for teaching basic hardware and software philosophy and applications are available separately or in combination with hands-on applications. These books provide students with a general overview of computer fundamentals including history, social issues, and a synopsis of software and

hardware applications. These books include *Understanding Information Systems*, by Steven C. Ross; *Management, Information, and Systems: An Introduction to Information Systems*, by William Davis; and *Understanding and Using Information Technology*, by Judith C. Simon.

3. A series of hands-on laboratory tutorials (*Understanding and Using*) is software specific and covers a wide range of individual packages. These tutorials, written at an introductory level, combine tutorials with complete reference guides. A complete list of series titles can be found on the following pages.

4. Several larger volumes combining DOS with three application software packages are available in different combinations. These texts are titled *Understanding and Using Application Software*. They condense components of the individual lab manuals and add conceptual coverage for courses that require both software tutorials and microcomputer concepts in a single volume.

5. A series of advanced-level, hands-on lab manuals provides students with a strong project/systems orientation. These include *Understanding and Using Lotus 1-2-3: Advanced Techniques Releases 2.2 and 2.3*, by Judith C. Simon.

    THE MICROCOMPUTING SERIES has been successful in providing you with a full range of applications books to suit your individual needs. We remain committed to excellence in offering the widest variety of current software packages. In addition, we are committed to producing microcomputing texts that provide you both the coverage you desire and also the level and format most appropriate for your students. The Executive Editor of the series is Rick Leyh of West Educational Publishing; the Developmental Editor is Sara Schroeder; the Consulting Editor is Steven Ross of Western Washington University. We are always planning for the future in this series. Please send us your comments and suggestions:

Rick Leyh
Executive Editor
West Educational Publishing
1515 Capital of Texas Highway South, Suite 402
Austin, TX 78746-6544
Internet: rleyh@research.westlaw.com

Sara Schroeder
Developmental Editor
West Educational Publishing
1515 Capital of Texas Highway South, Suite 402
Austin, TX 78746-6544
Internet: sschroed@research.westlaw.com

Steven Ross
Associate Professor/MIS
College of Business and Economics
Western Washington University
Bellingham, WA 98225-9077
Internet: steveross@wwu.edu

We now offer these books in THE MICROCOMPUTING SERIES:

General Concepts

Understanding Information Systems
Steven C. Ross

Understanding Computer Information Systems
Paul W. Ross, H. Paul Haiduk, H. Willis Means, and Robert B. Sloger

Understanding and Using the Macintosh
Barbara Zukin Heiman and Nancy E. McGauley

Operating Systems/Environments

Understanding and Using the Internet
Bruce J. McLaren

Understanding and Using Microsoft Windows 95
Steven C. Ross and Ronald W. Maestas

Understanding and Using Microsoft Windows 3.1
Steven C. Ross and Ronald W. Maestas

Understanding and Using Microsoft Windows 3.0
Steven C. Ross and Ronald W. Maestas

Understanding and Using MS-DOS 6.0
Jonathan P. Bacon

Understanding and Using MS-DOS/PC DOS 5.0
Jonathan P. Bacon

Understanding and Using MS-DOS/PC DOS 4.0
Jonathan P. Bacon

Networks

Understanding Networks
E. Joseph Guay

Understanding and Using NetWare 3.x
Larry D. Smith

Programming

Understanding and Using Microsoft Visual Basic
Jonathan C. Barron

West's Essentials of Microsoft Visual Basic
Jonathan C. Barron

Understanding and Using QBasic
Jonathan C. Barron

Word Processors

Understanding and Using WordPerfect 6.1 for Windows
Jonathan P. Bacon

Understanding and Using WordPerfect 6.0 for Windows
Jonathan P. Bacon

Understanding and Using WordPerfect for Windows
Jonathan P. Bacon

Understanding and Using Microsoft Word for Windows 95
Emily M. Ketcham

Understanding and Using Microsoft Word for Windows 6.0
Emily M. Ketcham

Understanding and Using Microsoft Word for Windows 2.0
Larry Lozuk and Emily M. Ketcham

Understanding and Using Microsoft Word for Windows (1.1)
Larry Lozuk

Understanding and Using WordPerfect 6.0
Jonathan P. Bacon and Robert G. Sindt

Understanding and Using WordPerfect 5.1
Jonathan P. Bacon and Cody T. Copeland

Understanding and Using WordPerfect 5.0
Patsy H. Lund

Desktop Publishing

Understanding and Using PageMaker 5.0
John R. Nicholson

Understanding and Using PageMaker 4.0
John R. Nicholson

Spreadsheets

Understanding and Using Microsoft Excel for Windows 95
Steven C. Ross and Stephen V. Hutson

Understanding and Using Microsoft Excel 5
Steven C. Ross and Stephen V. Hutson

Understanding and Using Microsoft Excel 4
Steven C. Ross and Stephen V. Hutson

Understanding and Using Microsoft Excel 3
Steven C. Ross and Stephen V. Hutson

Understanding and Using Quattro Pro 6.0 for Windows
Lisa L. Friedrichsen

Understanding and Using Quattro Pro 5.0 for Windows
Larry D. Smith

Understanding and Using Quattro Pro 4
Steven C. Ross and Stephen V. Hutson

Understanding and Using Lotus 1-2-3 for Windows Release 5
Dolores Pusins and Steven C. Ross

Understanding and Using Lotus 1-2-3 for Windows Release 4
Steven C. Ross and Dolores Pusins

Understanding and Using Lotus 1-2-3 Release 3
Steven C. Ross

Understanding and Using Lotus 1-2-3 Release 2.3 and Release 2.4
Steven C. Ross

*Understanding and Using Lotus 1-2-3: Advanced Techniques
Releases 2.2 and 2.3*
Judith C. Simon

Understanding and Using Lotus 1-2-3 Release 2.2
Steven C. Ross

Understanding and Using Lotus 1-2-3 Release 2.01
Steven C. Ross

Database Management

Understanding and Using Microsoft Access for Windows 95
Bruce J. McLaren

Understanding and Using Microsoft Access 2.0
Bruce J. McLaren

Understanding and Using Microsoft Access 1.1
Bruce J. McLaren

Understanding and Using Paradox 4.5 for Windows
Larry D. Smith

Understanding and Using Paradox 3.5
Larry D. Smith

Understanding and Using dBASE IV Version 2.0
Steven C. Ross

Understanding and Using dBASE IV
Steven C. Ross

Understanding and Using dBASE III Plus, 2nd Edition
Steven C. Ross

Integrated Software

Understanding and Using Microsoft Office for Windows 95
Emily M. Ketcham

Understanding and Using Microsoft Works for Windows 3.0
Gary Bitter

Understanding and Using Microsoft Works 3.0 for the PC
Gary Bitter

Understanding and Using Microsoft Works 3.0 for the Macintosh
Gary Bitter

Understanding and Using Microsoft Works 2.0 on the Macintosh
Gary Bitter

Understanding and Using Microsoft Works 2.0 on the IBM PC
Gary Bitter

Understanding and Using ClarisWorks
Gary Bitter

Presentation Software

Understanding and Using Microsoft PowerPoint for Windows 95
Lisa L. Friedrichsen

Understanding and Using Microsoft PowerPoint 4.0
Edna Dixon

Combined Books

Understanding and Using Microsoft Office for Windows 95
Emily M. Ketcham

Essentials of Application Software, Volume 1: DOS, WordPerfect 5.0/5.1, Lotus 1-2-3 Release 2.2, dBASE III Plus
Steven C. Ross, Jonathan P. Bacon, and Cody T. Copeland

Understanding and Using Application Software, Volume 4: DOS, WordPerfect 5.0, Lotus 1-2-3 Release 2, dBASE IV
Patsy H. Lund, Jonathan P. Bacon, and Steven C. Ross

Understanding and Using Application Software, Volume 5: DOS, WordPerfect 5.0/5.1, Lotus 1-2-3 Release 2.2, dBASE III Plus
Steven C. Ross, Jonathan P. Bacon, and Cody T. Copeland

Advanced Books

Understanding and Using Lotus 1-2-3: Advanced Techniques Releases 2.2 and 2.3
Judith C. Simon

Emily Ketcham earned a B.A. degree from Taylor University and an M.B.A. degree from Baylor University. She is a lecturer in Information Systems for the Hankamer School of Business at Baylor. Her responsibilities include teaching classes in advanced and introductory microcomputer applications and in managerial communications. Because Baylor's business school is quick to advance to the latest version of Windows software, Mrs. Ketcham, as course coordinator, is the first to learn new applications and explain the features both to her colleagues and to students. She also advises students interested in Information Systems courses and careers.

Mrs. Ketcham previously served as the information coordinator for the business school's Casey Computer Center, supporting faculty and staff in the use of micrcomputers and applications software. For many years she has participated in beta testing Microsoft applications and upgrades.

Students and faculty may contact the author with questions and comments via e-mail at emily_ketcham@baylor.edu.

Word Processing Basics

I

INTRODUCTION   *Introduction to Windows*

UNIT ONE   *Running Start*

UNIT TWO   *Entering Text*

UNIT THREE   *Documents and Disks*

UNIT FOUR   *Proofing Tools*

UNIT FIVE   *Printers and Printing*

■ **PART ONE** This is the first of three parts in this text. To use Word for Windows 95, it is essential that you master the material in this part. The skills in this part of the book concentrate on getting the writing done, the content edited, the files saved to disk for later use, and the output printed on paper.

The skills you learn in the Introduction will also allow you to learn how all Windows applications work. Then you will learn to enter text in a new document, edit text in an existing document, and save documents on a disk and open them again. You will learn to use proofing tools to ensure spelling and grammatical accuracy. The final unit in Part One shows you how to see which printers are set up in Windows, how to preview and print your document, and how to manage the printing process.

Introduction to Windows

Windows 95 is the foundation for Microsoft Word. In this unit, "Introduction to Windows," you will learn techniques that will be used throughout the rest of the book. This unit describes Windows and its four main advantages:

- Graphical user interface, using a mouse to point at pictures rather than typing commands

- Multitasking, the ability to have two programs working at the same time

- Sharing information among two or more programs

- Making previously difficult procedures easy to do, even for beginners

It contains a series of discussions and activities that provide practice in dealing with the different elements of windows and using the mouse. This unit also demonstrates how Windows makes it easy to work on several programs at once and to share information between the programs. Windows makes it simple to do difficult things, and you will learn how to customize the computer to fit your work habits, personality, and mood.

Learning Objectives

At the completion of this unit you should know

1. what Microsoft Windows 95 is and its four advantages,

2. the elements of the Windows screen,

3. how to start and exit Windows,

4. how to use a mouse,

5. how to move, size, minimize, maximize, restore, and close a window.

6. how to start programs,

7. how to share data among several programs,

8. how to customize Windows 95,

9. the elements of dialog boxes,

10. how to create shortcuts.

Important Commands

Start

Edit | Copy

Edit | Cut

Edit | Paste

Properties

What Is Windows 95?

Like its predecessors (Windows 3.0 and 3.1, and Windows 3.11 for Workgroups), Windows 95 offers definite advantages for computer users. Windows 95 is a type of software called an *operating system.*[1] This type of software is used by computers to start up, regulate their hardware components, and manage all the other software and information in the computer, its files. Other operating systems include DOS (rhymes with *toss*), which stands for Disk Operating System, used on typical IBM-compatible microcomputers; Apple System 7, used on Macintosh computers; Windows NT; UNIX; OS/2; and many others. Until Windows 3 appeared in 1990, DOS was the operating system on the vast majority of personal computers. Windows 3 offered numerous advantages over DOS, but actually ran on top of it rather than replacing the DOS operating system. In contrast, Windows 95 replaces DOS as the operating system.

Windows 95 maintains all the advantages of its predecessors while increasing their power and ease of use. In this chapter you will discover the ways it improves on DOS and earlier versions of Windows.

Windows 95 Interface

The first advantage of Windows 95 is its *graphical user interface* (abbreviated as *GUI*, pronounced *gooey*). A *user interface* is the way a computer allows people to interact with it. Traditional *character-based user interfaces* (*CUI*) such as DOS presented a blank screen and a blinking line called a *cursor*, and the computer user

---

1 In this section, we introduce a number of terms, typeset in *boldface italic*, that are defined in the text. The Key Terms section near the end of each unit lists the terms introduced in that unit.

FIGURE 1
DOS interface

```
C:\> COPY C:\LABS\WORDPAD.DOC A:\
```

needed to know exactly how to type in instructions or what special keys to press to make the computer do something. Figure 1 shows a typical example of this interface.

In contrast, Windows 95's graphical interface provides computer users more intuitive methods for working on personal computers as well as more visual cues. Windows puts elements on screen to give the user information on how to make things happen, including *icons* or pictures, *menu choices* that appear when a command is selected, and *buttons* that can be pushed with a pointing and clicking device such as a mouse.

Working with the Mouse

Because of the graphical interface of Windows 95, it makes sense to use a mouse or other pointing device for input, in addition to using the keyboard. Using a mouse has five basic procedures:

- point
- click
- double-click
- right-click
- drag

Hold the mouse by placing your right palm on the surface and positioning your index finger on the left button and middle or ring finger on the right button. (If you are left-handed, you can change the mouse so that the right button is the main one used with your left index finger. Instructions for doing this are found later in this unit.) By moving the mouse to the right or left, you move the *pointer* or arrow symbol on the screen right or left. When you move the mouse away from or toward you, the pointer moves up and down on the screen. When you move the mouse, keep the buttons and cord positioned straight away from you; don't turn or twist the mouse diagonally as you move it. When you are instructed to *point* the mouse, move it so that the arrow-shaped mouse pointer is on a specific part of the screen.

To *click* the mouse means to press the left button once and then quickly release it after you have pointed at something on the screen. With most mouse devices, this produces a "click" sound. You are instructed to click the mouse in order to choose or select something. For example, you click to instruct Windows to select a program, open a menu, execute a command, or pick an item from a list.

Double-click means to press the left mouse button twice, rapidly, while pointing at an object. To double-click successfully, you must hold the mouse completely still with your thumb and little finger. Double-clicking is a shortcut method for selecting and executing some commands. Throughout this book, you will be instructed where to use double-clicking.

Sometimes you use your middle or ring finger to click once on the secondary mouse button, located on the right side of the mouse. Later in this unit you will use a *right-click* to access *shortcut menus*, a handy way to invoke many commonly-used procedures.

Drag means to point to an object, and then press the active mouse button and hold it down while you move the mouse. You will drag with your mouse to move objects and text as well as to change sizes of windows and pictures. Dragging is also used to *highlight* text, which you will use later in this unit when copying. You can practice all these skills and take a look at Windows 95's graphical interface in the following Guided Activity.

GUIDED ACTIVITY 1

Starting Windows 95

The procedure for starting Windows varies from place to place and perhaps even from computer to computer. In this section we demonstrate a typical procedure for hard disk systems. If necessary, your instructor or system manager can assist you with any differences within your school or organization.

The following Guided Activity assumes that your system starts in Windows 95 when the computer is turned on. If this assumption is incorrect, your instructor or system manager will have to give you additional instructions in starting Windows.

1. Turn on your PC and monitor. Your computer will take several minutes to check its hardware components and load the various programs that the operating system requires. Instead of the mouse pointer, you will see an hourglass on the screen, which means to wait while the computer is busy.

2. The monitor will display the Windows 95 copyright screen. When you see this screen you are reminded that it is illegal and unethical to use this software unless it has been purchased for this machine. You must not copy or borrow it to install it on another computer without paying for it.

3. You might see a dialog box requesting your username and password. If this is the first time that you have used Windows 95, press the [Enter] key.

4. After a short pause, the Windows screen similar to the one shown in Figure 2 appears.

    The Windows screen might be a solid color, a design, or a picture, depending on your computer and your organization's preferences. You may have different icons than the ones shown on this screen. Keep Windows open while you read in the next section about the elements on the screen.

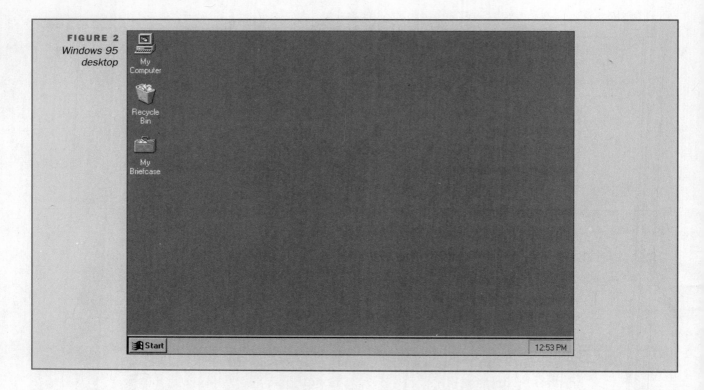

FIGURE 2
Windows 95 desktop

The Windows Desktop

The best analogy for learning how to use Windows 95 is to think of it as a desktop. Just as you keep handy on your desk your scissors, stapler, tape dispenser, and pen for frequent use, plus a clock for keeping your eye on the time, several elements always appear on the Windows screen, called the *desktop*. Along the bottom of the screen is the *taskbar*. In addition to the Start button and time displayed, the taskbar will contain buttons for every task you have opened on the desktop. A button, like the Start button, is a rectangular area that causes something to happen when you push it (that is, click on it with the mouse). Also on the screen are icons representing various handy tools. The one labeled *My Computer* is used for seeing the contents of your computer. It contains icons for each of the disk drives so that you can manage the files stored on each. If your computer is connected to other computers in a network, you will see the *Network Neighborhood* icon (not shown in these figures), which reveals the names of all the computers and printers that are connected to your computer. Otherwise you may see the icon for *My Briefcase*, which coordinates and updates copies of files between your computers at work and at home, or between your laptop and desktop computers. When you want to clean up the contents of your computer, throw them into the *Recycle Bin*, which stores them temporarily in case you want to retrieve them later. The Recycle Bin's icon changes depending on whether you have thrown things away or it is empty. In the next Guided Activity you will practice using your mouse with the objects on the desktop.

GUIDED ACTIVITY 2

Mousing Around

1. With Windows 95 already open on your screen, place your hand in the correct position on the mouse. Move the mouse in various directions and observe the way the pointer moves on the screen.

2. Move the mouse pointer so that it is on the Start button. The message `Click here to begin` appears on screen. Messages that appear when the pointer is on a button or object are called *ToolTips*, as you see in Figure 3. Their function is to help you know the button's function. They will disappear in a few seconds or whenever you move the mouse away.

FIGURE 3
ToolTips

3. Move the mouse pointer over to the time and pause there. The day and date appear just above the mouse pointer.

4. Move the mouse pointer up and click the icon labeled My Computer. To *select* something you must click on it. As soon as you click on it, the name is highlighted or selected.

5. Click on several different icons to observe that the highlight changes each time.

6. Click on the Start button and the Start menu appears as in Figure 4. A *menu* is a list of commands from which you may choose. Any time you want to access this menu, clicking on the button makes the menu appear. We'll discuss each of the features on the Start menu later. For now let's continue to try out the mouse.

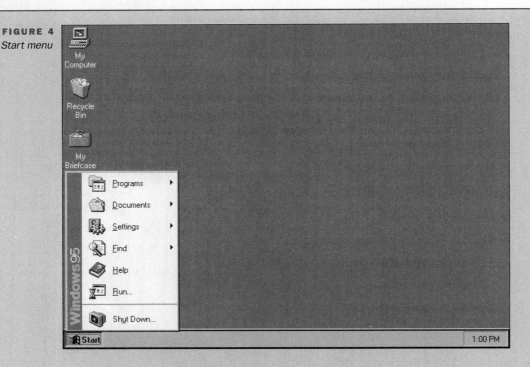

FIGURE 4
Start menu

7. Click on the Windows desktop, and the menu will disappear. To get rid of a menu without choosing anything, click somewhere else on the screen.

8. Drag the My Computer icon to another place on the screen. To drag, point at the icon, and then press and hold the left mouse button while moving the mouse to a new location. Release the mouse button to stop dragging.

   Depending on how Windows is set up, the icon may stay where you dragged it or it may jump back to the left.

9. Right-clicking opens a shortcut menu. Point at the Windows desktop and click on the right mouse button with your middle or ring finger.

10. Move the mouse pointer up or down to change which selection on the menu is highlighted. When you highlight any of the selections with the triangle pointing toward the right, another menu appears, as in Figure 5.

11. Look on the shortcut menu for a check mark next to Auto Arrange. If it is there, Windows will make your icons jump back to the left side of the desktop if you drag them around. Don't you wish all your belongings behaved so well?

12. If you do not see a check mark next to Auto Arrange, point the mouse at that selection and click on it. Once the selection is made, the menus disappear. If the check mark is already there, click on the desktop to make the menu disappear without selecting anything.

13. The last procedure is to double-click. Point the mouse at the My Computer icon and double-click. If you are successful, a rectangular box called a *window*

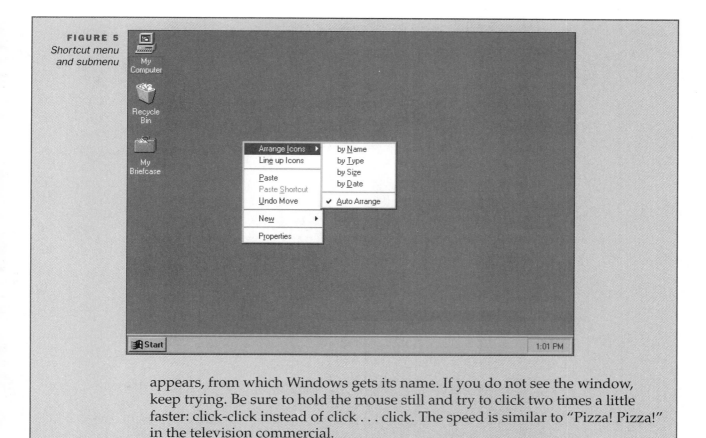

FIGURE 5
Shortcut menu and submenu

appears, from which Windows gets its name. If you do not see the window, keep trying. Be sure to hold the mouse still and try to click two times a little faster: click-click instead of click . . . click. The speed is similar to "Pizza! Pizza!" in the television commercial.

Components of a Window

Your desktop is not only a place to store your clock and office supplies, but also a place to spread out your work. Very tidy people work on only one task at a time, whereas people at the other extreme scatter papers around until the desktop is completely covered.

The Windows 95 desktop is just the same. You can open one window at a time or many simultaneously; you can move them around or stack them on top of each other. All windows have certain components in common that help you manipulate them. Compare your screen with Figure 6 to see the common elements of a window.

Across the top of the window is the *title bar*, which labels the window. While more than one window may be displayed at one time, you actually use only one window at a time. The window you are currently using is called the *active window*. When several windows are on screen at once, the active window will be identified with a brighter title bar, and its button on the taskbar will appear pushed in.

If you drag the title bar, the whole window moves. This allows you to see another Window beneath, just as you would move a sheet of paper aside to pick up a lower one. The size and contents of the window do not change; only its location does.

FIGURE 6
Typical window elements

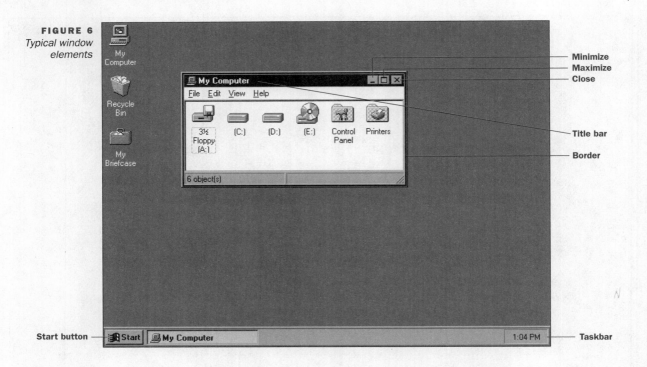

The thin frame around the window, called the *border*, is used to define the edge of a window. When you drag a border, you change the size of the window.

Occasionally you will want to make a window as large as possible to see as much information as you can. This happens many times when you are working in a single program and are not necessarily interested in viewing several programs at once. An application that completely fills the screen is said to be *maximized*. A maximized application cannot be moved or sized, and it has no borders. You can maximize a window two ways: click on the maximize button or double-click the title bar.

Other times you will want to move a window out of the way temporarily to perform another task. A simple way to do this is to *minimize* the program by clicking on the minimize button. When a window is minimized, it appears as a button on the taskbar. It is still running in the computer's memory and contains your data, but it is minimized to move it out of the way. To make the window visible again, click on the button on the taskbar.

Once a window has been maximized, the maximize button is replaced by the *restore* button. Clicking the restore button returns the window to its previous, intermediate size.

Many windows contain a selection of commands on a *menu bar*. Some commands are standard across Windows applications, although some commands are specific to the program contained in the window. (These commands will be printed in initial capitals in this text.). Whenever you click on one of the commands on the menu bar, a list of choices on a menu drops down. Just like the way you use the Start menu and the shortcut menu, you click on a command to make a selection, or click elsewhere to get rid of the menu without making a selection.

Sometimes, when the window containing an application or document is not large enough to display all the information, *scroll bars* (resembling vertical and horizontal elevator shafts) appear at the right side and bottom side of a window. Scroll bars are used to move other parts of a document into view when all the information will not fit in a window.

The last element all windows have in common is the *close button*. When you are through with your work, you can remove the window from the screen and also from the computer's memory by clicking on the close button. Another way is to select File on the menu and then click on the Close or Exit commands.

Just as you push papers out of the way to work on another task but still keep them out on your desktop, there will be times when you want to change the size and shape of the windows that are opened on your desktop. You can make a window occupy the entire screen so that you can have more room to work on it, you can have it take up only a portion of the screen, or you can even reduce it to a button on the taskbar. The following Guided Activity will step you through the process of manipulating windows using these common elements.

GUIDED ACTIVITY 3

Manipulating a Window

1. Continue from the previous Guided Activity. My Computer appears not as an icon but as a window on the desktop. Every window on the desktop has a corresponding button on the taskbar. Look for the button on the taskbar for the My Computer window, as shown previously in Figure 6.

2. Point at the title bar labeled My Computer and hold down the mouse button. Drag the window around on the screen. When you let go of the mouse button, the window is repositioned.

3. Move the mouse pointer over the bottom-right corner of the window until it changes to a two-headed arrow.

4. Hold down the mouse button and drag the window up and to the left to make the window much smaller. Make it so small that only two of the icons appear within the window.

FIGURE 7
Window with a scroll bar

As soon as you release the mouse button, a scroll bar appears on the side of the window, just as you see in Figure 7. Scroll bars resemble an elevator shaft with an elevator (the square box) that travels from one end to the other and stops anywhere in between. When you drag on the box within the scroll bar, the view of the window's contents moves up and down.

5. Drag the box on the scroll bar downward. The contents of the window change, showing the icons that were previously hidden from view.

    We could drag on the borders again to resize the window, but we can also change the size dramatically by clicking on buttons in the top-right corner of the window.

6. Click the maximize button to make the window expand so that it fills the entire screen.

    When a window is maximized, the other items on the desktop are covered, but the taskbar still resides at the bottom edge of the screen. The window's borders disappear and the maximize button is replaced by the restore button, as in Figure 8.

FIGURE 8
A maximized window

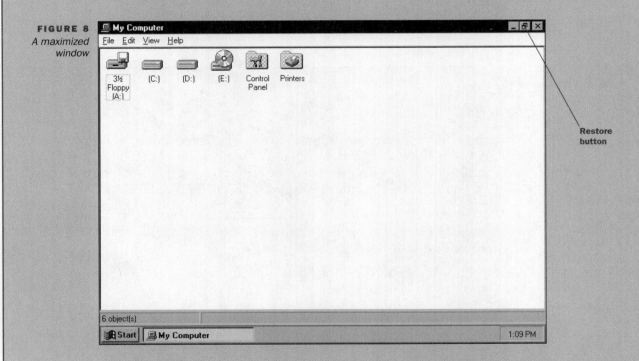

Restore button

7. Click on the minimize button. Now the window disappears from the screen so you can see the desktop again. The window is still running, however; it appears as a button on the taskbar. Minimized programs are accessed with the click of a button.

8. Click on the My Computer button on the taskbar. The window reopens to its previous size, which filled the screen.

9. Click on the restore button. This causes the window to shrink back down to the intermediate size. Now you can have the window open and still see other items on the desktop. Windows remembers what size you made the window when you dragged on its borders.

10. Drag the border to resize the window so that all the icons appear. The scroll bars disappear, as they are no longer needed.

11. Double-click on the Network Neighborhood icon to open a second window on screen. (If you don't have Network Neighborhood, use My Briefcase as shown here or some other icon or skip this step.) Each time you open another window, a button is added to the taskbar.

12. Double-click on the Recycle Bin icon. With three windows open, your desktop is getting cluttered. You could carefully rearrange and resize each window so that you could see the contents of all, but Windows gives a quick way to do it.

13. Position the mouse pointer on an empty area of the taskbar where no button is. You may have an empty space just to the left of the clock. Right-click (click on the right mouse button) to reveal a shortcut menu. The choices for arranging windows neatly on screen are Cascade, Tile Horizontally, Tile Vertically, and Minimize All Windows.

14. Select the command Cascade to arrange the windows in a neat stack with the title bars of each showing, just as in Figure 9. The active window, the one used most recently, is on top. Its title bar is a different color from the others, and its button on the taskbar appears pushed in.

15. Right-click on the taskbar again and click on Tile Horizontally. Now the windows fill the screen with boxes that stretch horizontally across the screen, as shown in Figure 10. Right-click and select Tile Vertically. Now the windows are arranged side by side. In both cases, you can tell which is the active window, the

FIGURE 9
Three windows cascaded

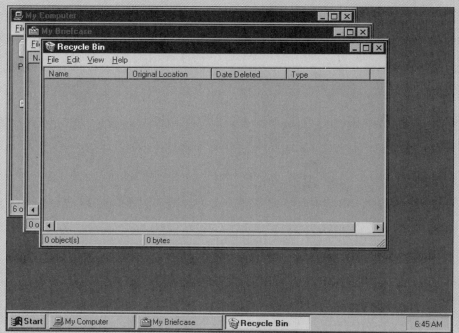

FIGURE 10
Tiled windows

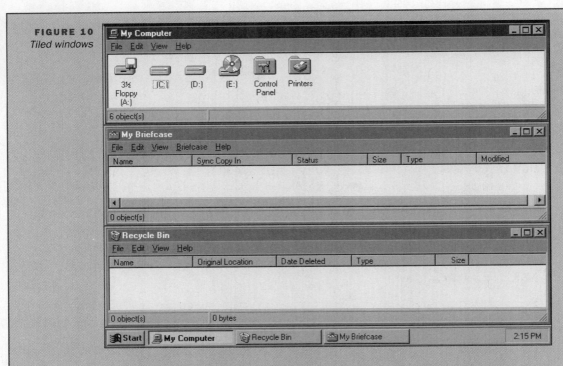

one used most recently, because of both the color of the title bar and the pushed-in appearance of its button on the taskbar.

16.   Right-click and then select Minimize All Windows as in Figure 11. The desktop is cleared off and the windows are minimized to buttons on the taskbar.

FIGURE 11
*Taskbar showing
shortcut menu
and minimized
windows*

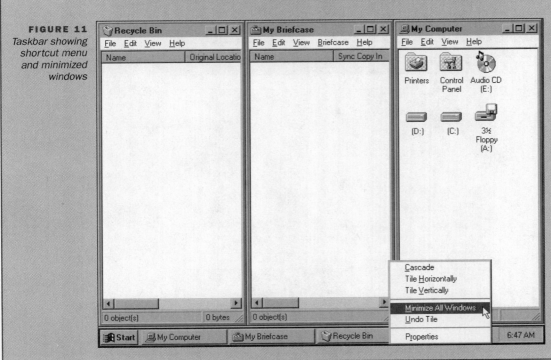

17. Click once on the My Computer button on the taskbar. The My Computer window reopens on the screen in the same size and shape it just had.

18. Right-click and select from the shortcut menu the command Undo Minimize All. This causes all the windows to reopen just as you last saw them.

19. Click the close button on the My Computer window. The window disappears from the screen and returns to being an icon on the desktop. Its button no longer shows on the taskbar.

When you are finished with a particular application window, it should be closed. Open applications, even those that have been minimized to buttons on the taskbar, take up computer memory and processing time, which makes other operations less efficient (especially on older computers with less memory). Closing a window is the equivalent of taking papers off your desktop completely and putting them away in a drawer.

20. Click on the close button on all the other windows on the desktop.

Multitasking

In the olden days of personal computers, if you were typing a document and you needed to check some figures on your financial statements, you had to interrupt your work on one task, close it down, and open the next task. You could only run one program at a time. With the advent of Windows version 3.x (and Apple System 7.0 on the Macintosh), computers were finally able to have more than one window open and a different program working in each window. This ability to have two or more programs running at one time is called *multitasking*. You have already seen how easy it is to open and manipulate several windows, although none of the windows were programs as such; they were merely views of information located on the computer, the network, and the Recycle Bin.

Windows 95 improves on the multitasking ability of Windows 3.x. Previously, if you started the computer on one process—say, copying information from one place to another—the computer was tied up until the task was completed, so you were still inconvenienced. No longer. Windows 95 allows you to begin one task, and then to switch to another window and keep working, while (without any direction from you) it manages the resources of the hardware.

Before we can try multitasking, you need to know the procedures for starting programs—all very simple, now that your mouse skills are developed.

Starting Programs

As you can guess, to start a program, you simply need to click on the Start button. This causes the Start menu to appear above the taskbar. Several choices are found on the Start menu.

PROGRAMS   Displays a menu of programs such as Word and Excel

DOCUMENTS   Displays a list of files you recently worked on

SETTINGS   Displays a list of items to customize Windows or to set up a printer

FIND   Allows you to search for a particular file or folder on the computer

HELP   Starts the Help feature so that you can find answers to questions and access further information about Windows 95's capabilities

RUN   Allows you to type a command like A:\INSTALL

SHUT DOWN   Allows you to shut down, restart, or log off of Windows

When you highlight the Programs choice (or any choice followed by ▶), you see yet another menu with a list of the programs that your computer can access, similar to what you see in Figure 12 (the items listed may be different on your computer). Some of the choices on this second list open yet more menus, and so on. This is one example of a *folder* being used to group several items together for easy access. As in a filing cabinet in an office, folders typically contain *files*—programs or documents stored on the computer. All folder icons on the Start menu show a picture of a manila folder with a group of tiny icons in a tiny window.

Other choices are programs, each with their own icon. Program names are not followed by a ▶. When you click on the name of a program, it opens a window on the desktop, just as you would expect.

Since the taskbar is always located at the bottom of the screen, even if the window is maximized, the Start button is available for you to start another program, and another. You can open as many as the memory of your computer can handle. Each time you open a window, its button appears on the taskbar at the bottom of the screen. Even though some windows hide other windows behind them, you can see at a glance what is running merely by looking at the taskbar.

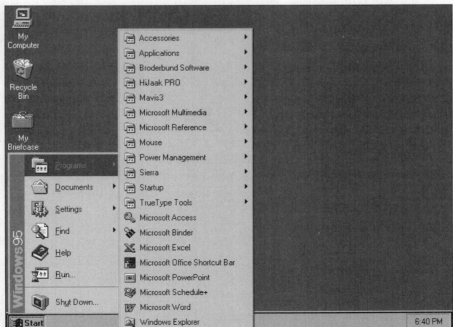

FIGURE 12
*Selecting
Programs on the
Start menu*

One analogy for the taskbar's use is that of a security guard keeping an eye on all the entrances for a building at one time by watching the monitors. Or perhaps you might compare the taskbar to a television director, who decides which image to broadcast by watching the images from every camera up in the director's booth. You will use Windows 95's taskbar not only to see all open windows at a glance, but also at any moment to bring forward any program you want to use, by simply clicking one button or another on the taskbar. If you begin a task that takes the computer some time to complete, you can click another button on the taskbar and work on something else while the computer keeps working on the first task.

GUIDED ACTIVITY 4

Starting Programs

1. Click on the Start button and move the mouse to highlight Programs.

2. Move the highlight to the top of the next menu and highlight Accessories. Since Accessories is a folder, it opens to another menu with more choices. Some of these choices are also folders, such as System Tools and Games. (With multitasking, you can start printing your research paper, and reward yourself for finishing by playing Solitaire while you wait!)

☞ TIP   *What should you do if you run out of room for your mouse? Lift the mouse off the table. The pointer will not move until you place the mouse back on the table, and you will be able to give yourself more room to roll.*

3. Click on the choice for Calculator. You can use this calculator by clicking on its buttons as you would a hand-held calculator.

4. Click on Start, and then highlight Programs, Accessories, and click on WordPad. WordPad is a program for typing short documents. Figure 13 shows both programs open on the desktop.

   With two programs open at once, you can view them all at once or you can maximize one to work on without being distracted by the other.

5. Maximize WordPad by clicking on the maximize button in the top-right corner of its window. Why do you suppose the maximize button is not available on the Calculator?

6. Click on the buttons, in turn, to bring each program to the top of the desktop. Keep this window arrangement for the next Guided Activity.

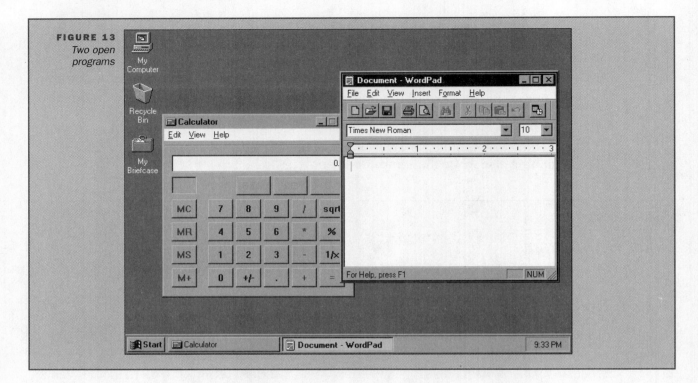

FIGURE 13
Two open programs

Using the Keyboard

The purpose of this section is not to teach you how to type. Rather, its purpose is to introduce you to the ways this book will refer to actions you will be instructed to perform with the keyboard. Whenever you are to type a single keystroke, this book will use the word *Press*, for example

Press Enter.

This means you press the Enter or Return key on your keyboard once. Three other keys (Alt, Ctrl, and Shift) are used in combination with a second key. For example, if instructed to press Alt Tab, you would hold down Alt, press the Tab key once, and then release Alt.

The word *Type* is used to indicate that multiple keystrokes must be entered on the keyboard. The specific text you should type looks different from the rest of the words, as you can see in the following sentence. In this case you would include the period at the end of the sentence:

Type I am learning to use Windows 95.

You will use these instructions to begin typing in the next Guided Activity.

Sharing Data

Windows makes it simple to share information from one program to another. By using three commands you can get numbers, text, and pictures from one place to another. Windows provides several handy ways to copy or move information from one place to another. One method you will learn here is to use commands on the menu.

To copy information from one place to another, either inside one document or between two different programs, you must follow these steps:

1. Highlight the material you want to move or copy by dragging the mouse across it.

2. Select the Copy command from the menu if you want to make a duplicate, or select Cut if you want to remove the material.

3. Move the cursor to the new location where you would like the information to appear.

4. Issue the Paste command.

This set of procedures involves the Clipboard, a temporary storage area provided by Windows. Each time you copy or cut, the material is moved to the Clipboard. When you paste, the material is moved from the Clipboard to the location of your cursor.

FIGURE 14
*Edit menu
selections*

Edit	
Undo	Ctrl+Z
Cut	Ctrl+X
Copy	Ctrl+C
Paste	Ctrl+V
Paste Special...	
Clear	Del
Select All	Ctrl+A
Find...	Ctrl+F
Find Next	F3
Replace...	Ctrl+H
Links...	
Object Properties	Alt+Enter
Object	

These commands—Cut, Copy, and Paste—are found on the Edit menu on the menu bar of the window shown in Figure 14.

Menu selections have certain things in common. First, some of the menu selections are gray (dimmed). This means that they cannot be selected at this time. Other selections, such as Find, are followed by an ellipsis (…) on the screen (ellipses are not printed in this book, however). This means you need to supply additional information in a *dialog box* ("Find what?," for example).

GUIDED ACTIVITY 5

Copying and Moving

1. Click on the WordPad button to bring this program to the top of the stack.

2. Type the following sentence into the document. The blinking line, the cursor, shows you where your next letter will appear.

   `If I work 15 hours per week at 4.25 per hour, before taxes I will earn`

3. It would be silly to rummage around to find a $10 calculator to find out your total pay when you are sitting in front of a $2,000 computer. Click on the Calculator button on the taskbar to bring it to the front.

4. Click `15*4.25=` on the buttons to make the calculations. When you get the answer, don't jot the numbers down and retype them—you might make a mistake. Windows will let you bring the results over into your text.

5. Click Edit on the menu bar of the Calculator, and then click Copy, as you see in Figure 15. A copy of the answer is stored in the Clipboard. (You don't need to highlight first, because there's only one thing you can copy from the calculator—the result.)

Calculator

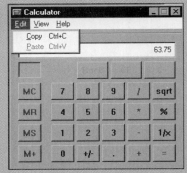

6. Click the WordPad button (labeled "Document-WordPad") on the taskbar to bring your document to the front.

7. Click Edit on the menu bar and select Paste. The number that was stored in the Clipboard is placed in the text, as you see in Figure 16.

8. Place a period after the number and press the key.

The Cut command works like Copy except that it does not leave the original in place. It removes the selected text and stores it in the Clipboard.

*Pasting the result
in the document*

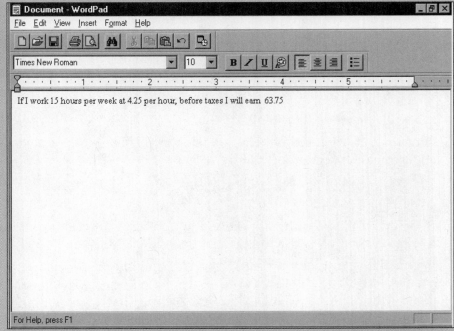

9. Drag the mouse over the sentence to highlight it. Click Edit on the menu. Select the Cut command.

    The sentence disappears, but it has not been deleted. The Clipboard now contains the paragraph that was just cut. It will stay there until some other piece of text is cut or copied or until you exit Windows.

10. Click on Edit on the menu bar and click Paste. From now on, when you are to click choices on a menu the instruction will be run together like this: Edit | Paste.

11. Select Edit | Paste from the menu again. The sentence is inserted from the Clipboard a second time, giving you the result shown in Figure 17. Close WordPad without saving your work. Then close Calculator.

    Windows also allows you to move and copy text without using any menu commands by a feature known as drag-and-drop. You will learn how in Unit 3. Later in this unit you will use the drag-and-drop technique to create shortcut icons on the desktop.

FIGURE 17
*Sentence pasted
a second time*

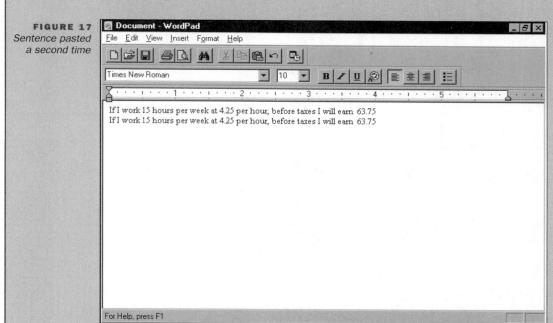

Doing Difficult Things Easily

When Windows 3.*x* offered the graphical interface and a multitasking capability, it seemed like a great leap forward in making computers easy to use. Because it operated on top of DOS, however, it was hampered by certain limitations, and many procedures were still difficult to do. Windows 95 takes the ease of use one step further so that complicated tasks are easily performed. Even novices can customize Windows, create shortcuts to programs and folders, set up hardware and software, manage network drives, and maintain their computers.

Customizing Windows Properties

One of the choices included on the shortcut menu and other menus is a selection for *Properties*. The properties are the features of objects that can be customized, such as the desktop, an icon, or the taskbar. Although the shortcut menu is one place to select the command to change properties, it is not the only one. Customizing the mouse is done through the Control Panel, which is a selection under Settings on the Start menu.

GUIDED ACTIVITY 6

Customizing the Mouse

1. Click on the Start button. Move the mouse upward to highlight the word Settings. Click on the choice for Control Panel.

   The Control Panel is a folder containing icons to customize many features of Windows, as you can tell from Figure 18.

FIGURE 18
Control Panel

2. On the Control Panel window, double-click the icon for Mouse.

   The window that opens, shown in Figure 19, is labeled Mouse Properties. Instead of icons inside, though, you are presented with many choices to make. This is more properly called a dialog box. All dialog boxes have certain features in common. Here you see *tabs*, each with certain categories of choices grouped together; *command buttons* to click with the mouse to make something happen (OK and Cancel); and *option buttons*, circles you fill in to make a single selection among two or more choices. Unlike windows, dialog boxes have no minimize or maximize button in the upper-right corner.

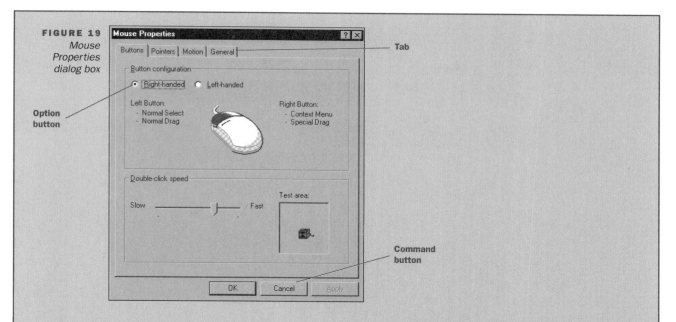

FIGURE 19
Mouse Properties dialog box

Tab

Option button

Command button

3. The tab labeled Buttons is the part of the dialog box in front. This is where you can swap the buttons, to work better if you are left-handed. If you are, you may want to click the option button labeled Left-handed.

 WARNING *If you share a laboratory computer with other users, swapping the mouse buttons will confound the right-handed users, who will think the mouse is broken. Always change it back when you are through.*

4. No doubt you are intrigued with the little handle cranking around. This is the place to test the speed of the double-click. Move the slide a little toward the Slow or Fast end, and then try out your double-clicking on the test area. If your double-clicking is fast enough for the setting, you will get a tiny surprise.

5. Click on the Pointers tab to bring a new part of the dialog box to the front, as in Figure 20. Windows provides choices for normal and also wacky symbols for your mouse pointer under different circumstances. You have already seen your mouse pointer look like an hourglass, an arrow, and a two-headed arrow. These typical shapes are displayed in the *open list box* of pointer styles. Click on the small downward-pointing arrow under the word Scheme to reveal a *drop-down list* of the many choices of pointer shape sets. If you want to try one of those, click on it and then click the Apply button. You may not see the new mouse pointers right away.

6. Explore the other two tabs in the Mouse Properties dialog box to see the customizing choices available to you. Notice on the Motion tab shown in Figure 21 a square next to Show Pointer Trails. *Check boxes* like this one allow you to select one, many, or none of the choices by clicking them, unlike option buttons, which require you to select one and only one of the choices.

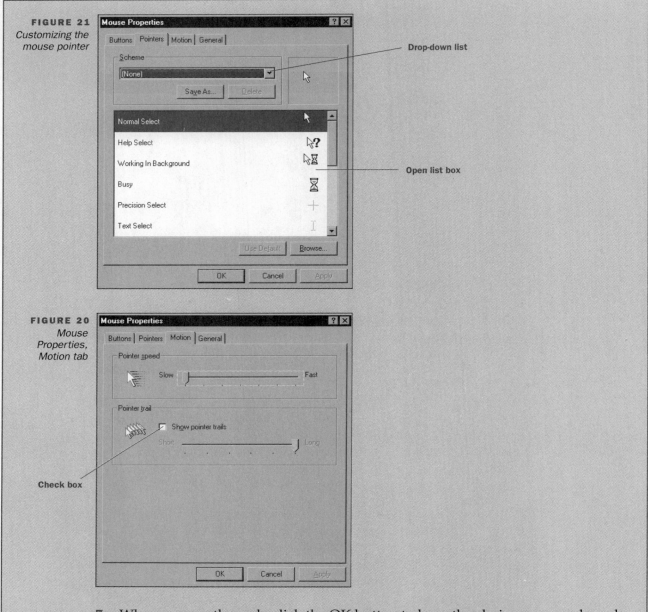

FIGURE 21
*Customizing the
mouse pointer*

Drop-down list

Open list box

FIGURE 20
*Mouse
Properties,
Motion tab*

Check box

7. When you are through, click the OK button to keep the choices you made and close the dialog box. If you want to leave a dialog box and *not* keep the changes, click the Cancel button or the close button in the upper-right corner. All dialog boxes have these or similar features.

8. Take note of the other items that can be customized in the Control Panel. Icons and dialog boxes make customizing these aspects of Windows 95 easy to do. Later you can explore the contents of these icons further. Close the window to return to the desktop.

Customizing the Desktop

Several features on the desktop can be customized. The way the desktop looks, its properties, can be customized to fit your personality and your mood or even the task at hand. You can change the colors and put a design or a picture on the background. You can install a *screen saver*, which keeps the monitor from shining brightly when your computer is idle.

GUIDED ACTIVITY 7

Customizing Desktop Properties

1. Place the mouse pointer on an empty part of the desktop and click the right mouse button. The shortcut menu that appears is the one we used before to arrange the icons.

2. Click the Properties selection on the shortcut menu. The Display Properties dialog box appears, as in Figure 22. You can also access this dialog box from the Control Panel.

FIGURE 22
Display Properties dialog boxes

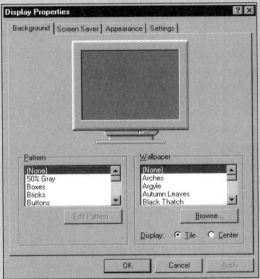

Two open list boxes show some of the choices for pattern and wallpaper. The top of the lists shows the selection [None]. If the wallpaper is set at any choice other than [None], you will be unable to see pattern choices.

3. Drag the scroll box on the scroll bar next to Wallpaper all the way to the top and click on [None] if it is not already highlighted, so that we can experiment with the patterns.

4. Click on the name of a pattern to view the sample in the picture of the monitor. To see more choices, click on the down arrow at the bottom of the scroll bar several times. When you see one you want to try, click Apply.

   When you click the Apply button, the pattern is immediately applied to the desktop, and the dialog box remains open. If you clicked the OK button instead, the pattern would still be applied, but the dialog box would close. If you clicked Cancel, none of your choices would be applied.

5. Scroll through the list of wallpaper choices and click on several names to preview the effect on the picture of the monitor. When you see one you like, click Apply. The background hides the pattern you previously picked.

   Both patterns and wallpaper consume some of the memory resources of your computer. If your computer seems to run slow or is unable to open multiple windows, you can conserve memory by setting both pattern and wallpaper to [None]. You can also create your own pictures or designs for the wallpaper in the Paint program, located on the Start menu, under Programs, Accessories.

6. Click on the tab for Screen Saver to see another part of the dialog box, as in Figure 23.

7. Click on the drop-down arrow to see more choices for screen savers. Flying Toasters, Fish, and Bad Dogs are separately purchased screen savers, but Windows 95 includes a few others to choose from.

FIGURE 23
Screen Saver tab with drop-down list displayed

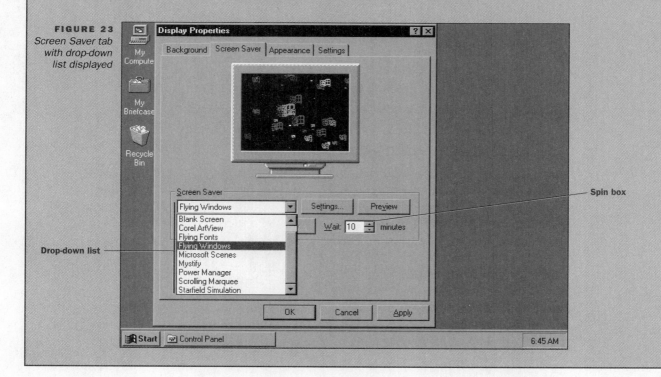

Drop-down list

Spin box

8. Click on the name of a screen saver and then click the Preview button to see its effect. When you wiggle the mouse again, or touch a key, the screen saver goes away.

9. Several of the screen savers have properties that you can customize by clicking the Settings button. For example, in the Scrolling Marquee you can type your own message to display on the screen saver and even specify its color and speed, plus specify whether you must use a password to stop the screen saver. For any screen saver, you can specify how soon it comes on. Change the number of minutes next to Wait by clicking the up or down arrows on the *spin box*. If one of the screen saver choices is Power Manager, use it to save electricity.

10. Click on the Appearance tab to customize the color scheme of the elements in Windows 95. The preview area at the top of the dialog box shown in Figure 24 displays all the items that can be colored. You can color each item individually or select a preset color scheme.

FIGURE 24
Customizing color schemes

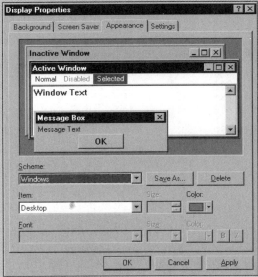

11. Click on the down arrow next to Scheme to reveal a drop-down list of selections. Click on various names to see a preview of the color scheme. When you see one you like, click Apply.

    The fourth choice, the one for Settings, provides an easy way to change the number of colors and the number of *pixels* (small *pic*ture *el*ements, rectangles of light) the screen can display. In older versions of Windows, you had to close Windows and reopen it before changes in these settings would take effect. Windows 95 makes these changes on the fly.

12. When all your settings are to your liking, click OK to close the dialog box.

Shortcuts

Another way to customize the desktop is to put items you use often at your fingertips. If you use a certain document often, you can place an icon for it right on the desktop. If you often look to see what information is stored on a certain disk drive, you can put an icon for it on the desktop. If you have favorite files or programs, you can place their icons into a folder and keep it on your desktop. These icons are called *shortcuts*, because they represent a fast way to access things. The normal, longer way to access them is still available.

Of course, the Start button itself is a shortcut, but you can customize the selections on the Start menu to make your favorite program available with a click of the mouse. You can change the appearance of the Start menu, as well as the menu selections.

GUIDED ACTIVITY 8

Creating Shortcuts on the Desktop

1. Suppose you want to create a shortcut to look at the contents of a disk drive. To begin, double-click on the My Computer icon on the Windows 95 desktop.

   All the disk drives available on your computer are represented by icons in the My Computer window.

2. Use the *right* mouse button to drag the icon for the 3½ Floppy [A:] from the window onto the desktop. When you release the mouse button, a message appears.

3. Click on the selection Create Shortcut Here, and a new icon appears on the desktop. Compare the icon you just created with the original in the window. The tiny arrow indicates that this is a shortcut.

4. To use the shortcut you must first insert a floppy disk into the disk drive. If you do not have a floppy disk handy, skip this step and the next.

5. Double-click on the shortcut icon to see the contents of the floppy disk. A window appears listing all the files it contains. Close all the windows on the desktop.

6. Delete the shortcut by dragging the icon (using the left mouse button) on top of the Recycle Bin. When the Recycle Bin appears highlighted, as you see in Figure 25, the icon will be thrown away.

FIGURE 25
Dragging to the Recycle Bin

   Now that you have the idea of right-dragging, you can foresee how easy it will be to find a program you like and drag its icon to the Start button. That customizes the Start menu so that it displays that program as one of the selections. The next task is to create a new folder into which you can drag shortcuts for several programs to keep them handy.

FIGURE 26

Creating a new folder from the shortcut menu

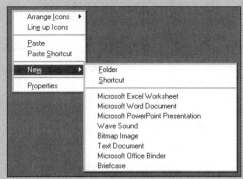

FIGURE 26

Creating a new folder from the shortcut menu

7. Right-click on an empty area of the desktop to reveal the shortcut menu, move the highlight to select New, and click on Folder. Figure 26 shows all the new things you can create from this shortcut menu.

8. An icon of a manila folder appears on the desktop with the name *New Folder* ready for you to name. Label the folder by typing your name.

9. Double-click the new folder icon to open its window. After you are proficient with Explorer and My Computer, you will be able to find your favorite programs and documents to drag into this folder with the right mouse button, just as you dragged the icon to the desktop. For example, you can see a folder created to keep all the games handy in Figure 27. For now, you will leave the new folder empty.

FIGURE 27

Sample folder with shortcut icons

☞ TIP *To create the folder shown in Figure 27, click on the Start button, highlight Find, and select Files or Folders. Type* Games *and click Find Now, and the computer will search for you and create a list of what it finds with that name. If any of the items found say File Folder, drag its icon to the desktop, and voilà—your Games folder. Double-click to open it and see the shortcuts.*

10. Close the window to return it to a folder icon. To remove the clutter of this new folder, drag the icon to the Recycle Bin to get rid of it. When the Recycle Bin is highlighted as in Figure 28, the item will be discarded.

11. To empty the Recycle Bin, point at it and click the right mouse button. On the shortcut menu that appears, click on the Empty Recycle Bin choice. Click Yes to

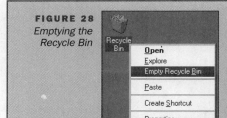

FIGURE 28
*Emptying the
Recycle Bin*

delete these items. When the process is complete, the computer makes a sound. Once you have emptied the Recycle Bin, discarded files may no longer be retrieved.

Exiting Windows

When your work day is done, your final task is to exit Windows 95 and shut down the computer. You should not just turn off the computer while Windows is still running. The shut-down process is important because the operating system needs to save any changes to your desktop and to manage any files it is using in its memory.

To exit Windows 95 so that you can turn off the computer, click the Start button on the taskbar, and then click the choice Shut Down. The desktop dims and a message appears giving you several choices and one last chance to keep working. Click on the choice Shut Down the Computer and click the Yes button. In a few seconds you will be given permission to turn off the computer.

GUIDED ACTIVITY 9

Exiting Windows

1. Close any programs that are running before leaving Windows. If any button appears on the taskbar besides Start, a window has been minimized. Click on it and close it as you have learned above.

2. Click on the Start button, and then click on Shut Down.

3. Click once on the Yes button to confirm your wish to shut down the computer.

4. Words appear on screen giving you permission to turn off your computer.

Summary

Windows 95 is software that runs an operating system, the kind of software a computer uses to start itself, manage the hardware, and keep track of all the information stored in its files. Unlike earlier versions of Windows, Windows 95 replaces DOS and greatly improves on its advantages and ease of use, features for which Windows is famous.

The first advantage to using Windows 95 is the graphical user interface (GUI). The icons, windows, and buttons on the desktop make it simple to visualize and access all the tools available. The taskbar contains a clock and Start button, which, when clicked, reveals a menu. The icon labeled My Computer shows the drives available on the computer, and Network Neighborhood displays all the resources available on other computers connected to your computer. The Recycle Bin is a temporary spot for information you wish to discard.

The user interface must be combined with using a pointing device such as a mouse. By moving the mouse on the table, a pointer moves on the screen. You manipulate items on the screen with these mouse techniques: point, click, right-click, double-click, and drag.

All windows have certain elements in common, such as the title bar and menu bar, borders, scroll bars, and the minimize, maximize, and close buttons. This makes it easy to learn to use all the programs in Windows 95, because once you learn how to use various features, they are used the same way everywhere else.

The second main advantage to Windows 95 is that it is a multitasking operating system. This gives you the ability to have two programs or two processes running at one time. To start one program or many, click on the Start button and highlight selections on the menu. Menu choices that are folders contain yet more choices on another menu, indicated by a folder icon and a right-pointing triangle symbol. Programs that are choices on the menu are indicated by their unique icons and a window that opens when each is selected.

A third advantage Windows 95 offers is the ability to share data among two or more different programs through the use of the Cut, Copy, and Paste commands, which are available on the Edit menu. This process is done through the use of the Clipboard, a temporary storage place provided by Windows.

The final Windows 95 advantage is its user-friendly interface, which makes formerly difficult processes easy to perform. A user can customize features through the Control Panel. For example, the mouse can be made to work better for left-handed people by swapping the functions of the right and left buttons. These changes are made in dialog boxes, which contain elements such as buttons, drop-down lists, option buttons, tabs, and check boxes. You can also customize the properties of the desktop to fit your mood and personality, or use the right mouse button to drag icons and folders to the desktop to create shortcuts.

EXERCISE 1

A Day in the Life of a College Student

1. Turn on your computer and start or log onto Windows, if necessary. Click on the Start button, then highlight Programs, Accessories, and then click on WordPad.

2. Type in the following sentence as best you can, filling in the appropriate numbers in place of the underlines.

    ```
    I am taking __ hours credit, and tuition for each credit
    hour is ___. The total tuition bill is $
    ```

3. Click on the Start button, then highlight Programs, Accessories, and then click on Calculator.

4. Click the buttons on the calculator to multiply the hours times the tuition rate. For example, 15*125=.

5. Click on Edit on the menu bar and select Copy.

6. Click on the WordPad button to bring it to the front.

7. Click on Edit on the menu and select Paste. Press ⏎Enter to start a new line.

8. Click on the Start button, then highlight Programs, Accessories, and then click on Paint. Paint is a drawing program that you can use to make pictures.

9. Draw a picture of yourself studying—it doesn't have to be good. To do this, click on the oval tool to draw your head, and drag on the page. Click on the button that resembles a pencil and drag on the page to draw the face and hair. Click on the rectangle button to draw a table top. Click on the straight line button to add shoulders and table legs, and so on. Click on a color and then click on the pouring bucket button to fill whatever shape you click on with the color. Any time you make a mistake, select Edit on the menu and click Undo.

10. When your picture is ready, click on the Select button, the one on the top that looks like a dotted rectangle. Click and drag down from the top-left corner of the picture to surround the entire picture with a dotted rectangle.

11. Click Edit on the menu and select Copy.

12. Click on the WordPad button on the taskbar to bring it to the front.

13. Select Edit | Paste.

14. If your computer is attached to a printer and the printer is on, print your document by clicking the Print button (the fourth from the left on the toolbar).

15. Close each window by clicking the close button. When the question appears each time asking if you want to save the document, click No.

16. Log off or shut down Windows 95.

The result should have the same elements as in Figure 29, except no doubt your picture won't be nearly as gorgeous as mine.

EXERCISE 2

Serious Business

1. Turn on your computer and log onto or start Windows, if necessary. Click on the Start button, then highlight Programs, Accessories, and then click on WordPad.

2. Type in the following sentence as best you can.

```
If I put $1000 in an interest-bearing account earning 10%
interest annually, at the end of two years I will have $
```

FIGURE 29

*Sample exercise
results*

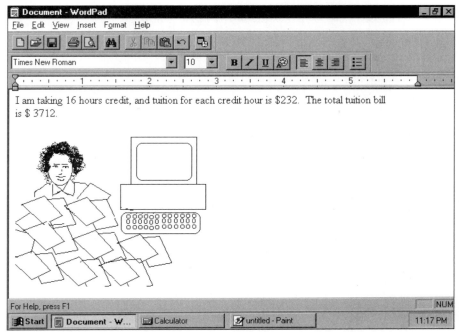

3. Click on the Start button, then highlight Programs, Accessories, and then click on Calculator. Select View | Scientific to see more calculator functions.

4. Click the following buttons on the calculator to find out the future value of your savings:

    1000*1.1 x^y 2 =

5. Click on Edit on the menu bar and select Copy.

6. Click on the WordPad button to bring it to the front.

7. Right-click to get the shortcut menu and select Paste. Press Enter to start a new line.

8. Click on the Start button, then highlight Programs, Accessories, and then click on Paint. Paint is a drawing program that you can use to make pictures.

9. Draw a picture of a dollar bill—it doesn't have to be realistic. To do this, click on the rectangle button to draw the general shape, and drag on the page. Click on the ellipse button to draw the ovals. Click on the button that resembles a pencil and drag on the page to draw George Washington. Click on the text button, and then click on the left side to type the number 1, and so on. Any time you make a mistake, select Edit on the menu and click Undo or click on the Eraser button and rub it out.

10. When your picture is ready, click on the Select button, the one on the top that looks like a dotted rectangle. Click and drag down from the top-left corner of the picture to surround the entire picture with a dotted rectangle.

11. Click Edit on the menu and select Copy.

12. Click on the WordPad button on the taskbar to bring it to the front.

13. Select Edit | Paste from the menu.

14. If your computer is attached to a printer and the printer is on, print your document by clicking the Print button (the fourth from the left on the toolbar).

15. Close each window by clicking the close button. When the question appears each time asking if you want to save the document, click No.

16. Log off or shut down Windows 95.

Review Questions

The answers to questions marked with an asterisk are contained in Appendix A.

*1. In what ways can Windows 95 be compared to a desktop?

2. What is an operating system? Compare and contrast Windows to DOS.

*3. What are the five different techniques in using a mouse?

4. What items are found on the Windows desktop? What is the function of each?

*5. What are the steps for starting Windows 95?

6. What is the function of My Computer? Network Neighborhood? Recycle Bin?

*7. What are ToolTips? When do they appear?

8. What is the procedure for shutting down Windows 95? Why is it important to shut down properly?

*9. Match the names of the elements with the numbers marked on Figure 30.

___ Border
___ Close button
___ Desktop
___ Menu bar
___ Maximize button
___ Minimize button
___ Scroll bar
___ Taskbar
___ Title bar

10. To access a shortcut menu, you must

a. Right-click.

b. Double-click.

c. Click.

d. Point.

FIGURE 30
Numbered
screen objects
for Review
Question 9

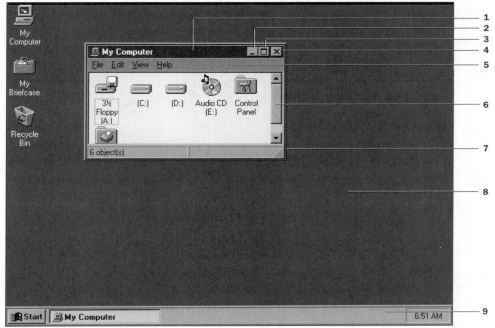

*11.   When several windows are open on screen, you can

   a.   Tile them so that they fit side by side to fill the screen.

   b.   Cascade them so that they are arranged neatly with their title bars showing.

   c.   Minimize them so that they appear as buttons on the taskbar.

   d.   All the above.

12.   To change the size of a window slightly,

   a.   Drag on the title bar.

   b.   Drag on the border.

   c.   Double-click on the title bar.

   d.   Click a button in the window's upper-right corner.

*13.   What are four advantages to using Windows 95?

14.   What feature allows you to see all the programs running at once? How can you tell which window is the active one?

*15.   What do the ▶ symbols on the Start menu mean?

*16.   What are the four general steps for bringing information from one place to another?

*17.   What is the Clipboard? What commands require it to be used?

18.   What do ellipses (…) on a menu selection mean?

*19.   How can the mouse be customized for left-handed people?

20.   What properties of the desktop can be customized? Why would you want to leave Pattern and Wallpaper set to [None]?

*21.   The command that erases material from one location and moves it to the Clip-board is

   a.   Copy.

   b.   Cut.

   c.   Delete.

   d.   Clear.

   e.   Paste.

22.   Match the numbers marked in Figure 31 with the following elements of dialog boxes.

   ___ Command button
   ___ Tab
   ___ Option button
   ___ Check box
   ___ Drop-down list
   ___ Open list box
   ___ Spin box

FIGURE 31
Dialog box elements to identify for review question 22

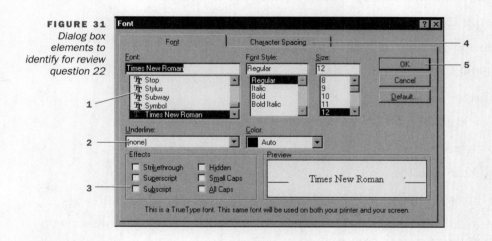

Key Terms

The following terms are introduced in this unit. Be sure you know what each of them means.

Active window	Character-based user	Click
Border	interface (CUI)	Close button
Button	Check box	Command button

Cursor
Desktop
Dialog box
Double-click
Drag
Drop-down list
File
Folder
Graphical user interface
   (GUI)
Highlight
Icon
Maximize
Menu
Menu bar

Menu choice
Minimize
Multitasking
My Briefcase
My Computer
Network Neighborhood
Open list box
Operating system
Option button
Pixel
Point
Pointer
Properties
Recycle Bin
Restore

Right-click
Screen saver
Scroll bar
Select
Shortcut
Shortcut menu
Spin box
Tab
Taskbar
Title bar
ToolTips
User interface
Window

Running Start

1

This unit gives both beginners and experienced computer users a sample of word processing with the easy-to-use features of Microsoft Word. You will put to work a few simple yet powerful techniques in creating your own business card. This unit should be used at the computer. Ordinarily you should read the units before performing the Guided Activities on the computer, but this unit is intended for you to use at the computer to introduce you to Microsoft Word and show you how simple it is to use a full-featured word processor. Some of these tasks can be used in any Windows application. Many steps in these Guided Activities will be explained in more detail in later units.

Learning Objectives

At the completion of this unit you should know

1. how to start and exit Microsoft Word,

2. how to create a simple document,

3. how to use buttons and menus,

4. how to get help.

Using Microsoft Word

The best way to appreciate the simplicity and power of a Windows program is to start it and use it. You will need a formatted disk if you want to save the document you will create in the Guided Activities. If you have not installed the software or need to format a disk, consult your Microsoft Word or Windows documentation for details about these procedures.

To start Microsoft Word, click on the Start button on the taskbar and select Programs. When the list of programs appears, click on the selection for Microsoft Word (shown in the margin). The screen in Figure 1.1 should appear. The Word screen contains certain elements common to every application that runs under Windows. You will see the title bar; the menu bar; the minimize, maximize, and close buttons on the upper right; and scroll bars on the right and bottom sides. The menu bar shows a list of commands that you can select to manipulate your document. As you click your mouse on the menu, a list appears with more specific commands, just as in Windows.

Several features are also found on the Word screen.

W7 Microsoft Word

- *Toolbars* just below the menu allow you to perform certain actions by clicking on their **buttons**.

- The *ruler* is used to change the margin and tab settings.

- The **status bar** gives information about your document or about the command you are performing. Word typically displays all of these screen elements. The following steps will help you set them up if your screen does not match the one in Figure 1.1.

FIGURE 1.1
Word screen

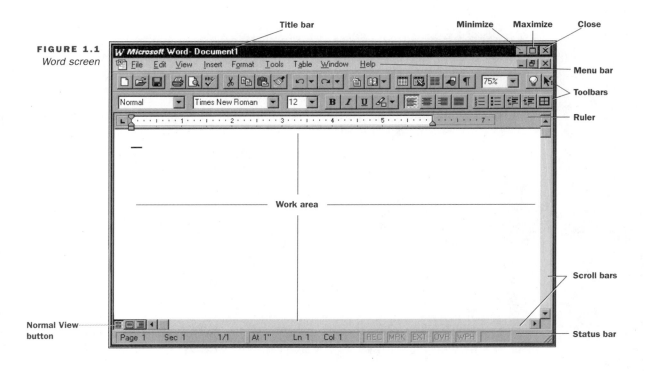

GUIDED ACTIVITY 1.1

Setting Up the Word Screen

1. Click once on the word View on the menu bar. The View menu drops down for you to select another command, as shown in Figure 1.2.

FIGURE 1.2
View menu

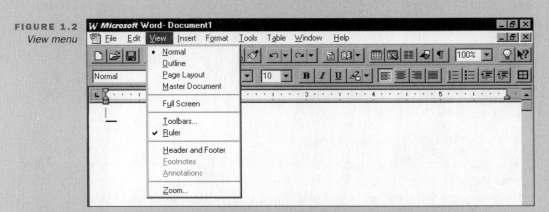

A list of commands appears below the word View. This list is called a drop-down menu. The area of the screen you clicked is called the menu bar. *Menus* display the commands available under a menu title such as View. To exit the menu without executing any of the commands, press [Esc] several times or click anywhere away from the menus and toolbars. If you ever open an incorrect menu or dialog box, pressing [Esc] several times will cancel the action.

2. If no check mark ✓ appears next to the word Ruler, click on Ruler, and the ruler will appear near the top of the Word screen. This command turns the ruler off or on, each time you select it. Click on the View menu and select Ruler several times to see the Ruler appear and disappear from the screen.

3. If no toolbars are visible at the top of the Word screen, select the View menu again, but this time click on the word Toolbars. Some commands in the menus, such as Toolbars, are followed by ellipses (…), which are not printed in this book. These commands will cause a dialog box to appear on the screen.

4. This time a dialog box appears for you to give additional information, shown on Figure 1.3. The boxes next to the words Standard and Formatting should contain a check mark, as should the ones at the bottom next to Color Buttons and Show ToolTips. If any of these check marks are missing, point the mouse at the empty box and click. You may also check the boxes labeled Large Buttons and With Shortcut Keys, but it isn't necessary to do so. When all are correct, click OK.

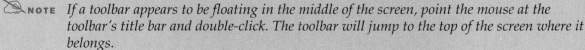

NOTE   *If a toolbar appears to be floating in the middle of the screen, point the mouse at the toolbar's title bar and double-click. The toolbar will jump to the top of the screen where it belongs.*

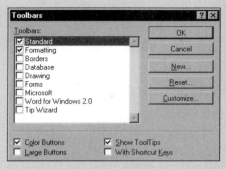

FIGURE 1.3
*Toolbars
dialog box*

5. Click on the Normal View button on the far left side of the status bar (refer back to Figure 1.1) to make sure you are in Normal view.

6. If a paragraph symbol (¶) appears next to the blinking cursor, click on the ¶ button on the toolbar and the symbol will disappear.

✎ **NOTE** *One other feature you may notice is an icon of a book with a red ✓ or ✗ located on the right side of the status bar on the bottom of the screen. This means that Automatic Spell Checking is turned on. This causes a wavy red line to appear below misspelled words. This feature will be explained further in Unit 2.*

GUIDED ACTIVITY 1.2

Entering Text

Let's begin with a unique word processing application—creating a business card. When Microsoft Word starts, it contains a blank document ready for new text. The cursor, a flashing vertical bar, is in the upper-left corner of the ***work area***, the area where text is entered and modified. The finished text will resemble Figure 1.4.

FIGURE 1.4
*Sample business
card*

1. The first step in this activity is to make the text only as wide as a standard business card, 3½ inches wide. To do this, place the mouse pointer over the triangle

FIGURE 1.5
Ruler setting

Drag triangle here

on the right side of the ruler, hold down the left mouse button, and drag the tri-angle to the 3½ inch mark on the ruler, as on Figure 1.5.

2. Type ---, and then press [Enter] 3 times.

    As soon as you press [Enter], Word automatically changes the three hyphens into a solid border across the top of the business card, 3½ inches wide.

    You may have figured out that, to get the cursor to the next line (as you are required to do in the previous step), you press [Enter].

3. Type in your first and last name. Press [Enter] again.

    If you make a typing error, erase it using [Backspace]. The [Backspace] key erases the character immediately to the left of the cursor.

NOTE *Wavy red lines appear under words the computer thinks are typing errors. Your name or your school's name may have this wavy underline because they are probably not found in the computer's dictionary. Use the wavy underlines to alert you to possible errors, but ignore them if the computer flags a word that is correct.*

4. Type in your position title, Computer Novice Extraordinaire.

5. Press [Enter] twice to leave a blank line between the title and what you are about to type.

6. Type your school name, and then press [Enter]. Type your school's address and press [Enter]. Type the city, state, and zip, and then press [Enter].

7. For the final line of text, type in voice and your telephone number. Press the [Tab] key twice and then type fax followed by your fax number. Press [Enter].

    If you would prefer, leave off the fax number and put in your E-mail address instead. You may have to use fewer tabs after your telephone number if your E-mail address is very long.

8. Type --- and then press [Enter]. The hyphens instantly expand to make a solid rule, or line, becoming the bottom border of the business card.

The text of your card is now complete. This is the first step involved in creating a word processing document. The preceding Guided Activity would work in most word processors. Sad to say, software engineers have not yet designed the software package that will enter the text for the user with perfect accuracy!

The next step in preparing the card involves changing the way the text appears, which is called *formatting*.

Formatting the Business Card

You will format the text of the business card so that it appears centered. You will also format your name so that it stands out. The first step in formatting is to indicate what words you wish to change by *highlighting,* or *selecting*, them.

1. To highlight, or select, the text, click on the word Edit on the menu bar, and then click on Select All. The text then appears in reverse color—white letters on black instead of black letters on white.

   Look at the area of the screen above the work area and ruler, shown in Figure 1.6. This area of the screen is called the Formatting toolbar, and is used for formatting text.

2. Click on the Center button on the Formatting toolbar.

   The text becomes centered on the business card, and the button appears pushed in, as in Figure 1.6.

FIGURE 1.6
Centering the text

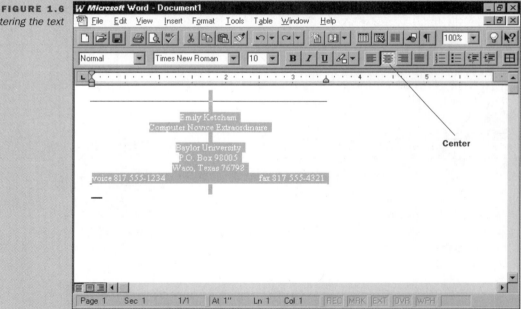

You may have discovered that, as you point with the mouse at any button on the screen, after a few seconds the name of the button appears. These are called *ToolTips*, and they will be of tremendous help as you learn your way around Word.

3. Click the mouse anywhere on the document to remove the highlighting.

4. To format your name so that it stands out, first highlight it. Place the mouse pointer on your first name and click and drag to the right until both your first and last names are selected.

5. Click on the Bold button on the Formatting toolbar. Then click the Italic button on the toolbar.

   When these buttons appear pushed in, as in Figure 1.7, anything typed will appear bold and italic.

FIGURE 1.7
Bold and Italic buttons appear pushed in

Your name now appears in bold, italic letters and will stand out from the rest of the text.

The letters in the school name, address, and phone number are too large to look nice on the small business card. The size of the letters is indicated by the number 10 on the Formatting toolbar. To make the letters smaller, this number must be smaller.

6. Highlight your school name, address, and phone and fax numbers. Use a click-and-drag technique as before.

7. Move the mouse pointer to the number 10 on the Formatting toolbar and click. This highlights (selects) the 10.

FIGURE 1.8
Changing the size of the text

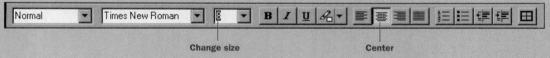

8. Type 8 (which replaces the number 10, as shown in Figure 1.8) and press . A smaller number means the typed characters will be smaller. Now the school name, address, and phone number are a little smaller than the name and title. Compare the sizes on the following sample:

This is size 10.

This is size 8.

GUIDED ACTIVITY 1.4

Enhancing the Design

The last task is to add the little picture design in the top-left corner. The picture will be inserted wherever the cursor is located, so you must first move the cursor to the correct position.

1. Click the mouse pointer on the center of the page in the area above your name and below the top border. The blinking cursor should be located just above your name and about a quarter of an inch below the border.

2. Click on Insert on the menu, and then click on Picture.

   A dialog box appears with a list of picture names as shown in Figure 1.9.

 The pictures are stored in a folder called Clipart. If that folder does not automatically open, you may have to double-click on it to see the list of picture names. The picture names may show other details about the files. Click on the Preview button to display a preview of the picture.

FIGURE 1.9
Inserting a picture

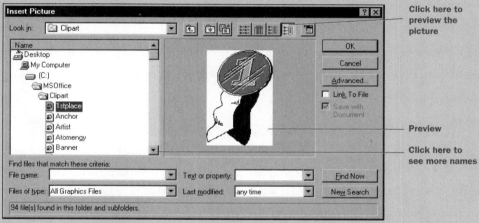

3. Click repeatedly on the arrow at the bottom of the scroll bar to scroll through the list of names. Click on the file names to see a preview of each picture.

   Any of the smaller pictures can be used on your business card. Choose one from this list:

   Celtic
   Checkmrk
   Deco
   Leaf
   Ornamnt1
   Ornamnt2
   Ornamnt3
   Ornamnt4

4. When you have the picture you want in the preview window, click OK or press Enter. The picture is inserted at the location of the cursor, and the text moves down to make room. The picture would look better on the top-left corner of the business card.

5. Click the Align Left button on the Formatting toolbar. To find which button this is, move the mouse pointer over each of the buttons on the toolbar and pause to see the ToolTips. The Align Left button is just to the left of the Center button you used previously, as in Figure 1.6.

   Although the business card is displayed on screen the way it will be printed, the entire page will not fit on the screen. To get an idea of how the page will appear, look at it with the preview screen.

6. Click on the Print Preview button, which has an image of a magnifying glass over a sheet of paper. It appears on the Standard toolbar shown in Figure 1.10.

   The Print Preview screen appears in Figure 1.11. This is the way your document will look on the page when you print it. The preview screen is meant only to display the position of the text on the printed page; the words are not really legible.

FIGURE 1.10
Standard toolbar

Print   Print Preview

FIGURE 1.11
Print Preview screen

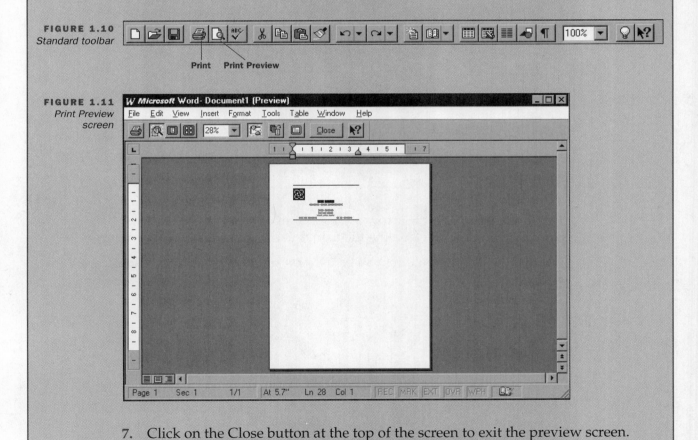

7. Click on the Close button at the top of the screen to exit the preview screen.

Ideally, you are finished; in all probability, you will decide to make changes to the text. For example, you wish to add your middle name to the business card, and the title `Computer Novice Extraordinaire` doesn't suit you. Therefore, you will need to edit the text.

GUIDED ACTIVITY 1.5

Changing Text

1. Move the mouse pointer between your first and last names and click once.

    The cursor is now positioned correctly to enter the new text.

2. Type in your middle name or initial. Make sure there is a space before and after.

    The second editing change to be made is to replace the title in the line under your name.

3. Click and drag across `Computer Novice Extraordinaire` to highlight it.

4. Type whatever title you prefer.

    Highlighted or selected text is replaced with whatever you type.

    The business card is correct. Now you need to print it.

 5. Click the Print button on the Standard toolbar. A message will appear on the status bar while the document is being printed, and soon you will have your printed card (assuming your printer is on and ready to work). With a fast computer, the message may be too quick to see.

You have successfully entered, edited, formatted, and enhanced text. The commands used were simple and intuitive. All of the formatting steps were performed by clicking buttons on the screen. Rather than requiring you to speak the computer's language by learning and remembering complicated codes or key sequences, Microsoft Word offers the use of commands in a manner that seems natural. This is typical of Microsoft Word specifically and of Windows software in general.

Executing Commands from the Keyboard

Any command that you execute with the mouse may also be executed with the keyboard. Users who type quickly may find it faster to use the keyboard for certain commands than to use the mouse, since they can keep both hands on the keyboard and their eyes on the screen. To access the menus, press and release the *Alternate* or Alt key (`Alt`) on the keyboard. Each menu selection contains one letter that is underlined, often the first letter of the menu's name. You may display the contents of that menu by pressing the underlined letter. Each command in the drop-down menu will also have one underlined letter or number that can be pressed to execute the command—in many cases, a mnemonic (as in `P` for `Print`). Any menu command can be executed by pressing three keys: `Alt`, the menu letter, and the command letter. For example, to print a letter, you would press `Alt` `F` (for the File menu), and then press `P` (for the Print command).

Executing Commands Using the Keyboard

If you have a mouse and will be using it to execute commands, you need not bother to complete this section. However, if you know how to execute commands from the keyboard as well as with the mouse, you will find yourself using both methods alternately, as convenient. When your hands are already on the keyboard (or if you have the misfortune of being stuck on a computer without a mouse), you will find this method of executing commands most helpful.

To preview the document with the keyboard, select the command File | Print Preview from the menu.

1. Press [Alt]. Press [F].

    The File menu drops down. The F in File was underlined, so when you pressed that key, the File menu opened. Both uppercase and lowercase letters are accepted when executing commands from a menu with the keyboard.

2. Press [V].

    The File | Print Preview command is executed immediately.

3. Press [Esc] to close the preview screen.

    Steps 4 through 6 are optional for this exercise.

4. Although it is not necessary, you may wish to save the document you created in this unit. To save, you must have a formatted disk and place it in drive A:.

5. Press [Alt]. Press [F]. The File menu drops down.

6. Press [S]. Type the file name A:Business Card, and press [Enter].

7. Close the file by selecting File on the menu and then Close.

Getting Help

If you need help in using Word, you do not have to find the manual or wait for someone to guide you. Help is available right on your computer screen. You can receive step-by-step verbal directions for using Word, and you can see visual examples and demonstrations as well. You can get help several ways:

■ Select Help from the menu.

■ Press the [F1] key.

■ Click the Help button on the toolbar.

■ Click the Help button in any dialog box to get further instructions.

1. Click on Help on the menu bar, and then select Microsoft Word Help Topics from the menu. This brings up the Help screen shown in Figure 1.12, which displays four tabs: Contents, Index, Find, and Answer Wizard. Any one of the four tabs may appear on screen, depending on which was used last, so your screen may not exactly match the one in Figure 1.12.

FIGURE 1.12
Microsoft Word Help Topics

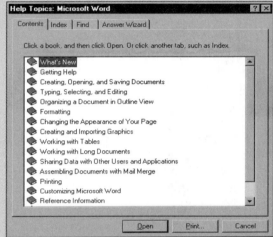

2. Click on the Answer Wizard tab on the Help screen. The Answer Wizard allows you to get answers by typing in a phrase. If you want information about printing your document, for instance, you would type the word `Print` in the box, as shown in Figure 1.13.

FIGURE 1.13
Answer Wizard

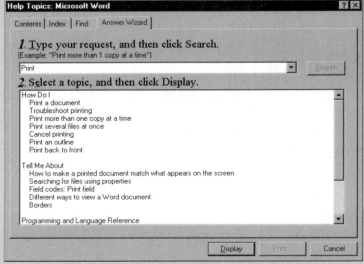

3. Type `Print`, and then press or click the Search button.

   Word lists related topics that may answer your question. When you click on the topic "How Do I Print a Document" and click Display, the Answer Wizard demonstrates selecting File and Print from the menu and explains more options.

4. Press OK if you want to print the document, or Cancel if you do not want to print.

   Another way to access information on Printing is to look in the Contents or the Index.

5. Select Help from the menu, and then select the Contents tab. This displays the table of contents of all the topics in Help, as shown in Figure 1.12.

6. To get information about printing, click on Printing, and then click Open.

7. This shows many more topics about printing, more than even the Answer Wizard. To specifically find how to print your work, take the next steps: select Print Your Work, then click Open, select Print a Document, and finally click Display. Finish up by clicking OK to print or Cancel to return to the document without printing.

   The Help button on the far-right side of the toolbar gives *context-sensitive* help. This means that when you click on the Help button, whatever you click on next—a button, a bar, any element of the Word screen—will be the subject of the Help screen that appears.

8. Click on the Help button. The mouse pointer changes to an arrow with a large question mark.

9. Click on the Print button (fourth from the left on the Standard toolbar). An explanation appears on screen, as shown in Figure 1.14.

FIGURE 1.14
Context-sensitive Help screen

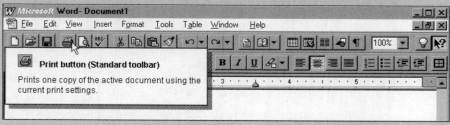

10. To get rid of the explanation, click anywhere inside it.

    A final way to get help is found in each of the dialog boxes. If you do not know what to do once you open a dialog box, click the Help button in its top-right corner.

11. Click on File on the menu bar, and then select Print. The dialog box that appears, shown in Figure 1.15, gives many more options about printing.

FIGURE 1.15
Help button in the Print dialog box

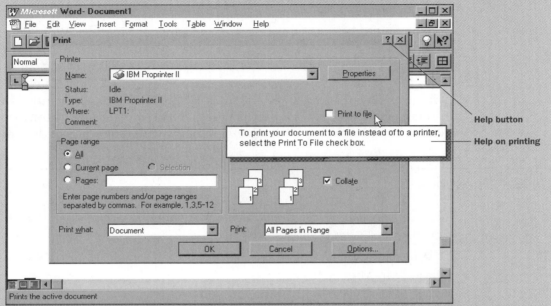

12. To find out what each item means, click the Help button in the top-right corner of the dialog box, and then point to any area of the screen. Click Cancel to return to the document.

13. One more way to get invaluable information about using Microsoft Word efficiently is through the TipWizard. Click on the TipWizard button on the right side of the Standard toolbar. Whenever you start Word, a new tip is displayed below the toolbars, as shown in Figure 1.16. Click the TipWizard button again to make the tip disappear.

FIGURE 1.16
Tip of the day

> 💡 1] Click the right mouse button on the red wavy underlined words to correct them.

The help within Microsoft Word is comparable to that found in books and is both convenient and easy to use. You can access it on screen by selecting from either the menu or the keyboard, or by clicking the Help button on the toolbar.

14. Exit Word by selecting File on the menu and clicking Exit. Another way to do this is to click the close button in the upper-right corner of the screen.

Summary

This unit led you through the steps of starting Microsoft Word and learning about the elements on the Word screen: the title, menu, and status bars; the buttons on the toolbars; the selections on the menu; and the dialog boxes. You stepped through typing and formatting a simple document, and then edited and embellished it. You previewed and printed the finished product. You also learned how to use the on-screen Help facility. Later units will give you much more information about creating, editing, formatting, and enhancing many different kinds of documents.

Review Questions

The answers to odd-numbered questions are contained in Appendix A. On multiple-choice questions, choose one or more answers.

*1. What parts of the screen are found in all Windows applications? What parts are found in Microsoft Word?

2. When is the ⏎Enter key used in typing?

*3. What is the single most important key to remember when executing commands from the keyboard?

4. What are four ways to get help? Which way gives context-sensitive help?

*5. The ruler is used for

   a. Measuring the size of typed characters.

   b. Changing the width of lines on the page.

   c. Telling the number of lines on the page.

   d. Accessing commands and dialog boxes.

6. If you want to get rid of a drop-down menu and not select anything from it,

   a. Press Esc.

   b. Press Ctrl Alt Del.

   c. Press M for Menu.

   d. Press Del.

*7. Changing the appearance of a document is called

   a. Highlighting.

   b. Editing.

   c. Formatting.

   d. Inputting.

8. You can tell the function of the buttons on the toolbars by

   a. Checking if they appear pushed in.

   b. Looking at the menu.

   c. Clicking on them.

   d. Pointing the mouse at them.

Key Terms

The following terms are introduced in this unit. Be sure you know what each of them means.

Alternate	Highlight	Status bar
Button	Menu	Toolbar
Context-sensitive	Ruler	ToolTips
Formatting	Select	Work area

2 Entering and Editing Text

Word processing can be divided into three general procedures:

- Entering and editing text
- Formatting text and paragraphs
- Using advanced features

This unit will cover the first of these procedures. This is the easiest part of word processing and is basically done the same way in any software package. You will learn how typing in a word processor is different from typing on a typewriter, how to correct errors as you type, how to move around in the document after information is entered, and how to manipulate and change text. These procedures are fundamental to word processing and must be mastered before continuing.

Learning Objectives

At the completion of this unit you should know

1. what general procedures are involved in word processing,
2. how to enter and correct text in a document,
3. the difference between using Backspace and Del,
4. how to move around in a document,
5. how to save a document.

Important Commands

> Edit | Clear
>
> Edit | Undo
>
> File | Save

Entering Text

The first task in creating documents in Microsoft Word is to type the content. Text is entered into a word processing document in much the same way as it is on a type-writer. Some differences will affect the way you enter text. Most of these arise from features designed to make typing faster.

A major difference between word processing and typing on a typewriter is the use of the *Enter* key (⌨Enter). Electric typewriters have a carriage return key that is used at the end of each line of text. Many first-time word processor users mistake the ⌨Enter key on the computer keyboard for the carriage return on the typewriter and use it to end each line of text. This is unnecessary because of a feature in word processors called *word wrap*, which automatically adjusts the text to fit between the margins.

As you approach the end of a line, the word processor monitors the length of each word that you type. When you enter a word that will go beyond the current right margin, that word is automatically moved to the beginning of the next line. There is no need to manually force the cursor to the beginning of the next line within paragraphs. The only time ⌨Enter is used is at the end of a paragraph or when the user wants to leave a blank line in the text.

The word wrap feature is invaluable because it allows you to concentrate on what you are typing without having to worry about how close the text is to the end of each line. This leads to greater typing speeds and minimizes the amount of time spent entering the document. Word wrap is also important when it comes to editing the text. Whenever you add or remove text, change the size of the typeface, or alter the margins, text flows between the margins. Pressing ⌨Enter at the end of each line would cause the lines to break at odd places after making changes like these.

Whatever your typing accuracy, you will eventually make an error as you enter text. If the Automatic Spell Checking feature is turned on, errors will be underlined with a wavy red line. If you notice the error when you make it, you can easily correct it by pressing the *Backspace* key (⌨Backspace) on the keyboard. The ⌨Backspace key always performs exactly the same function: it erases the character immediately to the left of the cursor.

If you notice an error farther back in the document, there are several ways to correct the mistake. You may use either the *arrow keys* (⌨←, ⌨↑, ⌨→, ⌨↓) or the mouse to move the cursor to the error. If you position the cursor immediately to the right of the mistake, you can erase it by pressing ⌨Backspace once for each incorrect character. After the incorrect text is removed, simply type the correct letters to fix the passage.

If the error is more than two or three lines away from the current cursor position, it may be more efficient to use the mouse to position the cursor to the right of the incorrect text. When the mouse pointer is moved into the work area, it will appear as an *I-beam* so that it can be easily positioned between characters. Move the mouse pointer to the right of the incorrect text and click once. The cursor will appear at the location of the mouse click. The procedure to correct the error is identical whether you use the arrow keys or the mouse to position the cursor.

GUIDED ACTIVITY 2.1

Entering Text

1. Start Microsoft Word. For this activity you will be typing an article. Since most teachers prefer that students turn in papers double-spaced, this is a handy skill to learn. To set up a document so that it will be automatically double-spaced, hold down the Ctrl key and press 2.

2. Type the following text into the document, with only a single word space between sentences. If you notice any keystroke errors as you type, correct them by pressing Backspace until the error disappears, and retype the text correctly. The misspelled words will be underlined with a wavy red line, as shown in Figure 2.1, if the Automatic Spell Checking is turned on. Remember not to press Enter at the end of each line. Let the word wrap feature take you to the next line instead. If you do press Enter inadvertently, press Backspace. At the end of each paragraph, press Enter once to end the paragraph and a second time to leave a blank line before starting the next paragraph.

FIGURE 2.1
Wavy red lines under misspelled words

This week I received a job announcement which contained several statements with errors: "Ideal canidate has software testing background. Neeed excellent spelling and grammer skills." No wonder they want to hire someone with those skills!

This example shows how important it is to edit and proofread your document. Once you have your text typed, it's time to read the whole thing over and look for anything that will distract from your message.

Word processing involves the tasks of entering text, editing the content, and formatting the appearance of the document. Which step is the most important in the process of creating a professional document?

Writing the first draft of a document can be a chore if you don't know exactly what you want to say or how to go about expressing it. In business writing, a chronological approach is often the most straightforward one. Gather your thoughts on what happens (or happened) first, and proceed through the "story" until you reach the end. Another model is to focus on a single outcome, then explain the reasons or causes for the outcome. To increase the reader's interest in your document, add specific examples or illustrations.

This week I received a job announcement which contained several statements with errors: "Ideal canidate has software testing background. Neeed excellent spelling and grammer skills." No wonder they want to hire someone with those skills!

This example shows how important it is to edit and proofread your document. Once you have your text typed, it's time to read the whole thing over and look for anything that will distract from your message. Distractions include not only spelling and grammar mistakes, but politically incorrect statements or personal, unkind remarks. Remove any sarcasm, as the reader might take it at face value and misunderstand your real meaning.

Formatting is the final consideration. An attractive document draws in the reader and supports the message you are trying to send. It only requires a few touches to increase the impact. Like junior-high girls with eye shadow, remind yourself that a little formatting goes a long way to increase appeal.

Oops! Pressing Enter in the middle of a paragraph causes the text to jump to the next line, leaving a short line of text, as shown in Figure 2.2. In a word processor, an Enter character is like any letter on the keyboard in that it can be added or removed. This character is not displayed on the screen. You can display it by clicking the Show/Hide ¶ button, which appears on the toolbar. When you click this, Enter characters appear as a ¶ (paragraph symbol), and spaces between words appear as small dots. To remove an incorrect ¶, use the arrow keys to move the cursor to the far left side of the line below the short line and press Backspace. If all those symbols and dots make the screen too cluttered, click the Show/Hide ¶ button again, and these symbols will disappear.

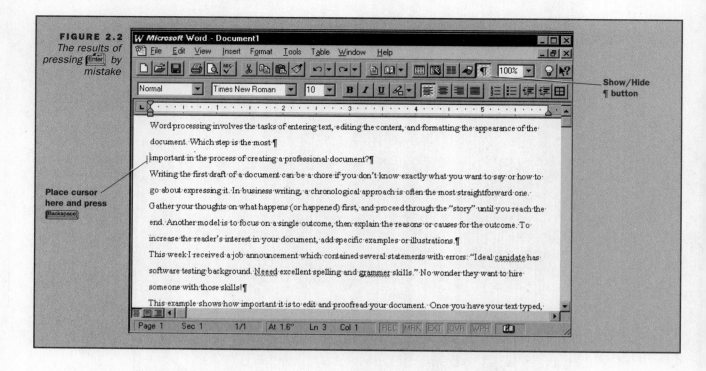

FIGURE 2.2
The results of pressing Enter *by mistake*

Place cursor here and press Backspace

Show/Hide ¶ button

Reviewing the Document

When you are done entering the text, the next step will usually be to read back through what you have written to proofread the document. This step often involves adding, deleting, or modifying text and can be considered your "second draft." An important element in editing text is moving around in the document. In essence, the screen is a window that allows you to look at only a portion of your text at once; thus, it is important to know how to see all parts of the document in the window.

The easiest way to move through your text is to use the arrow keys on the keyboard. If the cursor is at the top of a document, you can move down by repeatedly pressing the Down arrow key (↓). The cursor will move down one line at a time for each time you press ↓. Although this is a simple method to remember, it is cumbersome to read long documents one line at a time.

A more efficient method to review your text is to press the *Page Down* key (PgDn). This key will scroll down (move vertically) a document one screen length at a time and allow you to skim a few paragraphs at once. Rather than pressing ↓ once for each line of text, PgDn allows you to press a single key every eight or ten lines of text or more. This is less tiring for reading long documents and allows you to move much more quickly through several pages. The Up arrow key (↑) and the *Page Up* key (PgUp) work like the ↓ and PgDn keys, except that they scroll up through the document rather than down.

GUIDED ACTIVITY 2.2

Moving Within a Document Using the Keyboard

1. The cursor should still be at the end of the last paragraph you typed. If it is not, hold down the `Ctrl` key and press `End`.

2. Press `↑`. The cursor will move up one line. Continue pressing `↑` until the cursor is on the top line showing on the screen.

   So far the screen has not moved at all. All of the movements of the cursor have occurred on one screen.

3. Press `↑` one more time. This time the screen will scroll up one line.

   This is a good way to move a few lines of your document onto the screen, but not a good way for scrolling long distances in the text, unless you have a very fast computer. The `PgUp` key is better for this.

4. Press `PgUp`.

   Rather than moving up one line at a time, the screen has moved up to display the next 10 or 12 lines.

5. Press `PgDn` until the cursor reaches the end of the document.

   Each time you press `PgDn`, the screen moves down 10 to 12 lines.

6. Press the *End* key (`End`) on the keyboard. The cursor moves to the end of the current line. Press the *Home* key (`Home`) to move the cursor back to the beginning of the line.

   You can now move quickly up and down through the document as well as to the beginning and end of lines. It is also helpful to be able to quickly move to the middle of a line using the arrow keys. Use the *Control* or Ctrl key (`Ctrl`) in conjunction with the arrow keys to move along a line one word at a time.

7. Move the cursor to the top of the document. Hold down `Ctrl` and press `→` 5 times. The cursor moves a distance of five words along the first line.

   This is a much faster way to move through text than just using the `→` key.

8. Press `↓` once to get to the next line. Hold down `Ctrl` and press `→` several times until the cursor moves to the last word of the first line. Press `Home` to get the cursor to the beginning of the line.

9. Since using `Ctrl` with arrow keys augments their effect, you see that adding `Ctrl` to the `Home` and `End` keys will increase or exaggerate their effect as well.

10. Press `Ctrl``End` and the cursor jumps immediately to the very end of the document.

11. Press `Ctrl``Home` and the cursor jumps immediately to the very beginning of the document.

PRESS	TO MOVE
↑	up one line
↓	down one line
←	left one character
→	right one character
PgUp	up one screen
PgDn	down one screen
End	to end of the line
Home	to beginning of the line
Ctrl →	one word to the right
Ctrl ←	one word to the left
Ctrl Home	to beginning of the document
Ctrl End	to end of the document

Table 2.1 lists all the keys and their effect on the location of the cursor within a document.

The functions of the arrow keys and of the PgUp and PgDn keys can be duplicated by mouse movements. The *scroll bars* are used to move the screen position vertically or horizontally with the mouse. An important point to remember when using the mouse to move through your document is that, unlike when you use the keyboard, you are not changing the location of the cursor within the document. When you press ↓ or PgDn on the keyboard, you are forcing the cursor beyond the bottom of the screen; therefore, Microsoft Word scrolls down to show you the new cursor position. This is not the case when you use the mouse to move through the document. Using the mouse changes the part of the document being displayed but does not affect the position of the cursor *until* the left mouse button is clicked with the mouse pointer in the work area. The cursor is then positioned on screen.

The scroll bar allows you to move three ways through a document: one line at a time, one screen at a time, and globally (through the entire document). To move up or down a line at a time, click the scroll bar's up arrow or down arrow, respectively. This is equivalent to pressing the keyboard's ↑ or ↓ arrows. You can move quickly a line at a time by pointing at the mouse button at the arrows on either the top or the bottom of the scroll bar and holding down the left mouse button, but other ways are better used for scrolling through large segments of text.

The functions of the PgUp and PgDn keys can also be duplicated by using the mouse with the vertical scroll bar. Between the scroll bar's up and down arrows is a vertical strip with a box in it. The box is called the *scroll box* and represents the position of the screen you are viewing relative to the rest of the document. In the sample scroll bar, the user is viewing a screen of text approximately one-third of the way through the document. To perform the Page Up function, click anywhere in the vertical strip between the scroll bar's up arrow key and the scroll box. Page Down is performed by clicking between the scroll box and the scroll bar's down arrow. The document will move up or down one screen, respectively, to allow you to view other parts of your document.

You can move quickly across large distances inside your document by using the mouse to drag the scroll box on the scroll bar. The scroll box can be dragged directly with the mouse to any position in the vertical strip between the scroll bar's up and down arrows. You can immediately go to any location between the top and bottom of the document by dragging the scroll box toward the top or bottom of the scroll bar. In a multipage document, the page number appears next to the scroll bar as you drag, letting you know what will appear on screen when you stop dragging the scroll box.

GUIDED ACTIVITY 2.3

Moving Within a Document Using the Mouse

1. Click on the down arrow at the bottom of the scroll bar. The screen shifts down one line, but the cursor remains at the same position in the document. You can no longer see the cursor because the first line of the document has scrolled off the screen.

2. Click in the area between the scroll box and the down arrow at the bottom of the scroll bar. The screen shifts down just as though you had pressed `PgDn` on the keyboard.

3. Click on the up arrow at the top of the scroll bar.

   The screen moves back up one line at a time.

4. Click in the area between the scroll box and the up arrow at the top of the scroll bar.

   This is the equivalent of pressing the `PgUp` key.

Remember that, when you press the arrow keys (`←`, `↑`, `→`, `↓`) or the `PgUp` and `PgDn` keys, the screen moves because the cursor moves. When using the scroll bar to move through a document, however, the cursor remains in the last spot on the screen where you inserted or deleted text. If you edit a sentence on the last page and use the *global move* to move to the beginning of the document, even though the first page is displayed, the cursor is still located on the last page where you finished editing the sentence. This is the one major difference between using the keyboard and using the scroll bar to move through a document.

A touch typist can move around a document more quickly using the keyboard than the mouse, although using the mouse is more intuitive. Rather than having to remember which keys to use, many people find the mouse techniques easier to recall.

Editing Text

Once you have moved the screen to view an area of text that needs editing, the cursor is positioned by clicking with the mouse pointer in the work area wherever you want to add text. As you type, all characters to the right of the cursor will shift to the right to make room for the new text. The word processor is in the *insert mode* because the new text is inserted at the location of the cursor.

If you want the new text to replace the characters to the right of the cursor, you could use the *overtype mode*. In the overtype mode, each character you type will replace the character to the right of the cursor. To change between the insert and overtype modes, press the *Insert* or Ins key (⌷Ins⌷) on the keyboard. When the word processor is in the overtype mode, the letters OVR appear in dark letters on the status bar at the bottom of the screen, as shown on Figure 2.3. Another way to change between overtype and insert mode is to double-click the OVR on the status bar. Use the mode that requires the fewest keystrokes and is most suited to the editing that you are doing.

FIGURE 2.3
*Status bar
showing overtype
mode*

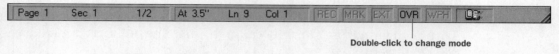

Double-click to change mode

The bottom line on the screen is the status bar. It gives several different items of information used periodically during editing. The first area gives information about the text that is visible on screen. The second box shows the position of the cursor on the page. The third area has several indicators, including the ones for overtype mode just discussed and Automatic Spell Checking.

In the status bar in Figure 2.3, the text on screen is on page 1 of a document 2 pages long (1/2). The first piece of information (Page 1) displays the same page number in this document, but this will not always be the case. The number here shows the page number that will be printed, even if the first page of the document is not page 1. (Page numbering is discussed in Unit 8.) The second box shows that the cursor is near the middle of the page, 3.5 inches from the top, on line 9 of the text, and on the far left side of the line, that is, in the first column. The OVR symbol is darker than the other mode boxes, showing that overtype mode is turned on.

GUIDED ACTIVITY 2.4

Using Overtype and Insert

1. Position the cursor to the left of the words An attractive that start the second sentence in the last paragraph of your document. Make sure the letters OVR appear gray (dimmed), and not dark on the status bar. If they are dark, press ⌷Ins⌷ once to make OVR turn gray (dimmed). (Make sure the *Numbers Lock* or Num Lock key (⌷Num Lock⌷) is off if ⌷Ins⌷ is combined with a number key on the numeric keypad portion of the keyboard.)

2. Type the following text:

    Italicizing, bolding, and adding bullets are examples of formatting.

The last sentences in the paragraph shift to the right to make room for the new text you have typed in. This is the insert mode.

3. Switch to the overtype mode by pressing [Ins] once, or by double-clicking on the status bar where the gray letters OVR appear. Now OVR appears in dark letters on the status bar.

4. Watch the screen to see what happens during this step. Type in the following text:

   Without formatting, documents may be easy to ignore.

   Some of the words in the third sentence in the paragraph were replaced by the new text you entered. The overtype mode can be helpful if you want to replace old text with new in a single step.

5. This process is inappropriate here. Remove overtype mode by double-clicking on the OVR on the status bar. Retype the text that was eliminated.

Selecting Text

Many editing procedures require you first to highlight (or select) various combinations of words, lines, sentences, and paragraphs. Both the keyboard and the mouse can be used to select text. Highlighting with the keyboard is performed by holding down the *Shift* key and pressing arrow keys. With the mouse, simply clicking and dragging over text highlights it.

 WARNING *When any amount of text is highlighted, any key that you press will replace the selected text, like the overtype mode. If that was the desired result, this feature is not a problem and is often beneficial. However, occasionally you may accidentally press a key with a large block of text highlighted, and the selected text will be replaced by the key you pressed. Do not panic. Should this happen, the deleted text may be retrieved by immediately using the Edit | Undo command or by clicking on the **Undo** button on the toolbar. Large blocks of selected text must be treated carefully to avoid losing them.*

GUIDED ACTIVITY 2.5

Selecting Text Using the Keyboard

1. Make sure the cursor is just to the left of the letter W at the very beginning of your document. Hold down the [Shift] key and press [→] once. The W is highlighted.

   At this point you could format the character by making it bold or underlined, or by changing its size. You could delete the character or replace it with other text.

2. Press ⬅ to remove the highlighting. Moving the cursor automatically removes the highlighting from text.

3. Hold down [Shift] and press [↓] to select the line. Keep holding down [Shift] and press the [↓] key or [↑] key to see how the highlighting is extended. Try holding down the [Shift] key and pressing [PgUp] and [PgDn].

4. Remove the highlighting by releasing the [Shift] key and pressing any arrow key.

Selecting text with the keyboard can take many taps of the arrow keys, but it is useful because of its precise control. Selecting text with the mouse is faster, although users sometimes feel that they have less control over the process.

GUIDED ACTIVITY 2.6

Selecting Text Using the Mouse

To highlight a single letter, position the mouse pointer to one side of it and click and drag it to the other side of the character. The character will appear highlighted.

1. Select the letter m in the word most in the second sentence of your document. Position the mouse pointer directly to the left of the letter m and drag the pointer to the right of the letter. Remember that dragging requires that you hold down the mouse button while moving the mouse pointer. It may be difficult to highlight a single character using the mouse, but with a bit of practice you will get a feel for it.

There is no difference between text selected with the arrow keys and text selected with the mouse. At this point you could format the letter m by making it bold or underlined or by changing its font or point size. You could delete the character or replace it with other text.

2. Double-click in the word most in the first paragraph of your document.

Individual words can be selected by positioning the mouse pointer anywhere over the word and double-clicking. Again, a word may be highlighted with either the arrow keys or the mouse.

3. To remove highlighting, click once on another area of the text.

To select more than one word, simply click and drag with the mouse.

4. Place the mouse over the middle of the word most and begin dragging to the right. As you drag to extend the highlight into the next word, the highlight automatically extends back to the beginning of most and continues to extend the highlight a word at a time. Remove the highlighting by clicking anywhere on the document.

Some selection procedures require you to use [Ctrl].

5. Select the first sentence in your document by holding down [Ctrl] and clicking anywhere on the sentence.

6. A single line of text is selected by clicking in the area to the left of the line. Move the mouse pointer to the far left and click once to highlight the first line in your document.

This selection technique requires you to click on the edge of the screen, outside the text area. You can tell when you are in the correct area because the mouse pointer will change from an I-beam to an arrow pointing up and to the right, as shown in Figure 2.4.

FIGURE 2.4
Selecting a line of text with the mouse

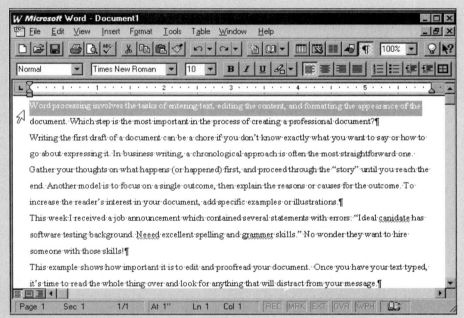

7. Select several lines in the document by clicking on the far left side of the screen and dragging carefully downward. *Watch out:* A fast mouse and a fast computer may quickly select more than you intend!

8. Double-click in the far left side of the screen to select an entire paragraph at once.

9. *Triple*-click on the far left side of the screen to highlight the entire document, or hold [Ctrl] and click in the left margin. This technique with the mouse has the same effect as selecting the command Edit | Select All.

10. Click once anywhere in the document to remove the highlighting.

A summary of the mouse actions to select certain parts of a document is given in Table 2.2.

TABLE 2.2 *Selection techniques*	TO SELECT	MOUSE ACTION
	Any amount of text	Drag over the text.
	Word	Double-click on the word.
	Sentence	Ctrl-click on the sentence.
	Entire line	Click on left side of screen.
	Paragraph	Double-click on left side of screen or *triple*-click on the paragraph.
	Entire document	*Triple*-click on the left side of screen or Ctrl-click on the left side of screen.

Delete and Undo

After you have reviewed your document, you may want to delete a large block of text. You could use Backspace to remove the text one character at a time, but this is a slow way to work. A faster way is to remove the text all at once. This can be done in two quick steps: (1) select the text, as you just learned, and then (2) press the *Delete* or Del key (Del) on the keyboard.

The Del key can also be used to remove individual characters. However, it differs from the Backspace key in that it deletes characters to the *right* of the cursor instead of to the left.

What if you delete text that you want back again? One of the nicest features of most Windows applications is the first command located under the Edit menu. The Undo command allows you to change your mind and reverse the action. For example, if you delete a large segment of text and subsequently decide that you needed that text after all, you could select Edit | Undo to recover the text. The Undo command works to reverse formatting, editing changes, deletions, and even typing. The action verb after the word Undo changes, based on the last thing you did.

The Undo button may be clicked once to undo the last action, or several times to undo the last several actions. If you click on the down arrow next to the Undo button, a list will drop down as in Figure 2.5, revealing the last 100 editing actions that you may undo in reverse order (with the most recent action listed first). Next to the Undo button is the *Redo* button that works in a similar way. If you Undo an action and change your mind, a single click on the Redo button reverses the undo. Clicking on the down arrow next to the Redo button drops down a list of actions. You can use the Undo and Redo buttons with typing, editing, and formatting actions, but not with some commands, such as printing and saving.

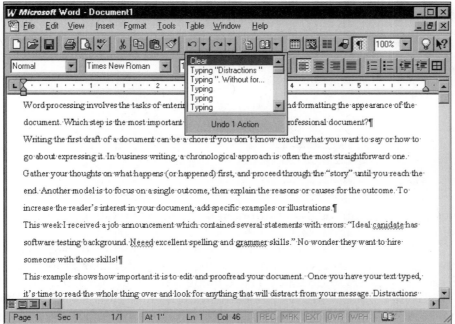

GUIDED ACTIVITY 2.7

Deleting and Undeleting

1. Highlight the entire last paragraph in your document. (Double-click in the area to the left of the paragraph.)

2. Press [Del] or choose the command Edit | Clear.

   The paragraph has been erased. If you change your mind, you can still retrieve it.

3. Click once on the Undo button or choose the command Edit | Undo.

   The paragraph reappears exactly as it was before [Del] (or Edit | Clear) was pressed. It is still highlighted and ready for the next function you will perform.

4. Remove the highlight by pressing the [→] key.

Saving the Document

When you begin word processing a new document, you can enter and edit text, and print a copy on paper. The document on screen is in the computer's random access memory (RAM, pronounced *ram*). Since RAM is only available when the computer is on, your document will turn to "electronic dust" when the computer is turned off. To keep a permanent copy of the document, you must save it to disk. To

FIGURE 2.6
*Save As
dialog box*

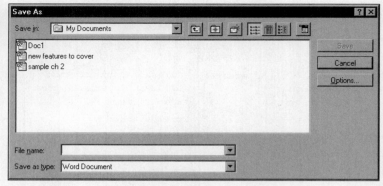

save a file, click on the Save button on the Standard toolbar or click on the File menu on the menu bar and select Save.

The Save button or command saves the active document being viewed on the screen under the name that appears in the window title bar. However, when you first create a document, it does not have a name. Microsoft Word gives it the name *Document1*. When you try to save a document for the first time, Microsoft Word opens a dialog box, shown in Figure 2.6, asking for further information before it can perform the command.

Type an appropriate name in the File Name box in the Save As dialog box. When you click Save, Word then stores the document under the name you supplied. The name that you entered is also placed in the Microsoft Word title bar. Later, whenever you click the Save button on the toolbar or select the Save command from the File menu again, Word will save the document under the same name without bringing up the dialog box.

GUIDED ACTIVITY 2.8

Saving Files

1. Place your formatted disk in drive A:.

   Your new document has not been saved, so it has no name. The title bar displays Document1 to reflect this.

2. Click on the Save button, or click on the File menu on the menu bar and select Save.

   Microsoft Word checks for the name of the document. When it discovers that the document is not yet named, it opens the dialog box to get more information.

3. Enter the file name A:Basics, and then press Enter. If the Summary Information dialog box appears, click OK.

   As the file is saved, the status bar displays a message and a graphical representation of the save process from start to finish. A light on the floppy disk drive comes on, indicating that the drive is working to save the document. After the file is saved, the cursor returns to the place you left it in the document. In the title bar, the name *Basics* appears. The file was saved on the disk in drive A: because you selected that drive. You could have selected any of the disk drives from the list available. However, placing a document on the hard disk of a computer other than your own is not recommended, because the document may not be there the next time you are.

4. In the document, press [Enter] and type in your name so that it is on the last line. Select Save to keep the changes you just made.

    This time Microsoft Word saves your file immediately, without showing you the dialog box, because the document already has a name.

5. Click on the Print button to get a copy of your document on paper.

6. Exit Word by selecting File on the menu and clicking Exit. Another way to do this is to click the close button in the upper-right corner of the screen.

Summary

In this unit you have learned that text is entered in much the same way it is typed on a typewriter. Errors made as you enter text can be corrected immediately with the [Backspace] key, or later with the [Del] key. After the text is entered, you can review the document by scrolling through it with the keyboard or the mouse. The arrow keys ([←] [↑] [→] [↓]) and page keys ([PgUp], [PgDn], [End], [Home]) are used to move the cursor with the keyboard. Clicking or dragging on the vertical scroll bar is the method to navigate through a document using the mouse.

Text can be selected with the [Shift] and arrow keys or with the mouse. There are shortcuts for selecting words, lines, sentences, paragraphs, and the entire document, with the mouse.

Text is added to a document in the insert mode. The text will be inserted at the location of the cursor in the work area. Characters can be replaced by new text if the word processor is placed in the overtype mode.

The [Del] key is used to erase large blocks of selected text. Deleted text can be recovered by immediate use of the Edit | Undo command or by clicking on the Undo button.

To keep a permanent copy of the document, you must save it to disk. Clicking on the Save button or selecting the File | Save command the first time brings up a dialog box. This dialog box is used to specify the name and place the file should be saved. As soon as a document is saved, its name appears on the title bar.

Exercises

Each of the following exercises requires you to save your file and print it. Before you save, place a formatted disk into drive A:. Before you print, make sure that a printer is attached to your computer and that the printer is on and has paper in it.

EXERCISE 2.1

A Day in the Life of a College Student

1. Start Word. Select Tools | Options and click on the Spelling tab. Make sure the box next to Automatic Spell Checking is checked.

2. Type the following information. Press [Enter] to leave a blank line for each ¶ symbol.

3. Look for wavy red lines under the words. Correct them if necessary by pressing [Backspace] and retyping.

   Today's date
   ¶
   ¶
   Your instructor's name
   Your instructor's address
   ¶
   Dear _____:
   ¶
   Type paragraph 1 with the following information included: your name, your hometown, the mascot of your high school, your local phone number, and the courses you are taking.
   ¶
   Type paragraph 2 telling about your current career plans and any computer experience you have.
   ¶
   Type paragraph 3 stating your interests and hobbies and any interesting facts about yourself.
   ¶
   Cordially yours,
   ¶
   ¶
   ¶
   Your name

4. Save to your Student Data Disk as *A:EX2-1*.

5. Highlight paragraph 1 (double-click on the left side) and delete it by pressing the [Del] key. Use the Undo button to restore it again.

6. Use [Ctrl] [Home] to move the cursor quickly to the top of the page. Type the following heading: Exercise 2-1, your class period, your seat number and press [Enter].

7. Click to the left of the word Cordially and press the [Ins] key. Use overtype mode to replace the word with Sincerely. Double-click the OVR on the status bar to change overtype mode back to insert mode.

8. Click on the Save button to save. Click on the Print button to print. Select File | Close to close the file.

9. Sign your name on the printed letter.

EXERCISE 2.2

Crusty's Pizza

1. Start Word. Select Tools | Options and click on the Spelling tab. Make sure the box next to Automatic Spell Checking is checked.

2. Type the following information. Press `Enter` to leave a blank line for each ¶ symbol.

3. Look for wavy red lines under the words. Correct them if necessary by pressing `Backspace` and retyping.

```
Hey, Kids! Welcome to Crusty's Pizza by the Pound
¶
Our Pizza is made every morning from only the freshest
ingredients:
¶
Homemade sauce
¶
Organically grown vegetables
¶
Hand-tossed crust
¶
Fat-free cheeses
¶
Make your selection of toppings, style of crust, and number
of pounds, and we will weigh it and prepare it just the way
you like it. Allow 1 to 2 pounds of pizza per person.
¶
Crusty
```

4. Save to your Student Data Disk as *A:EX2-2*.

5. Highlight the long paragraph (double-click on the left side) and delete it by pressing the `Del` key. Use the Undo button to restore it again.

6. Use `Ctrl` `Home` to move the cursor quickly to the top of the page. Type the following heading: Exercise 2-2, your name, your class period, your seat number and press `Enter`.

7. Click to the left of the term fat-free and press the `Ins` key. Use overtype mode to replace the word with natural. Double-click the OVR on the status bar to change overtype mode back to insert mode.

8. Click on the Save button to save. Click on the Print button to print. Select File | Close to close the file.

EXERCISE 2.3

The Internet

1. Start Word. Select Tools | Options and click on the Spelling tab. Make sure the box next to Automatic Spell Checking is checked.

2. Type the following information. Press ⌨Enter to leave a blank line for each ¶ symbol.

3. Look for wavy red lines under the words. Correct them if necessary by pressing ⌨Backspace and retyping. After you type the first line with the asterisk and press ⌨Enter, you will see the asterisk change into a bullet and the next line will automatically begin with a bullet.

    ```
    The Internet is an exciting online source of information.
    Connect to sites around the world to access interest groups
    on myriad topics: get up-to-the-minute stock quotes, read
    magazines that exist only in cyberspace, go shopping in
    Taos, hunt for job openings and apartment rentals in New
    York and Washington, D.C., and hear the meow of Socks the
    cat.
    ¶
    To view and retrieve information from the Internet you need
    three things:
    ¶
    * a modem
    an Internet access provider, such as America Online,
    Prodigy, or CompuServe
    a program to retrieve information such as Mosaic,
    CompuServe, or Microsoft's Internet Explorer
    ```

4. Save to your Student Data Disk as *A:EX2-3*.

5. Highlight the long paragraph (double-click on the left side) and delete it by pressing the ⌨Del key. Use the Undo button to restore it again.

6. Use ⌨Ctrl ⌨Home to move the cursor quickly to the top of the page. Type the following heading: Exercise 2-3, your name, your class period, your seat number and press ⌨Enter.

7. Click to the left of the word CompuServe in the third bullet and press the ⌨Ins key. Use overtype mode to replace the word with Netscape. Press ⌨Del twice to remove the remaining letters. Double-click the OVR on the status bar to change overtype mode back to insert mode.

8. Click on the Save button to save. Click on the Print button to print. Select File I Close to close the file.

EXERCISE 2.4

Thrill Seeker Tours

1. Start Word. Select Tools I Options and click on the Spelling tab. Make sure the box next to Automatic Spell Checking is checked.

2. Type the following information into a new document. Press [Enter] to leave a blank line for each ¶ symbol.

3. Look for wavy red lines under the words. Correct them if necessary by pressing [Backspace] and retyping. As you type, the double hyphen and asterisks will be automatically converted to a dash and bullets, respectively.

```
Thrill Seeker Tours
¶
Dive In--at Cozumel, Mexico
¶
Enjoy two dives on Palancar, Colombia, Santa Rosa or any of
our other beautiful sites and be back at the pool for
lunch! Del Mar Dive Shop is a fully equipped dive facility
with PADI and NAUI trained dive masters and custom dive
boats. Night dives are planned almost every night. Make
your adventure an underwater one!
¶
Dive packages include
¶
* Unlimited air fills for off-shore diving
Weights
Belts
Tanks and air
Souvenir T-shirt
¶
Standard 2-tank dive, only $60
```

4. Save to your disk as *A:EX2-4*.

5. Highlight the long paragraph (double-click on the left side) and delete it by pressing the [Del] key. Use the Undo button to restore it again.

6. Use [Ctrl][Home] to move the cursor quickly to the top of the page. Type the following heading: Exercise 2-4, your name, your class period, your seat number and press [Enter].

7. Click to the left of the term Del Mar and press the [Ins] key. Use overtype mode to replace the words with Seaside Dive Shop. Double-click the OVR on the status bar to change overtype mode back to insert mode.

8. Highlight the two lines of text from `Thrill Seeker` to `Mexico`. Make these lines larger and bolder by clicking on the 10 and changing it to `16` and clicking on the B button on the Formatting toolbar.

9. Click on the Save button to save. Click on the Print button to print. Select File | Close to close the file.

Review Questions

The answers to odd-numbered questions are contained in Appendix A. On multiple-choice questions, choose one or more answers.

*1. What are the three general procedures in word processing?

2. How is entering text on a word processor different from typing text on a type-writer?

*3. What keys are used to move through a document using the keyboard? What are their functions?

4. What screen area is used to move through a document with the mouse? How do the parts of this screen area work? What movement can you perform with the mouse that you cannot perform with the keyboard?

*5. What key is used in conjunction with the arrow keys and the page keys to select text with the keyboard?

6. What is the shortcut method to highlight a word with the mouse? To select a line? To select a sentence? To select a paragraph? To select the entire document?

*7. What is the difference between the insert and overtype modes? When is each used?

8. How is a block of text deleted? How can the action be reversed?

*9. What command does Microsoft Word execute if you select the command File | Save for a document that has not been saved (that is, does not have a name)?

10. How can you tell if the computer is in the process of saving your document?

*11. If you wish to remove a character just to the left of the blinking cursor, press

   a. Undo

   b. Del

   c. Esc

   d. Backspace

12. Press the Enter key whenever

   a. Your typing gets close to the right margin.

   b. You wish to start a new paragraph.

    c.   You want to access the menu selections.

    d.   You select text using the keyboard.

*13.   The key that augments or increases the movement of the arrow keys is

    a.   `Alt`

    b.   `Ctrl`

    c.   `Shift`

    d.   `Ins`

14.   Using the vertical scroll bar to move around in a document moves

    a.   The screen from place to place.

    b.   The cursor from place to place.

    c.   The highlighting from selected text.

    d.   The same amount as pressing `Home` or `End`.

Key Terms

The following terms are introduced in this unit. Be sure you know what each of them means.

Arrow keys	Home	Page Up
Backspace	I-beam	Redo
Control	Insert	Scroll bar
Delete	Insert mode	Scroll box
End	Numbers Lock	Shift
Enter	Overtype mode	Undo
Global move	Page Down	Word wrap

Creating a Name Tent

For this and all other Applications, you will receive general instructions to complete the task, but not complete steps. You will typically use skills you have mastered in the previous units. Use the Answer Wizard or online Help Topics to assist you if necessary.

The goal of Application A is to create a name tent. After folding it into a triangle, you can use the tent in class to display your name to help your teacher get to know you. Name tents like these are often used for formal business meetings where participants do not know each other, or during panel discussions so that members of the audience know to whom to address their comments and questions.

Your Name

1. Open Word and type your name.

2. Center your name horizontally on the page (press a button on the Formatting toolbar).

3. Change the size of the letters so that they are about an inch high (72 points) and make them bold (perform these changes on the Formatting toolbar).

4. Consult the online Help Topics or Answer Wizard to find out how to change the orientation of the page in order to print your name sideways on the page. (*Hint:* Two terms you might look for are "page orientation" and "landscape.")

5. In Print Preview, see where your name is vertically positioned on the page. Since it appears at the top of the page, move it down by pressing Enter a couple of times until it is approximately half-way down the page.

6. When the document is complete, save to drive A: under the name *Application A*.

7. Print the name tent. Fold into thirds so that it stands up like a tent. Display this on your desk in class.

Documents and Disks

In the previous unit you entered and edited text in a document and saved the information on a disk. This unit will cover how to use the File menu to create new documents, open previously saved documents from the computer's disk drives, and make backup copies of both documents and disks.

The first section discusses what types of disks there are, describe the advantages of each type, and tell how disks are prepared. The second section covers the commands available in the File menu used to manipulate Microsoft Word documents on disk. The third section deals with moving text and data from one place to another among documents. Finally, you will learn about the importance of making a backup copy of your documents and learn how to do so.

Learning Objectives

At the completion of this unit you should know

1. what kind of disks documents can be stored on,

2. how to create, open, and close files,

3. what wizards and templates are available,

4. how to work with several files at once,

5. the importance of making backups,

6. how to back up documents and disks,

7. how to rearrange text and data within a document.

Important Commands

IN WORD

Edit | Copy

Edit | Cut

Edit | Paste

File | Close

File | New

File | Open

File | Save As

Window | filename

ON SHORTCUT MENU ONLY

File | Send To

IN WINDOWS 95

Start | Programs | Accessories | System Tools | Backup

Start | Documents | *filename*

IN MY COMPUTER AFTER A DRIVE ICON IS SELECTED

File | Copy Disk

File | Format

Disks and File Names

Computers store information on magnetic storage devices called *disks*. Almost every application has some way to store the work you have done so that it does not have to be re-created every time the computer is turned back on. A computer uses a disk to store your work after it is created.

The computer places a magnetic head very close to the disk's surface to read the information stored on it. Any contaminants on the surface of the disk will get caught between the surface and the head and will make a scratch on the disk. This will cause the disk to be damaged and information to be lost. Substances that can contaminate disks are dust, smoke, hair, and water. Just touching the surface of the disk can place skin oils on the disk surface that will damage it when the head passes over that point. It is very important to handle disks carefully to avoid damaging the surface.

Because a disk is magnetic, placing the disk near a magnetic field may damage the information stored on it. Magnetic fields may be found near many electrical devices such as vacuum cleaners, televisions, ringing telephones, and even improperly shielded computers and monitors.

Disks must be maintained in a temperature- and humidity-controlled environment. Heat may cause the disk to warp and the chemicals on its surface to degrade. Cold may destroy the lubricants inside the disk's outer case, preventing it from spinning correctly. Excessively dry or wet atmospheres may also adversely affect the disk and its case. Even taking a disk from a cold area to a hot one may cause condensation to form on the disk surface, creating potential problems if the disk is used immediately.

Finally, disks fail with age. After several years of continuous use, a disk can lose information without warning. After the same surface is written to and read from many times, it loses its ability to be magnetized properly.

After all this is known, it seems incredible that anyone would trust a valuable document to such a volatile storage medium. In reality, though, disk storage is extremely reliable. Billions of disks are used on a daily basis for years without any failure. However, you must remember the limitations of the storage media. The likelihood of loss of information can be reduced to almost zero by keeping a backup copy of your important documents on a different disk. In this unit you will learn how to make backups to safeguard your documents.

Types of Disks

The three kinds of disks are hard disks, floppy disks (more properly called removable disks), and compact discs. *Hard disks* (also called hard drives or fixed disks) are attached to the inside of the computer and cannot be easily removed. *Floppy disks* (so called because early models had flexible covers) are more properly called removable disks because they are portable and can be used in many different computers. *Compact discs*, first popularized by the music industry, are also used to store large amounts of data, such as sound and video, and are increasingly being used to store programs and large help files for applications.

Floppy disks come in two sizes, 3.5-inch and 5.25-inch. The *5.25-inch* format has been popular for many years and is still available on some personal computers. The *3.5-inch* format is the standard in personal computers. Floppy disks have two capacities, *high-density* and *low-density*. The capacity of computer storage devices is abbreviated, using metric suffixes. The letter K (for kilo) stands for 1,000 in the metric system, while the letter M (for mega) stands for 1,000,000 and the letter G (for giga) equals a billion. Roughly, a single character (such as any character that can be typed from the keyboard) equals a byte, abbreviated B.

Using the abbreviations for kilobytes and megabytes, the capacities for the two kinds of 3.5-inch disk are 720KB (720,000 bytes) for low-density and 1.44MB (1,440,000 bytes) for high-density. (All of these values are approximate—1KB, for example, equals exactly 1,024 characters—but for convenience these numbers have been rounded to thousands and millions.)

FIGURE 3.1
*A high-density
3.5-inch disk*

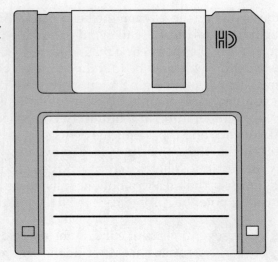

You can tell that the disk in Figure 3.1 is high-density (1.44MB) by two features: the letters "HD" and the extra square hole in the corner. These do not appear on a low-density disk. The disk has a metal shutter that covers part of the disk surface. When the disk is inserted into the *disk drive*, the shutter moves back to expose the disk to the drive head.

Disks also have mechanical means of preventing information from being written to or erased from them. On the back of the disk is a small plastic slide that either covers or uncovers a small hole in the disk cover, depending on its position. If the hole is uncovered, the disk is *write-protected* (safeguarded from being altered). When the slide is moved and the hole is covered, you can write information to and erase information from the disk.

The advantage to floppy disks is that they are transportable, but their drawback is that they do not hold very much information. Compact discs, abbreviated to CDs, on the other hand, are portable and have a large capacity for storage—626MB. A *CD-ROM*, which stands for compact disc read-only memory, is write-protected, which indicates that the information stored on it may not be changed once the disc leaves the factory.

Although floppy disks and CDs are useful for transporting information from one computer to another, hard disks can retrieve information more quickly and hold much more information than these removable disks. You will spend less time waiting for a document to be saved to or retrieved from a hard disk than a floppy disk or CD. The hard disk spins more quickly, so the computer can get the information from it in less time. Computers attached to a network have access to other hard disks, called network drives, which are located inside computers in another room or even another building. Hard disks come in many capacities, from 200MB (roughly 200 million characters) to 1.2GB (1,200 million characters, more than a billion) and even larger sizes.

Preparing Disks for Use

Before you can use a new floppy disk, it must be *formatted*. Formatting prepares a disk so that the drive in the computer can read from and write to it. If a disk is not formatted, the computer will be unable to use it for storage. Disk manufacturers commonly format floppy disks at the factory, and since formatting a disk takes time it may be cost-effective to pay the slightly higher price for preformatted disks. But sometimes you may wish to format a disk yourself, either because you purchased unformatted disks or because you want to completely empty a preformatted disk by reformatting it.

GUIDED ACTIVITY 3.1

Formatting a Disk

CAUTION *Formatting erases all information on the disk, so do not do this activity if you have documents or data on your disk that you wish to keep.*

1. Insert the disk you want to format into drive A:.

2. If you have already started Microsoft Word, minimize it by clicking on the down arrow at the top-right corner of the screen.

3. Double-click on My Computer.

4. Click *once* on the icon for the 3.5" floppy drive, usually labeled A:. Do not double-click and so open the window for drive A:.

5. Select from the File menu the command Format.

6. The Format dialog box will appear, as in Figure 3.2.

FIGURE 3.2
Format dialog box

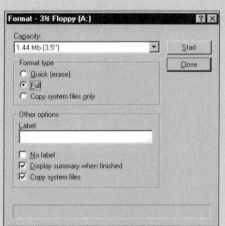

The dialog box offers you the option to select high or low capacity. Depending on whether your disk has the extra hole and the HD label, you may select either 1.44MB or 720KB capacity.

The Quick format option simply erases the files on a disk. The command will only work if the disk has been previously formatted.

The Full option deletes all data and scans for bad sectors on the disk's surface.

The Copy System Files options are used to make the disk into a *system disk*; that is, operating system files are incorporated into the disk. A system disk, placed in drive A: before the computer is turned on, is capable of starting the computer. Since the computer that you are working on probably starts from a hard disk, you will ordinarily not need to format disks with the system included. Placing the system on a floppy disk uses up some of the storage capacity that would otherwise be available on it.

The other options allow you to label your disk with an electronic name and to display summary information about the disk on completion.

7. Select Full and click on Start.

Windows will begin formatting your data disk in the drive, showing you a bar chart of the progress.

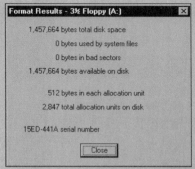

FIGURE 3.3
Display of results of formatting

If you want to cancel, click on Cancel to stop the format. If you do cancel, the disk will be unusable until you format it again.

The computer may take several seconds to format your disk. It is checking the entire usable surface of the disk for imperfections. If it finds any spots (sectors) on the disk that are bad, it will quarantine them from being used. When the computer has successfully formatted the disk, Windows displays the summary, as in Figure 3.3. If you do not type a label in the Format dialog box, a serial number appears on the Format Results. Read the information and click Close.

8. Click Close to close the Format dialog box. Close the My Computer window by clicking on the close box in the upper-right corner of the window.

    The disk is now formatted and prepared for the computer to store information on it.

Files and File Names

A *file* is the basic unit of storage, whether of a document (information you create) or a program (a computer application created by a manufacturer). Files are identified on disk by the *file name*. The file name is usually a word or words that represent something about the file being stored, one unique to that file. For example, the first assignment for a class may be a document saved as *Assignment1*. The more representative of the file the file name is, the easier the file will be to find and open later.

Windows 95 allows you to give names to files up to 255 characters long (including the pathname). Avoid using eight symbols in file names—the forward slash /, backward slash \, greater-than >, less-than <, asterisk *, question mark ?, quotation mark ", pipe |, colon :, or semicolon ;.

Depending on how you have Windows set up, you may not see the second part of the file name, the *extension*. The extension consists of up to three characters and is used to group files into types. For example, all Microsoft Word documents have the extension *.doc*. Excel spreadsheets have the extension *.xls*. Regardless, when you are saving documents in Microsoft Word, you will never have to enter the extension. The word processor appends the extension *.doc* automatically to the name you give the file, whether you see it or not. That is how the computer knows what type of file to list in Explorer and My Computer.

NOTE   *If you create a document and use it on a machine without Windows 95, a long file name will be **truncated** (chopped) to eight characters, and DOS will use both the file name and the extension to identify the document.*

The File Menu

The Microsoft Word commands dealing with files are located on the File menu, as shown in Figure 3.4. This menu allows you to create new documents, open documents already on disk, save documents you have created or edited, and close documents. These commands can be performed by simply clicking buttons on the screen.

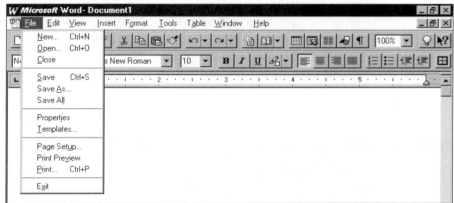

FIGURE 3.4
File menu

As handy as the buttons are, many people find that ***shortcut keys*** are even faster to use. Rather than moving your hand to the mouse, moving the mouse to a button, clicking the button, and returning your hand to the keyboard (and perhaps fumbling to find your place), you may like the convenience of using the shortcut key. To use the shortcut key, simply press and hold down the ⌃Ctrl key, type the letter, and then release the ⌃Ctrl key. Table 3.1 summarizes the methods available to perform each of these tasks.

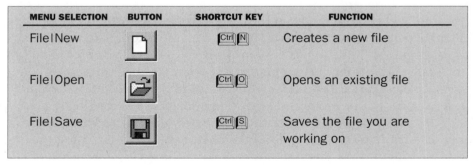

TABLE 3.1
File New, Open, and Save shortcut keys

MENU SELECTION	BUTTON	SHORTCUT KEY	FUNCTION
File|New		Ctrl N	Creates a new file
File|Open		Ctrl O	Opens an existing file
File|Save		Ctrl S	Saves the file you are working on

File\|New

When Microsoft Word is started, as you know, a new document called *Document1* gives you a blank sheet to begin typing. When you are working on a document and need to create a new one, you may begin in any of four ways:

- Click the New button on the Standard toolbar.

- Select File | New.

- Hold down the [Ctrl] key and press [N], to use the shortcut key.

- Click the Start a New Document button on the Microsoft Office Shortcut Bar.

Each of these commands offers slightly different options. Clicking the New button places a new blank document on top of the document you already typed and names it *Document2*. The shortcut key [Ctrl][N] acts the same way as the button.

The File | New command on the menu is followed by ellipses (…), which means you will need to supply additional information in a dialog box. (Ellipses are not printed in this text.) The New dialog box shown in Figure 3.5 asks you to choose what kind of document you would like to create.

This dialog box determines what kind of file will be opened, according to the option buttons at the bottom right. A ***document*** is a normal word processing file, one that will be unique and used for only one purpose. A ***template*** is a form document that is used many times and has built-in formatting and spaces in it for variable information. For example, a form letter that is sent on a regular basis can be saved as a template, allowing you to enter the name and address of the person to whom it is being sent without having to type the rest of the letter.

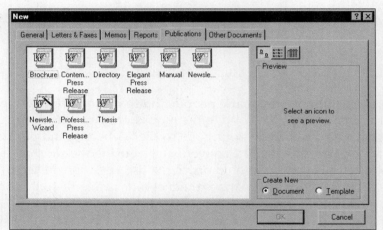

When you select the File | New command from the menu to begin a document, Word suggests the Blank Document, or normal, template—an empty template that sets up normal margins, page size, font, and size. Word provides several other templates that allow you to create and format documents quickly. Many of these templates come with wizards. Using a ***wizard*** is probably the simplest way to create a document. A wizard asks a series of questions and sets up the document according to your specifications.

Using any of these methods to start a new document while a document is already in the work area opens an additional document without closing the first one. The original document is merely hidden behind the ***active document***, or latest document. Commands on the Window menu, shown in Figure 3.6, allow you to view the names of all the ***open documents***, to bring another document to the front (by typing a single number) so that it becomes the active one, as well as to display more than one document at a time in the work area (the Arrange All option). The file names are listed in chronological order. The active document is marked with a check ✓ next to its name. Having more than one document open makes it simple for you to copy information from one document to another, as you will learn later in this unit.

FIGURE 3.6
Window menu

GUIDED ACTIVITY 3.2

Creating New Files

1. Start Microsoft Word.

    In the work area is a blank document for you to begin typing. If you look on the title bar, you see the name *Document1*. Until you save the file, this is its name.

2. Type your name.

3. With *Document1* on the screen, click the New button to create a new document.

    A blank document appears on the screen. Your other document is not gone from the screen; it is simply hidden behind the new one. The new one is called *Document2* until you save it.

4. Enter your street address.

    You now have two documents open at the same time. The Window menu will show you what documents are open.

5. Click on the Window menu.

    The bottom of the menu displays the names of the two documents you have created. You can tell that neither has been saved because they have the names given by Microsoft Word: *Document*, followed by a number. You can also tell which document is active by the check.

6. Select the file name *Document1*.

    Immediately, *Document1* becomes the active document and is displayed on screen, hiding the other document from sight.

7. Select from the menu the command File | New.

    The dialog box appears with all the choices of documents that are ready-made for you. Click on each of the tabs to see what is available.

8. Select the Letters & Faxes tab.

9. Click on each of the letters to see a preview of their appearance: Contemporary Letter, Elegant Letter, and Professional Letter.

10. Double-click on the Letter Wizard to have Microsoft Word automatically start a new document. The wizard asks a series of questions for you to answer and sets up the document according to your specifications.

11. The first screen asks what type of document you want it to create. Choose a Pre-written Business Letter and click the Next button.

12. The next screen offers 15 different prewritten letters. Choose the Letter to Mom. Click the Next button.

13. The next screen allows you to choose between printing on letterhead stationery and plain paper. Select Plain Paper. Click Next.

    The next screen allows you to type in the recipient's name and address and your return address.

14. Click and drag to highlight the recipient information. Press [Del] and type Mom's name and address. Change or delete the return address as well. Click Next.

15. Choose among the styles Professional, Contemporary, or Elegant. Click Next.

16. Select the choice Just Display the Letter and click the Finish button.

    Use the arrow keys or scroll bar to review the contents of your prewritten letter. If you want, you can edit or print this document.

    If the document is too small to read, select from the menu View | Normal.

17. Click on the Window menu. Now three documents are on the list of open documents. Select *Document1*.

    You can also start a new document through the Office Shortcut Bar.

18. If the Office Shortcut Bar shown in Figure 3.7 does not appear on the screen (perhaps in the top-right corner or elsewhere), click the Start menu, select Programs, and select Microsoft Office Shortcut Bar.

FIGURE 3.7
Microsoft Office Shortcut Bar

Start a New Document button

 NOTE *Some computers have Word only, while others have Microsoft Office. Computers with Microsoft Office may have the Microsoft Office Shortcut Bar start automatically every time the computer is turned on. The toolbar may appear in the top-right corner of the screen or in another place such as the side. It may be minimized and its button may appear on the taskbar. If you see another type of toolbar on the screen (other than the taskbar, of course), right-click on the Office button to switch to that toolbar. Your instructor will tell you where to access the Microsoft Office Shortcut Bar.*

19. Click on the Start a New Document button.

    The contents of the dialog box appear similar to those of the File | New dialog box in Microsoft Word. In fact, several of the same tabs and documents are included here. The difference is that this dialog box also contains templates for other types of files, including various Excel spreadsheets and PowerPoint presentations. When you start a New document by clicking the button on the Microsoft Office Shortcut Bar, Word opens automatically. You do not need to have Word open in order to start a new word processing document.

20. Click the Cancel button to return to Word.

File | Close

To remove the active document from the screen, select the File | Close command. This does not erase a saved document from disk, nor does it cause you to exit from Microsoft Word. It simply takes the current document and removes it both from memory and from the screen. If the document has not yet been saved, Word will give you one more chance to save, as in Figure 3.8, before the document is removed from the screen.

FIGURE 3.9
Reminder to save before closing files

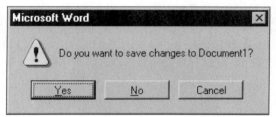

If you click on No to close the document without saving it, the document will be permanently erased, or any changes you made since last saving it will be lost. If you click on Yes, and the document already has a name, Microsoft Word will execute the File | Save command and save the document before closing it. If the document has not yet been saved and does not have a name, a dialog box appears to prompt you for a name for the file before closing it.

Another method for closing a file is to click on the close document button in the upper-right corner of the window. Two close buttons appear, one for closing the application (Microsoft Word), and one for closing the document—just as there are minimize and restore buttons both for the application as a whole and for the document by itself. These buttons are shown in Figure 3.9.

FIGURE 3.8
Title bar and menu bar showing two sets of minimize, restore, and close buttons

Affect Microsoft Word

Affect only the document

GUIDED ACTIVITY 3.3

Closing Files

1. With *Document1* on screen, select File | Close.

   Microsoft Word attempts to close the document, discovers that it has not been saved, and gives you a chance to save the changes. You can tell it has not been saved because the name Word gave it, *Document1*, still shows on the title bar.

2. Click on No, because you do not need to keep this document.

   Word removes the document from the screen without saving it. *Document2* is now visible on screen.

3. Close the *Document2* file also. Another way to close a file is to click on the Close button that appears on the menu bar (*not* the title bar). Click No so as not to save it.

   The last document on screen is the letter to Mom, which should be saved.

4. Click the Close button on the menu bar (*not* the title bar) or select File | Close, and at the prompt click Yes to save. The Save As dialog box appears.

5. Type A:Letter to Mom and press Enter.

   Word saves the document to your floppy disk in drive A: and then closes the file. Now that all the documents have been closed, Word is left with no document to work with. Consequently, the only menu commands that are available are File and Help. All the other commands may only be used on open documents.

File | Open

Just like creating a new file, opening a file you have previously saved to your disk can be performed several ways. You can open a file from Windows 95, which will cause Microsoft Word to open automatically and load the document, all in one step:

- Click the Open a Document button on the Microsoft Office Shortcut Bar.

- From Windows Explorer or My Computer, double-click the file name of a Word document.

If Word is already running, you do not have to go back to the Start menu or Explorer. You can also open a document with any of these methods:

 - Press the Open button on the Standard toolbar.

FIGURE 3.10
File menu in Word lists the last four most recently used files

■ Select File | Open.

■ Hold down the [Ctrl] key and press [O], the shortcut key.

Word provides users many handy shortcuts for working with documents. Users commonly modify a document that was recently closed. Rather than forcing you to look through lists of drives, folders, and file names, Word lets you open your file from a list of the most recently used documents in two ways:

■ The names of the four most recently used Word documents are listed at the bottom of the File menu, as in Figure 3.10.

■ Recently used files of all types, including Word documents, are located on the Start menu under Documents.

FIGURE 3.11
File|Open dialog box

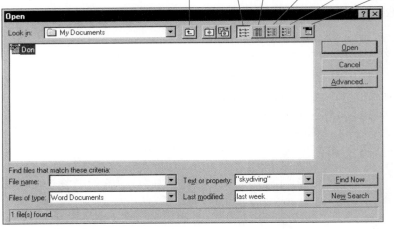

These methods for opening files (other than the ones accessing the recently used files) use the Open dialog box shown in Figure 3.11. The Open dialog box contains four main areas: a graphical list of the folders and files, a preview of the document, buttons that allow you to customize the appearance of the folders and files within this dialog box, and places to type information needed to search for a document. The Open dialog box works the same whether you are using the Office Shortcut Bar, Word, Excel, PowerPoint, or other Windows 95 applications. The only difference is what types of files are listed. When you open this dialog box in Word, as opposed to any of the other Office programs, the list of files includes only Word documents. Click on the down arrow next to Word Documents in the Files of Type list box to reveal the various types of files.

NOTE *File names are shown in upper- or lowercase letters in the Open dialog box. In this book, they are printed in italics with initial capital letters, for readability.*

The Open dialog box displays a list of files contained in the *My Documents* folder matching the description in the type box. A **folder** was called a directory (or subdirectory) in earlier versions of Windows. If there are more files in a folder than can be displayed on one screen, you can scroll through the list of files by dragging the scroll box on the scroll bar. If you wish to see file names in another folder, click the Up One Level button. You may change to higher and higher levels of folders by clicking the button repeatedly or by pressing the [Backspace] key. By clicking on the down arrow next to the Look In box, you can select other drives and see the contents of the folders there.

You can customize the way the files and folders are listed through the buttons on the dialog box:

 The List button causes the dialog box to display a list of file names only.

 The Detail button causes the dialog box to include the file names, as well as the size, type, and date and time the file was last modified.

 The Properties button lists the files only, on the left, but opens a new box with a summary of facts about the file, such as the file's author and the number of words or pages in the document.

 The Preview button on the Open dialog box allows you to look at a portion of the document whenever you highlight a file name. This feature helps you know whether you are going to open the correct file.

 The Commands and Settings button allows you to specify several options. One handy command is the Print command, which may be used to print a document directly to the printer without even opening it (saving you a bit of time). Another is the ability to access network drives. To shorten the time it takes to list the files in the dialog box, remove the check from the Search Subfolders option. When the check is removed, only the files from one folder—the current folder—are listed in the dialog box.

GUIDED ACTIVITY 3.4

Opening Files

1. Click on the File menu to drop down the list of menu choices.

   On the bottom of the menu is a list of the four most recently used files. This list includes only files that have been saved to the disk, *not* those that were closed without saving.

2. Click *Letter to Mom.* After a few seconds the file appears on screen.

3. Click the Open button to access a file not on the list of recently used files. We will try to find the business card you created in Unit 1 and saved to your floppy

disk. If you did not save the business card to a floppy disk, you may wish to step through this activity to see what other documents are on the disk.

Before looking for a particular document, we will try the functions of each button in the dialog box.

4. When the Open dialog box appears, click the Preview button on the dialog box. Click on any file name to see a preview of the file.

5. The list of file names may look different from those shown in Figure 3.10, depending on which of the buttons you have selected. Click the List button and the Details button to see how each changes the appearance of the file list on the Open dialog box.

6. You can also choose the option to show or not to show the entire contents of the disk at once, including the subfolders and files within them. Click the Commands and Settings button, and then select Search Subfolders.

The next step shows you how to see the folders and files on the hard disk.

7. Click the Up One Level button to see the contents of the hard disk (drive C:).

8. Click on the down arrow next to My Computer to display a list of available drives. Select 3½ Floppy [A:].

9. Click once to highlight the file named *Business Card*. (If you formatted your disk earlier in this chapter, it will show only one file, *Letter to Mom*. Select it instead.) A portion of the file contents appears in the preview part of the dialog box. To open the file, double-click the file name.

10. With the document open on screen, press Spacebar once.

Although this is just a single character, it is in fact a change to your document. Microsoft Word will not let you close it without first warning you to save the changes.

11. Select File | Exit or click on the Close button on the title bar to exit Microsoft Word. Exiting Microsoft Word automatically closes your documents, so Microsoft Word gives you a warning.

12. Click on Yes to save the document. Microsoft Word will close, returning you to Windows 95.

13. Click on the Start button and select Documents.

14. Select the file name *Letter to Mom*.

This time, Microsoft Word is opened and, rather than displaying a blank document on screen, the letter to Mom appears immediately.

15. Close the file.

Searching for Files

While you may have some of your documents saved in the *My Favorites* folder, if you work on shared computers in a laboratory you will probably save your files to the floppy disk or to a network drive instead. If you work at home on your own computer, you may put files in other folders to keep them organized. To open these files later, you can search for these files on your disks several ways:

- If you know the exact name of the file and in which folder it is located, you can type the complete file name and *path*, which consists of the drive letter, the folder name(s), and the file name.

- If you think you know which folder the file is located in and think you will recognize the file when you see the name and look at the text in the preview window, you can look through the folders until you find the file.

- If you can only remember that it was a file you worked on last Monday or that it contained the unique text `skydiving`, you can search for it by specifying the time period in the Last Modified box, or by typing the phrase in the Text or Property box in the File | Open dialog box, as in Figure 3.12.

FIGURE 3.12
Searching for a file

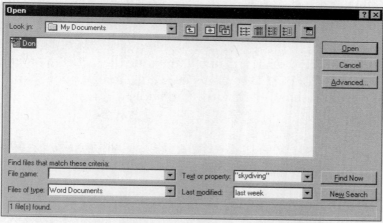

In addition to searching for and opening files, another function available in the File | Open dialog box is to manage files just as you can in Explorer or My Computer. After highlighting a file name, you can rename the file, move or copy the file to a new location, create a backup copy of a file, and delete or print a file, all from within the dialog box.

To access these commands, highlight a file name and then click the right mouse button to reveal the shortcut menu, just as you did in using My Computer and Explorer in Windows 95. You will use this feature later in this unit for backing up a file.

GUIDED ACTIVITY 3.5

Searching for a File

1. Select File I Open or click the Open button or press the shortcut key [Ctrl] [O].

2. Click in the box labeled Text or Property. Type the quotation marks and the phrase "Dear Mom" to find all files containing that phrase within the text of the document.

3. To restrict the search to documents on drive A:, select 3½ Floppy A: in the Look In box.

    Word searches the contents of all the files for the text Dear Mom and compiles a list of the documents. *Letter to Mom* is displayed on the list.

    Word also makes it easy to specify the time frame of when you last worked on the document. The Last Modified box allows you to select today, yesterday, this week, last week, this month, or last month, and to narrow the search.

4. Click New Search to clear the text Dear Mom.

5. Click on the down arrow next to Any Time and select This Week. Click Find Now.

6. Word compiles a list of all the documents that have been modified this week. Double-click the file *Letter to Mom* to open the document.

Cut, Copy, and Paste

Several commands are used often in rearranging text in a document. To copy or move text from one place to another, first select the text, and then issue the command Edit I Cut or Edit I Copy. Move the cursor to the new location where you would like the text to appear, and issue the command Edit I Paste. Using these commands involves the **Clipboard**, a temporary storage area provided by Windows. Each time you copy or cut, the material is moved to the Clipboard. When you paste, the material is moved from the Clipboard to the location of your cursor. The difference between cut and copy is that the cut command removes the original material and places it on the Clipboard, whereas the copy command makes a copy of the material, places it on the Clipboard, and leaves the selected material in place.

These commands—Cut, Copy, and Paste—are so commonly used that Word provides four different ways to access these commands. The first way is to choose them from the Edit menu on the menu bar. Another, faster, way is to click their buttons on the Standard toolbar. In addition, each of these commands has shortcut keys. A summary of these methods is shown in Table 3.2.

Because these commands are so commonly used, Word places these commands on the **shortcut menu**, which is accessed by clicking the *right* mouse button within the document, as shown in Figure 3.13.

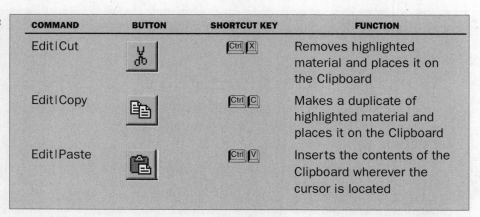

TABLE 3.2
*Cut, Copy,
and Paste
shortcut keys*

COMMAND	BUTTON	SHORTCUT KEY	FUNCTION
Edit|Cut	✂	Ctrl X	Removes highlighted material and places it on the Clipboard
Edit|Copy	▤	Ctrl C	Makes a duplicate of highlighted material and places it on the Clipboard
Edit|Paste	▤	Ctrl V	Inserts the contents of the Clipboard wherever the cursor is located

FIGURE 3.13
Shortcut menu

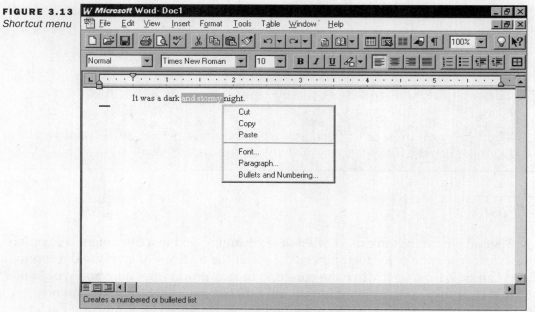

Word allows you to move and copy text without using any menu or button commands. This feature is known as *drag-and-drop*. To move text using this method, you must first highlight it. Then move the mouse pointer over the highlighted area so that it changes shape from the typical I-beam to an arrow, as in Figure 3.14. Finally, drag the highlighted text to move it to its destination, and release the mouse button to drop it in place. If you want to copy text using the drag-and-drop technique instead of moving it, hold down the Ctrl key on the keyboard while dragging it. It's easy to remember that Ctrl is for Copy because they both start with C.

GUIDED ACTIVITY 3.6

Copying and Moving Text

1. Select the command View | Normal so that the document is easier to read.

2. Select the middle paragraph beginning with `In fact, I just bought a great program` by double-clicking in the left margin. Choose the command Edit | Copy.

   A copy of the paragraph is stored in the Clipboard.

3. Position the cursor below the return address at the beginning of the first paragraph of the body text. To insert at this location a copy of the material in the Clipboard, select Edit | Paste.

4. Click on the Undo button. Redo steps 2 and 3, accessing the commands from the shortcut menu by clicking the right mouse button with your middle or ring finger.

5. Position the cursor at the end of the document.

6. Click the Paste button on the toolbar.

   The same paragraph you pasted at the beginning of the document is now duplicated at the end. You can paste as many copies of the text contained in the Clipboard as you like. Simply place the cursor where the new copy is to be inserted, and choose the Paste command or click on the Paste button.

   The Edit | Cut command works like Edit | Copy except that it does not leave the original in place. It removes the selected text and stores it in the Clipboard.

7. Select the third paragraph in the document (it should begin with `I'm sorry`). Select Edit | Cut.

   The paragraph disappears, but it has not been deleted. The Clipboard now contains the paragraph that was just cut. It will stay there until some other piece of text is cut or copied or until you exit Microsoft Word. (Unlike Undo, the Clipboard holds only one block of text at a time.)

8. Position the cursor at the end of the document.

9. This time use the shortcut key for Paste. Hold down [Ctrl] and press [V].

   The paragraph that was cut in step 8 has been moved to the end of the document.

   Edit | Copy and Edit | Cut both place the selected text in the Clipboard. The text can then be pasted to the location of the cursor in the document. Edit | Copy does not affect the original selected item, whereas Edit | Cut removes it.

10. Highlight the paragraph that was pasted in step 10.

11. With the mouse directly over the highlighted text, press and hold down the left mouse button. Notice that the mouse pointer looks like an arrow with a dotted rectangle attached, as in Figure 3.14.

FIGURE 3.14

The drag-and-drop technique

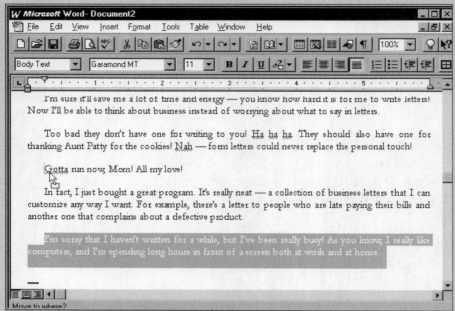

With the mouse button held down, carefully drag the mouse pointer upward. As you do so, you will notice a dotted or gray insertion point moving upward. Move this gray insertion point until it is at the beginning of the Gotta run paragraph. When you let go of the mouse button, the highlighted text is inserted at the location of the gray insertion point.

You can copy information from one document to another using Edit | Copy and Edit | Paste.

12. Select the text in the document and select Edit | Copy.

13. Click on the New button to create a new blank document.

14. With the new document now the active one, issue the Edit | Paste command, and the information is transferred to the new document.

15. To return to the original document, click on the Window menu, and select *Letter to Mom* by either typing the number shown or clicking on the name.

16. To view both documents at once, select the command Window | Arrange All.

Both documents are visible on screen. Each document is contained in a separate window with separate title bars, rulers, and scroll bars. You can tell which document is the active document by the color of the title bar; the inactive document's title bar is gray or a lighter color.

With both documents visible, you can use drag-and-drop to move information from one document to another.

17. Highlight text in the active document and, with the mouse pointer over the highlighted area, drag it to the document in the other window.

18. To view only one document on screen at once, click on the maximize button in the upper-right corner of the title bar of the desired document. Close both files.

File | Save As

The File | Save command saves the active document being viewed on the screen under the name that appears in the window title bar. As you know, when you first create a document, it does not have a name. Microsoft Word gives it the default name *Document1*. When you select File | Save for a document that does not have a name, Microsoft Word executes instead the File | Save As command. On the File menu the Save As command is followed by ellipses (…). This means that Word will open a dialog box, shown in Figure 3.15, asking for further information before it can perform the command.

FIGURE 3.15
*Save As
dialog box*

File | Save As stores the document in the active window under a name supplied by the user. Word uses the first line of text as a suggested file name. If you wish to give it another name, you must type a name in the File Name text box in the Save As dialog box. The file name that you enter then appears in the Microsoft Word title bar instead of the default name, *Document1*.

The File | Save As command is also used when you have opened an existing document from disk, have modified it, and now want to save it under a different name or in a different location. If you select File | Save (or click the Save button), the original document on disk will be replaced by the modified version. To preserve the original, use the File | Save As command to store the modified document under a different name.

The Automatic Save Feature

Anyone who has worked on personal computers for any length of time knows that, for one reason or another, on occasion, they may temporarily stop working. You may call this "freezing," or "locking up," or any of several other colorful terms. Power may even suddenly go out. When this happens, the information you were working on, regardless of the application, is usually gone, and you will need to completely redo any work you have done since the last time you saved. This often causes wailing and gnashing of teeth, and, at worst, tragically loses what you wrote in a rare flash of brilliance.

Microsoft Word has a life-saving feature called Automatic Save. This feature automatically saves your document after a time period that you determine. If you turn on the feature and select five minutes, every five minutes Word will save your document. The time period you pick is entirely up to you. If you are a fast typist, the period should probably be relatively short. If it takes you several minutes to type a sentence or paragraph, the period could be longer.

To turn on Automatic Save, select File | Save As, and click on the Options button on the dialog box. The Save tab of the Options dialog box appears, as shown in Figure 3.16.

FIGURE 3.16
Options for saving

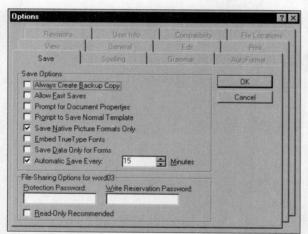

Click the up or down arrow in the box to the right of the Automatic Save Every __ Minutes section to set the number of minutes in the Automatic Save period. Click OK to exit the Options dialog box and click Cancel to exit the Save As dialog box. Your document will now be saved automatically after every time period you specified.

You must still save the file yourself when finished with it (or before you answer the phone or go to lunch) by selecting File | Save or clicking the Save button on the toolbar. Using Automatic Save will just prevent the tragedy of lost information in case of unforeseen circumstances.

Backing Up Files and Disks

Although AutoSave protects you from losing the information you are working on in case of power loss or a bolt of lightning, you must still safeguard your data from the tragedy of losing information that is stored on disk. Because you never know when you will lose a floppy disk or the hard disk will fail, you must *back up* your files onto another disk. You may back up a single document, a single floppy disk, or the entire hard disk. Windows 95 makes it easy to back up files, folders, and disks.

You can back up a single file from the hard disk or a network drive onto a floppy disk whenever you see a list of file names. My Computer, Windows Explorer, and even the File | Open and File | Save As dialog boxes list the names of files. To back up the file, place a disk in drive A:, highlight the file name on the list, and click the right mouse button to access the shortcut menu. Select the command Send To 3½ Floppy [A], as in Figure 3.17.

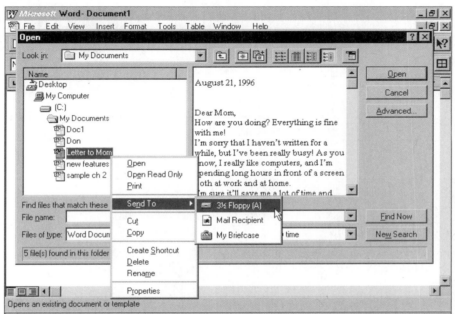

FIGURE 3.17
Backing up an individual file

If you work primarily from floppy disks, you may want to keep an identical copy of the disk just in case you lose or damage it. You must have two disks in order to back up: the source disk containing your files, and a destination disk to receive the backup. Close Word and then open My Computer and highlight the 3½ Floppy [A:] drive. Issue the command File | Copy Disk. Step-by-step instructions to complete the task are given on screen.

Backing up data on the hard drive of a computer is also simple through the backup program provided by Windows. Because hard drives contain such massive amounts of data, they are usually backed up to a special tape drive rather than to floppy disks. If you have access to the tape backup apparatus, you may begin the backup process by clicking the Start menu, selecting Programs, Accessories, System Tools, and Backup, as shown in Figure 3.18. The programs listed on your computer will not exactly match the list on the figure.

FIGURE 3.18
*Accessing the
backup program*

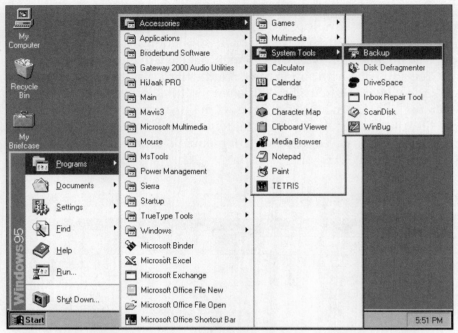

GUIDED ACTIVITY 3.7

Making a Backup Copy of a Single File

1. To back up a single document from the hard disk to a floppy disk, insert into drive A: the disk you wish to receive the backup file.

2. Click the Open button to reveal the Open dialog box.

3. If drive A: is selected, click on the down arrow next to Look In and select drive C:.

   Highlight from the list the name of any file you wish to practice backing up.

4. Click the right mouse button to reveal the shortcut menu.

5. Select Send To 3½ Floppy [A]. You briefly see a copying message box, and the light comes on, indicating that drive A: is working.

6. Click Cancel to remove the dialog box from the screen.

GUIDED ACTIVITY 3.8

Making a Backup Copy of a Floppy Disk

1. To back up the contents of a floppy disk, you must have two disks. Insert into drive A: the disk you wish to copy.

2. Minimize Microsoft Word by clicking on the minimize button on the title bar.

3. Double-click the My Computer icon on the desktop.

4. Click once to highlight 3½ Floppy [A:]. Do *not* double-click to open a window.

5. Select from the menu File I Copy Disk, as shown in Figure 3.19. Follow the instructions on screen as to when to remove the source disk and insert the destination disk, the one that will receive the backup files.

6. Close the My Computer window and click on Microsoft Word on the taskbar to return to Word.

FIGURE 3.19
Copying a floppy disk

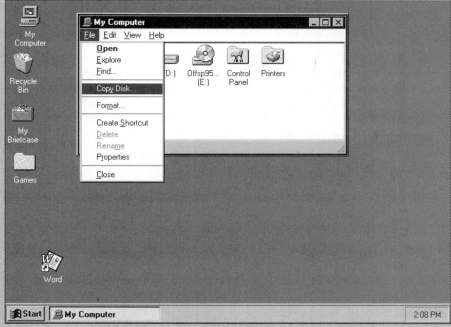

Summary

Disks are a magnetic medium used to store information from computer applications. Two types of disks are available: removable and fixed. Many environmental factors cause a disk to fail, although proper handling and backups can virtually eliminate data loss.

Floppy disks, which come in two sizes (3.5-inch and 5.25-inch) and two densities (low and high), can be taken easily from one computer to another. Hard disks are installed in the computer itself and are not easily transportable, but they hold much more information than floppy disks. The information on a hard disk can be retrieved more quickly than information from removable disks. Compact discs combine the advantages of large storage size and portability.

Windows 95 identifies files with a unique file name. Although Windows 95 allows long file names of up to 255 characters, certain characters may not be used. The names of any files used in computers running the older operating system DOS will be limited to eight characters and must be identified by both file name and extension of up to three characters.

Microsoft Word manipulates files by commands in the File menu. File | New is used to create new documents and to access templates and wizards. File | Open opens a file that was previously saved to disk. File | Close removes the current document from the screen and from memory. File | Save saves the current file under the name shown in the title bar of the window. File | Save As saves the current file under a new name that you supply.

The Automatic Save feature automatically saves your document to keep you from losing any changes if your personal computer shuts down for any reason. For truly safeguarding disks and data, make a backup copy often, using one of the methods supplied by Windows 95.

Finally, large blocks of text can be copied or moved to other locations in a document. The Edit | Copy command is used to make a duplicate of the selected characters to the Clipboard. The Edit | Cut command removes the selected text and places it in the Clipboard. Edit | Paste copies the contents of the Clipboard to the document at the location of the cursor. These commands may also be accessed from the shortcut menu, from buttons on the toolbar, and through shortcut keys. In addition, Word allows you to drag and drop text to a new location without using any menu commands or buttons. Text or data may be copied or moved between two or more open documents.

EXERCISE 3.1

Using the File Commands

1. Start Word.

2. Use the command File | New on the menus to start a new document using the templates.

3. Select the Letter Wizard for prewritten business letters.

4. Select the choice for résumé cover letter and complete the steps through the Letter Wizard.

5. When the document appears on screen, select View | Normal to make it easier to read.

6. Type your heading on the top of the page (name, class, date, and so on). Wherever necessary, type appropriate information or remove the underlining by highlighting and clicking on the U button.

7. Exit Word. Do this by clicking on the close button on the title bar or by selecting File | Exit.

   Because you have not yet saved the document, Word warns you to save first.

8. Click Yes to save, and type in the file name A:Job Letter. Click Save or press [Enter]. The light on the floppy disk drive will come on, indicating that the file is being saved, and then Word will close, returning you to Windows 95.

9. Click on the Start button, and then select Document and highlight the name of the file you just created, *Job Letter*.

   Word starts and immediately opens the letter.

10. If you are stopping here, exit Word. Otherwise continue on to Exercise 3.2.

EXERCISE 3.2

Using Cut, Copy, and Paste

1. If you are not continuing from Exercise 3.1, start Word and open the *Job Letter* file.

2. Click the down arrow next to the Look In box to reveal available drives. Select the one labeled 3½ Floppy [A:]. If you created one of the documents for the exercises in Unit 2, open it. It should be named *EX2-1* (or *EX2-2*, *EX2-3*, or *EX2-4*). If none of these are available, pick *Letter to Mom*, which you created in the Guided Activities in this unit.

3. Highlight the first two paragraphs (not including the heading with your name, class, and so on) and copy them. Use the command Edit | Cut, or use the shortcut key ([Ctrl][X]), or click the Cut button on the toolbar.

4. Use the Window command on the menu to switch to the *Job Letter* document.

5. Move the cursor to the end of the document. Paste, using the command Edit | Paste, or the shortcut key ([Ctrl][V]), or the Paste button on the toolbar.

6. Highlight the third paragraph, beginning with As a senior programmer (or however you edited the text to read in the last Guided Activity), and use the drag-and-drop technique to move this paragraph above the second paragraph.

7. Highlight the bottom paragraph (the one that was pasted from the other document). Copy it, by selecting Edit | Copy, or pressing [Ctrl][C], or clicking the Copy button.

8. Move the cursor to the top of the document above the first paragraph of the body of the letter. Paste.

9. Save the document and print. Exit Word.

EXERCISE 3.3

Backing Up a Single Document and a Floppy Disk

1. Open Word. Select File | Open or click on the Open button. Insert a floppy disk into drive A:.

2. Click once to highlight the name of a file on the list in the My Documents folder.

3. With the mouse pointing at the file name, click the right mouse button. From the shortcut menu, select Send To and click on 3½ Floppy [A].

4. Close the Open dialog box and exit Word.

   You need two floppy disks for the next step. With your data disk in drive A:, create a backup onto another disk.

5. Double-click My Computer, and then click *once* on 3½ Floppy [A:]. Do *not* double-click and open a window for the floppy disk.

6. Select the command File | Copy Disk. Follow directions on screen to complete the process.

Review Questions

*1. Why are disks used to store information?

2. What types of disks are available? What are the advantages and disadvantages of each type? How much information can be stored on each type?

*3. What types of environmental factors can damage a disk?

4. How do you format a floppy disk? What options are available?

*5. What limitations does Windows 95 place on file names? How do file names differ in DOS?

6. What is the difference between using the File | New command from the menu bar and pressing the New button on the toolbar?

*7. What happens when you attempt to close a file that has not been saved? What command does Microsoft Word execute if you then elect to save the file?

8. What is a wizard? What wizards are available with File | New?

*9. Explain the functions of Edit | Cut, Edit | Copy, and Edit | Paste. What is the Clipboard?

10. What two commands perform the same function as drag-and-drop editing?

*11. What are four methods to execute many commands?

12. Backups

    a. Can be performed by clicking the B button on the toolbar.

    b. Must be made on the same size disk.

    c. Are unnecessary if Automatic Save is turned on.

    d. Can be done for a single document, floppy disks, or hard disks.

*13. To open a file you closed a few minutes ago, you can

   a. Select it from the bottom of the File menu.

   b. Click on the Start button, and then Documents, and find its name on the list.

   c. Click the Open button and find its name on the list.

   d. Do any of the above.

14. The quickest way to move highlighted text from one place to another is to

   a. Drag and drop.

   b. Click and copy.

   c. Cut and paste.

   d. Click the Move button on the toolbar.

*15. When two documents are open at the same time,

   a. Use the Window menu to move from one to the other.

   b. The active document is on the bottom.

   c. Only one can be displayed at a time.

   d. All of the above.

Key Terms

3.5-inch disk	Drag-and-drop	Open document
5.25-inch disk	Extension	Path
Active document	File	Shortcut key
Back up	File name	Shortcut menu
CD-ROM	Floppy disk	System disk
Clipboard	Folder	Template
Compact disc	Format (disks)	Truncate
Disk	Hard disk	Wizard
Disk drive	High-density disk	Write-protect
Document	Low-density disk	

Proofing Tools

While a document is being written, in the flurry of creativity, it is easy to make errors. Microsoft Word provides several tools to help you ensure that the final draft is free of mistakes in typing, spelling, or grammar. These tools automate some of the proofreading tasks you need to perform when editing a document.

The spelling checker has a large dictionary against which it checks each word. Spelling may be checked while you type each word or all at once when the document is finished. Although the spelling checker picks up most spelling and typographical errors, it ignores even the most obvious grammatical error. Word provides a grammar checker to uncover mistakes in both grammar and writing style as well as to give suggestions for changes.

Using certain words many times throughout a document can make the text seem repetitive. A thesaurus can be used to find synonyms for words that are used often in a document. Microsoft Word has a built-in thesaurus to help you find synonyms. Finally, requirements may demand that the document be a certain size—no more than 150 words, for example, or at least 5,000 words. The Word Count tool helps you know whether you have met the specified length.

These four features make it easier to ensure that you have a correct and more professional document. They will not guarantee an error-free document, although each assists in the proofreading process. This unit will cover the use of the spelling checker, the grammar checker, the thesaurus, and the word counter.

Learning Objectives

At the completion of this unit you should know

1. three ways to check the spelling in a document,

2. how to customize the AutoCorrect feature,

3. the limitations of the spelling checker,

4. how to check for errors in grammar or writing style,

5. how to find synonyms for words,

6. how to replace multiple occurrences of text,

7. how to count the number of words in a document.

Important Commands

Edit | Replace

Tools | AutoCorrect

Tools | Grammar

Tools | Spelling

Tools | Thesaurus

Tools | Word Count

Spell Checking

When a document is first created, making errors in spelling or typing is common. Part of the proofreading procedure should be to thoroughly review the document for these mistakes. To reduce the number of errors you must catch, Microsoft Word's *spelling checker* verifies the words in the document with three features:

- Automatic Spell Checking, which flags errors as you type

- AutoCorrect, which automatically changes certain mistakes on the fly

- Checking spelling in the entire document all at once

The three features of the Microsoft Word spelling checker work together to make finding and correcting spelling or typographical errors as simple and hassle-free as possible.

Automatic Spell Checking

If the Automatic Spell Checking feature is turned on, this icon appears in the status bar. *Automatic Spell Checking* examines each word *as you finish typing it* against the dictionaries. If the word does not occur in its dictionaries, Word flags the word with a wavy red line, as in Figure 4.1. At this point, you can press Backspace and retype the word correctly, or you can get suggestions from the spell checker. Suggested corrections are accessed from the shortcut menu (always available in Windows applications with the click of the right mouse button). Point the mouse at the word and click the right mouse button to access the shortcut menu. From there you can select from

FIGURE 4.1

The automatic spell checker at work

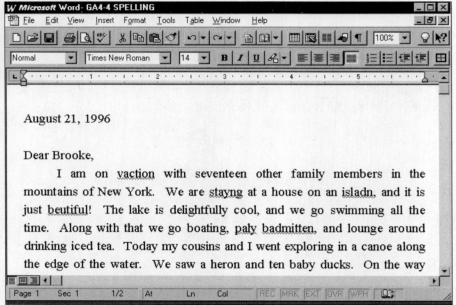

suggested alternatives, ignore the word (that is, accept it as it is currently spelled), or add the word as spelled to the dictionaries.

Word uses two types of dictionaries to search for correct spellings: the main dictionary, and a custom dictionary for your own name and technical terms you commonly use. The standard custom dictionary is *Custom.dic*, but you may also use a different custom dictionary that you create or purchase.

GUIDED ACTIVITY 4.1

Turning on Automatic Spell Checking

1. Open Word. To make sure that Automatic Spell Checking is on, follow these steps. Click on Tools on the menu, and then selection Options. You will see several tabs in the Tools|Options dialog box, with options for customizing many different features of Microsoft Word.

2. Click on the tab labeled Spelling to bring it to the front. The results are shown in Figure 4.2.

3. Click on Automatic Spell Checking so that a check appears in the check box.

4. Click OK or press [Enter] to return to the document. As soon as you start typing, the icon will appear on the right side of the status bar, as in Figure 4.3.

FIGURE 4.2
*Spelling options
dialog box*

Check this box

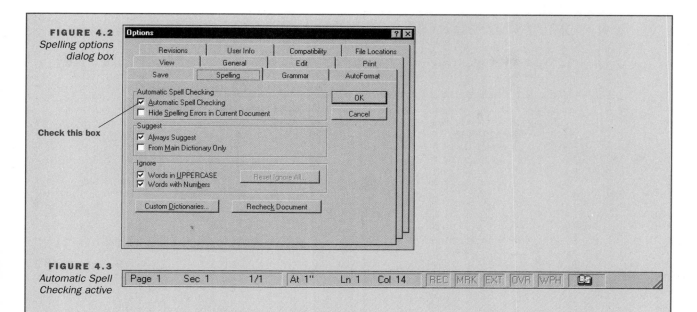

FIGURE 4.3
*Automatic Spell
Checking active*

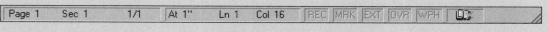

GUIDED ACTIVITY 4.2

Working with Automatic Spell Checking

1. Type in the following quote, deliberately making mistakes as you go. Make sure you type a period and space after `Shakespear`:

   `The wordl is a book, and the person who stays at home reads but one page. William Shakespear.`

   As soon as you press the `Spacebar` after the mistakes, the automatic spell checker flags the word with the wavy red line, and the icon on the status bar changes, as shown in Figure 4.4. Do not press `Backspace` and retype.

FIGURE 4.4
*Automatic Spell
Checking has
found an error*

Page 1   Sec 1   1/1   At 1"   Ln 1   Col 16   REC MRK EXT OVR WPH

2. Point the mouse at the first wavy red line and click the right mouse button. The shortcut menu appears with several choices for likely replacements, as in Figure 4.5.

3. Click the choice `world` to fix the error. The text in the document is immediately changed, and the shortcut menu disappears.

 TIP *If you are reviewing your document and correcting words with the wavy red underline, you can jump quickly to the next misspelled word by double-clicking the Automatic Spell Checking icon on the status bar.*

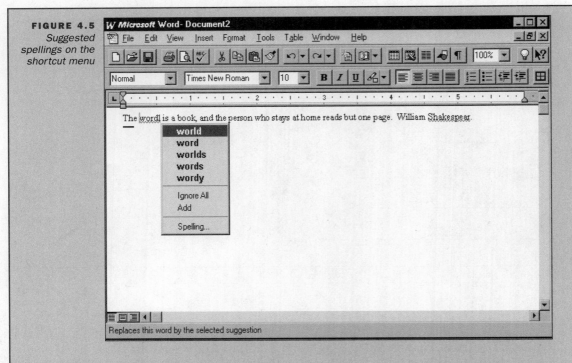

FIGURE 4.5
Suggested spellings on the shortcut menu

4. Double-click the Automatic Spell Checking icon on the status bar to jump to the next flagged word, and choose the correction on the shortcut menu. When all misspellings are either corrected or ignored, the wavy red lines disappear and the status bar's icon has a red check instead of the red X.

AutoCorrect

Microsoft Word includes a feature called *AutoCorrect*. This feature can be customized to fix your most common typographical errors for you while you type, without your having to make any changes. AutoCorrect automatically changes straight quotations marks (like ") to "curly" ones (often a dead giveaway that a published document has been "desktop published" rather than professionally typeset). It may also fix certain capitalization errors and change awkward symbols to nice ones, such as ==> to →.

GUIDED ACTIVITY 4.3

Watching AutoCorrect Work

1. Make sure AutoCorrect is turned on. To do this, select Tools | AutoCorrect and check the box next to Replace Text as You Type.

2. Move the cursor to the end of the document, either by clicking to the right of the last period or by pressing Ctrl End.

3. Add the following text, and watch carefully to see what happens as you type each error:

    ==> Pack all teh adventure yuo cna into yuor next vacation wiht an all-inclusive package from Back Road Travels!

    As soon as you press the [Spacebar] after typing a mistake, AutoCorrect changes the word.

    What happens if you go back and change a word during editing?

4. Double-click on the auto-corrected word *your* and change it to *yuor*. Notice that, since you are not pressing the [Spacebar] after completing the word, AutoCorrect doesn't make the change for you. However, the Automatic Spell Checking feature is still on the job and flags the word with a wavy red line.

If you find yourself making the same typographical errors time after time, you can instruct Word to correct them automatically *while you type* by customizing AutoCorrect. To manage which errors are automatically corrected, select the command Tools | AutoCorrect from the menu.

GUIDED ACTIVITY 4.4

Customizing the AutoCorrect Tool

1. Select from the menu Tools | AutoCorrect.

2. In the text box under Replace, type informaiton, as in Figure 4.6.

3. Press [Tab] to move the cursor to the With text box. Type information.

4. Click the Add button to add both these words to the list, and then OK.

FIGURE 4.6
*Customizing
AutoCorrect*

Check this box

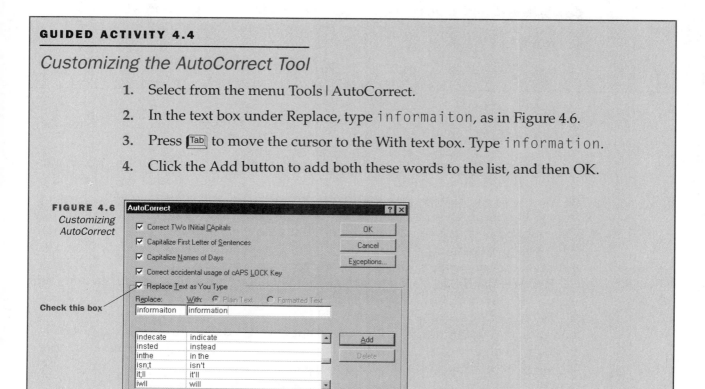

5. Press ⌈Enter⌉ at the bottom of the document. Type the following words and watch Word automatically correct the mistakes:

    `ONe excellent source of informaiton on traveling is Rick Steves, author of teh "Through the Back Door" book series.`

    The straight quotes are changed to curly ones, the capitalization is corrected, and the spelling of `informaiton` and `teh` is changed while you type.

    Some words or phrases are simply long and difficult to type, such as `Environmental`, even with Word correcting typing errors for you. AutoCorrect can also be used to automatically expand certain abbreviations into a word, phrase, or sentence.

6. Select Tools | AutoCorrect, in the Replace box type `callif`, and in the With box type `Please call if you have any further questions`. Click Add.

    Of course, you must be careful to use a unique word in the Replace box. In this case, using the word `call`, for example, would automatically expand to the phrase even if you didn't intend it to.

7. Add another abbreviation in the Replace box: `EPA`. In the With box, type the full name: `Environmental Protection Agency`. Click Add and then OK to register your addition and close the dialog box.

8. Press ⌈Enter⌉, and then type `callif` and `EPA` and watch AutoCorrect expand each word to a phrase or sentence. Type a space after each word for AutoCorrect to happen.

9. Select File | Close to close the file. No need to save.

Checking Spelling All at Once

Sometimes the wavy red lines may be a distraction during the writing stage, particularly if you are doing a list of proper nouns that the spell checker does not find in its dictionaries. You may wish to turn off the automatic spell checking feature and instead check the spelling of all the words at one time when you are finished writing. This method of "create first, polish later" is used by many professional writers, and it gives you an easy way to catch errors in your document at the appropriate time, without constantly interrupting your train of thought.

To begin the process of checking spelling all in one pass, click on the Spelling button on the standard toolbar or select from the menu Tools | Spelling.

Microsoft Word compares each word in the document against entries in its dictionaries, and if it finds a word that does not match, a dialog box appears. At this point, you can type in the correct spelling, select from suggested alternatives, ignore it (that is, accept it), or add the word to the dictionaries.

GUIDED ACTIVITY 4.5

Checking Spelling All at Once

1.   Open the file *GA4-4 Spelling*.

2.   Press [PgDn] several times to skim through the document. At the end of the docu-ment, replace Leina's name with your first and last name.

3.   Select the command Tools | Spelling.

Rather than using the Tools | Spelling command, you may click the Spelling but-ton on the toolbar. Word looks up the word in both its standard dictionary and any custom dictionaries selected.

The first misspelling found is vaction. For each word the spelling checker does not find in the dictionary, the Spelling dialog box will open to give you a chance to review the word. Since the word vacation is misspelled, it was not found in the spelling dictionaries. Microsoft Word opens the dialog box shown in Figure 4.7, and offers a list of suggestions for the word you intended to type. Most of the time, the first word in the list is correct. If there is more than one suggestion, you can click on the up and down arrows to the right of the Sugges-tions box to scroll through the list of possibilities.

FIGURE 4.7
Spelling dialog box

4.   Since the correct spelling is already highlighted, just click on Change.

The suggestion you selected replaces the incorrectly spelled word, and Microsoft Word continues to check the document.

5.   Continue to find and correct the next three errors: stayng, isladn, and beutiful.

Whenever the spelling checker tries to find suggestions for a misspelled word, it must pause as it looks through the dictionary. To speed up the process, you may tell Microsoft Word not to make suggestions each time. For simple mis-takes, you may wish to type the corrections yourself.

6.   When the dialog box appears at the next misspelled word, paly, click Options. A new dialog box appears, as shown in Figure 4.8.

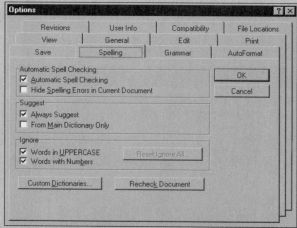

FIGURE 4.8
Spelling options

7.   Click on the check box next to Always Suggest to turn this feature off. The check should disappear from the box. Click OK, and then correct the word in the dialog box.

8.   The Spelling box appears more quickly the next time because the spelling checker does not have to look up suggestions for the misspelled word. (With a fast computer it may not make much of a difference.) Correct the word yourself by typing `badminton` in the Change To box. Click Change to continue to check the spelling.

If you would like to see suggestions for the correct spelling, that option is still available.

9.   When the dialog box appears with the next misspelled word, `embarassing`, click on the Suggest button.

A list of suggestions appears. However, the next time you check the spelling of a word, the list will not appear unless you again click on Suggest.

10. Turn on the Suggestions again. To do this, click on Options, put a check in the box Always Suggest, and click OK to return to the spelling checker.

Since the correct spelling of the word in the Suggestions box is already selected, click on Change. Continue to check the spelling in the remainder of the document.

One of the words that does not appear in the dictionary is `Theround`. The dictionary has no suggestions for a correct spelling, since it is two words combined without a space. You may correct it without completely retyping.

11. Correct this error by clicking the mouse in the Change To box to the right of the `e` and inserting a space between the words. Click Change to continue.

12. The spelling checker also picks up repeated words such as `the the`. To correct this error, click Delete.

> ✎ **NOTE**   *Some repeated words are not errors, as in the phrase* `It is ludicrous that that Senator claims he is innocent.`
>
> **13.** The next item found is `Adirondack`. This word is not an error; it is a proper name.
>
> When this word appears in the Spelling dialog box, click on Ignore All to tell the spelling checker that this and all subsequent occurrences of the word in the current document are not misspellings.
>
> **14.** Occasionally, you will place a word in documents you create that is not in the spelling dictionary. A perfect example of this is a name. While common names may appear in a spelling dictionary, `Leina` is included in very few. To avoid Word's having to list this as a misspelling in every document where it appears, it can be added to a special dictionary. This option is only available when *Custom.dic* is in the Add Words To box.
>
> **15.** Word encounters your name at the end of the document. If your name is uncommon, it appears in the Spelling dialog box. Click on Add. (If *Custom.dic* is not available, click Ignore.)
>
> You have added your name to the custom dictionary named *Custom.dic*. Now, whenever a document is checked that contains your name, the spelling checker will not consider this a misspelling.
>
> When the spelling checker reaches the end of the document, it jumps to the beginning of the document. The spelling checker stops when it reaches the position of the cursor from which you first started checking, and displays a dialog box telling you the spelling check is complete. Click OK.
>
> **16.** Select from the menu File | Save As (do NOT click the Save button). Give the corrected document the name *GA4-4 Correct*. Close the file.

Limitations

The spelling checker and AutoCorrect can be very useful when you are editing and proofreading a document, but they are limited in what they can correct. The spelling checker finds words that do not appear in its dictionary and suggests alternative spellings, and AutoCorrect fixes specified typographical errors, but neither can find every mistake in a document. For example, the word `of` may be typed incorrectly as `or`, but Microsoft Word will not find this error because both words appear in its dictionary. You cannot assume that a document is correct simply because the spelling checker does not find any misspelled words. You must carefully proofread each document to find such mistakes.

Grammar Checking

The *grammar checker* is another tool provided by Microsoft Word to aid in proofing your document. It performs three useful functions:

- Flagging questionable grammar and writing style
- Checking spelling
- Providing readability statistics

Like the spelling checker, Word's grammar checker normally examines the entire document beginning at the location of the cursor. When it finds a sentence with questionable grammar or writing style, it displays the sentence in a dialog box. Directly underneath the questioned sentence is a box containing a suggested way to correct the error. The buttons on the right side of the dialog box, shown in Figure 4.9, give you several alternative ways to deal with the grammar checker's findings—Ignore, Next Sentence, Change, Ignore Rule, and Cancel.

FIGURE 4.9
Grammar checker

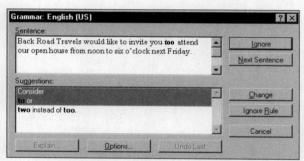

The grammar checker follows certain grammatical and stylistic rules. It may be quite permissible to use language informally for personal letters, but usually not for business writing. To select whether the grammar checker should be strict or lenient, choose Options and set your preferences. Even so, in some cases the grammar checker questions phrases that may be correct. The Explain button gives an explanation of the suspected error.

Choosing Ignore causes the grammar checker to skip the questioned word or phrase without making any changes. Choose Ignore Rule, on the other hand, to skip this and similar occurrences for the remainder of the document. Next Sentence causes the grammar checker to leave the entire sentence unchanged. If you have made an error, you may accept the suggested correction by selecting Change. If the Change button is unavailable, type your correction in the Sentence box, and then click Change to continue checking the remainder of the document.

Word's grammar checker has several advantages and even drawbacks. One advantage is that, because it also checks spelling, you can perform two functions with one step. Furthermore, if you substitute `there` for `their` by mistake, the grammar checker will find the error, whereas the spelling checker will not.

The drawbacks are serious, however. The process of grammar-checking a long document is quite tedious. The grammar checker flags the use of the word

FIGURE 4.10
Grammar options

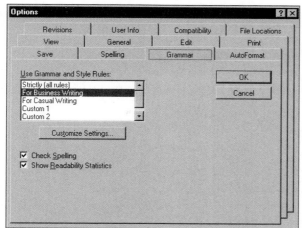

personal, for example, and warns you not to confuse it with personnel. In addition, some perfectly correct sentences are flagged as errors. For example, sentences using helping verbs are sometimes thought to be passive, and long sentences are just too much for the grammar checker to analyze. Nevertheless, using the grammar checker can assist in the proofreading task.

The grammar checker can be customized for several different kinds of text, including formal, business, and casual writing. The customization can be performed by clicking Options in the Grammar Checker box to reveal the dialog box shown in Figure 4.10. Additional customization is available by clicking Customize Settings.

GUIDED ACTIVITY 4.6

Using the Grammar Checker

1. Open the file *A:GA4-5 Grammar*. Select Tools | Grammar.

2. The homonym too has been substituted for the correct to. Click Change to fix the error.

3. The *spelling* checker (at work during the *grammar* checking process) highlights an unknown word, Steves. Click Ignore.

4. Continue checking the document, making the following changes to the flagged selections:

who	Click Change.
with	Click Next Sentence (consider rewording this later).
Information	Click Ignore (it is correct as it stands).
you're	Select your and click Change.
receives	Click Change.
passive voice	Click Ignore (a few passive verbs are acceptable; more than two or three means you should rewrite in active voice).
we're	Correct the capitalization.
We're	Click Ignore to keep the contraction.

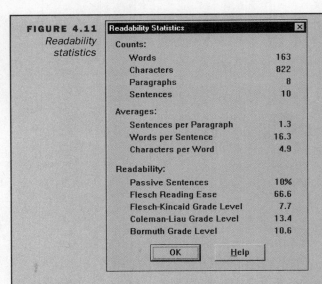

FIGURE 4.11
Readability statistics

5. At the end of the grammar checking process, the readability statistics are displayed, as shown in Figure 4.11. You will read about these statistics in the next section, so click OK to finish.

6. Select from the menu File|Save As (do NOT click the save button). Give the corrected document the name *A:GA4-5 Correct* and click Save. Keep the file open for the next Guided Activity.

Readability Statistics

The grammar checker also provides information about the readability of a document. At the end of the grammar checking process, Readability Statistics are displayed, as shown in Figure 4.11. These indexes measure how many long words and complicated sentences are in the document. Several of the indexes are referenced to grade level. A Flesch-Kincaid Grade Level of 7, for instance, would be considered readable by the average reader who has completed seventh grade. Thus, the higher the number, the more difficult the material is to read.

The Flesch Reading Ease index is the only exception. This score ranges from 100 (corresponding to a fourth grade reading level) to 0 (which is college graduate level or very difficult reading). This score tells the percentage of people who can likely understand the document readily, so a higher number here means that the document is less difficult to read.

The Thesaurus

A *thesaurus* is used to find synonyms for words in a document. The thesaurus tool in Word is very (*extremely, quite, awfully*) useful when a word is repeated many times and should be replaced by another word with the same or a similar meaning. Sometimes you are searching for a word with a particular shade of meaning. Other times, a word is too difficult or is otherwise inappropriate for the reader. To use the thesaurus, click in a single word and select Tools | Thesaurus.

GUIDED ACTIVITY 4.7

Using the Thesaurus

1. Continue using the file from the previous activity. Click in the word `indigenous` in the first sentence of the sample document. Select Tools | Thesaurus to see the dialog box shown in Figure 4.12.

FIGURE 4.12
Thesaurus dialog box

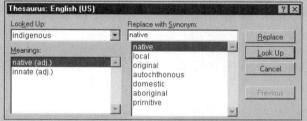

Microsoft Word provides a list of alternatives in the Replace with Synonym box. `Local` is the best choice. Select `local` and click Replace.

2. Click in the word `plan` in the same sentence, and then select Tools | Thesaurus.

The synonyms listed on the right all loosely match the definition in the Meanings box. However, `plan` is not always a noun.

3. Click on the verb definition in the Meanings box to see more definitions for the word `plan`.

New synonyms now appear in the Replace with Synonym box. These are the synonyms for `plan` when it is used as a verb.

4. Highlight `arrange` in the Replace with Synonym box and click the Replace button.

Word returns to the work area and replaces `plan` with `arrange`.

The thesaurus allows you to find all of the possible definitions of a selected word, to select from the definitions the correct one, and to choose an alternate word. This will help reduce repetition of commonly used words in your documents, although you should still use discretion when substituting synonyms to avoid the writing fault called "elegant variationism."

5. Save the document. Keep the file open for the next Guided Activity.

Search and Replace

Text that occurs several times throughout a document can be changed with very little trouble by using the command Edit | Replace. Although AutoCorrect replaces such text while you type, for a one-time use the Replace command is more appropriate. For example, a standard letter may be sent each month to various departments in a business. Perhaps the only change is every occurrence of the month or the department name throughout. Rather than skimming through the text, highlighting and typing the new text, you can specify the text you wish to search for and the text with which it should be replaced in the Edit | Replace dialog box, shown in Figure 4.13. Then replace one at a time or all at once.

Replace can be used to change not only a whole word or phrase, but all forms of a word. For example, if you want to change the word buy to purchase, if you check the box Find All Word Forms, you will also change bought to purchased and buying to purchasing. (What a smart program!) When you replace words, however, you have to watch out or you may replace text you don't intend to change. For instance, if you replaced can with can't throughout a document, the word cannon would change to can'tnon by mistake.

FIGURE 4.13
Replace dialog box

GUIDED ACTIVITY 4.8

Replacing Text

1. Use the document from the previous Guided Activity. The company has changed its name from Back Road Travels to Thrill Seeker Tours. In a small document like this, making the change could be done easily without using Edit | Replace, but let's practice the skill in this document regardless.

2. Select the command Edit from the menu, and then select Replace. The dialog box in Figure 4.13 appears.

3. In the box labeled Find What, type Back Road Travels. Press Tab to jump to the next box, labeled Replace With, and type Thrill Seeker Tours.

4. Click the Replace button. This replaces the first occurrence of the name and automatically jumps to the next occurrence.

5. Click the Replace All button. Now all the occurrences are changed at once, and a message appears telling how many replacements were made. Click OK.

6. The Replace dialog box stays open in case you want to make other changes. Click Close to return to the document.

Save the document.

Counting Words

As you create a document and change the formatting of the text, the paragraphs, and the page as a whole, you are probably wondering how long the document has become. Since the number of pages a document fills depends on the style and size of the font, the spacing of the paragraphs, and the width of the margins, the best measure for the length of a document is the number of words it contains. The formatting of the document has no effect on this statistic. Rather than counting the words yourself one by one, issue the command Tools | Word Count. Pages, words, characters, paragraphs, and lines are counted automatically, and the results appear as in Figure 4.14. This *Word Count* tool is very useful for those times when you are asked to write an article of exactly so many words for an article or a term paper.

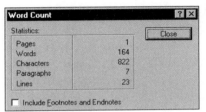

FIGURE 4.14
Word Count dialog box

Summary

Microsoft Word features a spelling checker that flags mistakes while you type or all at once. The spelling checker can offer alternatives to words it cannot find in the dictionary, either on the shortcut menu or in the Spelling dialog box. You may select one of the alternatives or type in the correct spelling yourself. You may also add words (such as your name or technical words) to the dictionary that are not already there but that may appear in many of your documents. AutoCorrect is useful for correcting specific typographical errors and for automatically expanding abbreviations into words or phrases. While AutoCorrect replaces text automatically, the Edit | Replace command is better for one-time changes that occur throughout a document.

The grammar checker goes one step further. It will help correct simple grammatical mistakes and flag text of questionable style. If you use the grammar checker, it performs the spell check function at the same time.

The thesaurus offers synonyms for repetitive words in a document. This allows you to replace these words with other words of similar meaning. The thesaurus in Microsoft Word maintains all the possible meanings for each word in the dictionary and offers a different list of synonyms for each one. You can also instruct Word to count the number of words in a document to determine how long it is.

The proofing tools provided by Microsoft Word will not ensure a perfect document. It is still your responsibility to make sure that there are no errors in the text before giving the document to its intended recipient.

EXERCISE 4.1

A Day in the Life of a College Student

1. Open the document *A:EX4-1 Proofing*.

2. Add your class heading to the top of the document (for example, name, date, class time, seat number) and press `Enter`.

3. Click the Spelling button on the Standard toolbar and check for errors. Any misspelled words should be corrected by clicking on one of the suggested spellings or by retyping. If a proper noun is flagged in error, click Ignore. Any repeated words should be deleted.

4. Run the grammar checker to detect any grammatical errors. Ignore flagged stylistic suggestions that are not actual errors. *Watch out:* The grammar checker makes mistakes, too! Click OK when finished.

5. Find a synonym for the word `proffered`. Look under the related word `proffer`. Remember to change the new word to past tense.

6. Use the command Edit | Replace to change all occurrences of the words `University Program` into `College Program`. Click Replace All. Click OK and then Close.

7. Issue the command Tools | Word Count to find out how many words are in the document. Type a sentence at the bottom of the page giving the total word count.

8. Save and print the document.

EXERCISE 4.2

Crusty's Pizza

1. Open the document *A:EX4-2 Proofing*.

2. Add your class heading to the top of the document (name, date, seat number).

3. Click the Spelling button on the Standard toolbar and check for errors. Any misspelled words should be corrected by clicking on one of the suggested spellings. If any proper nouns are flagged in error, click Ignore.

4. Run the grammar checker to detect any grammatical errors. Ignore flagged stylistic suggestions that are not actual errors. *Watch out*: The grammar checker makes mistakes, too! Click OK when finished.

5. Find a synonym for the word `modicum`. When you change to the synonym, you may have to delete the word `of` that follows.

6. Use the command Edit | Replace to change all occurrences of the words `Pizza King` into `Crusty's`. Click Replace All. Click OK and then Close.

7. Issue the command Tools | Word Count to find out how many words are in the document. Click Close. Type a sentence at the bottom of the page giving the total word count.

8. Save and print the document.

EXERCISE 4.3

The Internet

1. Open the document *A:EX4-3 Proofing*.

2. Add your class heading to the top of the document (name, date, seat number).

3. Click the Spelling button on the Standard toolbar and check for errors. Any misspelled words should be corrected by clicking on one of the suggested spellings. If any words are flagged in error, click Ignore.

4. Run the grammar checker to detect any grammatical errors. Ignore flagged stylistic suggestions that are not actual errors. *Watch out:* The grammar checker makes mistakes, too! Click OK when finished.

5. Find a synonym for the word `roam`.

6. Use the command Edit | Replace to change all occurrences of the word `facts` into `information`. Click Replace All. Click OK and then Close.

7. Issue the command Tools | Word Count to find out how many words are in the document. Click Close. Type a sentence at the bottom of the page giving the total word count.

8. Save and print the document.

EXERCISE 4.4

Thrill Seeker Tours

1. Open the document *A:EX4-4 Proofing*.

2. Add your class heading to the top of the document (name, date, seat number) and press [Enter].

3. Click the Spelling button on the Standard toolbar and check for errors. Any misspelled words should be corrected by clicking on one of the suggested spellings. If any words are flagged in error, click Ignore. *Watch out*: The grammar checker makes mistakes, too! Click OK when finished.

4. Run the grammar checker to detect any grammatical errors. Ignore flagged stylistic suggestions that are not actual errors.

5. Find a synonym for the word `concomitant`.

6. Use the command Edit | Replace to change all occurrences of the word `Eurorail` into `Eurail`. Click Replace All. Click OK and then Close.

7. Issue the command Tools | Word Count to find out how many words are in the document. Type a sentence at the bottom of the page giving the total word count. Click Close.

8. Save and print the document.

Review Questions

*1. How can you tell if Automatic Spell Checking is turned on?

2. How do you find suggestions for ways to correct a word flagged with a wavy red underline?

*3. What kinds of things can AutoCorrect change?

4. How do you check the spelling of the entire document at one time?

*5. Why is there an option to turn off the suggestions in the spelling checker?

6. What is the purpose of the grammar checker? What other functions does it perform?

*7. What triggers the changes made by AutoCorrect?

8. Is everything that is highlighted by the grammar checker in error? Why or why not?

*9. What functions does the thesaurus perform?

10. What should you do if the synonyms that are listed under the first definition in the Meanings box do not match the usage of the word in the document?

*11. The quickest way to change occurrences of the word `January` to `February` in a long document is to

   a. Customize the AutoCorrect tool to replace `January` with `February`.
   b. Use the Edit | Find command to search for `January` and retype.
   c. Use overtype mode.
   d. Select Edit | Replace.

12. The grammar checker flags

   a. Misspelled words.
   b. Casual writing style such as contractions.
   c. Run-on sentences, subject-verb agreement problems, and use of homonyms.
   d. All of the above.

*13. To find suggestions for correcting the spelling of a word with the wavy red line,

    a. Double-click the word.

    b. Click the right mouse button.

    c. Click the Spelling button.

    d. Select Edit | Suggest.

14. You can tell if Automatic Spell Checking is active by

    a. Clicking the Spelling button on the toolbar.

    b. Double-clicking the Spelling icon on the status bar.

    c. Misspelling a word on purpose.

    d. Double-clicking a word with the right mouse button.

Key Terms

AutoCorrect	Grammar checker	Thesaurus
Automatic Spell Checking	Spelling checker	Word Count

5 Printers and Printing

The goal of word processing is to get a document on paper. This unit will discuss the details of the printing process for the documents you have created in Microsoft Word.

Before you print for the first time in Word, you must have a printer connected directly to your computer or to the network to which your computer is attached. Second, you must have the printer set up correctly in Windows settings. Third, you must select which printer you will use for a particular document, if more than one printer is available.

The first section discusses the various types of printers that are available to you. The printer you use will determine the quality of the printed document and some of the fonts available. The second section covers the way the printer is attached to your computer. It is important to understand how your computer communicates with the printer and the name of the connection to the printer, as well as how Windows handles the printing for all applications. Finally, the Microsoft Word print commands will be covered in this unit.

Learning Objectives

At the completion of this unit you should know

1. what types of printers are available,
2. what kind of printer you have,
3. how printers are attached to computers,
4. how to set up Windows for different printers,
5. how to preview and print both documents and envelopes,

6. how to control the printing process.

Important Commands

File | Print

File | Print Preview

Tools | Envelopes and Labels

FROM THE TASKBAR

Start | Settings | Printers

Types of Printers

Several popular types of printers may be attached to your computer. They are generally classified by how they print characters on paper and by the quality of the print they produce. The printer to which you have access will determine the quality of the output you produce and the fonts that are available to you for use in documents.

Dot-matrix printers produce characters by printing a series of dots in the shape of letters. For example, the letter m when greatly enlarged would look like Figure 5.1.

FIGURE 5.1
Dot-matrix character

At their actual size the dots are so small that the eye does not distinguish between them. When you look at a character, you simply see the shape created by the dots, not the dots themselves. The more dots a printer can place in a specific location on a page, the smoother the characters will appear. This principle is the same one that underlies the pixels on a computer monitor. A finer image can be produced by making the dots (or pixels) smaller and placing them closer together. The popular models of ***dot-matrix printers*** are 24-pin printers, capable of producing characters with 24 vertical dots. These printers are called *NLQ* (near letter quality) because the quality of the text closely resembles that of a typewriter. Most NLQ printers can print graphics in addition to text. The print heads pass across the page line by line to print the document, and it takes several minutes to print each page.

Though more expensive to operate than dot-matrix printers, ***laser printers*** are the standard. The laser technology, similar to that of a photocopy machine, increases both print speed and print quality. Although these printers also create letters by joining a series of dots, the dots are so tiny that they are indistinguishable to human eyes. Typical laser printers can print 300 or 600 dots per inch (dpi) and can print 4 to 16 pages per minute or more.

Another printer type is the ***inkjet*** or bubblejet ***printer***, some models of which print in color as well as black ink. Inkjet printers work by injecting black or colored inks onto the paper surface. This requires special ink cartridges and sometimes special types of paper. Inkjet printers are less expensive to purchase and use than laser printers, so they are increasingly popular. Color inkjet printers now are quite reasonably priced, making the ability to print in color accessible to many. Microsoft Word allows you to format text in different colors as well as to include pictures and graphics to take advantage of color printers.

The latest printer technology combines the functions of a fax machine, copier, scanner, and color inkjet printer into a single unit. These *multifunction printers* are ideal for small-office or home use.

Computer Connections

Peripheral devices, such as printers, scanners, and modems, are connected to computers by plugging them into *ports* (plug-in sockets) on the back of the computer. There are several different kinds of ports, but printers can be connected into either *parallel ports* or *serial ports*. The large majority of printers attach to the parallel port, but a few attach to the serial port. Since the configuration of different computers varies so much, it is impossible to tell exactly where the parallel and serial ports will be on your computer. To find these ports, consult the documentation for the particular computer you are using, although you may be able to tell by looking. A

FIGURE 5.2
Parallel port has holes

parallel port on the back of a computer is typically about 1½ inches long and ¼ inch wide, and contains 25 holes in two rows, as in Figure 5.2. A serial port, on the other hand, may be approximately the same size, but instead of 25 holes it contains 25 pins in two rows. Some serial ports are only half as long and have only 9 pins in two rows, as in Figure 5.3.

FIGURE 5.3
Serial port has pins

The computer has names for each of the ports available in its configuration. The parallel port is called *LPT1:*, and the serial port, *COM1:*. If the computer has more than one parallel or serial port, these additional ports have the same name with the number increased by one. For example, if a computer had three parallel ports, the second and third ports would be called LPT2: and LPT3:, respectively. If the computer had a second serial port, it would be called COM2:.

You can determine which port your printer is connected to by tracing the cable that attaches the printer to the computer, noting the location of the port where it is attached, and consulting your computer's manual to find out what port it is. This information is necessary to allow Windows to operate the printer and to make sure your printouts go to the right printer when you select the Print command.

You may be able to use a printer that is attached not directly to your computer but rather to a *network*. A computer network allows several computers to be connected to each other so that they may share information and peripherals. It is cost-effective to buy one expensive printer, attach it to a network, and share it with 20 or 30 other computers. If you use a printer from a network, it may appear to the computer that you are using the LPT2: or LPT3: port even though your computer does not actually have these ports. You should not have to set up Windows yourself to make your computer communicate with a network, but you should know how to tell what printers are available on your computer.

Windows 95 maintains a list of printers available for use in all Windows applications. Every Windows application has access to the same set of printers. Printers are defined from the Settings selection from the Start menu on the taskbar.

GUIDED ACTIVITY 5.1

Setting Up Printers in Windows

1. Start Windows 95. Click the Start button on the taskbar. Select Settings, and then select Printers, as in Figure 5.4.

FIGURE 5.4
*Setting up
printers from the
Start menu*

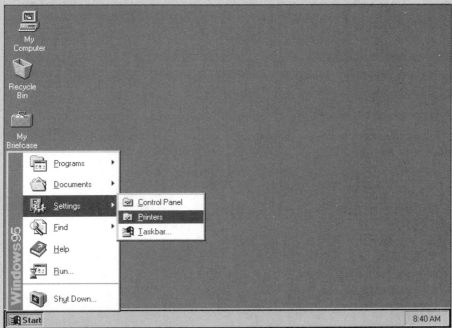

The Printers window appears, showing icons or a list of currently installed printers, as in Figure 5.5. The names of the printers on your screen will differ from what is shown in the figure.

From this window you can add and delete printers, see what printers are available, and tell what documents are currently being printed.

You will not actually add or delete printers at this point because Windows has probably been set up for the printers attached to your computer and because the original Windows 95 disks or CD may be needed to complete the process. However, you can easily change the port to which the printer is assigned without permanently damaging the setup.

Select the first (and possibly only) printer listed in the Printers window by clicking on it.

FIGURE 5.5
Printers window

2.   Select File | Properties from the menu, then click on the Details tab to reveal the dialog box shown in Figure 5.6.

FIGURE 5.6
Printer Properties dialog box

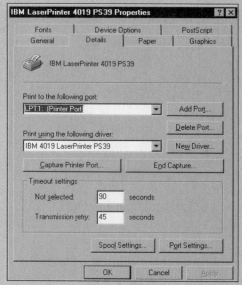

The Print to the Following Port text box contains information about the port to which the printer is connected. Make a note of which port is selected in that box so that you can change the printer back to the correct port later.

3.   Click on the down arrow to the right of the current port, and select one of the ports that was not selected in step 2 (such as COM1: or LPT2:). Press [Enter] or click on OK.

Windows returns to the Printers window. The list of printers in the Installed Printers box is still the same, but the port has been changed. Whenever you select this printer from any application and print to it, Windows will attempt to send the information for the printout to this port.

Since this is not actually the correct port for this printer, change the port back to its original setting.

4. Select File | Properties again and the Details tab to change the port back.

5. Click on the original port to which the printer was connected in the Print to the Following Port box.

6. Press or click on OK.

   The selected printer is now changed back to the original port.

7. Click the Close button. We will return to this Printers window later to learn how to control the printing process.

Print Commands

Once you have correctly set up the printers from the Start menu, you are ready to print from any Windows application. The commands in this section relate specific- ally to Microsoft Word, but you will find them in many different Windows applica- tions in nearly the same form. If you know how to print in Microsoft Word, you know how to print in almost any Windows application. The File menu contains sev- eral commands that give the user control over the printing function.

Since Microsoft Word will format and display your document based on the printer that you have selected, the next step is to verify which printer will be used to print the document. To select or verify which printer will be used, first select the File | Print command, which brings up the dialog box shown in Figure 5.7. Clicking the down arrow next to the printer name drops down a list of available printers from which you select the one you wish to use in printing your document.

Once the printer is selected, you could print the document to see what it looks like. However, doing this frequently wastes paper, for, in most cases, minor changes need to be made to produce a document that looks right. Some of these needed changes can be seen when you preview the entire document on the screen before

FIGURE 5.7
Print dialog box

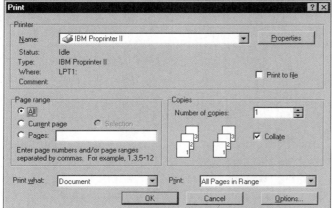

printing it. Microsoft Word allows you to do this with the File | Print Preview command. Print Preview will show you what each page of your document will look like. The actual text in the document cannot usually be seen from Print Preview, but the shape of the paragraphs and their position on the printed page are displayed. This is a very useful feature that shows, for example, whether what you intend to be a one-page letter fits on one page, or whether individual pages in a multiple-page document appear correct and balanced.

GUIDED ACTIVITY 5.2

Preparing the Printer

1. Start Microsoft Word.

2. Select File | Print. At the top of the dialog box, Word shows the selected printer and the port to which it is connected.

3. Click on the down arrow next to the name of the printer to display a drop-down list of all available printers.

4. Click on the name of the printer you want to use. Click Cancel to exit the dialog box and return to the document.

   The printer is now ready to produce your document. However, before putting your document on paper, you should preview it on the monitor.

GUIDED ACTIVITY 5.3

Previewing a Document

1. Click the Open button and select the file *GA4-4 Correct* (or *GA4-4 Spelling*, if you do not have the other) from the Student Data Disk. This is the sample file you will print in this Guided Activity.

 2. Select File | Print Preview or click the Preview button.

   Word creates a picture of how the entire page will look and displays a new toolbar with buttons specific to the Preview mode, as shown in Figure 5.8.

   You can see what the paragraphs will look like when you print the document. However, the actual text is not legible. Your mouse pointer now appears as a magnifying glass.

3. Click on the document with the magnifying glass to examine the text at a legible size.

   If you have additional corrections you need to make before you print the document, you can make them here in Preview. In the sample document, the letter appears to be too high on the page.

FIGURE 5.8
Print Preview

Magnifier

Previous page
Next page

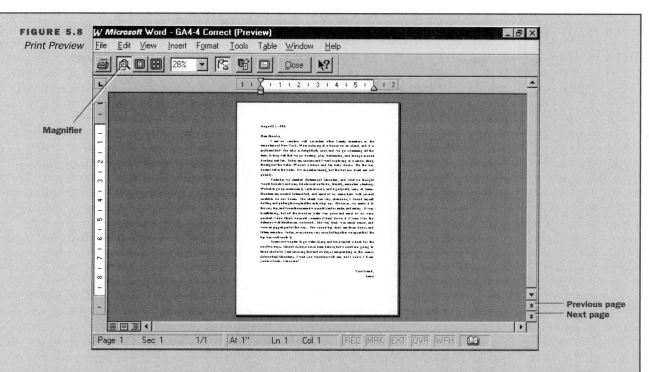

4. Click on the Magnifier button on the Preview toolbar. The button no longer appears pushed in, and the mouse pointer changes into an I-beam. Click on the page to place the cursor back at the beginning of the document. Press Enter 5 times.

5. Click on the Magnifier button to turn the mouse pointer into the magnifying glass again, then click on the document to zoom back out to see the entire page. Now the letter does not appear so high on the page, but instead it drops off the bottom of the first page and continues on a second. Notice that the status bar shows 1/2, meaning that the screen shows page 1 out of 2 total pages, as in Figure 5.9.

FIGURE 5.9
Status bar

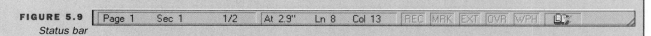

6. Click the next page arrow on the scroll bar at the right of the screen (or press the PgDn key) to view the second page of your document, and then click the previous page arrow (or press the PgUp key).

7. To view more than one page at a time, click the Multiple Pages button on the toolbar. Highlight the number of pages you wish to view at once by dragging across the sample pages, as shown in Figure 5.10. Select 1x2 Pages.

8. Change the preview back to a single page by clicking on the One Page button.

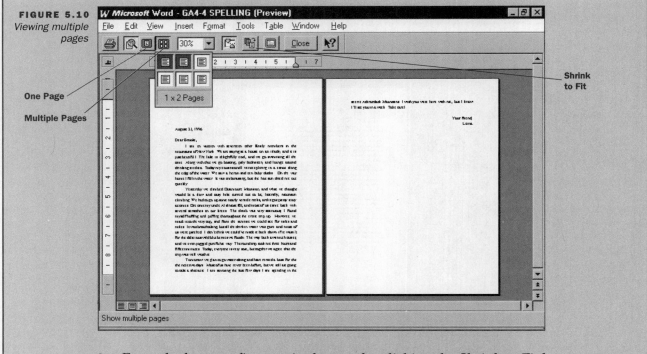

FIGURE 5.10
Viewing multiple pages

One Page

Multiple Pages

Shrink
to Fit

9. Force the letter to fit on a single page by clicking the Shrink to Fit button. Notice that the status bar now shows 1/1, telling us that the document is now only one page long.

    How does the Shrink to Fit button work? It reduces the size of the font and the amount of spacing between the lines. A better solution in this case would have been to remove the empty lines we inserted at the top of the document. In other cases, narrowing the margins or rewording the text could change the length of the document. The Shrink to Fit button is always a quick solution for a document that runs a few lines over onto the next page.

10. Click Close to close the Print Preview.

Printing

After you preview the document on the screen and make any changes that are necessary, you are finally ready to print. Word offers five ways to print a document.

- Click the Print button on the Standard toolbar.

- Click the Print button in Print Preview.

- Select File | Print from the menu.

- In My Computer, Explorer, or dialog boxes, highlight the file name and select Print from the shortcut menu.

- Drag the file name from My Computer or Explorer to a printer shortcut icon on the desktop.

Pressing the Print button, either in Normal view or in Print Preview, bypasses the Print dialog box and immediately sends the entire document to the selected printer. It is the fastest way to print a single copy of your document to the default printer.

When you select the File | Print command from the menu, however, the Print dialog box appears (refer back to Figure 5.7), providing several options for printing. Besides being able to select the name of the printer, you can also specify the number of copies to be printed. The default is 1, but you could enter a different number. You could either type in the number of copies to print, or use the mouse to increase or decrease the number of copies by clicking on the up or down arrows next to the box.

This dialog box also lets you define the range or amount of the document to print. There are three options you can select. The default is to print the entire document: the option button next to All is filled in. The second option is to print only the page where the cursor is located by clicking on the option button next to Current Page. The third option is to specify certain Pages of the document to print. When you have made all your choices, click OK to begin the printing process.

Word handles printing in the background. That is, the printing is handled by the hard disk and the CPU (central processing unit) without making you wait until the job is finished before you can continue to work on a document. To let you know how the background printing is proceeding, the status bar shows a tiny, animated picture of pages spooling off a printer next to the number of the page currently being printed. To turn on the background printing option, select Tools | Options, click on the Print tab, check the box labeled Background Printing, and click OK.

If your printer is set correctly and ready to print, the document should begin to print within a few seconds. Network printers may take longer to print, depending on how many other people are also using the same printer.

Once a document has been sent to the printer, you still have control over the printing process through Windows 95. Double-click the printer icon on the status bar (NOT the button on the toolbar) and the Printer window shown in Figure 5.11 appears. In this window you will see a list of the documents in the process of being printed to it, called the ***print queue***. You can rearrange the order of printing, pause the printer, or cancel printing from menu selections in this window.

 You can also access the Printer window from the Start menu. Click the Start button, select Settings, Printers, and then double-click the name of the printer to which your document was printed.

FIGURE 5.11
Printer window

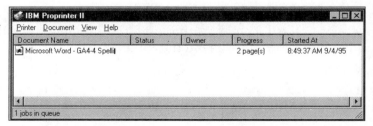

What should you do if the document does not print at all or prints incorrectly?

The mistake could be a user error, that is, you clicked the wrong button or selected the wrong printer. Other sources of the problem may be harder to detect. The problem may be any one of the following:

- *Printer is not turned on.*
- *Printer is offline or not ready.*
- *No paper is in the printer.*
- *Printer cable is not plugged securely into the computer or printer.*
- *Printer is not correctly configured in Windows 95.*
- *Network connections are not set up correctly.*

For additional hints, check your printer's control panel or look in the Answer Wizard under "Troubleshoot Printing."

If you made a mistake and wished to stop the printing process or delete a print job from the queue, you could do so with these steps:

- Highlight the name of the document being printed.
- Select from the menu Document | Pause, Document | Delete, or just press the [Del] key.

GUIDED ACTIVITY 5.4

Printing

1. Select the command File | Print from the menu, and the Print dialog box appears. Select 2 copies and All pages.

2. Make sure your printer is ready, and then click on OK to print the document.

3. If your printer is not extremely speedy, you will have time to examine the printing process through the Printer window in Windows 95. Double-click on the tiny printer icon on the status bar or access it from the Start menu. If printing is still under way by the time you open this window, you will see your document listed here.

4. Another way to print the document is through Print Preview. Click the Print Preview button or select from the menu the command File | Print Preview.

5. Click the Print button on the Preview toolbar. This button has the identical function as the Print button on the Standard toolbar, bypassing the dialog box and printing a single copy of the entire document.

6. Click Close to close Print Preview.

7. Click the Open button and highlight the file name *GA 5-6 Correct*, but do *not* double-click or click OK to open it.

8. With the file name highlighted, *right*-click to access the shortcut menu. Click the Print command. When the Print dialog box appears, click OK to print the document. Word automatically begins background printing the document without even opening the file.

Printing Envelopes

Since printing a letter is a common task, Word makes it simple to print the envelope or mailing labels to go along with the letter. To create and print an envelope, simply choose Envelopes and Labels from the Tools menu, and then click on the Envelopes tab. Word examines the letter to find text that is most likely an address, and inserts it into the Envelopes and Labels dialog box, as shown in Figure 5.12. From this dialog box you may change the recipient and the return address. Clicking on Options will change the direction the envelopes feed into the printer. If you are using envelopes with a preprinted return address, click in the check box next to Omit to keep from printing over it. Note that a sample of the elements to be printed is shown in the Preview area. You may need to experiment to find the correct way to feed the envelope into your printer.

FIGURE 5.12
Envelopes dialog box

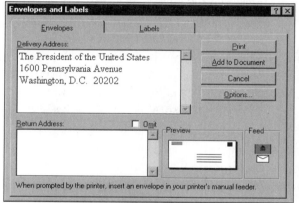

Summary

Several types of printers are available, including dot-matrix, laser, and multifunction inkjet printers. Each produces a different kind of print quality and is used for different reasons. Printers are attached to the computer by means of ports, or sockets, located on the back of the computer. There are two kinds of ports: parallel and serial.

Windows maintains a list of printers that are available to all Windows applications. The list of printers is maintained from the Printers window, which is accessed from the Start button. The Printers window is used to add, delete, or configure printers by changing the port to which they are attached. During the printing process the Printers window lets you change the print order or discontinue printing files that have been sent to the printer.

Printing in Microsoft Word is a simple process. Print Preview is used to view the document on the monitor to check that the appearance of each page is correct. To view or change the target printer, check the Print dialog box through the File | Print command. Use File | Print also to specify what portion of the document and how many copies to produce. Click on the Print button on the toolbar to bypass the dialog box and print a single copy of every page in the document. Located under the Tools menu is a command that allows you to print an envelope or mailing labels with ease.

Exercises

1. Open the file *A:EX5 Printing*. Enter the standard heading at the top of your document.

2. In Print Preview, preview two pages at once. Click the Shrink to Fit button to force the text to fit on one page. Click the Print button to print the document. Close Print Preview.

3. Click on the Start button on the taskbar and select Settings | Printers to see what printers are available. Leave the Printers window open and return to the Word document to type the names of the printers at the end of the document.

4. Return to the Printers window by clicking the button on the taskbar, and select one of the printers. Click on its icon and select Details to find out what port the printer is attached to. Click Cancel to close the Properties dialog box. Close the Printer window. Return to the Word document and type the port information for the appropriate printer.

5. Print the document. While it is printing, access the Printers dialog box through the Start menu (or double-click on the Print icon on the status bar) and note the information about this document on the print queue.

6. Click in the Word document window. Press [Ctrl] [End] to jump to the end of the document and press [Enter]. Type the information from the job queue noted in step 5.

7. Select File | Print and select only page 2 to print. Save the file under a new name.

8. Address and print an envelope using the command Tools | Envelopes and Labels. (Consult your printer documentation if necessary to determine how to feed the envelope.)

Review Questions

*1. What types of printers may be attached to a computer? What kind of printer are you using?

2. What are the two kinds of ports to which printers may be attached? How is yours attached?

*3. What is the difference between clicking the Print button on the toolbar and selecting the command File | Print?

4. What menu selections do you make to set up printers in Windows 95?

*5. What does double-clicking on the Printer icon on the status bar do?

6. What are the advantages of using Print Preview?

*7. What should you check if the document does not print?

8. How do you pause or cancel the printing of a document?

*9. The type of printer that is most often used in business is

    a. Dot matrix.

    b. Laser.

    c. Inkjet/bubblejet.

    d. Multifunction printer.

10. Printers are plugged into the back of a computer via a(n)

    a. Port.

    b. Serial capture.

    c. NLQ.

    d. LPT1:.

*11. The Printers window, accessed through the Start menu, can be used to

    a. Add printers.

    b. Change the port.

    c. Cancel printing.

    d. Do all of the above.

12. The Print Preview screen

    a. Lets you see only one page at a time.

    b. Helps you shrink a slightly too long document to fit on one page.

    c. Is accessed by clicking the View buttons on the status bar.

    d. Removes the ruler and toolbars from the screen.

Key Terms

COM1:	Multifunction printer	Port
Dot-matrix printer	Network	Print queue
Inkjet printer	NLQ	Serial port
Laser printer	Parallel port	
LPT1:	Peripheral device	

Creating a Memo

As a young executive with Thrill Seeker Tours, one of your responsibilities is to develop new tours. Create a trip that would fit with the Thrill Seeker Tours image. Research a location for your activity, and get information on lodging, restaurants, and approximate costs. Using a memo template, type up your proposal for your manager.

1. Select File | New and access a memo template. Customize the information at the top of the page following the To:, From:, and Subject: lines. Backspace to remove the CC: line completely.

2. Replace the directions below the line with the text for your memo. In the first paragraph, describe in colorful terms the trip's activities and features. Try to write as though the reader is experiencing what your customers will experience.

3. In the second paragraph, describe specific locations and lodging and meal arrangements.

4. Itemize the costs for the customer. Use the Calculator accessory to total the costs for the trip and paste the answer in place.

5. In the final paragraph, explain to your manager the benefits to the company of offering such a trip, including the projected demand. Offer to lead the tour, and urge the manager to implement this trip in the near future.

6. Proofread, save as *Application B*, and print.

Formatting

UNIT SIX   *Formatting Characters*

UNIT SEVEN   *Formatting Paragraphs*

UNIT EIGHT   *Formatting Documents*

■ **PART TWO** of this manual helps you change your documents to enable you to better convey your intended meaning to the reader. Different formats affect the way the reader's eyes move across a page of text and can enhance the reader's comprehension and retention of a document. Different character sizes and attributes such as bold, italics, and underline can draw attention to important words or letters in a document. Changing the way a paragraph looks can emphasize a section of text by making it stand out from the rest of the document. You can use formatting commands to make more or less information fit on a page, to create a certain impression, or to follow specific styles required by some organizations.

Useful documents can be created without using any formatting commands. However, formatting will make documents more effective and can be the single most important step that you can take (aside from writing the content) to make sure that your document communicates your intended message.

6 Formatting Characters

Formatting a document is like getting dressed in the morning. What you put on gives others a message about the kind of person you are (punk rocker, police officer, executive) and what your destination is (beach, work, wedding). Likewise, the way you "dress" or format a document sends a message to the recipient beyond the words on the page. The document's appearance not only helps communicate what kind of company or individual the sender is and what the intended audience or purpose of the document is, but also invites the reader in to grasp the verbal message without distractions.

Three levels of formatting are applied to every page: character, paragraph, and document. Because formatting is done so often, Word makes the commands easy to access. Formatting commands are available through buttons on the Formatting toolbar, through commands on the Format and shortcut menus, and through the use of shortcut keys. This unit covers the first of the three levels of formatting commands.

The most specific level of formatting is character formatting. Once the actual text in a document has been established, the way the words look may be changed to emphasize their meaning. Characters may be made **bold**, <u>underlined</u>, or *italic*, or may be ^{super}scripted or $_{sub}$scripted. Character formats may be combined for added effect.

Learning Objectives

At the completion of this unit you should know

1. how to format existing or new text,

2. what character formats are available,

3. how to apply character formatting,

4. how to copy formats,

5. how to change the default font,

6. how to insert special characters into a document.

Important Commands

Format | Font

Insert | Symbol

Formatting Characters

Four methods may be used to format selected characters or words:

■ Click buttons on the Formatting toolbar.

■ Select commands located on the Format menu.

■ Use commands located on the shortcut menu.

■ Press the shortcut key combinations.

The most commonly used commands are located on the Formatting toolbar. Less frequently used formatting commands are accessed by selecting Format | Font from the menu.

Text may be formatted either after it has been entered or as it is typed into the work area. To format text that is already entered, you must first highlight (select) it before executing the format command. After you choose the command, the high-lighted characters will display the new format. This formatting method, known as *direct formatting*, is ordinarily used when you are trying different format attributes on a portion of text to see which will best convey the message the passage is meant to send.

If you already know which format a word or sentence should have, you can apply it to the text before you begin to type. With the cursor positioned where the text is to go, turn on the desired format and begin typing. Every character typed will have the format *attribute* (characteristic) you selected. Eventually, you will probably want to type text without this formatting. To continue typing text without the selected format attribute, you turn off the format again. This method of formatting is known as *indirect formatting*.

Font and Point Size

The first and most common character attributes formatted are the font and point size. Microsoft Word uses the word *font* as a name for the shape of a character. While the actual name of the shape of a character is its typeface, for the sake of consistency with the program it will be called a font. The *point size* of a font is its size. One vertical inch is equal to 72 points; the normal point sizes of text in documents are 10 and 12, with levels of headings perhaps in 14, 16, and 20.

Different fonts are used to convey different messages with the same text. A legal brief does not (and should not) look the same as a child's storybook. A wedding invitation has a different appearance than a business plan. A company's annual report certainly does not resemble its newspaper advertising circular.

Fonts affect the legibility of a document and give a certain image to a document. Plain, unobtrusive fonts are generally more readable than unusual or eye-catching fonts. The more noticeable fonts call attention to themselves, thus slowing the eye. While there are times you may want this to happen (to call attention to a particular word or phrase), overuse can decrease the readability of your document.

Styles in fonts change over the years, just as styles in colors do. For example, fat, rounded overlapping letters remind us of the 1960s as much as the earth-tone colors then in fashion. In the early 1990s, tall delicate fonts were considered chic. Take a look at magazines, newsletters, and recently published books to see the latest trend in the shapes of the letters.

Fonts are classified into two broad categories, *serif* and *sans serif*. A serif is a small line used to finish off a main stroke of a letter, as at the top and bottom of the letter M. Paragraphs of text are easier to read in serif fonts because the serifs guide the reader's eyes along the line of text. They are often used in books and newspapers with long, narrow columns to read. Examples of serif fonts include Times Roman, Times New Roman, Palatino, and Courier.

Sans serif fonts, without the serifs, are slower to read. That is what makes them good for titles, headings, and STOP signs because, in slowing the eye, they stand out better. Helvetica and Arial are examples of sans serif fonts.

Fonts are further classified as *proportional* and *nonproportional*. If a font is proportional, each of the letters in that font has a different width. These fonts are very pleasing to look at because each character has an individual shape and width. Capital letters in a proportional font are much wider than lowercase letters.

By contrast, nonproportional fonts (also called monospaced fonts) force every character to be exactly the same width. While these fonts are not beautiful, they are easy to work with when creating tables or any other application that requires letters to be vertically aligned. The example in Figure 6.1 illustrates the difference between widths of characters in the Times Roman and Courier fonts. The characters in both samples are the same point size.

FIGURE 6.1
Font samples

Courier:
```
The quick brown fox jumped over
THE QUICK BROWN FOX JUMPED OVER
```

Times Roman:
The quick brown fox jumped over
THE QUICK BROWN FOX JUMPED OVER

All the Courier characters line up. There are 31 characters on each line of the Courier sample. The capital letters are the same width as the small letters. Because nonproportional fonts have a fixed spacing, they are often measured in characters per inch (CPI), rather than points.

In the Times Roman sample, neither line matches the other or the lines in the Courier sample, even though they are the same point size. The Times Roman uppercase letters are much wider than the lowercase letters, and the W is more than four times wider than the I because of its shape. When you are working with a document that will require you to line up characters in any kind of tabular form, it is easier to use a nonproportional font, although paragraphs of text look more attractive—and are more legible—in a proportional font.

Many different fonts and sizes are available for use in documents. Windows provides several fonts called *TrueType* fonts, including Times New Roman, Arial, Courier New, and Symbol. These fonts are scalable, that is, they can be made any size (even half size, as in 8.5 point). TrueType fonts appear the same on screen as they will on the printed page, which is termed *WYSIWYG* (pronounced *wiz-ee-wig*, for "what you see is what you get"). Other fonts are unique to the printer you use, and still others are appropriate for on-screen use but not for printing. These may be limited in the sizes available.

Times New Roman is the *default* font in Word, and 10 points is the default size. A default is the normal setting that is used in the program unless you specify another. The font and size can be easily changed from the Formatting toolbar. As you click on the arrow next to the font name Times New Roman, an alphabetical list of other fonts appears. You can tell which fonts are TrueType, screen, or printer fonts by the symbols next to the font name, as in Figure 6.2. Your computer may be configured to display only TrueType fonts.

FIGURE 6.2
Font choices

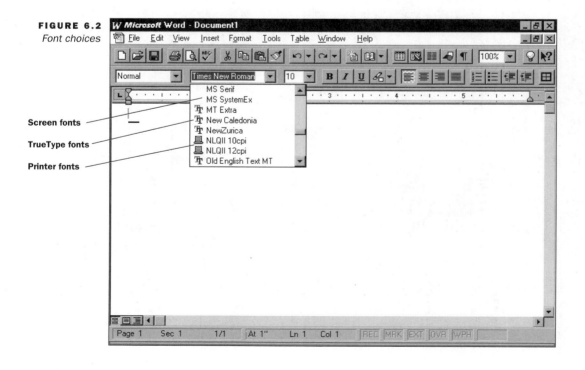

Screen fonts

TrueType fonts

Printer fonts

What character formats increase readability?

- *Use ordinary fonts more than extreme fonts for large amounts of text.*

- *Utilize serif fonts rather than sans serif for large amounts of text.*

- *Employ upper- and lowercase letters more than all caps.*

- *Make sure fonts are large enough to be read easily (or small enough to be difficult to read, if you're typing the fine print on the back of a contract you don't want people to notice!). For business cards, use 8 or 9 points; books and letters need 10 to 12 points; overhead transparencies should have letters at least 16 or 24 points; the fonts on billboards and highway signs should be ... enormous.*

- *Save extra-bold and italic for accents.*

- *Use contrasting, distinctive fonts only for headings and titles.*

GUIDED ACTIVITY 6.1

Changing Font and Size

1. Start Word.

   The default font is displayed in the Font box on the Formatting toolbar, as in Figure 6.3.

FIGURE 6.3
Formatting toolbar

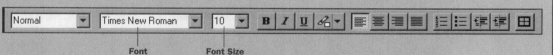

Font   Font Size

2. Type the words This is Times New Roman.

   Any text that you enter will be in the font and point size listed on the Formatting toolbar. You may select any font or size by selecting from the drop-down list.

3. Press twice. Click on the down arrow to the right of the Font box.

   The list of fonts is displayed in alphabetical order. If the list is too long to fit in the Font box, a scroll box will appear to the right of the box to allow you to scroll through all the available fonts. The most recently used fonts are listed above the alphabetical list.

4. Select Arial as the new font by clicking on Arial in the font list. Type This is Arial.

The words appear in a new font. Using this method, you may position the cursor anywhere in a document and begin typing in any font available on this list.

5. Press twice. Type the words new text.

These words appear in the same font you used in the previous line. However, you can change this.

6. Select the entire line you just typed (click to the left of the line). Click on the down arrow next to the Font box to see the list of fonts again. Select Courier New.

The words on the last line change to the Courier New font. You could just as easily have changed them to any other font on the list.

In addition to changing the font, you may select a different size.

7. Select the first line in the document. Click on the down arrow next to the Font Size box.

A list of the sizes available for the selected font appears, as shown in Figure 6.4. The current size is listed in the box at the top of the list and is also highlighted in the list itself.

FIGURE 6.4
Formatting toolbar showing point sizes

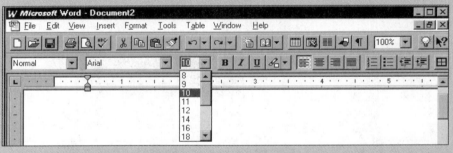

8. Select a different size from the list in the Font Size box by clicking on any size in the list.

Because Word is a WYSIWYG word processor, you can actually see the text change sizes on the screen after you change the format. The printed output will match the document's on-screen appearance.

To see a sample of the fonts before applying them to text, you may also use the Format | Font command.

9. Position the cursor at the end of the document by clicking anywhere below and to the right of the bottom line. Press twice to start a new line. Select Format | Font to see the dialog box shown in Figure 6.5.

You may select a new font and size from the Font dialog box by scrolling through the available options and selecting your choice.

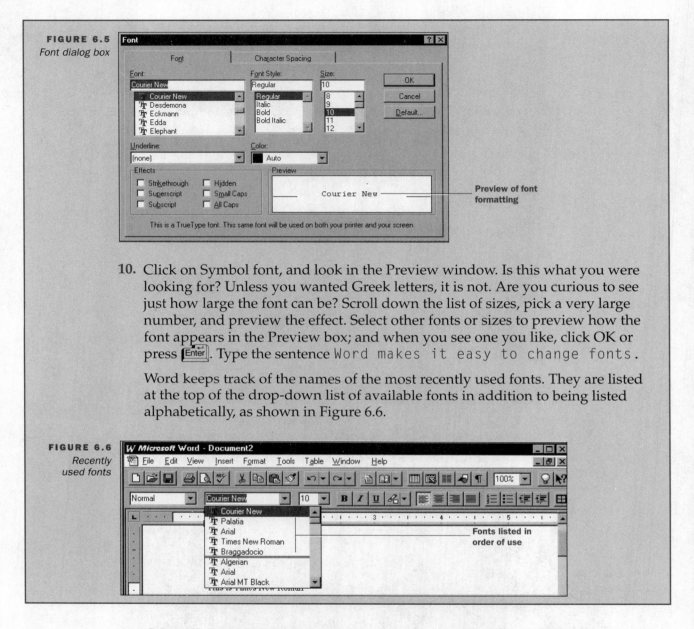

FIGURE 6.5
Font dialog box

Preview of font
formatting

FIGURE 6.6
*Recently
used fonts*

Fonts listed in
order of use

10. Click on Symbol font, and look in the Preview window. Is this what you were looking for? Unless you wanted Greek letters, it is not. Are you curious to see just how large the font can be? Scroll down the list of sizes, pick a very large number, and preview the effect. Select other fonts or sizes to preview how the font appears in the Preview box; and when you see one you like, click OK or press [Enter]. Type the sentence Word makes it easy to change fonts.

Word keeps track of the names of the most recently used fonts. They are listed at the top of the drop-down list of available fonts in addition to being listed alphabetically, as shown in Figure 6.6.

Generally it's a good idea to limit the number of fonts in a document. One serif and one sans serif font offer plenty of contrast and variety, if you discreetly vary the point sizes and judiciously add in bold, italic, or both. Too many fonts cause confusion and clutter and can be in bad taste, just like mixing plaid, checks, and stripes in clothing.

In addition to changing the font in small segments of text, it is possible to change the basic font for the document. As you know, the default font for Word is Times New Roman, 10 points. As you experiment, you may find that you prefer a slightly larger size or an entirely different font for your documents. Change the default font and size setting by making the selections you want and then clicking on the Default button in the Font dialog box.

Bold, Italics, and Underline

In addition to changing the font and point size of text, the Formatting toolbar has three other formatting attributes to choose from. These are normally used to make certain characters stand out from the others around them. Because they are the most frequently used character format attributes, they are available from the Formatting toolbar, as in Figure 6.7.

The attribute buttons on the Formatting toolbar normally appear to be three-dimensional, that is, to stick out from the surface of the toolbar. When one of these attributes is selected, its button will appear to be pressed in. The buttons themselves also give you a quick preview of the function they perform. The B on the Bold button is itself bold, the I on the Italic button is italic, and the U on the Underline button is underlined.

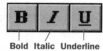

FIGURE 6.7
A portion of the formatting toolbar

Bold Italic Underline

The *bold* attribute makes letters darker by thickening the lines that compose the letters. Bold words will immediately stand out on a printed page, so they are easy to find. Highlighted text in Word can be easily made bold by clicking once on the Bold button on the Formatting toolbar. *Italics* also make words stand out from the text around them, though not as much as the bold attribute. The italics attribute slants characters to the right. To make words appear with the italics attribute, click once on the Italic button on the Formatting toolbar.

Sample text regular:	sample
Sample text in bold:	**sample**
Sample text in italics:	*sample*
Sample text in bold italics:	***sample***
Sample text with underline:	<u>sample</u>

Many writing style manuals indicate that bold or italics may be used in place of underlining when creating references like footnotes or endnotes for passages from other texts. This is desirable because underlining certain letters alters their appearance. The strokes of characters that extend beneath the line of text (as in the letters g and p) are called *descenders*. Descenders can be overwritten by the underline attribute, as shown on the sample text with underline; therefore, it is advantageous to use bold or italics whenever possible to avoid underlining text.

The *Underline* button is used to add or remove the Single underline attribute from selected text. There are three other kinds of underlining, available only in the Font dialog box, shown in Figure 6.8. The Words Only underline attribute places a single underline under only the actual characters

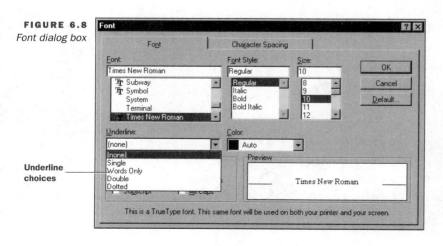

FIGURE 6.8
Font dialog box

Underline choices

selected, excluding spaces. The Double underline attribute places two lines under selected text. Another option is the Dotted underline.

Sample text underlined:	This text is underlined.
Sample text word-underlined:	This text is word-underlined.
Sample text double-underlined:	This text is double-underlined.
Sample text dotted-underlined:	This text is dotted-underlined.

GUIDED ACTIVITY 6.2

Applying Bold, Italics, and Underline

1. Highlight Times in the first line in your document. Click on the Bold button on the Formatting toolbar to make the word bold. Click elsewhere in the document to remove the highlighting from the word.

2. Highlight the second line and make it italic by clicking on the Italic button.

3. Highlight the fourth line of text in the document and underline it by clicking on the Underline button.

   As with the font and point size format commands, you may either format existing text or type in new, formatted text.

4. Position the cursor at the end of the document by clicking anywhere below and to the right of the last line. Turn off the underline by clicking on the Underline button. Click on the Bold button to turn on Bold and press [Enter] twice. Type in your name.

   Using the shortcut keys turns attributes on and off and makes the buttons appear pushed in, just as if you clicked the button.

5. Press [Enter] twice. Hold down [Ctrl] and press [B] to turn off the bold attribute. You will notice that the button does not appear pushed in anymore. Hold down [Ctrl] and press [I] to turn on the italics. Type in your name again.

6. Press [Enter] twice. Turn off the italics with the [Ctrl][I] shortcut key, and use [Ctrl][U] to turn on the underline. Type in your name a third time.

7. Highlight the first line with your name on it. Click on the Underline button on the Formatting toolbar to underline it.

   The entire line is underlined, including spaces.

8. Highlight the second line with your name on it. Select Format | Font, and from the Font dialog box in the Underline section select Words Only and click OK. This turns on the word-underline attribute.

   All letters on the line are underlined, but spaces are not.

You also may use the shortcut menu to quickly access the Font dialog box.

9. Highlight the third line with your name on it. With the mouse pointer over the highlighted text, click the right mouse button to access the shortcut menu. When the menu appears, click on Font using either mouse button.

10. From the Font dialog box, select Double from the Underline section to turn on the double-underline attribute. Click OK.

The entire line is double underlined. The attributes that are in effect at the location of the cursor will continue to be in effect as you type in new text.

11. Press ⏎.

The highlighting on the last line disappears, and the cursor should appear at the end of the line. The double underline attribute is still on. As you type new text, it will be double underlined.

12. Press `Enter` twice. Type `Accountants often use double underline for final totals.`

13. Highlight the words `double underline`. Select Format|Font and then choose (none) in the Underline section of the Font dialog box to remove the double underline from these two words. Click OK.

The Underline button may also be used to turn off all types of underlining.

14. Highlight the entire sentence beginning with `Accountants`. Click on the Underline button twice to turn off all underline formats.

Commands in the Font Dialog Box

Several other character format commands are found only in the Font dialog box. These functions are not often used and therefore are not included on the Formatting toolbar. The Color selection area in the dialog box allows you to select a color for text in a document. Using color is an excellent way to get words to stand out in a document that others will be reading, and some very attractive effects can be achieved by matching colored text with pictures.

A second feature available only from the Font dialog box is the ability to introduce certain effects to the formatted font. These effects include *strikethrough*, used in marking revisions; *superscript* and *subscript*, used in formulas; and *hidden* text, used in making comments that will not appear in the printed version. Characters that have been typed in lowercase may appear in all *capitals* or in *small capitals*, which combines normal-size initial capital letters with all lowercase letters converted to capitals in a smaller point size. Clicking in the check box next to the attribute desired will make a check mark appear in the box. When you then click OK, the format attribute will be in effect. You may format text that has been highlighted, or you may execute a command and enter new text that has the format attribute.

Sample text with strikethrough:	~~Sample text~~
Sample text superscripted:	x^2
Sample text subscripted:	H_2O
Sample text in all caps:	SAMPLE TEXT
Sample text in caps and small caps:	SAMPLE TEXT

Superscripting is often used when referencing a passage from another author's text. A superscript number, keyed to a note at the foot of the page or at the back of the text, is placed at the location in your document where you wish to give credit to another person or source. Word handles footnote and endnote marks automatically, so there is no need to use superscripting for this purpose. However, writers commonly use superscripting and subscripting when creating mathematical expressions in a document. When raising a number to a power, it is necessary to use superscripting. The variable expression x^2 is created by using superscripting. The number 2 is superscripted and automatically formatted to a smaller size. The formula H_2O is created by subscripting the number 2, which automatically makes the font smaller. There are other uses for superscripting and subscripting, but these are the most common.

Character Spacing

The Format Font dialog box contains a tab for setting *character spacing*, which is shown in Figure 6.9. This section of the dialog box gives you control over both the vertical and horizontal spacing of highlighted characters. To change the vertical position of a character, select Raised or Lowered in the Position box. If you select a higher value next to Position By, the character will be moved further from the line; a lower number will move it closer to the line.

To *condense* or *expand* a series of characters, you choose Expanded or Condensed in the Spacing box, shown in Figure 6.9. Selecting Expanded puts spaces between the selected characters. The default amount of space by which to expand each character is 1 point. The higher the number in the By box, the more space is added between each character. Condensing text removes space from around selected characters. The higher the number in the By box, the more space is removed. *Kerning* is a method to force letters to fit more closely together. It is often used to improve the appearance of letters with diagonal strokes, in headings, or in large fonts.

Sample raised by 1 point:	xy
Sample raised by 3 points:	xy
Sample raised by 5 points:	xy
Sample condensed by 1 point:	Sample condensed text
Sample expanded by 1 point:	Sample expanded text
Sample text without kerning:	AWAY
Sample text with kerning:	AWAY

Changing from Capital to Lowercase Letters

By mistake you may have typed in a title or heading and forgotten to capitalize it. Word provides a handy way to change the case of letters. The Format | Change

FIGURE 6.9
Character Spacing tab of the Font dialog box

Expand or condense

Raised or lowered

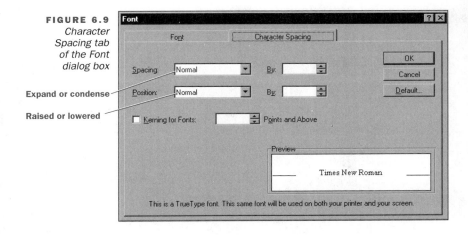

Case command is a real time-saver, allowing you to select the correct case from a dialog box without having to retype the material.

The dialog box shown in Figure 6.10 shows the choices of case you may apply to highlighted text. Sentence case applies a capital letter to the first letter highlighted and lowercase to the rest. The lowercase and UPPERCASE choices change the highlighted material to all lowercase and all uppercase letters, respectively. Title Case capitalizes the first letter of each highlighted word and places the other letters in lowercase. The tOGGLE cASE choice changes all capital letters to lowercase, and all lowercase letters to capitals. The shortcut key to *toggle* (switch between several choices) the case is Shift F3. Shortcut keys for this and many other character formats are given for reference in Table 6.1.

FIGURE 6.10
Change Case dialog box

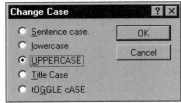

Readability is a key concern with capital letters. A significant factor in being able to read quickly is recognizing words by their shapes. When all uppercase letters are used, every word is shaped like a rectangle and the reader has to carefully read letter by letter rather than a word or phrase at a time. It's important to get the message STOP or WARNING, and not to skim too quickly across the words. The uppercase letters slow the reading process and perhaps cause you to think about the consequences of not stopping or not heeding the warning.

GUIDED ACTIVITY 6.3

Changing the Case of Text

1. Use the text from the previous Guided Activity. Highlight the top line with the words This is Times New Roman. Click the Bold button twice to apply bold to the rest of the words and then remove it from all.

2. Select the command Format | Change Case. In the dialog box that appears, choose lowercase and click OK.

TABLE 6.1
Font formatting shortcut keys

SHORTCUT KEY	FORMAT
`Ctrl` `B`	Bold
`Ctrl` `U`	Underline
`Ctrl` `I`	Italicize
`Shift` `F3`	Toggle case
`Ctrl` `Shift` `F`	Change font
`Ctrl` `Shift` `P`	Change point size
`Ctrl` `Shift` `A`	All capitals
`Ctrl` `Shift` `W`	Word underline
`Ctrl` `Shift` `D`	Double underline
`Ctrl` `Shift` `K`	Small capitals
`Ctrl` `=`	Subscript
`Ctrl` `Shift` `=`	Superscript
`Ctrl` `Spacebar`	Plain text, default font and size

The words change to resemble this: `this is times new roman.`

3. Select the command Format | Change Case. In the dialog box that appears, choose Sentence case.

    The result looks like this: `This is times new roman.`

4. Select the command Format | Change Case, and select Title Case. Now the text appears as this: `This Is Times New Roman.`

    Next use the shortcut key to toggle the case.

5. With the words still highlighted, hold down the `Shift` key and press the `F3` key. Now the sentence appears in all capital letters: `THIS IS TIMES NEW ROMAN.`

6. Repeat the last step, using the `Shift` `F3` shortcut key. The letters all appear in lowercase.

7. Hold down the `Shift` key and press `F3` 6 or 7 times, while observing the effect on the highlighted characters. The case of the letters cycles through three choices. This process is called toggling.

Copying Formats with Format Painter

If you have gone through several steps in applying formats to a segment of text, it can be troublesome to repeat the steps to format another portion of the document. You might think that using the Edit | Copy command could accomplish the task, but that command copies actual text and not just the formatting. Word provides an easy method to copy only the formats of characters to other text. The Format Painter button on the Standard toolbar may be used to pick up and apply character formatting.

Copying character formatting involves three steps. First, highlight the text with the formats you like. Second, click on the Format Painter button. At this point, the mouse pointer displays a paintbrush and Word registers the current formatting. Finally, highlight the text you wish to format. The text is formatted with the new attributes and the mouse pointer automatically changes back to normal.

To apply the formats several times, double-click on the Format Painter button in the second step. This allows the mouse pointer to keep the paintbrush and apply formatting to everything you highlight until you click again on the Format Painter button to turn it off.

GUIDED ACTIVITY 6.4

Using the Format Painter

1. Continue working with the document from the previous Guided Activity.

2. Select a few characters from the second line with your name. This line has received formatting that changed the font name and added words-only underline.

3. Click on the Format Painter button on the Standard toolbar. The mouse pointer changes to display a paintbrush next to the I-beam.

4. Highlight the text that says New text with the I-beam part of the mouse pointer. The character formatting now matches the other text.

Inserting Special Characters

Word provides numerous special characters in addition to the letters, numbers, and punctuation marks shown on the keyboard. You may wish to type letters with accent marks, cent signs, or trademark or copyright symbols. The command Insert | Symbol reveals a dialog box, shown in Figure 6.11, that provides these special characters and more.

The dialog box has information under two tabs: Symbols and Special Characters. The symbols available under the Symbols tab depend on the font selected. The (normal text) choice provides letters with accents (diacritical marks) for whatever font is used, as well as common fractions and British pound and Japanese yen symbols.

FIGURE 6.11
*Symbol
dialog box*

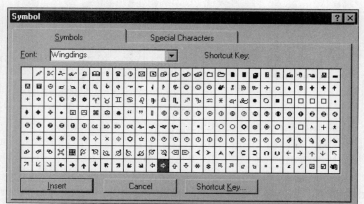

Changing the font to Symbol reveals Greek letters and several mathematical symbols, such as summation and infinity. The Wingdings font provides small shapes and pictures to add sparkle to the page.

GUIDED ACTIVITY 6.5

Inserting Special Characters

1. Start a new document. Type the following text, leaving out the symbol:

   Windows® 95 is a registered trademark of Microsoft Corporation.

2. Place the cursor just to the right of the word Windows but before the space.

   Select Insert | Symbol and click on the Special Characters tab.

3. Click on the ® symbol and click Insert. Click Close to return to the dialog box.

   You can insert more than one symbol at a time. Type the following text on a new line, leaving out the e's in résumé:

   Enlosed is my résumé.

4. Select Insert Symbol, and click on the Symbols tab.

   If (normal text) does not appear after Font, drop down the list and scroll to the top to select it.

   Some of the symbols are too small to see clearly. As you click on a symbol, Word doubles its size. Select the é symbol.

5. Instead of closing the dialog box, click Insert again to put in another é, and then click Close to return to the document.

   Your text now appears like this:

   Enclosed is my rsuméé.

6. Using cut-and-paste or drag-and-drop, move the symbols to their proper position.

If you examined the contents of the Special Characters tab, you probably noticed symbols that are commonly used in business, such as the © symbol. Word has set the AutoCorrect feature to automatically change simple keystrokes into these profes-sional symbols. For example, typing (c) will automatically produce ©. Consecutive hyphens--like these--are converted into real dashes—like these—automatically. Likewise, typing a typical *emoticon*—a series of punctuation marks that look like a sideways facial expression—such as :) automatically becomes a smiley face ☺. In the Tools | AutoCorrect dialog box, you can see all the symbols that will be substi-tuted for normal keystrokes.

The Highlighter

One final character formatting feature of Microsoft Word—one that does not appear in the Format | Font dialog box—is the highlighter pen which, like a real high-lighter, is useful for emphasizing text you want to work on, or perhaps wish to have a colleague review on screen. Click the Highlight button on the Formatting toolbar to turn on the highlighter. The mouse pointer changes shape so that it resembles the picture on the Highlight button. Drag across text to highlight certain areas. Highlight will remain active until you begin typing or click the Highlighter pen button again to turn it off. To change the color of the highlighter pen, click on the down arrow next to the button and select the desired color. To remove highlighting from text, select None from the color choices and drag across the text again.

Highlighting is best used for text that is going to be edited on screen; when printed, some color choices may be so dark as to obliterate the words.

Summary

Character formatting is the most specific of the three formatting levels (character, paragraph, document). Formats may be applied in four different ways:

- Click on buttons on the Formatting toolbar.

- Select the Format | Font command.

- Use the shortcut menu to select Font.

- Use shortcut keys.

The Formatting toolbar allows you to change the font and point size and to add bold, italic, and underline formatting with a click of the mouse.

The Font and Point Size boxes change the actual appearance of the characters by allowing the user to select the shape and size of the letters. The use of bold, italics, or underline does not change the shape of the characters, but rather adds emphasis to them to make them stand out on a printed page. Several types of underlines and other formats such as color and customized character spacing are available from the Font dialog box. These commands are seldom used and therefore are not included on the Formatting toolbar.

Word provides several other tools to make complex formatting simple. Character formats may be copied from one selected segment of text to another with the Format Painter button. You can also choose from an array of special characters and symbols to insert into your document. And you can apply highlighting in a color of your choice to any text, using the highlighter pen.

EXERCISE 6.1

A Day in the Life of a College Student

1. Open the file *EX6-1 Formatting*.
2. Insert your name, class time, and date at the top of the page. Double-underline the date.
3. Highlight the title and make it bold. Change the font to Arial. Click on the Center button.
4. Use the Format I Change Case command to capitalize the title in title case.
5. Insert the ™ symbol after `Mrs. Field's`.
6. Find $E=mc2$. Highlight the 2 and make it superscripted.
7. Select the words `tips to academic success` and apply words-only underlining.
8. Change the formula $E=mc^2$ to small caps.
9. Change to a different color each item in the list of ways to impress your professor.
10. Select the list and change the point size to 10.
11. Highlight the words `positive academic rewards` with the highlighter pen.
12. Select the word `College` in the title, and use the Format Painter to apply the same formatting to the words `you can still have fun.`
13. Print the document. What happens to the colored items if you print to a black-and-white printer?

EXERCISE 6.2

Crusty's Pizza

1. Open the file *EX6-2 Formatting*.
2. Insert your name, class time, and date at the top of the page. Double-underline the date.
3. Highlight the title and make it bold. Change the font to Arial. Click on the Center button.
4. Insert the symbol ™ after the word `Crusty's`.

5. Use the Format | Change Case command to capitalize the title in title case.

6. Find H20 in the first paragraph. Highlight the 2 and make it subscripted.

7. Select the words Be sure to check the screen and apply words-only underlining.

8. Add the ñ to jalapeños.

9. Change each item in the list of toppings to a different color.

10. Select the list of toppings and change the point size to 10.

11. Highlight the instruction do not let it sit on the cut table with the highlighter pen.

12. Select the word Crusty's in the title, and use the Format Painter to apply the same formatting to the words deliver to the customer as soon as possible.

13. Print the document. What happens to the colored items if you print to a black-and-white printer?

EXERCISE 6.3

The Internet

1. Open the file *EX6-3 Formatting*.

2. Insert your name, class time, and date at the top of the page. Double-underline the date.

3. Highlight the title and make it bold. Change the font to Arial and change it to 14 points. Click on the Center button.

4. Use the Format | Change Case command to put the title in all uppercase.

5. Use the Edit | Find command to search for the words surfing the 'Net. Replace the ' symbol with ' by using the Insert | Symbol command.

6. Find all instances of acronyms (such as ARPA) and change them to small caps. You will first need to change to lowercase, and then apply small cap formatting.

7. Select the words What would we do without e-mail? and apply words-only underlining.

8. Change the words president@whitehouse.gov to italics.

9. Change each item in the list of tips to a different color.

10. Select the list of tips and change the point size to 10.

11. Highlight the warning Don't write anything you don't want to see in a court of law with the highlighter pen.

12. Select the title and use the Format Painter to apply the same formatting to the words `Individual Use of the Internet`.

13. Print the document. What happens to the colored items if you print to a black-and-white printer?

EXERCISE 6.4

Thrill Seeker Tours

1. Open the file *EX6-4 Formatting*.

2. Insert your name, class time, and date at the top of the page. Double-underline the date.

3. Highlight the title and make it bold. Change the font to Arial. Click on the Center button.

4. Use the Format | Change Case command to capitalize the title in title case.

5. Use the Edit | Find command to search for the word `degree`. Delete it and insert the ° symbol in its place.

6. Find `H20` in the first paragraph. Highlight the 2 and make it subscripted.

7. Select the words `work together as a team` and apply words-only underlining.

8. Change the word `kevlar` to small caps.

9. Change each item in the list of river classes to a different color.

10. Select the list of classes and change the point size to 10.

11. Highlight the warning `Experts only` with the highlighter pen.

12. Select the word `Canoeing` in the title, and use the Format Painter to apply the same formatting to the words `pray the river doesn't rise`.

13. Print the document. What happens to the colored items if you print to a black-and-white printer?

Review Questions

*1. What are the three levels of formatting?

2. What is the difference between using the Formatting toolbar and using the Font dialog box to format text? What determines which method you use to execute a command?

*3. What is the difference between formatting text that already exists and formatting text that is being typed?

4. What is the difference between a proportional and a nonproportional font? Between a serif and a sans serif font? What uses are appropriate for each?

*5. Why are some commands included on the Formatting toolbar, while others are available only from the Font dialog box?

6. What commands are available only from the Font dialog box?

*7. What is the default font for Word? How may it be changed?

8. What is the Format Painter used for?

*9. What special characters are available in Word, and how are they accessed?

10. To apply a format to make a highlighted word appear dark and emphasized,

    a. Click the D button on the Formatting toolbar.

    b. Select Bold from the shortcut menu.

    c. Press Ctrl B or select Format | Font.

    d. Double-click on the word.

*11. To make a business letter easy for an executive to read,

    a. Use a serif font, 12 points.

    b. Use a sans serif font, 10 points.

    c. Use all capital letters.

    d. Use italics so that it looks very classy.

12. Fonts that appear exactly the same when printed as they do on screen are called

    a. Serif fonts.

    b. Scalable fonts.

    c. Printer fonts.

    d. TrueType fonts.

*13. The category of fonts in which every letter takes up the same amount of space is

    a. Serif.

    b. Kerned.

    c. Nonproportional.

    d. Proportional.

Key Terms

Attribute	Font	Small capitals
Bold	Hidden	Strikethrough
Capitals	Indirect formatting	Subscript
Character spacing	Italics	Superscript
Condense	Kerning	Toggle
Default	Nonproportional	TrueType
Descender	Point size	Underline
Direct formatting	Proportional	WYSIWYG
Emoticon	Sans serif	
Expand	Serif	

7 Formatting Paragraphs

The second level of formatting your documents is paragraph formatting. Paragraph format commands are used to change the way a paragraph looks. This may be done by changing the paragraph's indentation, alignment, spacing, and other attributes. These commands affect any paragraphs where the cursor is located or paragraphs that are partially or completely highlighted. This unit covers paragraph formatting using the toolbar, the ruler, and the menu commands. You will also learn to copy these attributes and to combine them into a style.

Learning Objectives

At the completion of this unit you should know

1. how to format existing or new paragraphs,

2. what paragraph formats are available,

3. six ways to execute paragraph format commands,

4. how to copy paragraph formatting.

Important Commands

Format | Borders and Shading

Format | Bullets and Numbering

Format | Paragraph

Format | Style

Format | Tabs

Insert | Break

Formatting Paragraphs

The paragraph format commands are accessed in many of the same ways as character format commands, and one new way. The six methods for applying formatting commands are as follows:

- Click buttons on the toolbars.
- Select Format on the menu.
- Use the Paragraph command on the shortcut menu.
- Press shortcut keys.
- Click and drag settings on the ruler.
- Type a few sample characters to cause borders, bullets, and numbering to be applied automatically.

Paragraph formatting may be applied to one or more existing paragraphs. If no text is currently highlighted, only the paragraph where the cursor is located will be affected by the command. If a paragraph is partially or completely highlighted, the entire paragraph will be changed to reflect the format command. This is known as direct paragraph formatting.

In addition to formatting paragraphs that have already been entered, you may select the format command before typing. If you already know how the paragraph is to be formatted, this is usually faster than entering the text and formatting it later. This method of formatting, called indirect formatting, is accomplished by selecting the desired format attribute as you start a new paragraph, and then typing the text. Indirect formatting stays in effect as you start new paragraphs until you turn it off.

Several paragraph formats may be changed from the Format | Paragraph dialog box. Alignment, spacing, and indentation are all found under the Indents and Spacing tab, shown in Figure 7.1. Other options are found under the Text Flow tab. Just like the Format | Font command, the Format | Paragraph command is found on the shortcut menu, accessed by clicking the right mouse button with the middle (or ring) finger.

FIGURE 7.1
Paragraph dialog box

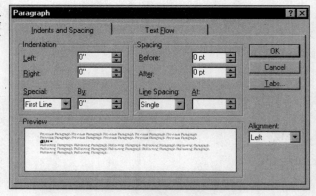

Alignment

A paragraph's *alignment* refers to how it is aligned relative to the page margins. A paragraph may be aligned against the left margin, the right margin, or both margins—or it may be centered between the margins. These alignment options are changed with buttons on the Formatting toolbar, shown in Figure 7.2. Examples of each of the four alignment options are shown below:

Align   Center   Align   Justify
Left   Right

Left-Aligned: When a paragraph is left-aligned (like this one), the left edge of the paragraph is even against the left margin of the page and the right edge is uneven (also called *flush left* or *ragged right*). This alignment method is commonly used in letters and reports.

Justified: Justified paragraphs (like this one) are aligned against both left and right margins so that both edges of the paragraph are straight. If a line of text is not exactly long enough to fill the space between the two margins, space is added between the words to make the line longer. However, this alignment method does not increase the length of documents. Many newspapers, magazines, and books are justified.

Centered: Center alignment is usually not used for long paragraphs
because it makes large amounts of text hard to read. This alignment method
is used for titles, dates, and other short items that need to be centered
between the left and right margins. Centering is done by clicking
on the Center button on the toolbar.

Right-Aligned: Right alignment causes paragraphs to be flush along the right margin
of the document (also called *flush right* or *ragged left*). It is not generally used to align
long paragraphs, but instead is suitable for copy in an advertisement or mailing
piece.

The alignment options can also be selected from the Format | Paragraph dialog box in the Alignment section. Select the alignment desired from the drop-down list in the dialog box, and click on OK to execute the command. The shortcut keys for alignment are fairly easy to remember: [Ctrl][L] for Align Left, [Ctrl][E] for Center, [Ctrl][R] for Align Right, and [Ctrl][J] for Justify.

GUIDED ACTIVITY 7.1
___

Aligning Paragraphs

1.   Start Word. Open the file *GA7 Paragraphs*.

2.   Click on the Center button on the toolbar.

The title, which started out on the left margin, moves to the center of the page.

3. Highlight the first long paragraph, and then click on the Justify button.

   Now both edges of the paragraph are lined up with the document margins. The words are spaced out slightly.

4. Highlight all or part of the last two lines, beginning with This service announcement.... Click on the Align Right button to right-align the paragraphs.

   Right alignment is not usually intended to be used for full paragraphs of text several lines long, but only for short lines like these.

5. Position the cursor at the end of the last paragraph. Press [Enter] twice to leave a blank line. The cursor stays on the right edge of the page as the format is carried on to the next paragraph.

6. Check the toolbar to see that the Align Right button is pressed in. The cursor should appear on the right side of the document.

7. Save the document.

Line Spacing

In addition to altering the alignment, you may change the *line spacing*. The line spacing refers to the amount of space between one line of text and the next. Single-spacing places lines of text close together and allows you to get the most information on a page. Double-spacing places a full blank line between each line of text. While this takes up more space on a page, it is easier to read and is the required format for reports, term papers, material submitted for publication, and other such documents.

Word allows the user to format the line spacing from the Format | Paragraph dialog box, as shown in Figure 7.3. The first setting, Single, is the default mode for Word. Single-spacing allows just enough height to contain the font size selected and to separate it from the lines above and below it. If the size of even one letter on a line is larger, the spacing automatically increases to accommodate it. Spacing is measured either in lines, relative to the largest letter on the line, or in points, which is exact. (You may recall that there are 72 points to the vertical inch.) Double-spacing makes the lines twice as high, 1.5 Lines spacing allows a line and a half, and Multiple is used to select triple-spacing or larger.

You might think that single-spacing a line of 10-point text would be 10-point line spacing. As a matter of fact, Word gives an extra bit of white space between each line to enhance legibility. This extra white space is known as *leading* (pronounced *led-ing*) because, in the days of hot-metal typesetting, typesetters used to place a thin strip of lead

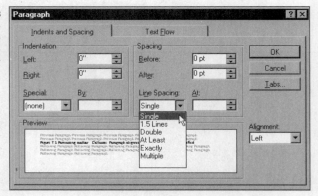

FIGURE 7.3
Changing line spacing from the Paragraph dialog box

between lines of type. Leading is typically 20 percent of the base points. Thus, a line of 10-point text has 12-point line spacing, 12-point text has a little more than 14-point line spacing, and so on. To achieve a true single space, select Exactly and specify the number of points in the At box.

The At Least setting allows you to set the minimum number of points for the line height. Objects taller than the minimum setting will make the line higher. Problems arise when, in the midst of nicely flowing text, you have a few lines that are widely spaced because of a large item on that line. The Exactly selection overcomes this effect, forcing each line to be exactly the line height you specify, regardless of the height of objects on the line.

The shortcut keys are Ctrl 1 for Single spacing, Ctrl 5 for 1.5 Lines spacing, and Ctrl 2 for Double spacing. (Use the number keys at the top of the keyboard, rather than those on the keypad at the right side of the keyboard, since using Ctrl with the 5 on the keypad is the shortcut key for selecting the entire document.)

Another spacing option available in Word is to automatically place a space before each paragraph. This is a useful feature when you are entering a long single-spaced document and do not want to press Enter twice after each paragraph. The word processor automatically adds a blank line before each paragraph. Type the number of points in the Spacing section of the Format | Paragraph dialog box, shown in Figure 7.4, to turn on this option. You may also toggle this feature on and off with the shortcut key Ctrl 0 (zero).

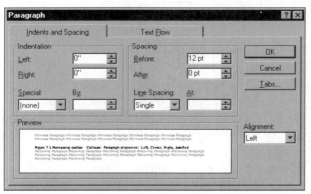

FIGURE 7.4
Adding a blank line before the paragraph

Additionally, you may change the amount of space added above the paragraph or may elect to place the blank line after the paragraph rather than before. Use the up or down arrow to the right of the Before or After box, or type the number of points of space to leave before or after each paragraph. Click on OK to apply the format.

GUIDED ACTIVITY 7.2

Setting Line Spacing

1. Position the cursor anywhere in the first long paragraph. Make sure the spacing is set to Single by using the shortcut key Ctrl 1.

2. Position the cursor in the second long paragraph. Change the spacing to Double by using the shortcut key Ctrl 2.

   A full blank line is inserted after each line in the paragraph. The paragraph takes up twice as much room as before, but it is easier to read because the lines are farther apart.

3. Position the cursor in the third long paragraph. Select Format | Paragraph.

4. Under the Line Spacing section of the dialog box, select Multiple. Check that the At box is set to 3 lines. Notice the sample of this triple-spacing in the Preview window. Click OK.

    The height of each line of text is now 3 spaces. There are two full blank lines between each line of text.

5. Having several line spacings is silly. Highlight the entire document and press `Ctrl` `1` to change back to single-spacing.

6. Press `Ctrl` `0` (zero) to open a space between paragraphs. Now the document is easier to read.

7. Highlight the six short lines at the end of the document.

8. Select Format | Paragraph and change Spacing Before back to 0 and Line Spacing to 1.5 lines. Click OK.

9. Save the file.

Tabs

A *tab* is a marker that you define to allow you to move quickly to a specific horizontal position along the line. Tabs are used to align text at a location measured from the left margin of a document. When aligning a column of text or numbers formatted to a proportional font, you will find it is more accurate to use a tab than to try to line up the characters by pressing the `Spacebar` repeatedly. If you always use tabs to align numbers and text, you will save time later if you decide to change the font or point size of characters in the document, or if you modify column widths.

What paragraph formats increase readability?

- *Either indent the first line or leave a blank space between, not both.*

- *Keep line spacing (leading) at least 20 percent more than the size of the font. More crowded lines decrease readability.*

- *Adjust column width to keep the line length to approximately 5 to 10 words across. Very short lines are choppy to read; very long lines may cause the reader's eye not to track all the way across.*

- *When justifying alignment, watch that no large gaps appear between words.*

- *Don't center or right-align large amounts of text.*

- *Use bullets or numbers any time you have lists or steps.*

- *Keep bullet items consistent—either all sentences or all phrases.*

By default, if you press the [Tab] key, the cursor will jump one-half inch to the right. The arrows in Figure 7.5 indicate where the [Tab] key has been pressed. It is displayed in the same way as the Enter character, by clicking on the Show/Hide ¶ button on the toolbar. The tabs by default are set every half-inch along the ruler, indicated by tiny dots at the bottom edge of the ruler, shown in Figure 7.5. You may use the *default tabs* to align columns of information by pressing the [Tab] key once or several times, or you may create custom tab settings.

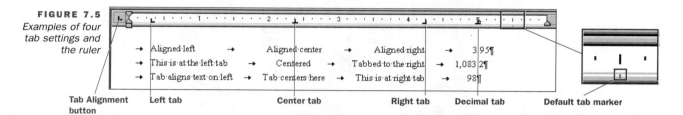

FIGURE 7.5
Examples of four tab settings and the ruler

Tab Alignment button   Left tab   Center tab   Right tab   Decimal tab   Default tab marker

Custom tabs are placed on the ruler by clicking along the ruler's bottom edge under the measurement marks. Four kinds of tabs can be set from the ruler.

The first and most commonly used is a left tab. A column of text typed from a left tab will be left-aligned (aligned along its left side) at the location of the tab.

Right tabs are used to right-align a column of words (that is, to align it along its right side) at the location of the tab.

Center tabs are used to center columns of text at the location of the tab stop.

Decimal tabs align a column of numbers by their decimal points at the tab location.

The tab type is selected by clicking on the Tab Alignment button on the left side of the ruler until the desired type is displayed. The picture of the screen in Figure 7.5 gives examples of each of the four types of tabs.

It is easy to set, move, and remove tabs on the ruler:

■ To place a tab on the ruler, check to see that the tab type is displayed on the Tab Alignment button. If it is not, click on it to change the type of tab, and then click on the bottom edge of the ruler at the location where the tab is to be set. A marker representing the type of tab will appear at the bottom of the ruler at that location.

■ To move a tab marker, place the mouse pointer on it and drag to the right or left along the ruler.

■ To remove a tab marker, click and drag it down off the ruler.

Remember that only the paragraph containing the cursor, or any paragraphs highlighted completely or partially, will be affected by the new or changed tab settings. Before setting or changing a tab for an entire document, you must highlight the entire document by selecting Edit | Select All or by triple-clicking in the left margin.

GUIDED ACTIVITY 7.3

Creating Tabs

1.   Open a new document by clicking the New button on the left side of the toolbar. If the ruler is not visible, select View | Ruler to turn it on.

2.   Click on the Tab Alignment button 3 times to select a decimal tab. Click on the bottom edge of the ruler directly below the number 2.

     The default tab markers from the left margin to your tab, which were located every half-inch on the ruler, are now gone. When the tab is removed from the ruler, the default tabs will return.

3.   Press [Tab] on the keyboard.

     The cursor jumps to the location of the decimal tab.

4.   Enter the number 3.1416. Press [Enter] and press [Tab] again.

     The cursor again lines up directly below the tab marker you inserted on the ruler.

5.   Enter the number 100.5. Press [Enter], press [Tab], and type the number 0.386.

     All the numbers you have just typed are aligned with their decimal points directly below the decimal tab you defined at 2" on the ruler.

6.   Highlight all the lines, and then drag the tab marker to the right one inch.

     That moves the tab so that it is set at 3" rather than 2".

7.   Click on the decimal tab marker on the ruler, and drag it off the bottom of the ruler.

     The decimal tab disappears and is replaced by default left tabs at every half-inch.

8.   Place the cursor at the end of the last line and press [Enter] twice. Click on the Tab Alignment button to select a left tab. Click on the bottom edge of the ruler directly below the 1" mark. Click on the Tab Alignment button twice to select a right tab, and place a right tab below the 5" mark.

9.   Press [Tab] to position the cursor at the first tab marker. Enter the text Chapter One. Press [Tab] to position the cursor at the second tab marker. Type 1.

     You now have the first line of a table of contents. Chapter One begins on page 1.

10. Press [Enter] and press [Tab]. Type Chapter Two. Press [Tab] and type 23.

11. Enter Chapters Three through Five. Invent your own page numbers for these chapters.

     No matter what values you assign the page numbers, they will align on their right-hand sides because they are lined up on a right tab.

The table of contents looks good, but it could look better. It is difficult to tell which chapter name goes with each page number when there is so much *white space* between the names and the numbers, especially if the contents are listed single-spaced. To avoid this, you can attach a *leader* (not to be confused with leading) to the second tab. A leader is a character, typically a dot or a dash, that leads the eye by filling the white space from the point where the cursor was located when you pressed the [Tab] key to the next character in the text (often a page number) lined up at the tab. Leaders cannot be added from the ruler. They are defined only in the Format | Tabs dialog box, shown in Figure 7.6.

FIGURE 7.6
Format|Tabs
dialog box

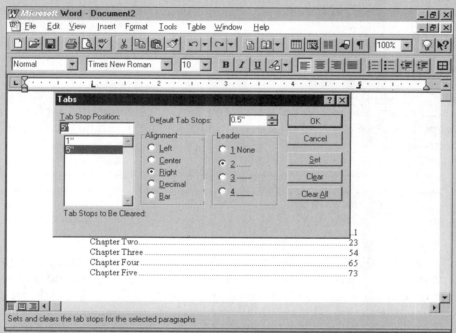

12. Highlight all the lines in the table of contents. Select Format | Tabs to display the dialog box shown in Figure 7.6.

You may reach the same dialog box by double-clicking the ruler or by selecting Format | Paragraph and clicking on the Tabs button. This box can be used to set tabs if you prefer not to use the ruler: you enter a new position, select the alignment, and click on Set to set the tab. However, you have already set up the tabs you need. You just need to modify one.

13. In the Tab Stop Position box, click on 5" to highlight it.

The circle next to Right in the Alignment box is filled in because the tab is a right tab.

14. Click on the circle next to 2 in the Leader box to set the dot leader. Click on OK.

The dots lead from the chapter name to the page number, the white space between the two columns having been replaced by dot leaders.

15.   Close the file. Save it if you want to keep it; otherwise, click No.

A final element available in the Format | Tabs dialog box is the spacing of default tabs. When Word is first installed, a left tab is located by default every half-inch from the left to the right margins. These default tabs show up as tiny dots at the bottom edge of the ruler. You can change the spacing between the default tabs in your document by selecting a different value in the Default Tab Stops section of the Format | Tabs dialog box.

Paragraph Indents

Individual paragraphs can be indented from the left or right margins of the document, or both. You may *indent* the entire paragraph, only the first line, or all lines except for the first. Indentation is controlled by the ruler and the Format | Paragraph command.

FIGURE 7.7
Ruler

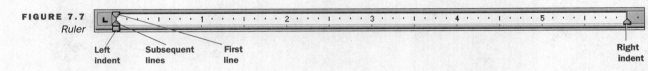

Left indent   Subsequent lines   First line   Right indent

The triangular markers on the left and right sides of the ruler, shown in Figure 7.7, are used to set the indent amounts for each paragraph. To indent the right side of a paragraph, click on the right paragraph indent marker at the right side of the ruler and drag it to the position where you want the new right side to be. The ruler is calibrated in inches by default, so it should be easy for you to indent a specific amount. Word will figure the new places for word wrap for each line and redisplay the paragraph.

The marker that represents the left paragraph indent, located at the left edge of the ruler, consists of three parts. The upper triangle is the indent amount for the first line of the paragraph. The lower triangle is the indent amount for all lines but the first. The small square below the lower triangle on the left moves both the upper and lower triangles at the same time.

To indent the first line of every paragraph in a document, you could press Tab at the beginning and then type the paragraph. Instead, Word allows you to indent the first line automatically by setting the indentation from the ruler. To indent only the first line of the paragraph one-half inch, you would drag the upper triangle to the right to the tick mark halfway between the 0 and the 1. The lower triangle stays in place; therefore, the second and subsequent lines of the paragraph are not indented, as in Figure 7.8.

Like all paragraph format commands, indentation affects only the paragraph containing the cursor or any paragraphs partially or completely highlighted. All other

FIGURE 7.8
*Ruler with first
line indent
settings*

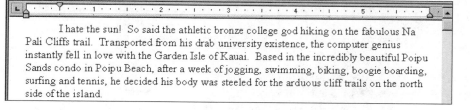

paragraphs are unaffected. Paragraph indents only affect the entire document if it is completely highlighted first.

Indenting the first line of every paragraph increases readability by giving the eye a place to rest. Because indenting serves the same function as leaving a blank line between paragraphs, these two formats are not usually used together.

Word also includes a way to quickly indent (or unindent) all the lines on the left side of a paragraph to the next (or previous) tab stop. To indent a paragraph to the next tab stop, press the Increase Indent button on the toolbar. All of the lines in the paragraph will be indented to the next tab stop to the right. If no tab stops are set, the indent will be set to the default tab stop. The Decrease Indent button shifts the paragraph indent one tab to the left. The shortcut keys for these operations are [Ctrl][M] to increase indent, and [Ctrl][Shift][M] to reduce indent. The triangles on the ruler, shown in Figure 7.9, are set just as if you had dragged them by hand.

FIGURE 7.9
*Sample of ruler
with indented
paragraph*

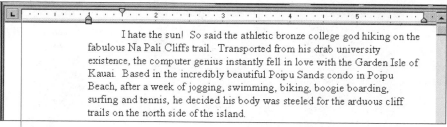

Left margin

Sometimes the first line of a paragraph is not indented, but the remaining lines are. For example, a numbered list has the number at the left margin, but the rest of the paragraph is indented, as in the Guided Activities in this book. To set this type of indentation, move the lower triangle on the left indent marker, but leave the upper triangle at the margin, as in Figure 7.10. This is termed a *hanging indent* because the first line is flush with the margin and succeeding lines are indented (called "flush and hung" in book production) to hang beneath it. Word automates this operation with the shortcut key [Ctrl][T], which indents the lower triangle to the first tab stop or

FIGURE 7.10
*Sample hanging
indented
paragraph with
first line flush to
left margin*

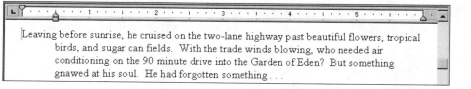

SHORTCUT KEY	FORMAT
Ctrl E	Center
Ctrl J	Justify
Ctrl L	Left-align
Ctrl R	Right-align
Ctrl M	Increase indent
Ctrl Shift M	Reduce indent
Ctrl T	Hanging indent
Ctrl Shift T	Reduce hanging indent
Ctrl Q	Remove all paragraph formatting
Ctrl 1 *	Single space
Ctrl 2 *	Double space
Ctrl 5 *	Space-and-a-half
Ctrl 0 (zero)*	Add and remove blank line preceding paragraph

* Use the numbers along the top row of the keyboard.

default tab, if none is set. The shortcut key Ctrl Shift T removes the hanging indent. The shortcut keys used in formatting paragraphs are shown in Table 7.1.

GUIDED ACTIVITY 7.4

Indenting Paragraphs

1. If you closed the original document in this unit, open *GA7 Formatted*.

2. Position the cursor in the first long paragraph. Drag the right indent triangle one inch to the left. If the right side of the ruler does not appear on the screen, click on the horizontal scroll bar at the bottom of the screen until it comes into view.

   The right side of the paragraph moves to the left one inch.

3. Click the Increase Indent button on the toolbar *twice*.

   The left side of the paragraph and the left indent triangles all move to the one-inch mark on the ruler, if you are using the default tabs.

4. Click the Reduce Indent button on the toolbar.

   The left edge of the paragraph moves back under the half-inch mark on the ruler, and so do the triangles.

5. Drag the square on the left indent marker one-half inch to the right.

   The paragraph is again indented one inch on both sides. This format may be used with long quotations in a research paper.

6. Click anywhere in the second paragraph to position the cursor there. Drag the lower triangle on the left indent marker one-half inch to the right.

    To get exact measurements on the ruler (as in Figure 7.11) rather than the usual eighth-inch marks, position the mouse pointer over the marker, and hold down both mouse buttons at once.

FIGURE 7.11
Ruler measurements with both buttons held down

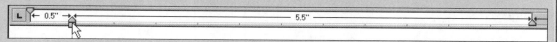

The first line of the paragraph is not indented, but the rest of the paragraph is.

It is not mandatory to use the ruler to set the indent amounts.

7. Position the cursor in the third paragraph. Select Format | Paragraph.

8. Use the up arrows next to the Left box to enter 0.5". Select First Line in the Special box under Indentation and 1" in the By box, as shown in Figure 7.12. A preview of this indentation format shows in the preview area of the dialog box. Click on OK to execute the command.

FIGURE 7.12
Paragraph dialog box showing settings for first line indent

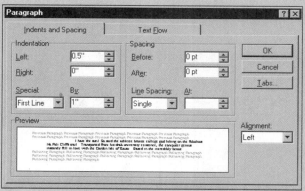

Either method of paragraph indenting will work. Using the ruler allows you to see the text as you position the indent markers, but the dialog box allows you to specify the measurements more accurately.

Text Flow

A long document flows from one page to the next, with the division between pages happening automatically. Word designates the places where the new page begins by a light dotted line extended across the screen. This is called a ***soft page break*** because it occurs automatically whenever a page is full. Occasionally, you may create a paragraph that you do not want separated at the end of a page. For example, a heading may happen to fall on the last line of the page, so that the following text displays at the top of the next page. How can you solve this problem?

You could press [Enter] a few extra times to force the heading onto the next page. Another solution is to insert a *hard page break* that forces a new page to begin at that point. Insert a hard page break with the shortcut key [Ctrl][Enter] or by selecting Insert | Break and picking Page Break. The hard page break appears as a dark dotted line labeled Page Break, as in Figure 7.13.

FIGURE 7.13
*Soft and hard
page breaks*

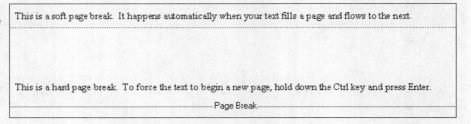

The disadvantage of using hard page breaks is that, after editing, perhaps both the heading and the following text could fit on the previous page but the hard page break prevents it. To avoid this disadvantage, Word gives the user control over how the text flows between pages, from the Text Flow tab of the Paragraph dialog box, shown in Figure 7.14. You may elect to keep a paragraph intact by checking the Keep Lines Together check box. Rather than breaking your paragraph at the end of a page, Word will move the entire paragraph to the top of the next page.

FIGURE 7.14
Text Flow tab

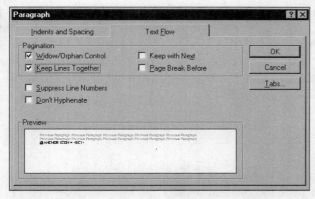

A second option is to keep a paragraph together with the next paragraph. This helps avoid having headings appear alone at the bottom of a page or having a chart get separated from an explanatory caption or paragraph. To prevent these kinds of occurrences, check Keep with Next. The Page Break Before option may be used with headings that must always begin at the top of a page, regardless of the amount of text before them. Widow/Orphan control prevents a single line of a paragraph from appearing at the top of a page separate from the rest of the paragraph on the previous page.

FIGURE 7.15
*Borders toolbar
with Line style
choices*

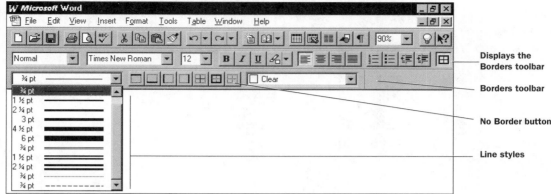

Borders and Shading

Another useful paragraph attribute is the ability to create a rule (a line) above, beside, or under a paragraph or any other object like a picture or graphic, or to set apart a portion of text with shading. Like other paragraph formatting, *borders* and *shading* affect paragraphs that are partially or completely highlighted, or the paragraph where the cursor is located.

Clicking the Borders button on the Formatting toolbar causes a new toolbar to be displayed on the screen. The Borders toolbar, shown in Figure 7.15, contains buttons for adding a border to the top, bottom, left, or right side of a paragraph, as well as to the inside (if several paragraphs are highlighted) or outside of a paragraph or paragraphs. The No Border button removes any borders that have been applied. The drop-down box to the left of the toolbar gives choices for the line style of the border, from thin to thick, and single, double, dotted, or dashed.

Word makes applying borders even easier than clicking buttons—it automatically adds borders for you. Type three hyphens at the beginning of a line and press Enter, and a thin line called a *rule* instantly extends between the margins of the page. Type three equal signs (=) and press Enter and a double-line rule appears; type three underscores and press Enter and a bold rule appears.

The drop-down list box on the right side of the Borders toolbar sets the shading behind the paragraph. Shading may be very light (5%) through very dark (90%) or even patterned. Not all these effects are available on every printer. To remove shading, select the choice Clear, which is the default. Adding a solid black shading on a paragraph and formatting the font to the color white (instead of Auto) creates a very nice effect called *reversed text*. For example, the Microsoft Word title bar at the top of the screen has reversed text. Shading and reversing text are eye-catching formats that add impact to a page, so use them in moderation and always test them on a printout. Sans serif fonts and block fonts are best for reversing.

When you are through formatting the borders and shading, you may remove this toolbar from the screen by clicking again on the Borders button. Adding color to the borders and shading is only done through the Format | Borders and Shading dialog box.

GUIDED ACTIVITY 7.5

Adding Borders and Shading

1. At the top of the document type three hyphens (- - -) and press ⏎Enter.

    A single border (rule) appears above the title.

2. Press the ⬆ key to move the cursor above the line. Click on the Borders button to reveal the Borders toolbar. The button denoting the bottom border appears pushed in.

3. Move the cursor to the document's last line. Type three underscores (_ _ _) and press ⏎Enter. This time a heavier rule is placed below the paragraph.

4. Press ⏎Enter again. Unlike all other font formatting, the automatic borders are not repeated on the following paragraph.

5. Highlight the paragraph beginning with `Years later. . .` and click the Outside Border button to place a box around the paragraph.

6. With the paragraph still highlighted, change the line style of the border to double lines, and click the Outside Border button again.

7. Access the command Format | Borders and Shading. Choose the Shading tab, and then change the color of the Foreground color to blue and the Shading to 20%. Click OK.

8. Remove the shading by changing back to Clear on the Borders toolbar.

9. Remove the borders from the document by highlighting the whole document and clicking on the No Border button on the Borders toolbar. Remove the toolbar from sight by clicking on the Borders button.

Placing Numbers and Bullets on Paragraphs

It is an easy process to place bullets or numbers alongside paragraphs with a word processor. Word makes it even easier with two buttons on the Formatting toolbar, plus the Bullets and Numbering command found on both the Format menu and the shortcut menu.

To place numbers automatically on lines or paragraphs, highlight the paragraphs in the document that are to be numbered and click on the Numbering button. A number appears at the beginning of each of the selected paragraphs. Word will automatically apply this numbering format to your paragraphs if you begin the paragraph with a number.

Once you turn on numbering format, as you press ⏎Enter, each paragraph is automatically numbered and formatted with a hanging indent of .25 inch. If the paragraphs are later rearranged, the paragraphs are automatically renumbered. You can specify the numbering scheme through the Bullets and Numbering dialog box. The Numbered tab is shown in Figure 7.16. The Modify button opens a dialog box where

FIGURE 7.16
Numbered tab of the Bullets and Numbering dialog box

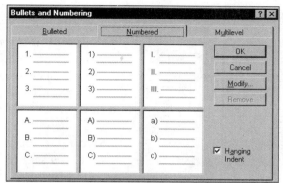

FIGURE 7.17
Modify Numbered List dialog box

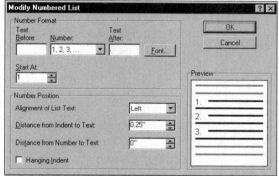

FIGURE 7.18
Bulleted tab

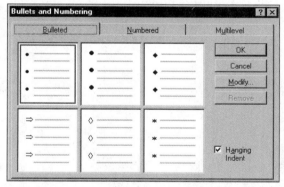

FIGURE 7.19
Modifying bullets

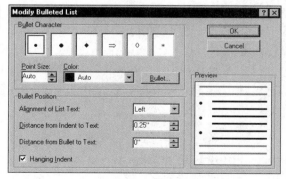

both the starting number and the size of the hanging indent may be changed, as shown in Figure 7.17. To remove numbers, highlight the paragraphs and click on the Numbering button again.

A *bullet* is a small symbol generally placed at the left of several lines to catch the eye and visually separate and emphasize each line. Placing bullets at the left edge of a series of paragraphs is similar to placing numbers there. It is accomplished by clicking on the Bullets button on the Formatting toolbar.

Word automatically applies a bullet to every paragraph that is begun with an asterisk (*). A small round symbol appears at the left margin, and the paragraphs are given a hanging indent format.

The Bulleted tab portion of the Bullets and Numbering dialog box, shown in Figure 7.18, also contains a Modify button. This button reveals a dialog box, shown in Figure 7.19, with several additional options for modifying bulleted paragraphs. It is a simple matter to choose a color, to specify a different style of bullet (such as diamond, arrow, or asterisk), or to change the size of the available bullets by increasing or decreasing their point size.

Sometimes you need a special symbol to be used as a bullet, such as a check mark or a check box. To get other choices for bullets, click the Bullets button. The Symbol dialog box shown in Figure 7.20 appears (similar to the one that appears when you select Insert | Symbol), in which you may change the font to find new bullet choices.

The TrueType font Wingdings is a set of symbols—some quite

FIGURE 7.20
Wingdings bullet choices

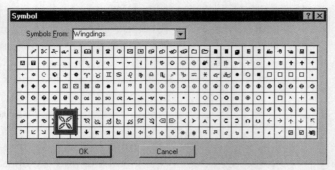

decorative—suitable for use as bullets. Clicking on a symbol you think you will like enlarges it, making it easier to view. Selecting one of the symbols, numbers, or images from the fonts available and clicking OK will cause the new symbol to replace the bullet that was highlighted when the Bullet button was pressed.

GUIDED ACTIVITY 7.6

Adding Numbers and Bullets to Paragraphs

1. Create a new document. Enter the following text:

   ```
   Paragraph One
   Paragraph Two
   Paragraph Three
   ```

2. At the beginning of the next line, type `1. Paragraph Four`. Press `Enter`.

   As soon as you press `Enter`, the last line and current line automatically are numbered 1 and 2 and the text is indented .25 inch.

3. Add the following text:

   ```
   Paragraph Five
   Paragraph Six
   ```

   Since the Numbering format was turned on, each of these paragraphs is numbered immediately.

4. Highlight the first three lines and click on the Numbering button.

   The paragraphs are immediately renumbered in order.

5. Using cut-and-paste or drag-and-drop, move Paragraph Four above Paragraph Three.

   The paragraphs are automatically renumbered.

6. Highlight all six paragraphs. Use the shortcut menu to open the Bullets and Numbering dialog box. Change the numbering scheme to ABC, and click OK.

7. Click Undo to change back to Numbers. Select File | Close to return to the *I Hate the Sun* document. No need to save.

8. Highlight the four sun-safety tips near the end of the document.

9. Click the Bullets button to add bullets to emphasize these lines.

10. With the paragraphs still highlighted, select the command Format | Bullets and Numbering, choose the Bulleted tab, and click the Modify button.

11. When the dialog box appears, change the color of the bullets and increase the point size, and then click OK.

12. Select the command Format | Bullets and Numbering, click on Modify, and then click on Bullets.

13. In the Symbol dialog box that appears, change the font to Wingdings. Select one of the shapes to be the bullet, and click OK twice to see the changes to the paragraphs.

14. Click Undo to change back to regular bullets, so this new symbol will not remain in effect.

Checking and Copying Formats

Paragraphs may have several formats, such as indents, tabs, alignment, and borders, which have taken several steps to apply. You may wish to see all the formatting that has been applied to a section of text. To do this, simply click on the Help button, and then click on the text where you wish to see the formatting. A window appears describing the paragraph and the font formatting for that segment of text, as in Figure 7.21.

Word stores the paragraph formatting in the ¶ symbol at the end of each paragraph, which denotes when the Enter key was pressed. Sometimes the Enter character

FIGURE 7.21
Reveal formats of text

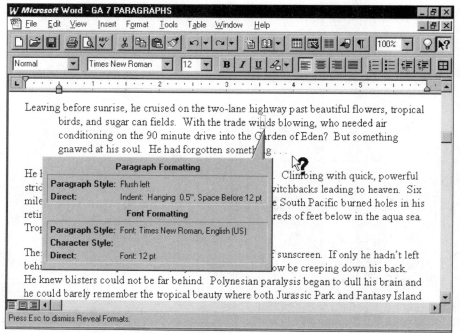

is invisible on the screen, and it is never printed: it is meant to separate paragraphs and terminate lines, not to be visible. However, you may see the exact location of the Enter symbol in Word by clicking on the Show/Hide ¶ button on the toolbar. This button displays or hides special characters in the work area that are normally hidden. These characters include spaces, Enter characters, and tabs. With this feature turned on, a paragraph symbol (¶) will appear at each location where the [Enter] key was pressed. Even though the special characters are displayed in the work area, they will never print. To make the special characters invisible on the screen again, click on the Show/Hide ¶ button once more.

To copy the paragraph format from one paragraph to another, simply click the Show/Hide ¶ button to reveal the nonprinting characters. Copy the ¶ symbol from the end of the correctly formatted paragraph and paste at the end of the paragraph that needs to be formatted, or use the Format Painter to copy the formats from the ¶ symbol.

Style

The Style feature in Word can save you a tremendous amount of time and ensure that paragraphs are formatted consistently. When you get a paragraph formatted the way you want it (indents, tabs, alignment, spacing, and so on), you may discover that you need other paragraphs in your document formatted exactly the same way. You could execute all of the necessary format commands, one by one, each time to get the desired effect, or you could carefully copy ¶ symbols; however, Word allows you to save the format attributes under a new *style* name that you select, enabling you to use it many times in a document with accuracy and ease. Several styles are predefined and listed in the drop-down box on the Formatting toolbar, as shown in Figure 7.22.

FIGURE 7.22
Formatting toolbar showing styles

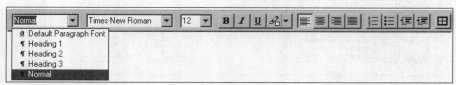

GUIDED ACTIVITY 7.7

Defining and Applying Styles

1. Position the cursor in the first long paragraph of your document. Click the Style box at the left-most edge of the Formatting toolbar. The word Normal will be highlighted. Type the word New and press [Enter].

2. Position the cursor in the fifth paragraph. Click on the down arrow to the right of the Style box on the toolbar.

3. Select New from the list by clicking on it.

All of the format attributes from the first paragraph are applied to the fifth paragraph. You can position the cursor in any paragraph and select the New style to immediately apply the format attributes from the first paragraph. The paragraph containing the cursor and any completely or partially highlighted paragraphs will be formatted with the attributes defined for the style. To apply the style to the entire document, you must highlight the document before selecting the style.

Styles can also be defined from the menus, by selecting Format | Style.

Styles are saved as part of the template. Word provides many preformatted styles that you may view by selecting Format | Style Gallery. The Style feature can save you time and aggravation while ensuring consistency when you have many paragraphs that require the identical paragraph format attributes.

Summary

Paragraph format commands affect the paragraph where the cursor is located or any paragraph that is completely or partially included in a highlighted segment of text.

Many paragraph format commands are available from the toolbar, including alignment, indentation, bullets, numbering, borders, and shading. The ruler can be used to change indents and tabs. These functions can also be performed from the Format | Paragraph, Format | Bullets and Numbering, and Format | Borders and Shading dialog boxes. The dialog boxes offer more options for commands than are available from the ruler or the toolbar. Some formats, such as numbering, bullets, and borders, are applied automatically by Word when you type sample characters. Copy paragraph formatting by copying and pasting the ¶ paragraph symbol at the end of the paragraph, or by creating a new style and applying the style elsewhere.

Use Insert | Break to specify where a page breaks, for better text flow, and use the options in the Paragraph dialog box to keep a paragraph with its headline and to avoid widows.

EXERCISE 7.1

A Day in the Life of a College Student

1. Open the file *EX6-1 Formatting*.

2. Insert your name, class time, and date at the top of the page.

3. Highlight the entire document by triple-clicking in the left margin. Click the Justify button.

4. Right-align the heading with your name, class time, and date. Center the title.

5. Double-space the first long paragraph.

6. Apply space-and-a-half line spacing to the second paragraph.

7. Remove the automatic leading from the third paragraph. Select Format | Paragraph and change the line spacing to exactly 12 points.

8. Highlight the teacher-pleaser list. Number each paragraph by clicking the Numbering button.

9. Change the numbers to bullets.

10. Indent the list of items 1".

11. Highlight the entire document and add a line space before each paragraph.

12. On a blank line at the bottom of the document, set the following tabs:
    left   3"
    right   3.5"

    Add the following grading scale, pressing [Tab] as indicated by the → symbol:

    A   →   90- →   100.
    B+ →   88- →   89.9
    B   →   80- →   87.9
    C+ →   78- →   79.9
    C   →   70- →   77.9
    D   →   60- →   69.9

13. Highlight the grading scale and select Format | Tabs. Change the 3.5" right tab to a decimal tab. Add a dot leader to the 3" left tab.

14. With the grading scale selected, drag the decimal tab marker on the ruler so that it fits closely with the previous text.

15. Select the grading scale and place a box around the outside. Save and print.

EXERCISE 7.2

Crusty's Pizza

1. Open the file *EX6-2 Formatting*.

2. Insert your name, class time, and date at the top of the page.

3. Highlight the entire document by triple-clicking in the left margin. Click the Justify button.

4. Right-align the heading with your name, class time, and date. Center the title.

5. Double-space the paragraph about the dough temperature.

6. Apply space-and-a-half line spacing to the next paragraph.

7. Remove the automatic leading from the sauce paragraph. Select Format | Paragraph and change the line spacing to exactly 12 points.

8. Highlight the instructions down to the list of toppings. Number each paragraph by clicking the Numbering button.

9. Highlight the last two instructions and apply a number here also. Select Format | Bullets and Numbering, select the Numbered tab, click Modify, and change the Start At number to 7. This way the steps are numbered sequentially.

10. Indent the list of toppings 1".

11. Highlight the entire document and add a line space before each paragraph.

12. Highlight the list of toppings and set a right tab at 4" and 5".

13. Add a dot leader to the 4" tab. Move it to 4.5".

14. Place a heavy (6-point) border above the title and below the last line.

15. Print and save.

EXERCISE 7.3

The Internet

1. Open the file *EX6-3 Formatting*.

2. Insert your name, class time, and date at the top of the page.

3. Highlight the entire document by triple-clicking in the left margin. Click the Justify button.

4. Right-align the heading with your name, class time, and date. Center the title.

5. Double-space the first long paragraph.

6. Apply space-and-a-half line spacing to the second paragraph.

7. Remove the automatic leading from the third paragraph. Select Format | Paragraph and change the line spacing to exactly 12 points.

8. Highlight the list of tips at the end of the document. Place a bullet on each paragraph by clicking the Bullets button.

9. Change the bullet symbols to diamonds.

10. Indent the list 1".

11. Highlight the entire document and add a line space before each paragraph.

12. Select the title. Select Format | Font and change the format to Arial Bold Italic 16 points and the color to white. Add solid shading to the paragraph.

13. Use the format painter to copy the title's paragraph and font formatting (¶ symbol) to `Individual Use of the Internet`.

14. Print and save.

EXERCISE 7.4

Thrill Seeker Tours

1. Open the file *EX6-4 Formatting*.

2. Insert your name, class time, and date at the top of the page.

3. Highlight the entire document by triple-clicking in the left margin. Click the Justify button.

4. Right-align the heading with your name, class time, and date. Center the title.

5. Double-space the first long paragraph.

6. Apply space-and-a-half line spacing to the second paragraph.

7. Remove the automatic leading from the third paragraph. Select Format | Paragraph and change the line spacing to exactly 12 points.

8. Highlight the rapids classification list. Place a bullet on each paragraph by clicking the Bullets button.

9. Change the bullet symbols to diamonds.

10. Indent the list 1".

11. With the list still highlighted, set a left tab at 2".

12. Move the tab to 3". Add a dot leader.

13. Highlight the entire document and add a line space before each paragraph.

14. Select the title. Select Format | Font and change the format to Arial Bold 16 points and the color to white. Add solid shading to the paragraph.

15. Copy the title's paragraph formatting (¶ symbol) to the `Rapids Classification`. Use the format painter to copy the font formatting from the title to the words `Rapids Classification`.

16. Print and save.

Review Questions

*1. What determines which paragraphs will be formatted when a paragraph format command is executed?

2. Which methods may be used to apply paragraph formatting?

*3. What are the four paragraph-alignment methods available in Word? What is each one used for?

4. What is leading? Why does Word include leading by default? How is leading modified?

*5. What is a tab? How are tabs set? How do the four different types of tabs work? What is the purpose of a leader? What kinds of leaders are available?

6. Explain the functions of the triangular markers at the right and left edges of the ruler. How are the same functions performed using the Format | Paragraph dialog box?

*7. What is the purpose of the Keep Lines Together and Keep with Next commands?

8. What are bullets? How are they applied? What choices in bullets are available? Which paragraph indent is automatically applied?

*9. Which new toolbar appears when you click a button on the Formatting toolbar? Which formats may be applied or removed from the new toolbar?

10. How can you view the formatting of a certain segment of a document? How can paragraph formatting be copied?

*11. What is a style? How are styles defined?

12. To format the paragraphs of a memo to make it very easy for an executive to read,

   a. Keep the line spacing at least 120% of the font size.

   b. Keep lines approximately 5 to 10 words long.

   c. Place bullets or numbers on short paragraphs of lists or steps.

   d. Do all of the above.

*13. The kind of tab most often used to align page numbers in a table of contents is a

   a. Dotted tab.

   b. Right tab.

   c. Center tab.

   d. Default tab.

14. To display the actual measurements of the ruler while dragging the indentation markers,

   a. Drag with the right mouse button.

   b. Double-click on the ruler first.

   c. Drag with both mouse buttons.

   d. Hold down the [Shift] key and drag.

*15. When the Bullets button is clicked, the paragraph automatically

   a. Receives a hanging indent.

   b. Is indented .5 inches.

   c. Is justified.

   d. Undergoes all of the above changes.

Key Terms

Alignment
Border
Bullet
Centered
Default tab
Hanging indent
Hard page break

Indent
Justified
Leader
Leading
Left-aligned
Line space
Reversed text

Right-aligned
Rule
Shading
Soft page break
Style
Tab
White space

Formatting Documents

This unit describes document-level formatting, the third and most general level of formatting. These commands will not change the appearance of the words or paragraphs but *will* change the way the pages as a whole look, by allowing you to select the paper size, margins, and other items affecting the entire document or sections of the document.

A document may be viewed in several ways. You may view a page in closeup to see details, or far away to get the overall appearance of the page. You may wish to view the entire page to see how the text fits within the margins. The various views Word provides are useful for seeing formatting at the document, or page, level.

Learning Objectives

At the completion of this unit you should know

1. how to format the layout of a page,

2. several ways to view a document,

3. how some typical documents are formatted.

Important Commands

File | Page Setup

Insert | Page Numbers

View | Full Screen

View | Page Layout

View | Zoom

Formatting Documents

Document format commands may be used to change the look of a page or an entire document. You may have a document with an attractive font style and size, the paragraphs with the correct indent and line spacing, but to finish the formatting you need to establish the layout of the pages. The document may be printed on standard 8½"×11" paper or on another size, such as legal-size paper (8½"×14"). The text may be printed sideways on a page rather than vertically. The document may be bound and, if so, may be formatted so as to look correct when printed (or duplicated) on both the front and back of the pages. Page numbers will be needed for documents over two pages long. Word provides several simple procedures to establish these types of document formatting.

Margins

The margins are the distance between the edge of the paper and the printed text. They are independent of the size of the paper and any format attributes of the text on the page. Margins are set in two ways: with the ruler, and from the Margins tab of the File | Page Setup dialog box.

This command gives you the choice of displaying four different dialog boxes. To see the Margins section, click on the Margins tab. As you can see in Figure 8.1, the default margins are 1 inch at the top and bottom of the page and 1.25 inches at the left and right edges. You may change any of the margins by clicking the up or down arrow next to the Top, Bottom, Left, or Right box until the desired number appears or by double-clicking in the box and typing a new number.

FIGURE 8.1
Margins tab of the Page Setup dialog box

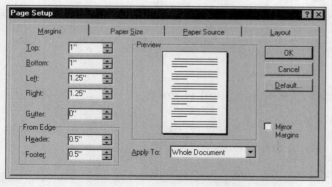

If a document is to be bound, you need to leave extra space along the edge of the paper where the binding will go so that the text will not be hidden by the binding. Word provides a specific setting, the **gutter**, that is used to allow extra space along the side of the page for binding. When a document is bound that has been printed on the front of the page only, the gutter makes the left margin a specific distance wider than normal to allow for the binding. However, when a document that will be printed on both sides of the page is bound, some document pages will be bound on the left and others on the right.

Word allows you to set up different margins for even-numbered (left-hand) and odd-numbered (right-hand) pages in a document by using the *Mirror Margins* feature. This allows you to specify margins for documents printed on both sides of the page. In the File | Page Setup dialog box, click in the box next to Mirror Margins. The words Left and Right are replaced by Inside and Outside. You may now set the inside and outside margins for each page. The inside margin is the margin that will be against the binding, while the outside margin is the one at the outer edge of the document.

In the Guided Activity below, you will set up the page to have asymmetrical margins, and then add a gutter to leave room for the binding. Both odd and even pages will print correctly, with extra space left along the right or left margin, whichever is against the binding for each page.

GUIDED ACTIVITY 8.1

Setting Margins Using Page Setup

1. Open *GA8 Margins*.

2. Position the cursor in the first paragraph. Change the left paragraph indent by moving the square at the left side of the ruler and dragging it 1 inch to the right (or click the Increase Indent button twice). Select File | Print Preview.

   The left edge of the first paragraph is indented 1 inch more than the second. Paragraph indentation is different from margins in that indentation only affects the highlighted paragraph, while margins affect the entire document.

3. Select File | Page Setup. Change the left margin to 1.5 inch by clicking 3 times on the up arrow next to the Left box. Press OK.

   The new margin you selected increases the space between the edge of the paper and the closest text to 1.5 inches. The left edge of the first and second paragraphs are one-quarter inch farther to the left than previously. However, the first paragraph is still indented on its left edge 1 inch farther than the second. It is indented 1 inch from the left margin, regardless of the margin setting.

4. Select File | Page Setup. Double-click in the Left box of the Margins section of the dialog box. Type 2.25 and press Enter.

   Wherever the left margin is placed, the first paragraph will appear 1 inch farther to the right than the second.

5. Close the preview screen.

6. Select File | Page Setup and click in the box next to Mirror Margins to place a check in the box, as shown in Figure 8.2.

   With Mirror Margins selected, the words Left and Right change to Inside and Outside. This feature is used to set the margins for a document that will be printed on both sides of the page and be bound.

FIGURE 8.2
Mirror Margins
and Gutter
settings

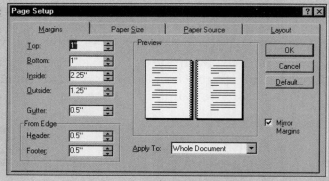

7. Use the up arrow to increase the value in the Gutter box to . 5. The gutter appears in the Preview section of the dialog box as a shaded area on the inside margin. Click OK.

8. Position the cursor at the top of page 1. Click on the Print Preview button. Click and drag on the Multiple Pages button to view two pages at once on the preview screen.

    The first page is displayed on the right-hand side of the screen.

9. Click on the Next Page button in the lower-right corner to view pages 2 and 3.

    In a bound document, page 2 would be on the left and page 3 on the right. The right margin for page 2 and the left margin for page 3 are wider than the outside margins to allow extra room for the binding. The gutter is added to the inside margin to allow room for the binding. You can see the difference in size between the two margins in Print Preview, but the gutter appears only as part of the inside margin.

10. Click on Close to exit the preview screen.

Paper Size and Orientation

Word offers you complete flexibility in selecting a size of paper. The Paper Size tab on the Page Setup dialog box allows you to enter any height and width, as shown in Figure 8.3.

The default values are 8.5" wide by 11" high, the dimensions of a standard sheet of typing paper. You may pick one of the standard paper sizes by selecting from the Paper Size list or enter any values by double-clicking in either the Height or Width box and typing in a new number.

While the word processor may allow you to change these settings to any value, your printer may require certain paper sizes. Pin-feed paper used by some dot-matrix printers only comes in certain sizes. Laser and inkjet printers often will only accept paper of specific sizes. Check your printer manual for more details.

You may also select the print *orientation* of the document from this section of the dialog box. Orientation refers to the direction of the sheet of paper with the text right

FIGURE 8.3
Paper Size tab

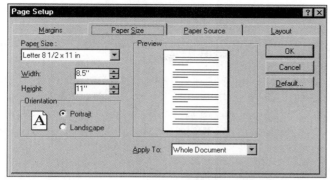

side up. If the paper is taller than it is wide, that is termed ***portrait*** orientation, just as a portrait of a person is generally taller than it is wide. If the paper is wide rather than tall when the text is right side up, this is termed ***landscape*** orientation, just as landscape paintings are most often horizontal. Wide tables of information may fit better on a page in landscape orientation. In Microsoft Word 7.0, the orientation is stored along with the document, not as a printer setting. This allows you to work with both portrait and landscape documents at the same time—or in both orientations within one document—without having to worry about changing the printer setting.

GUIDED ACTIVITY 8.2

Changing Paper Size and Orientation

1. Use the document from the previous Guided Activity. Click on the Print Preview button to view a picture of the standard-size page. Click the One Page button.

2. Select File | Page Setup and select the Paper Size tab. Select `Legal 8½ x 14 in` from the list of paper sizes. Click on the OK button.

   The picture of the page is now three inches longer than before you changed the page size.

3. Select File | Page Setup, and change the paper size back to 8½ by 11 inches. Select Landscape and click OK.

   Now the page is wider than it is long. The text automatically wraps to fit the wider page.

4. Select File | Page Setup, and change the orientation back to Portrait. Click OK. Click on the Close button to exit the preview screen.

Paper Source

Another section of the Page Setup dialog box allows you to select the paper source for your document. Many printers have more than one paper source, perhaps two paper trays plus a place to feed a sheet of paper by hand. These various paper trays are particularly useful for long business letters where the first page would print on letterhead and the rest on plain stationery. Students in computer labs desiring to print on special paper may wish to manually feed it into the printer. Word allows you to take advantage of the capability of printers to feed different kinds of paper from different sources. To change the paper source, select File | Page Setup and select the Paper Source tab to see the result shown in Figure 8.4.

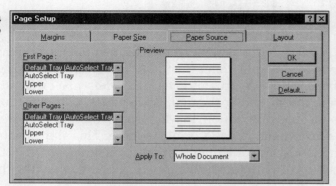

FIGURE 8.4
Paper Source tab

The different paper sources available for your printer will be displayed in both the First Page and Other Pages boxes. Select the paper source for the first and other pages in your document and click OK. Make sure the proper paper types are in the bins you selected before printing.

Numbering Pages

Documents that are more than one or two pages long will most likely require page numbers. Word automatically numbers pages when you issue the command Insert | Page Numbers. The dialog box that appears is shown in Figure 8.5. You must specify the position and alignment of the page numbers on the page.

Page numbers may be placed within either the top margin or the bottom margin of every page. Once that position is specified, the alignment must be chosen. Page numbers may be at the left side, the center, or the right side of the page. If Mirror Margins is checked in Page Setup, then the page numbers may also be placed on the inside (where they are hard to spot quickly) or outside of the page. The Format button on the dialog box allows you to specify the starting page number, in cases where the document does not start on page 1, as well as the numbering sequence, such as Arabic or Roman numerals, or alphabetic letters. Page numbers may also be combined with text, such as chapter titles. Look under Headers in the Answer Wizard.

FIGURE 8.5
Page Numbers dialog box

Click here to access more options

GUIDED ACTIVITY 8.3

Inserting Numbers on Pages

1. Use the three-page document from the previous Guided Activity. Select the command Insert | Page Numbers.

2. Select Top of Page (Header) from the Position drop-down box.

3. Select Right under Alignment and Click OK.

4. Use Print Preview to see the page numbers on each page.

   They are almost too small to read.

5. Place the mouse pointer over the page number, and click. Now you can see the page number clearly.

6. Press ⟨PgDn⟩ or click the Next Page arrow on the scroll bar to view the page numbers on pages 2 and 3.

   Click Close to exit Print Preview.

   Page numbers may also be inserted and modified as headers and footers.

Working in Other Views

Word provides more than one way to accomplish many tasks. Some tasks of document formatting can be performed more easily if you change to a different view. Until now, you have been working in *Normal view*, which shows a many-paged document as a seamless flow of text broken only by dotted lines showing where pages break. To see the actual pages, you use Print Preview. Buttons on the Print Preview toolbar allow you to zoom in for a close-up view of the page, to zoom out again, or even to view multiple pages at a time.

A hybrid of Normal view and Print Preview is *Page Layout view*. Page Layout view is accessed by selecting from the menu View | Page Layout or by clicking the Page Layout View button, which is in the middle of the three view buttons in the lower-left corner of the screen. To return to Normal view, click the button on the left. The button on the right displays the document in Outline view.

Like Print Preview, Page Layout view shows the page exactly as it will appear when printed, including the margins and page numbers. Also like Print Preview, Page Layout view displays a vertical ruler and the two arrow buttons on the vertical scroll bar that allow you to jump quickly to the next or previous page. (If the vertical ruler does not appear, select Tools | Options, choose the View tab, and click in the check box next to Vertical Ruler.)

As in Normal view, the Standard and Formatting toolbars appear in their usual place. Unlike Normal view, however, Page Layout view allows you to see the entire width and length of every page, so that the bottom margin of the first page is

FIGURE 8.6
Page Layout view

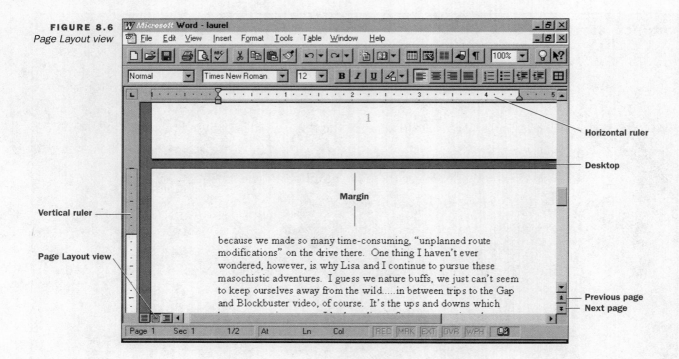

followed by the top margin of the next page against a darker desktop. The features of Page Layout view, shown in Figure 8.6, make it easier to apply document formatting and quickly see the effects.

Page Layout view allows you to change the margins of a document by dragging the margin settings on the ruler. The part of the document between the margins shows on the ruler in white; the shaded parts of the ruler are the margin area. On the vertical ruler, the top of the document is set at the zero mark on the ruler. When you place the mouse at the top of the vertical ruler on the line between the white and shaded parts, the mouse pointer changes to a two-headed arrow. As you drag on the boundary to change the top margin, the rulers reflect the new measurement.

The horizontal ruler changes the left and right margins. Place the mouse pointer on the line between the white and shaded parts of the horizontal ruler in order to turn it into a two-headed arrow. To view the measurement of the margins in numbers, rather than ruler markings, hold down both mouse buttons.

GUIDED ACTIVITY 8.4

Changing the Margins with the Ruler

1. Using the document from the previous Guided Activity, press `Ctrl` `Home` to place the cursor at the top of the first page.

2. Click on the Page Layout View button on the horizontal scroll bar, or select View | Page Layout.

You may need to move to the left to see the left margin. If so, click on the left side of the horizontal scroll bar. If you move to the right you may see the page numbers in gray within the top margin.

3. Place the mouse pointer at the top margin on the vertical ruler. Drag the margin down until the top margin is set to 1.5 inches. Look at the inch tick marks on the ruler, as in Figure 8.7, or hold down both mouse buttons while dragging, to

FIGURE 8.7
Changing the
margin setting
on the ruler

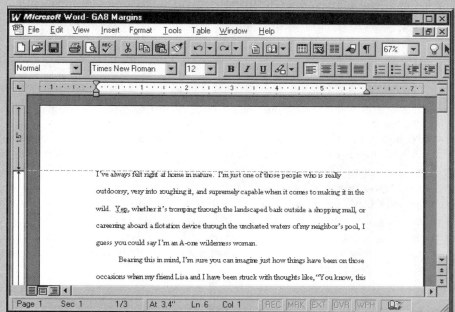

see the measurements between margins in numbers, as in Figure 8.8.

4. Change the left margin to 1.25 inches. Carefully place the mouse pointer on the left side of the horizontal ruler on the line between white and gray parts, as in Figure 8.8. When it changes to a two-headed arrow, drag to the left until the margin displays 1.25". Be careful not to get the indentation markers by mistake.

FIGURE 8.8
Changing the left
margin with the
ruler in Page
Layout view

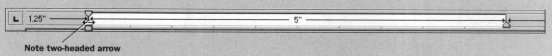

Note two-headed arrow

5. Changing the margins from the ruler may also be done in Print Preview. Click on the Print Preview button. If the rulers are not showing, click the View Ruler button on the Preview toolbar. Drag the top side of the vertical ruler down until

the top margin is set at 4". Click on the Next Page button at the bottom of the scroll bar.

The change is immediately apparent on all pages of the document. The rulers disappear when you view a page that does not contain the cursor.

6.   Go back to the first page. Drag the right side of the horizontal ruler to set the right margin at 1.5 inches.

Because Mirror Margins is selected, Word adjusts the document to keep the left page symmetrical to the right page. That is, changes to the right margin of right pages are mirrored on the left margin of left pages.

7.   Click Close to exit Print Preview. Change back to Normal view and save the document.

Word has several other views that enable the user to see the document in different ways. At the right side of the Standard toolbar is the Zoom Control box, shown in Figure 8.9. You may type a percentage to shrink or enlarge the document, or click on the down arrow next to it and select a setting. This feature allows you to *zoom* in to see detail or zoom out to see the entire page. The menu command View | Full Screen allows the maximum space for editing and entering text. In *Full Screen view*, the title bar, menu bar, toolbars, ruler, status bar, and scroll bars are all removed from the screen. To restore them, click on the Full Screen button, the only thing remaining on the screen besides the text.

FIGURE 8.9
*Zoom Control
box in Page
Layout view*

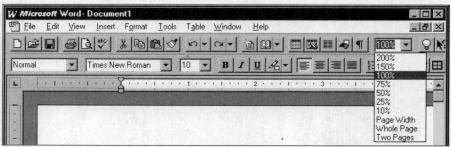

GUIDED ACTIVITY 8.5

Using Other Views of a Document

1.   Use the document from the previous Guided Activity. Select from the menu View | Full Screen.

The usual elements of the Word screen disappear, allowing the maximum amount of space for entering and editing text. The only new feature is the Full Screen button.

2.   Click on the Full Screen button to restore the usual elements of the Word screen.

3.   Click on the down arrow next to the Zoom Control box. Select 200%. The fonts appear twice their normal size. This feature allows you to see even the smallest font clearly.

4.   Click on the down arrow next to the Zoom Control box. Select Page Width.

     In Normal view, zooming to Page Width does not display the margin area, but the document is reduced or increased to a certain percentage to allow you to see both the right and left edges of the ruler. In documents with narrow margins, the text may extend beyond the right side of the screen. Using this view allows you to see all the text within the window.

5.   Change the Zoom back to 100%. This is the default setting for Word documents.

6.   Change to Page Layout view by clicking on the Page Layout View button.

7.   Zoom to Page Width.

     In Page Layout view, the document is reduced to a percent that allows you to see not only the text area of the page, but also the entire left and right margins against a dark desktop. This view gives you a good idea of how the proportions, spacing, and margins of the document will appear when printed.

8.   While still in Page Layout view, click on the down arrow by the Zoom Control box and select Two Pages. This option is only available in Page Layout view. Compare this view to Print Preview.

9.   Click on the Print Preview button. Click and drag on the Multiple Pages button to view two pages at once.

     Note that the two pages and the rulers look nearly the same as in Page Layout view. The difference is that the Print Preview toolbar appears, and the other toolbars disappear.

10. Click Close to exit Print Preview. Select from the menu View | Zoom. Select 100% and click OK. Using the dialog box has the same result as using the Zoom Control box on the toolbar.

11. Select from the menu the command View | Normal. This has the same effect as pressing the Normal View button.

Summary

Document format commands affect the entire document or large sections of it. They are the most general of format commands. The File | Page Setup command is used to access the Page Setup dialog box. All document format commands are located in this dialog box. Since they are generally used only once when creating each document, these format commands are not located in a prominent location like the toolbar or the ruler.

The commands in the Page Setup dialog box affect the entire document (unless you select Apply to This Point Forward). The Margins tab allows you to set the margins and gutters for the document. The margins are the distance between the edge of the paper and the printed text. The Paper Size tab allows you to enter the paper size and print orientation for the document. Another tab allows you to select the paper source used when your document is printed. You may select a different source for the first page and for the remaining pages of the document. Using Insert | Page Numbers, you can instruct Word to number pages automatically within the top or bottom margins of multipage documents.

Word provides several views to help you to accomplish your formatting and editing tasks:

- Normal view lets you see the font and paragraphs the way they will appear on paper.

- Page Layout view lets you see the formatting of the entire page as it will appear on paper.

- Full Screen view lets you enter and edit text with the maximum amount of space in the work area.

- Zoom view lets you move closer in to see details and farther out to see the overall effect.

- Print Preview lets you view multiple pages on screen at one time, and displays a different toolbar.

EXERCISE 8.1

Printing Pages for Two-Sided Bound Documents

1. Open *EX8 Margins*. Assume that the document will be printed on both sides of the page and bound in a book with other articles.

2. Switch to Page Layout view and drag on the vertical ruler to set the top margin to 1.5".

3. Select File | Page Setup and check Mirror Margins. Set the margins to an inside margin of 2 inches and an outside margin of 1 inch. Add a ½-inch gutter to allow for the binding.

4. Use Insert | Page Numbers to add page numbers at the outside bottom corner of all pages, including the first.

5. Print the document. (You will not actually print on both sides of the page. Pages 1 and 2 will appear on separate pages on your printout.)

EXERCISE 8.2

Using Manual Feed

1. Print page 1 of *EX8 Margins*, if this option is available on your printer.

2. Set the paper source to manual feed.

   Use the File | Print command to print only page 2. Manually feed page 1 so that page 2 prints on the back of page 1 (you may have to experiment with which direction to feed the paper to get this correct).

EXERCISE 8.3

Printing Sideways

1. In a new document, create a jazzy cover for the booklet created in Exercises 8.1 and 8.2. Type the title `Adventures in the Great Outdoors`. Format these lines to 36 points and right-align them. Add a heavy (6-point) border to the top.

2. Set the paper source to default. Change the orientation to Landscape.

   Print the cover. Yes, the title will be sideways, but it will make an impact. Staple down the left side to bind the cover and pages together.

Review Questions

*1. Why are the format document commands intended for the most general level of formatting?

2. Why are the format document commands not located in a prominent place in the work area?

*3. What is the limitation when setting the paper size in the File | Page Setup dialog box? What is the default paper size?

4. What are the margins? What are two methods for changing margins?

*5. How are margins different from paragraph indents? How do margins affect paragraph indents?

6. When is the Mirror Margins option used? What changes when Mirror Margins is selected?

*7. What is a gutter? When is a gutter used? How does the effect of the gutter differ when Mirror Margins is on or off?

8. In what different ways can a document be viewed?

*9. What features appear in Page Layout view that are not visible in Normal view?

10. The view resembling Print Preview in which you can change margins by dragging on the ruler is

   a. Normal.

   b. Page Layout.

   c. Zoom.

   d. Full Screen.

*11. If you wish to copy your document on both sides and bind it, you should

   a. Use Mirror Margins.

   b. Insert page numbers.

   c. Use manual feed.

   d. Work in Page Layout view.

12. The File | Page Setup command allows you to

   a. Set orientation.

   b. Specify the preferred view.

   c. View the text with the margin settings.

   d. Control the page numbers.

Key Terms

Full Screen view	Mirror Margins	Page Layout view
Gutter	Normal view	Portrait
Landscape	Orientation	Zoom

Creating a Flyer

While flyers often contain pictures and drawings, you can use simple font and paragraph formatting to create an eye-catching flyer. Make a flyer advertising your ideal vacation—whether part of Thrill Seeker Tours or Luxury Seeker Tours. Identify several features of the vacation, including destination, activities, eating, and sleeping, each on separate, short lines. Include the dates and price.

Make the fonts the appropriate size for your flyer, and put key words or phrases in a unique font that helps convey your message. For example, you could use the following kinds of fonts for these phrases:

Elegant Dining Rooms

OLD FASHIONED COUNTRY COOKIN'

50 miles of Mountain Bike Trails

You know the rule of using only two fonts at a time, but if you're going to break a rule, as Martin Luther said, sin bravely. Vary the text as much as possible in terms of font, size, color (if you have access to a color printer), and paragraph alignment. Make some paragraphs reversed; that is, format the font as white within dark-shaded paragraphs. Change the margins and page orientation if necessary. Proof the text carefully, print (on colored paper, if you like), and save as *Application C*.

III
Advanced Word Processing

UNIT NINE   *Tables*

UNIT TEN   *Desktop Publishing*

UNIT ELEVEN   *Chart and Draw*

UNIT TWELVE   *Headers and Footers*

UNIT THIRTEEN   *Mail Merge*

UNIT FOURTEEN   *Working with Long Documents*

UNIT FIFTEEN   *Macros and Customizing*

■ **PART THREE** of this manual gives you techniques that are used to make complex tasks simple. Many features in Word are as complete as those in desktop publishing software, such as those that place text into columns or tables and insert pictures and charts. Word greatly reduces the effort required to produce headers and footers, which are required on many documents. The advanced functions automate the process of mail merge to create customized form letters, envelopes, and mailing labels. The outline feature organizes the creation of long documents. Word simplifies footnoting reference material and preparing a table of contents and an index. Word may be fully customized to your liking, including creating your own selections on the menus and toolbar.

The advanced word processing features are not necessary to produce useful documents, but they can save you a great deal of time by taking the difficult work out of your hands and letting the computer do it for you.

Tables

This unit presents techniques for creating and formatting tables, used to store text and pictures in row-and-column or side-by-side format. The purpose of a table is to allow fast and easy access to information that fits into two categories. The reader can follow a row and column, representing two categories, to their intersection to quickly find an individual piece of information.

Word allows you to easily create, maneuver through, and modify tables. Existing text can be placed into a table, as can portions of spreadsheets, pictures, and any other item that can be cut and pasted. The dimensions of the rows and columns can be changed to allow for the most effective presentation of the information in the table. Items in a table can be formatted, like any other selection of text, with bold, italics, small caps, and any other attribute. Predefined borders and styles may be added with the AutoFormat command.

Learning Objectives

At the completion of this unit you should know

1. what a table is,

2. what kind of information fits best in a table,

3. how to create and enter information into a table,

4. how to modify and format a table,

5. how to sort and calculate information in a table.

Important Commands

Edit | Copy

Edit | Paste Cells

Format | Borders and Shading

Table | Cell Height and Width

Table | Delete

Table | Formula

Table | Gridlines

Table | Insert

Table | Merge Cells

Table | Select

Table | Sort

Table | Split Cells

Table | Split Table

Table | Table AutoFormat

Purpose of Tables

A *table* is a rectangular text structure that holds information in rows and columns. Tables are used to allow readers to look up pieces of information that fall into two intersecting categories. In a catalog, you might look up a type of product and a price range to decide which brand to buy. The two categories, type and price, allow you to narrow your choices. Using the table method, you can find individual items from a large set of information.

The table in Figure 9.1 allows you to look up quickly the average temperature of regions of the country by one of two seasons, summer and winter. If you know two pieces of information, the region and the season, you can quickly find the average temperature.

FIGURE 9.1
A table used for finding temperatures

	North	South	East	West
Summer	75	95	80	80
Winter	20	40	30	50

Tables are also useful for aligning any information that is most effectively presented side by side. While setting tabs may also achieve this for a small amount of text or numbers, tables can align paragraphs, graphics, or any amount of text with flexibility and ease of handling.

FIGURE 9.2
A table used to align paragraphs side by side

Artist	Compact Disc
Take That	'Nobody Else' © 1995 by BMG Records &U.K.) Ltd.
Chicago	'If You Leave Me Now' © 1983 CBS Records, Inc.
The Weavers	'The Best of the Weavers' © 1994 Vanguard Records
Handel	'Water Music - Concerto Grosso' © 1990 Delta Music

The table structure is very flexible. The table in Figure 9.2 shows the way Word can align even longer amounts of text in rows and columns. Any set of information that needs to be arranged side by side will fit into a table.

Tables have several other uses. Any portion of a spreadsheet that is inserted into a Word document will automatically become a table. Tables are also used during mail merge operations for holding names and addresses as well as for creating mailing labels.

Creating Tables

There are two ways to create a table. One method requires that you create the table and enter information yourself. The other allows you to select existing text or numbers separated by tabs and create a table that will fit the items.

Creating an Empty Table

To create a table from scratch, position the cursor where the table is to be placed, and then click on the Table button on the toolbar. On the Table button grid that drops down, drag the mouse to select the number of rows and columns you want in the new table, as shown in Figure 9.3.

FIGURE 9.3
Selecting the size of a new table

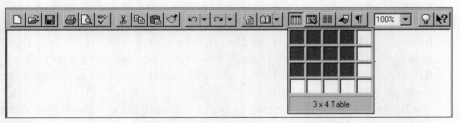

Another method for creating a table is to select from the menu Table | Insert Table. The dialog box that appears allows you to select the Table Wizard or to specify the number of columns and rows, as shown in Figure 9.4. The Table Wizard is a great time-saver for creating and formatting standard tables containing dates and numeric data. Many of the features incorporated into the wizard will be explained in this unit.

FIGURE 9.4
Insert Table dialog box

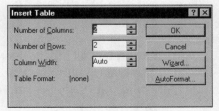

When creating a table using the dialog box, you need to enter only the number of columns you require in this table. Entering the number of rows is optional, since the table will automatically add new rows to the bottom of the table as you type and you may not know the number of rows you need.

The default value for the column width is Auto. This value will cause Word to make the width of each column equal to the total distance between the left and right margins divided by the number of columns specified. Each column will be the same width, and the table will fill the space between the margins. If the columns must all be a specific width, enter that value in the Column Width box before continuing. If not, accept the Auto default and continue, since the column width can be changed later.

GUIDED ACTIVITY 9.1

Creating a Table

1. Start Word and create a new document.

2. Click the Table button on the toolbar and drag to create a 1×3 table.

   Another method is to select the command Table | Insert Table.

3. Turn on the gridlines, if you can't see them on your table, by selecting Table | Gridlines.

4. Click Undo. This time use the command Table | Insert Table to create a table.

   The default values for the number of columns and rows are 2 and 2.

5. Change the value in the Number of Columns box to 3. Click on the OK button.

The empty table structure appears at the point where the cursor was located before executing the command. The lines in the table are called *gridlines*. The gridlines will display in the work area but will not print. They are displayed only to make working with the table easier. Gridlines define the edges of the *cell*, the intersection of a row and column. Cells can contain text, pictures, or any other item that can be cut and pasted in Windows. If you press the Show | Hide ¶ button, the *cell marks* appear within each cell and at the end of each row, as shown in Figure 9.5. You can turn the gridlines off and on with the Table | Gridlines command.

At this point the table is ready for you to type information into each cell. The cursor is in the top-left cell of the table, the point from which you would normally begin to add data.

FIGURE 9.5
An empty table

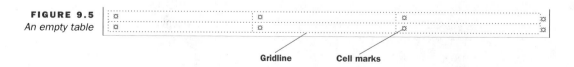

Gridline   Cell marks

GUIDED ACTIVITY 9.2

Entering Text into a Table

1. Type Schedule of Train Departures from Amsterdam.

   When the cursor reaches the right-hand edge of the cell, a second line will appear in the cell to hold the extra text, as shown in Figure 9.6.

FIGURE 9.6
Word wrapping when text is wider than the cell

Schedule of Train Departures from Amsterdam		

Entering text into a cell is much like entering items directly into the work area. As you move the cursor to the edge of the cell, word wrap moves the next word to the beginning of the next line. You can enter several paragraphs into the same cell, and Word will continue to increase the cell's height to hold them.

The Tab key ([Tab]) is used to advance the cursor to the next cell in a table.

2. Press [Tab].

   The cursor moves to the second cell in the top row.

3. Type the day of the week.

   You can move the cursor to a second line inside a single cell by pressing [Enter].

4. Type today's date.

   You can continue to make the cell taller by pressing [Enter] at the end of the last line in the cell.

5. Press [Tab] to advance to the last cell in the first row. This cell will remain blank. To move to the beginning of the next row, press [Tab] again.

6. Type the following three column headings on the second row of the table. The abbreviation fl stands for guilders (formerly florins). Remember to use [Tab] to advance the cursor to the next cell and row.

   Destination   Departure   Price (fl)

7. Press [Tab].

   When you press [Tab] from the last cell in a row, the cursor is moved to the beginning of the next row. If you are in the bottom-right corner of a table and press [Tab], a new row appears in your table. Although you originally created a table with only two rows, rows will be added as you enter information into the table. Each time you press [Tab] from the last cell in the table, a new row will be added, and the cursor will move to the left cell of the new row. This means you need not know beforehand how many rows will be in a table. You can always add rows to any existing table in this fashion.

8. Type the following information on new rows.

```
Paris                 8:26        65
Interlaken           12:49        87
Luxembourg City      10:02        36
```

You may edit text in a table just as though it were outside the table and in the work area. Simply move the cursor to the location of the text to be edited and perform the function necessary to edit the text.

9. Highlight `Interlaken`. Type `Geneva`.

The original city name is replaced by `Geneva`. This is the same procedure you would use if you were editing text outside the table.

Text can also be formatted inside the table.

10. Move the cursor to the first cell of the second row. Highlight the entire row. Make the text bold by clicking on the Bold button on the toolbar or by using the Format | Font command.

Any character format attribute can be given to selected text in a table. Paragraph format commands also work.

11. Center the titles in the cells by clicking on the Center button on the toolbar or by using the Format | Paragraph command.

The column titles are centered, but not between the page margins. They are centered between the left-hand and right-hand edges of each cell.

When the Guided Activity is complete, you should have a table that looks like the one in Figure 9.7.

FIGURE 9.7
Results of
Guided
Activity 9.2

Schedule of Train Departures from Amsterdam	Friday October 22, 1996		
Destination	**Departure**		**Price (fl)**
Paris	8:26	65	
Geneva	12:49	87	
Luxembourg City	10:02	36	

Modifying Tables

Word provides several commands to modify tables by adding, deleting, rearranging, and formatting rows and columns. These features allow you to quickly modify a table so that it is presented most effectively.

The Table | Insert and Table | Delete commands are used to add and delete cells, rows, and columns from a table. The command changes, depending on whether a row, a column, or a cell is highlighted before the command is selected.

FIGURE 9.8
*Shortcut menu
when the pointer
is on a table*

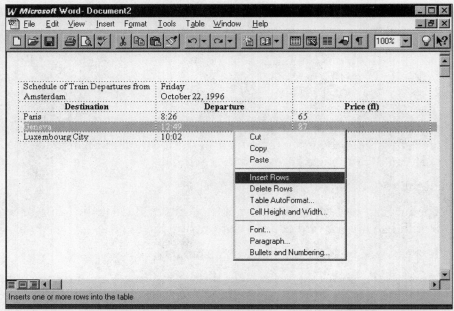

Adding and Deleting Rows and Columns

In Guided Activity 9.2, you added a row to the end of the table by pressing [Tab] with the cursor in the last cell of the last row. If you want to add a row in the middle of the table, place the cursor at the desired location of the new row and select the Table | Insert Rows command. When the mouse pointer is positioned within a table, you can click the right mouse button to access this command on the shortcut menu, shown in Figure 9.8. The row containing the cursor moves down to make room for the new row.

To insert new cells or new columns, you must select either a cell or a column first. To select a cell, place the mouse pointer at the left edge of a cell until it changes from the I-beam into an arrow pointing up and to the right, and then click. To select a column, move the mouse pointer over the top border of the column until it changes into a small down-pointing arrow, and then click. The entire column is highlighted. You can also select rows, columns, or the entire table with the Table | Select command.

After highlighting, new cells or columns are added by selecting the Table | Insert Cells or Table | Insert Columns command from the menu. This command changes, depending on what is highlighted. New cells or columns are added above or to the left of the highlighted items.

Rows and columns are deleted in the same manner from the Table menu. Select the cell, column, or row to be deleted, and then issue the Table | Delete command. The cell, row, or column where the cursor is located will be deleted. Rearranging rows and columns may be done by simply using either the cut, copy, and paste commands or the drag-and-drop method.

GUIDED ACTIVITY 9.3

Adding and Deleting Rows and Columns

1. Position the cursor anywhere in the row that contains the data on Paris.

   The new row will be added *above* the location of the cursor. Placing the cursor here will cause a new row to be inserted between the existing second and third rows.

2. Select Table | Insert Rows.

   A new row appears above where you positioned the cursor, as shown in Figure 9.9. The rest of the table moves down.

FIGURE 9.9
Table with new row inserted

Schedule of Train Departures from Amsterdam	Friday October 22, 1996	
Destination	**Departure**	**Price (fl)**
Paris	8:26	65
Geneva	12:49	87
Luxembourg City	10:02	36

3. Type the following data into the blank cells, pressing [Tab] to move to the next cell.

   ```
   Athens    6:42    138
   ```

4. You can delete cells by using a process similar to inserting. Highlight the entire Athens row by clicking at the far left side of the row outside of the gridlines.

5. Select the command Table | Delete Rows. The new row has now been deleted.

   Information is copied from one cell, row, or column to another by using the copy command with the Paste Cells, Paste Rows, or Paste Columns commands. These last commands only appear on the Edit or shortcut menus when the cursor and mouse pointer are located in a table, in which case they replace the Paste command, as shown in Figure 9.10.

   To highlight a row with the mouse, move the mouse pointer to the far-left side of the row and click, or position the cursor in the row you want to highlight and select the command Table | Select Row.

FIGURE 9.10
Shortcut menu with Paste Rows command

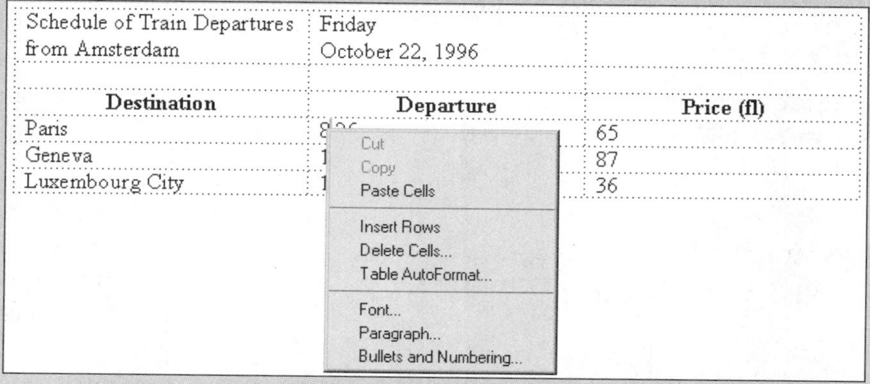

Schedule of Train Departures from Amsterdam	Friday October 22, 1996	
Destination	**Departure**	**Price (fl)**
Paris	8:26	65
Geneva	1	87
Luxembourg City	1	36

Cut
Copy
Paste Cells

Insert Rows
Delete Cells...
Table AutoFormat...

Font...
Paragraph...
Bullets and Numbering...

6. Highlight the row that contains the Geneva information. Select Edit | Copy.

7. Position the cursor in front of `Paris`. Select Edit | Paste Rows.

    The information from the Geneva row is copied into a new row, moving the Paris row down. You now have two rows containing the Geneva information.

8. Highlight the entire second Geneva row. Press `Del`.

    The Geneva information disappears, but the empty row is still there. The only way to remove the empty row is with the Table | Delete command.

9. Click Undo to get the information back. With the row highlighted, select Table | Delete Rows. The original Geneva information is deleted along with the row that contained it.

    You can also insert more than one row or column at a time by highlighting the areas where you want the new rows inserted. To highlight more than one row, position the mouse pointer to the left of the first row, and then drag down to the last row to be highlighted. You can also position the cursor within the first row, select Table | Select Row, and then press and hold `Shift` and press `↓` to highlight another row below the first.

10. Highlight the two rows below the Geneva information, and press the Table button on the toolbar or select Table | Insert Rows.

    Two new rows appear at the highlighted location. The Paris and Luxembourg City rows move down to make room for the new rows, as shown in Figure 9.11.

FIGURE 9.11
Table with two new rows inserted

Schedule of Train Departures from Amsterdam	Friday October 22, 1996	
Destination	**Departure**	**Price (fl)**
Geneva	12:49	87
Paris	8:26	65
Luxembourg City	10:02	36

11. Add the following information to the appropriate cells in the new rows.

    ```
    Milan         21:14    114
    Copenhagen    22:07    95
    ```

    Columns can also be added to an existing table. To add a column, highlight the column at the desired new location and either click the Table button or use the Table | Insert Columns command.

12. Carefully place the mouse pointer over the top of the Price column until the pointer turns into the small down-arrow, and then click. You may also select a column by positioning the cursor within the column and using the command Table | Select Column. Click the Table button on the toolbar and a column of blank cells appears to the left of the Price column.

13. Add the following text to the blank cells in the new column. Use the ⬇ key to move from one cell to the next in the column.

```
Arrival

8:32

7:39

9:40

14:48

14:16
```

The table is now too wide to fit in the work area or on the page. Each of the original columns took up one-third of the width of the page. The new column is the same width as the others; therefore, the last column extends beyond the right margin. You will adjust this in the next Guided Activity.

14. Columns may be rearranged using cut and paste or drag-and-drop. Highlight the Departure column.

15. With the mouse pointer positioned over the column, drag the cursor to the far-left side of the word `Schedule` on the table, and then release the mouse button.

The second column has been dragged to the left of the first column.

Formatting Tables

Once the rows and columns in a table are positioned where you want them, you can change the width, height, borders and shading, and alignment of the cells in the table.

Column Width

The width of the columns is set when the table is first created. However, the table may need to be modified so that it better fits the information, the page, or the document. The table you created in Guided Activity 9.3 extends beyond the right margin by one column. It is therefore necessary to change the column width after modifying the table.

As soon as a table is inserted in a document, the ruler changes to display column markers to denote the edges of the columns, as shown in Figure 9.12. The width of a column may be changed with the mouse by dragging the column markers on the ruler or dragging directly on the column's right-hand gridline.

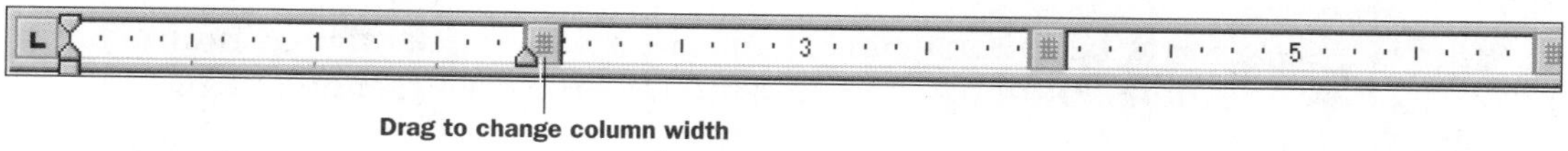

FIGURE 9.12
Ruler showing column markers

Drag to change column width

More precise measurements may be obtained by using the Cell Height and Width dialog box. Highlight the column to be changed, select Table | Cell Height and Width (you may access this command also from the shortcut menu), and view the Column tab in the dialog box. Type the desired column width into the Width box, as shown in Figure 9.13, and press Enter.

Once in the dialog box, you may change widths of other columns in the table by clicking on the Next Column button or on the Previous Column button. Using this method, you can format the width of all the columns in the table without having to exit the dialog box for each one.

Word provides a handy way to make cells fit the contents of the cell—wider for long text, narrower for short. To apply AutoFit from the dialog box, click on the AutoFit button on the Column tab, as in Figure 9.13.

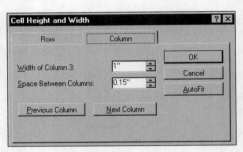

FIGURE 9.13
Column tab of the Cell Height and Width dialog box

When you change the width of a column by dragging either the gridlines or the column markers on the ruler, all columns to the right are changed in size to accommodate the change in width, so that the table overall retains its size. When you hold down the Shift key and drag the column, the single column just to the right of the changed column adjusts to be wider or narrower to accommodate the change, and the table's overall size remains unchanged. The only ways to change the size of the table as a whole are to hold down both the Shift and Ctrl keys while dragging, or to drag the right-most gridline. You can see what results when you hold each key when dragging in Figure 9.14.

FIGURE 9.14
Effects of narrowing column 2

Original column width			
After dragging to make second column narrower			
	narrower	wider	wider
Shift+dragging			
	narrower	wider	same as original
Ctrl + Shift + dragging			
	narrower	same as original	same as original

GUIDED ACTIVITY 9.4

Changing Column Widths

1. The table in Guided Activity 9.3 is too wide to fit between the margins now that we have added a column. Highlight the entire table by selecting Table | Select Table from the menu. Remember that the cursor must be positioned within a table for this choice to be available.

2. Select Table | Cell Height and Width and click on the Column tab. Click on the AutoFit button. Click anywhere on the document to remove the highlighting.

FIGURE 9.15
*Column widths
after using
AutoFit*

Friday October 22, 1996	Schedule of Train Departures from Amsterdam		
Departure	**Destination**	**Arrival**	**Price (fl)**
12:49	Geneva	8:32	87
21:14	Milan	7:29	114
22:07	Copenhagen	9:40	95
8:26	Paris	14:48	65
10:02	Luxembourg City	14:16	36

This makes the columns just wide enough to display the contents of the cells without wrapping, as shown in Figure 9.15. AutoFit adjusts the column widths to the different length of the headings, and the result is not very attractive in this case.

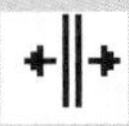

3. Place the mouse over the gridline just to the right of the Destination column. When it changes to a double line with two arrows, drag the gridline to the left to narrow the Destination column.

Note that the table as a whole remains the same size, but both the Arrival and Price columns widen to accommodate the change, as in Figure 9.16.

FIGURE 9.16
*Changing one
column width
changes the
width of all
the columns
to the right*

These columns are affected

Friday October 22, 1996	Schedule of Train Departures from Amsterdam		
Departure	**Destination**	**Arrival**	**Price (fl)**
12:49	Geneva	8:32	87
21:14	Milan	7:29	114
22:07	Copenhagen	9:40	95
8:26	Paris	14:48	65
10:02	Luxembourg City	14:16	36

4. Undo the last action. This time hold down Shift while narrowing the Destination column. This time, just the Arrival column is changed, while the table as a whole is not changed.

5. Highlight the Arrival and Price columns. To make these columns all the same width, use the command from the menu.

6. Select Table | Cell Height and Width, and click on the Column tab. Set the column width at 1" and click OK. The two columns should be the same width, wide enough to accommodate the heading. Click elsewhere to remove the highlighting.

7. Save the table and leave the document open.

Column Alignment and Tabs Within a Table

By default, the contents of a table are left-aligned within each column. Sometimes, such as in the case of numbers, it is more appropriate to right-align (or in the case of titles to center-align) the text within the column. This formatting is done the same way as formatting ordinary text, by simply clicking the Left, Center, and Right alignment buttons on the toolbar, or by using the Format | Paragraph command.

Likewise, indentation applied to the paragraphs affects the indentation of the text within the column itself. The indentation of text within a column may be changed by dragging the indent markers on the ruler. In addition, it is possible to set tabs within a table to align text in columns within a table. Specifically, adding a decimal tab to a column causes numbers to *automatically* align at the decimal point. To align text at any other kind of tab within a table, you must press Ctrl Tab, since pressing Tab alone will jump the cursor to the next cell.

GUIDED ACTIVITY 9.5

Changing Column Alignment

1. Select the columns for Arrival and Price.

2. Change the alignment to right alignment. With the mouse, click on the Align Right button on the toolbar. The contents of the cells move to the far right side of the columns. Now the numbers are properly aligned, but the titles are not, as in Figure 9.17.

FIGURE 9.17
Effect of changing alignment

Friday October 22, 1996	Schedule of Train Departures from Amsterdam		
Departure	**Destination**	**Arrival**	**Price (fl)**
12:49	Geneva	8:32	87
21:14	Milan	7:29	114
22:07	Copenhagen	9:40	95
8:26	Paris	14:48	65
10:02	Luxembourg City	14:16	36

3. Change the alignment to Center. This alignment looks a little more attractive at a glance, but the numbers look awkward being centered in a column.

4. Change the alignment to Left, and then click elsewhere to remove the highlighting.

   Set the alignment of the numbers in the Arrival column, using a decimal tab in the next step.

5. Highlight the Arrival column by clicking on the top border or by selecting Table | Select Column. Click 3 times on the Tab Alignment button on the far-left side of the ruler until a decimal tab is displayed. Click on the ruler to set the tab in the center of the column, as in Figure 9.18.

FIGURE 9.18
Aligning numbers in a table by setting a decimal tab

Click here to display decimal tab

Friday October 22, 1996	Schedule of Train Departures from Amsterdam		
Departure	**Destination**	**Arrival**	**Price (fl)**
12:49	Geneva	8:32	87
21:14	Milan	7:29	114
22:07	Copenhagen	9:40	95
8:26	Paris	14:48	65
10:02	Luxembourg City	14:16	36

6. Highlight the Price column and set a decimal tab in this column by clicking again on the ruler.

7. In the Departure column, highlight only the cells containing numbers. Set a decimal tab.

Center the headings only in the Arrival and Price columns. Highlight these two cells only, and center by clicking on the Center button on the toolbar. The results of this Guided Activity should look something like Figure 9.19.

FIGURE 9.19
The formatted table

Friday October 22, 1996	Schedule of Train Departures from Amsterdam		
Departure	**Destination**	**Arrival**	**Price (fl)**
12:49	Geneva	8:32	87
21:14	Milan	7:29	114
22:07	Copenhagen	9:40	95
8:26	Paris	14:48	65
10:02	Luxembourg City	14:16	36

Row Height and Alignment

Ordinarily, the height of the row in the table is set to the minimum value needed to contain everything in the row. You can override this default through the Row tab in the Table|Cell Height and Width dialog box, shown in Figure 9.20, or by dragging the settings on the vertical ruler in Page Layout view. You can select any of three options: Auto (the default), At Least, or Exactly. The At Least option sets a minimum value for each row, but allows the cell to expand if the contents of a cell exceed the minimum height. The Exactly option sets the row height to a fixed amount, and if the cell's contents exceed this amount they may appear cropped (trimmed) on the screen and when printed.

FIGURE 9.20
Row tab of the Table|Cell Height and Width dialog box

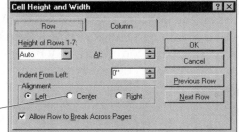

Click here to center the whole table

How can you center the table as a whole on the page? You know that pressing the Center button causes the text to be centered within the cells. To center or indent the entire table between the margins of the page, you must change the indent or alignment from the Row tab of the Cell Height and Width dialog box.

GUIDED ACTIVITY 9.6

Setting Row Height and Alignment

1. Continue to use the table from Guided Activity 9.5. To create more space in the heading of the table, change the row height from the default Auto setting.

Select the top row by clicking the mouse pointer on the far-left side of the row or by placing the cursor within the top row and issuing the Table | Select Row command.

2. The only way to change the automatic row height is to access the dialog box. Select Table | Cell Height and Width and click on the Row tab.

3. Click the down arrow under Height of Row 1 and select At Least.

4. Set the minimum height of the row by double-clicking on the value in the At text box and changing it to 28 points. Click OK.

Change the alignment of the entire table so that it is centered between the margins rather than left-aligned. This will *not* affect the text within the columns.

5. Highlight the table with the command Table | Select Table, and then issue the command Table | Cell Height and Width. On the Row tab, click on the option for Center under Alignment, and then click OK. The table is centered between the two margins, the way you would want it to be if it were presented in a paper or report.

6. Save the table.

Borders, Shading, and AutoFormat

The dotted gridlines that surround the cells in a table are there to show you the edges of the cell. They will not appear on paper when the document is printed. However, some tables are easier to read if the cells are separated by some type of line or rule. You may add borders as well as shading to the cells in a table by using the Format | Borders and Shading command or buttons on the Borders toolbar, just as you apply borders and shading to paragraphs of normal text.

Borders and shading may be added to individual cells in the table as well as to the entire table. It is not difficult to format the borders and shading, but Word makes it even easier by providing 37 predefined formats to choose from. These are applied with the Table | Table AutoFormat command. This command may be used to apply several types of formatting, including borders, shading, font, color, and AutoFit, as shown in Figure 9.21.

The type of data in the table determines what the correct formatting should be. Simple contrast between titles and the main text is the main purpose. Borders, shading, spacing, and color may be used to provide contrast—but not all are needed at once.

FIGURE 9.21
Table AutoFormat dialog box

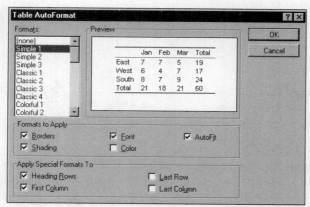

What formatting increases readability for tables?

- *Use horizontal borders on the top and bottom of rows if the table is to be read horizontally. If the table reads vertically, use vertical borders on the left and right sides.*

- *Place a box around the outside of vertical tables. Horizontal tables look cleaner without vertical lines.*

- *Add shading for more emphasis than borders or to add contrast to table headings.*

- *Avoid shading darker than 20% because text and numbers will be too difficult to read. Exception: for reversing (white letters on dark), the shading should be 80% or more.*

- *Use reversing for maximum attention to columns or rows.*

- *Add 2 to 4 points of space between the paragraph and any top or bottom border. Do this by formatting the paragraph with extra space above or below, or by changing the row height.*

- *Format headings and totals in bold, italic, or a different font to contrast with the data in the text.*

Source: Daniel Will-Harris, "Format a Table," *Technique* (May/June, 1994): 58.

GUIDED ACTIVITY 9.7

Using Cell Borders

1. Select the command Table | Gridlines to remove the check mark so that the non-printing gridlines disappear from the screen.

2. Highlight the entire table by selecting Table | Select Table or by using the mouse.

3. Create a border that will print gridlines between all the cells of the table, by issuing the command Format | Borders and Shading and then selecting Grid under Presets, and click OK.

   This places a heavier border around the outside of the table and thinner gridlines inside the table. Check Print Preview to see that these gridlines will print. Close Print Preview. These borders may be enough to complete the table. Using AutoFormat will replace these borders with new ones.

4. Select the command Table | Table AutoFormat. Click on each choice in the list of formats to see the effect of each on the sample table. Highlight the choice List 3. Do not press OK yet.

   Click the Color check box to show the color formatting of several of the choices. The colors are mostly used for on-screen viewing or printing in color. Adding color to a table that you plan to print on a black-and-white laser printer will sometimes make the table too dark and hard to read.

5. Click next to AutoFit to remove the check from the box. You previously went to a great deal of trouble fixing the column widths when AutoFit did not give attractive results in this case.

6. Click to remove the check in Heading Rows to see the effect on the sample. Check the Heading Rows choice again. When you have made all your choices, click OK to see the results on the train schedule.

7. Since the Table AutoFormat command overrides the previous formatting on the column titles, highlight the column titles again and bold them.

8. If you like the way the table appears, save it. Otherwise click Undo and try other choices.

Sorting and Calculating

Tables often hold numeric or financial data that need to be totaled or averaged. You could use a hand-held calculator to tally the numbers, or you could switch to the Calculator by clicking the Start button and choosing Programs, Accessories, Calculator. Both operations, though, require typing the same numbers over again. Word allows you to perform simple calculations such as these with the command Table | Formula.

The Table | Formula dialog box, shown in Figure 9.22, gives several simple formulas for use with data in tables, including SUM and AVERAGE.

FIGURE 9.22
Table Formula dialog box

These and other formulas are available

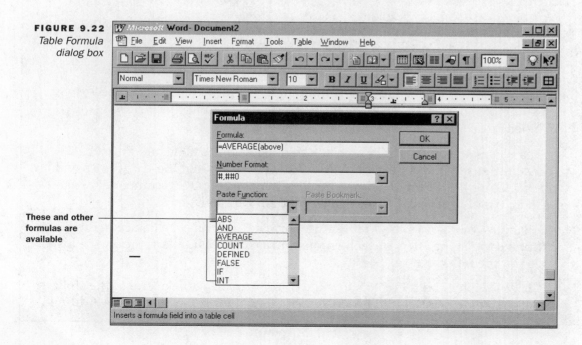

After typing the data in a table, you may find that you would like to have the data sorted. It would be time-consuming to drag and drop them piece by piece to get everything in order. The Table | Sort command sorts a table automatically, in ascending (A–Z, 1–10) or descending (Z–A, 10–1) order, on one or more columns in the table.

In the table with the departure times, the hours are not listed in numerical order. With a small table like this one, it would be simple to use drag-and-drop to rearrange the data, but let's try the sorting function on the data anyway.

GUIDED ACTIVITY 9.8

Sorting and Calculating

1. Highlight the bottom five rows of departure data in the Train Schedule table, not including the headings. Issue the command Table | Sort. The dialog box in Figure 9.23 appears.

FIGURE 9.23
Table|Sort dialog box

Word guesses that Column 1 is the item you wish to sort on. In the station, trains are listed in order of departure time. The default sort order is Ascending, which is A-to-Z, lowest to highest order.

2. Make sure that No Header Row is selected because you have not highlighted the column headings.

3. Change the data Type to Date. Click OK to sort the data.

The formatting of borders and shading may get mixed up as a result of sorting. For this reason, it's a good idea to sort *before* applying the formats to a table.

4. Place the cursor in the bottom-right cell of the table and press [Tab] to add a new row at the bottom of the table.

5. Press [Tab] again and enter Average ticket price in the second cell. Press [Tab] twice to get to the last column.

6. Issue the command Table | Formula. Word guesses that you wish to total, or sum, the numbers above it within the column. Replace the word SUM with AVERAGE and click OK. The average ticket price appears in the cell. Save the table.

    The number representing the average ticket price is not just typed digits. It is actually a field code showing the results of the formula. When you select it, the number turns gray (dimmed). To view the formula behind this number, point the mouse at the shaded area and click the right mouse button to access the Toggle Field Codes from the shortcut menu. You can also press [Alt][F9].

Merging Cells in a Table

Another table feature allows you to merge cells on the same row into one cell. The new cell contains the contents of the original cells and is as wide as the original cells combined.

To merge cells in a table, highlight the cells and select Table | Merge Cells. If cells contain text, such as the cells containing 5 and 6 in Figure 9.24, the result of merging is a single cell twice as tall, with the contents of the original cells in separate paragraphs. Empty cells that are merged, on the other hand, become a single, wide cell without the extra height. To split a cell into two, highlight the cell and issue the command Table | Split Cells.

FIGURE 9.24
When merged, two cells become one cell two lines tall

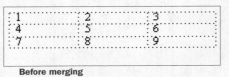

Before merging

After merging

GUIDED ACTIVITY 9.9

Merging Cells

1. Highlight the four cells in the top line of the train schedule, beginning with the day of the week.

2. Select Table | Merge Cells. The result is a single cell stretching across the entire table.

3. Move the title Schedule of Train Departures from Amsterdam to the top, above the day of the week. Center the text in the merged cell.

4. To put blank lines above the table, place the cursor at the top-left corner and press [Enter] several times to move the table lower on the page.

5. Select Table | Table AutoFormat and reapply List 3 to correct the borders. The result should resemble Figure 9.25.

Schedule of Train Departures from Amsterdam
Friday
October 22, 1996

Departure	Destination	Arrival	Price (fl)
8:26	Paris	14:48	65
10:02	Luxembourg City	14:16	36
12:49	Geneva	8:32	87
21:14	Milan	7:29	114
22:07	Copenhagen	9:40	95
	Average ticket price		79.4

6. Save and close the file.

The table is now complete. It was created with Table | Insert Table, where you set up the original dimensions and entered information into the table. You used Table | Insert and Table | Delete to add, delete, and move rows and columns in the table. The Table | Cell Height and Width command allowed you to change the height of rows and the width of columns, as well as to align the table in the center of the page. Format | Borders and Shading and Table | Table AutoFormat put on the finishing touches. Table | Formula and Table | Sort simplified the process of putting departure times in numerical order and averaging the ticket prices. Table 9.1 summarizes the hard-to-remember techniques for tables.

TABLE 9.1
Techniques
for tables

ACTION	RESULT
Tab	Moves cursor forward to the next cell or down to a new row.
Shift Tab	Moves cursor backward to the preceding cell or upward to the previous row.
Ctrl Tab	Moves cursor to a tab set within a cell.
Drag column width	Changes the current column, affects all columns to the right. Entire table remains the same size overall.
Shift and drag column width	Changes the current column, affects also the adjacent column to the right. Entire table remains the same size overall.
Ctrl Shift and drag column width	Changes only the current column. Overall size of the table is affected.

Summary

Tables are rectangular text structures used to contain information that can be presented effectively in a two-dimensional format. Tables are created and placed into documents with the Table button on the toolbar or the Table | Insert Table command. They may be created from scratch or from information that already exists in a document. You may maneuver the cursor through a table with the [Tab] key, with arrow keys, or with the mouse. The intersection of a row and a column in a table is a cell. Text in cells may be formatted like any other text by using the buttons on the toolbar or the Format | Font command.

The Table | Insert and Table | Delete commands are used to add and delete cells, rows, and columns. Rows and columns can be added or deleted one at a time or several at once, depending on what is highlighted before the command is executed.

Once a table contains the desired information, you may change the column width, row height, and alignment with the Table | Cell Height and Width command. These functions are used only to alter the appearance of the table and do not affect the information inside the cells. Cells may be merged to span two or more columns. The appearance of a table may be enhanced by the use of borders and shading, or with a preset AutoFormat. Data in tables may be sorted and totals and averages calculated automatically.

EXERCISE 9.1

A Daily Schedule in the Life of a College Student

1. Insert a table nine columns wide.

2. Highlight the left-most column and insert a new column.

3. Type in your typical daily schedule for Monday through Friday following the model shown in Figure 9.26. If certain days are similar, you may wish to highlight the rows and use the Copy and Paste Rows commands.

FIGURE 9.26
A sample of the daily schedule

day	9	10	11	12	1	2	3	4	5
Monday	get up	ACC	eat breakfast		MGT	Study	play intramurals		
Tuesday	sleep in	get up	FIN	computer lab		ECO	laundry	go shopping	

4. Use the Merge Cells command to allow activities to span several hours.

5. Apply the AutoFormat that you think looks the best. If you don't like the results, click Undo and try again. Apply or remove borders, or format the font to customize the appearance.

6. Place the cursor in the top-left corner of the table and press [Enter]. On the new line above the table, type your name, class time, and date. Save and print.

EXERCISE 9.2

Work Schedule for Crusty's Pizza

1. Insert a table four columns wide.

2. Type the following work schedule into the table, pressing ⎡Tab⎤ to go to the next cell. When you type Kay's split shift, press ⎡Enter⎤ after 12:00 noon and 2:00 p.m. to type the next time in the same cell.

Management	start time	stop time	hours
Kenny	5:00 p.m.	12:00 midnight	7
Curtis	10:00 a.m.	7:00 p.m.	9
Randy	11:00 a.m.	8:00 p.m.	9
Tom	5:00 p.m.	12:00 midnight	7
D. J.	5:00 p.m.	11:00 p.m.	6
Kay	12:00 noon	2:00 p.m.	
	5:00 p.m.	9:00 p.m.	7
Shelly	4:00 p.m.	11:00 p.m.	7
Esperanza	5:00 p.m.	10:00 p.m.	5

3. Select the entire table and apply outside and inside borders.

4. Highlight the start time column. Apply a decimal tab near the center to line up the times. Highlight the stop time column and apply a decimal tab.

5. Center the contents of the hours column. Drag the right gridline to make the hours column narrower.

6. Place the cursor in the top-left corner of the table and press ⎡Enter⎤. On the new line above the table, add the heading Work Schedule for Thursday and center it.

7. Use the Table AutoFormat command and apply a List 4 format.

8. Select the headings row, and center the column headings within the column.

9. Add a new bottom row and add the word Total. In the hours column use the Table I Formula command to add a formula to sum all the above numbers.

10. Highlight the Kenny row and insert a row between Management and Kenny. Move the word Management to the new row. Insert a row above Randy and type Delivery Personnel. Insert a row above Kay and type Inside Personnel.

11. Select the Management row and merge the cells to become one long cell. Remove the extra paragraph mark inside the merged cell. Repeat for the Delivery Personnel and Inside Personnel rows.

12. Highlight the entire table and center it between the margins of the page. To do this, find the choice for Centered in the Row Height tab of the Table | Cell Height and Width dialog box.

13. Place your name, class time, and date on the top of the paper, and print.

EXERCISE 9.3

The Internet: Comparing Internet Access Providers

1. Do some research to find out the following information about the four providers listed plus one local provider in order to complete the table.

2. Insert a table five columns wide.

3. Type in the following information and fill in the correct data.

```
Provider            Monthly Fee   Number of Users   Advantages   Phone Number

Prodigy             ??            ??                ??           1-800-PRODIGY
America Online      ??            ??                ??           1-800-827-6364
CompuServe          ??            ??                ??           1-800-487-6227
Microsoft Network   ??            ??                ??           1-800-386-5550
```

4. Highlight the Number of Users column, and center.

5. Highlight the Monthly Fee column and place a decimal tab near the center to align the numbers.

6. Highlight the Advantages column and apply a ¼-inch indentation to the first line of the paragraphs.

7. Highlight the Prodigy row and insert a row above it. Enter the heading Local Provider and fill in the information.

8. Select the entire table and use Table AutoFormat to apply a List 3 format to the table.

9. Insert a new row at the bottom of the table. In the left column type Total number of users. In the third cell of that row insert a formula with the command Table | Formula that will sum the above numbers.

10. Place the cursor in the top-left corner of the table and press [Enter]. On the new line above the table, type your name, class time, and date. Save and print.

EXERCISE 9.4

Thrill Seeker Tours

1. Insert a table three columns wide.

2. Type the following information into the table, pressing [Tab] to advance to the next cell.

Whale watching 800-WHALING	Open sea excursions to meet the magnificent humpback close up.	April to October
Saltwater fishing 800-ASK-FISH	Party and charter boats from 27 ports provide some of the finest angling in the country.	April to October
Whitewater rafting Inflatable kayaking 800-553-7238	Outdoor adventures in the Berkshires. Beginner and advanced rafting trips available.	April to October
Cross-country skiing Hiking	Over 9 miles of trails. Boardwalk trail runs through a quaking bog.	Year-round

3. Insert a row above the table and enter the following text:

    Massachusetts tours   Description   Best times

4. Insert a column in the table and enter the following price information:

    Price per person
    $20
    $75
    $75
    $3

5. Format the width of all the columns to 1.5".

6. Insert a decimal tab in the center of the price column to align the numbers.

7. Move the price column to the right edge of the table.

8. Sort the tours alphabetically. With the cursor inside the table, issue the command Table | Sort. Since the entire table is automatically highlighted, click the My List Has Header Row option and click OK.

9. Add a new row to the bottom of the table and type Total. In the price column insert a formula that will calculate the total price per person for these tours.

10. Use Table AutoFormat to apply a Contemporary format to the table.

11. Place the cursor in the top-left corner of the table and press [Enter]. On the new line above the table, type your name, class time, and date. Save and print.

Review Questions

 *1. For what kind of information is a table best suited?

  2. What is a cell? What kind of information can be stored in a cell?

 *3. How is a table created from scratch? What kind of information must you supply when creating a table?

  4. What is the default width of a table column in Word?

 *5. What happens when the text typed into a cell is too wide to fit in the cell?

  6. How is the keyboard used to move the cursor forward and backward through a table?

 *7. How is a new row added to the bottom of a table?

  8. How are characters in a cell formatted?

 *9. How are rows and columns added to the middle of a table? What procedure is used to move a row or column?

 10. What elements are found on the ruler when the cursor is within a table?

*11. How are cells in a table merged? When is it appropriate to merge cells in a table? What criteria must cells meet before they can be merged?

 12. How are the row height and column width changed using the mouse? Using the keyboard? What is the default row height?

*13. How do cell borders differ from gridlines? How are they activated? What formatting does AutoFormat do?

 14. Why is the Alignment section of the Table | Cell Height and Width dialog box necessary? Aren't these functions already available?

*15. What are tabs used for within a table? Which keys must be pressed to move the cursor to a tab setting in a table?

 16. What calculations may be performed on numeric data in a table?

*17. If you highlight a table and press the Center button,

  a. The titles will be centered above the columns.

  b. The text will be centered within the columns.

  c. The entire table will be centered between the margins.

  d. All of the above will happen.

 18. To add a new row at the bottom of the table, place the cursor in the bottom right cell and

  a. Press Enter.

  b. Press Tab.

     c. Select Table | Insert Row from the menu.

     d. Select New Row from the shortcut menu.

*19. To remove a single row from a table entirely, select the row and

     a. Press [Del].

     b. Click the Cut button.

     c. Select Edit | Undo.

     d. Select Delete Rows.

20. To change the width of a highlighted column,

     a. Select Format | Table.

     b. Drag the gridlines.

     c. Drag the triangles on the ruler.

     d. Do all of the above.

Key Terms

Cell	Gridline
Cell mark	Table

Using Tables to Create a Résumé

Create a résumé by inserting a table into an empty document. Use merged cells to create the wide cells (like the one containing the Objective) and the cells to the right of Education, Work Experience, Honors and Awards, Computer Skills, and References. In the sample résumé in Figure D.1, the gridlines show the cell widths. Do not include borders in your résumé. You may include a bulleted list for subpoints within the right column. Be sure to carefully proofread your document; then print and save as *Application D*. Absolutely no mistakes are tolerated on a résumé.

FIGURE D.1
Sample résumé layout

FIRST AND LAST NAMES Street address either here or below City, State Zip Phone number		
Present address Street City, State Zip Phone number		Permanent address Street City, State Zip Phone number
Objective: to obtain a full-time position with XXX company working in the field in which you are trained		
EDUCATION		
WORK EXPERIENCE		
HONORS AND AWARDS		
COMPUTER SKILLS		
REFERENCES		

Desktop Publishing

The word processing expertise you have gained in earlier units enables you create many useful documents. By utilizing Word's ability to produce text in several columns and to display pictures, you can create even complex and professional documents. You do not need to purchase and learn to use a separate desktop publishing program to create newsletters and brochures. This unit will tell you how to create such documents with multiple columns as well as how to insert pictures into a document and adjust them to your needs.

While Word's table feature provides the capability of printing parallel, side-by-side columns of information, some types of documents such as newspapers, brochures, and newsletters require you to enter text into "snaking" columns on a page, where the text flows from the top to bottom of one column, and then from top to bottom in the next column. Newspaper-style columns are easy to create and format. Text can be entered directly into multiple-column format and will automatically scroll from one column to the next. If changes need to be made in the text, the word processor reorganizes the columns to reflect the changes in much the same way that it moves text from one page to another when lines are added or deleted. The Newsletter Wizard incorporates many of the elements explained in this unit.

How good can a newsletter or brochure be without pictures to create interest? You probably have an idea from the junk mail that crosses your desk. Word makes it easy to insert pictures and graphics directly into documents. There they may be selected, cropped, and resized to fit the space available, and then placed on the page so that text flows around them. Word has several sources for pictures for your documents. In addition, you can place pictures from numerous other sources into Word documents through the simple process of cutting and pasting.

Learning Objectives

At the completion of this unit you should know

1. how to place a document into newspaper-style columns,

2. how to place part of a document into several columns when the rest is regular single-column text,

3. how to balance and manipulate the format of the columns,

4. several sources for graphics and pictures,

5. how to insert pictures into a document,

6. how to manipulate and position pictures and graphics in a document,

7. how to use text as graphic images.

Important Commands

File | Page Setup

Format | Columns

Format | Drop Cap

Format | Frame

Format | Picture

Insert | Break

Insert | Frame

Insert | Object

Insert | Picture

Tools | Options | View

Columns

We use columns in documents for several reasons. In newspapers and magazines, we find it is much easier to align articles and advertisements in multiple-column format. This particular style gives greater flexibility when laying out pages. Since more headlines and articles can fit on a single page, the page is more inviting for the reader to browse here and there.

Also, the reader's eye can scan narrow columns more quickly than lines the width of a full page. This means that more text can be read in the same amount of time if it is printed in multiple-column format. However, when columns are less than about two inches wide, the text in them begins to look choppy because of loss of continuity in sentences and paragraphs. There is an optimum range of widths that provides the easiest and fastest reading, usually 30 to 65 letters across (roughly 5 to 10 words).

A picture positioned between columns of text illustrating the content of the text is a very efficient means of conveying information. The combination of text and graphics not only increases eye-appeal and makes the page more inviting and interesting, it can also help the reader remember the point of the document. For these reasons, many publications use multiple-column format exclusively. Word allows you to create a document in multiple-column format as well as to change existing documents to multiple-column format.

Creating Columns

You may enter text directly into columns, or take existing text and change it into multiple-column format. Word provides a button on the Standard toolbar to format the document into several columns. Click on the Columns button and drag to highlight the number of columns desired, as in Figure 10.1. If nothing is highlighted before you drag on the button, the entire document is placed into columns.

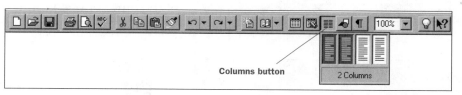

FIGURE 10.1
Inserting multiple columns

Columns button

The width of the columns is determined by dividing the distance between the margins by the number of columns and allowing for a space of one-half inch (as a default) between the columns.

After text is placed into several columns, Normal view displays it in a single, long, narrow column on the left of the work area. While Normal view shows a narrow column width and is easy to use for text entry and editing, it does not display the columns as they will print.

Page Layout view, on the other hand, displays the columns side by side. Because text flows from the bottom of one column to the top of the next, Page Layout view may be awkward for text entry and editing, but it is excellent for final viewing to see the format of the columns on the page.

Changing Column Widths

The widths of columns are determined by three factors: the margins, the number of columns, and the amount of space between columns. Changing any of these elements affects the column width. The ruler, shown in Figure 10.2, displays markers that may be dragged to change the settings for the document. Dragging these markers left or right affects the widths of the columns in the document, or the width of the space between the columns.

FIGURE 10.2
*Ruler with equal
column markers*

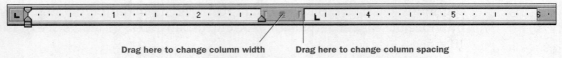

Drag here to change column width   Drag here to change column spacing

Columns may also be formatted to unequal column widths through the Format | Columns dialog box, shown in Figure 10.3. This dialog box allows you to specify the exact widths of the columns and the space between them. Clicking the Line Between check box places vertical lines between the columns. To see the columns and vertical lines as they will appear when printed, select Page Layout view or Print Preview.

FIGURE 10.3
*Format Columns
dialog box*

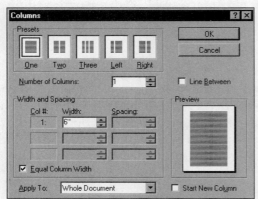

To remove the multiple-column formatting and return to a single, wide column, click the Columns button and drag to highlight only one column. Another method is to select Format | Columns and set the number of columns to 1.

GUIDED ACTIVITY 10.1

Creating Columns

1. Start Word and open *GA10 Columns*.

2. Click on the Columns button and drag the highlight across two columns. Press **PgDn** a few times to see the long, single column.

   The ruler shows the width of the two columns with column markers, as in Figure 10.4.

3. Click on the Page Layout View button at the bottom of the screen, or select View | Page Layout to see the two columns side by side, as in Figure 10.5. Press **PgDn** a few times to view the bottom of the first column. Nothing happens when you press **PgDn** again to see the next part of the text. Because of the way it shows the flow of the text, Page Layout view is best for seeing the format of the column, but it is awkward for editing text.

4. Press **Ctrl** **Home** to jump to the beginning of the document. Click on the Columns button and drag the highlight across three columns. Notice the change in the width of the columns, both in the text and on the ruler.

5. These columns are really too narrow, and the paragraphs are too choppy to be read easily. By changing the margins we can make the columns wider.

FIGURE 10.4
*Multiple columns
in Normal view*

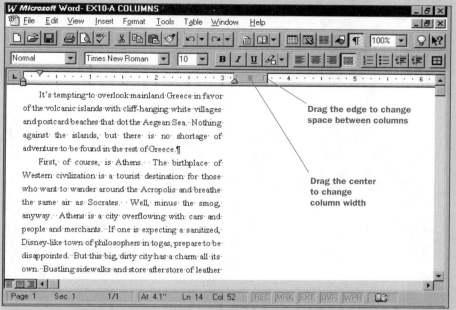

FIGURE 10.5
*Page Layout view
showing columns
side by side*

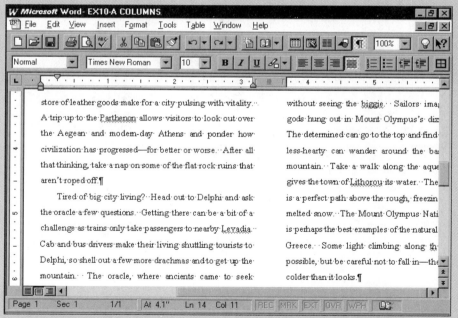

6. Carefully place the mouse pointer at the left edge of the ruler between the indentation markers. When you see the two-headed arrow, drag to make the margin .5" wide. You can click both mouse buttons to see the measurements. Repeat for the right margin. The width of the columns adjusts to use the space available. (If you want, you can set the margins in the File | Page Setup dialog box.)

If you drag the indentation triangles on the ruler by mistake, the paragraphs in the column will be indented. This also affects the width of the text within the column, but only one paragraph at a time.

7. Drag the edge of a column marker to make the space between the columns narrower. Drag the center crosshatched area of a column marker to change the widths of the columns.

8. Select Format | Columns. In the dialog box, click on Left to change to two unequal column widths. Click on the box next to Line Between to place lines between the columns. Click OK.

There are now two columns, the left one narrower than the right, with a vertical line drawn between them.

9. Change to Normal view. The vertical line disappears, and the text is displayed in one long column. The column width of the text does not reflect the width of either the narrower left column or the wider right column. The ruler still reflects the actual column width, however, as shown in Figure 10.6.

10. Change back to Page Layout view to see the unequal columns just as they will print. Drag the crosshatched area on the column marker to the right so that the left column is roughly twice as wide as the right. This changes the unequal column widths so that the left column is wider and the right column is narrower.

FIGURE 10.6
Unequal columns in Normal view

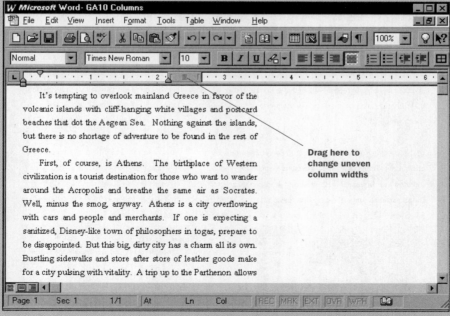

Separating Sections

Usually, an entire document does not appear in multiple-column format. For example, most documents have a title that appears centered above the text; the title does not appear in multiple-column format, even when the text does. Such a title on a newspaper or newsletter is termed a *masthead* (from sailors' practice of raising their flag to the top of the mast).

To create several column formats like this within a single document, it is necessary to break the document into separate sections. Each section, separated by a *section break*, may be formatted to have a different number of columns, different margin settings, or a different orientation.

Changing the Columns in One Section

To change only a section of a document to a different number of columns, you must first highlight the section. Click the Columns button and select the desired number of columns, and the column formatting is applied immediately to the highlighted portion of the text without affecting the rest of the document.

Behind the scenes, so to speak, Word has placed a section break above and below the highlighted area. These section breaks appear in Normal view as double lines across the text, labeled End of Section, as in Figure 10.7, or they may be viewed in Page Layout view by clicking the Show/Hide ¶ button.

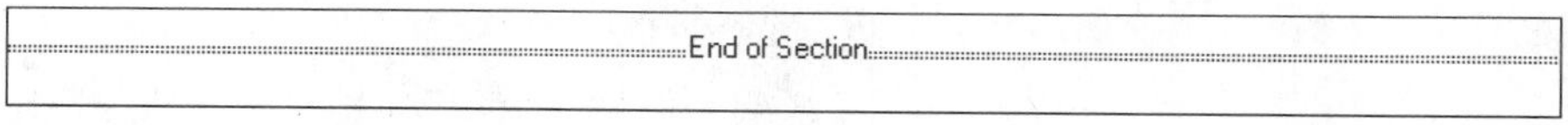

FIGURE 10.7
Section break in
Normal view

End of Section

A section break is inserted to separate those portions of the document that have a certain column or page format from those that have another. Section breaks may be manually inserted in a document by selecting Insert | Break. Each section may be formatted separately, without affecting other sections. Sections are formatted with settings in the File | Page Setup dialog box as well as with Format | Columns.

Word makes it simple to create a masthead in one section of a document and continue with several columns of text in another section on the same page. If you begin with the multiple-column text, as you did in Guided Activity 10.1, you can later highlight the text for the masthead and format it to a single column, and Word will insert a section break for you. If you are starting a document from scratch, you may want to first create the masthead, and then select the Format | Columns dialog box and specify the number of columns, changing the Apply To setting from Whole Document to This Point Forward. Word automatically inserts a section break and formats the following section for the desired number of columns.

A common problem with multiple columns is that the last column may not reach the bottom of the page to end evenly. When a multiple-column format document ends in the middle of a page, the columns on that page should ordinarily be the same length. This is known as ending with a balanced page. To balance a page, position the cursor after the last text on the page and insert a section break. (You may also have to add or delete a few words of text or break one paragraph into two, to create an equal number of lines in each column.)

GUIDED ACTIVITY 10.2

Creating an Article with a Headline

1. Place the cursor at the beginning of the document. Type `Back Doors into Greece` and press `Enter`. Type the ***byline*** by `Thomas Bartlett` and press `Enter`. Format the title to 32 points bold, and the byline to 14 points bold.

2. Move the mouse pointer to the left margin area and click and drag to highlight the headline and the byline and the blank line below. Click on the Columns button and drag across one column only.

3. Change to Normal view to see the section break that Word has applied. Change back to Page Layout view.

4. With the headline and byline still highlighted, click the Right Align button and apply a border below the text.

5. See the results of your work in Print Preview, and then close to return to the document.

   It is also simple to begin with the headline or masthead, and then create the multiple-column text.

6. Create a new document. Select View | Normal.

7. Enter the title `Desktop Publishing News`. Center the title at the top of the page. Press `Enter`, and then type the date and press `Enter`. Right-align the date by pressing `Ctrl` `R` or by clicking the Right Align button on the toolbar. Click on the Border button and apply top and bottom borders to the date paragraph.

8. Put the cursor below the ruling line (border) under the date paragraph. Left-align the current paragraph by pressing `Ctrl` `L` or by clicking on the Left Align button on the toolbar.

9. Select the command Format | Columns and select 2 next to Number of Columns. Change the setting next to Apply To from Whole Document to This Point Forward and click OK. A section break appears across the document.

10. Enter the following text.

    `Using multiple columns allows you to place several small articles on the page instead of one long one. Add interest by having a headline, a phrase or sentence as a teaser, and then the main article.  Divide out part of a long article and place it in a sidebar.  Include a pull quote or illustration.`

```
Using multiple columns gives the page the flexibility of
having several elements on a single page.  Having a num-
ber of places for the eye to land makes the page more
inviting and adds to the likelihood that people will actu-
ally read your article, rather than skimming on by.
```

11. Select Page Layout view to see the columns as they will print. The text appears in a single narrow column on the left side of the page.

12. To balance the text in two columns, insert a section break at the end of the document. To do this, position the cursor at the end of the document. Press ⏎Enter to place the cursor in an empty paragraph. Select Insert | Break, fill in the option button next to Continuous, and click OK.

    The columns are now balanced on the page. If you add or delete text, the column lengths will adjust to remain approximately equal.

13. Close the document and return to *GA10 Columns.*

Pictures

Besides offering the obvious advantage of providing something to look at on the page, ***pictures*** can greatly enhance the presentation of information in a document. Icons, graphs, charts, drawings, images, lines, and shapes can all be used to illustrate a complex topic and enhance the reader's comprehension.

One process of inserting pictures is familiar to you. You already know that items that are cut or copied from the Edit menu are placed in the Clipboard. The contents of the Clipboard can then be pasted to the location of the cursor in your document. Therefore, any picture viewed on screen that can be copied to the Clipboard can also be pasted into Word. This paste procedure has been demonstrated in several Guided Activities that you have completed in previous units.

Another method for inserting pictures is to import them with the Insert | Picture command. There are several sources for pictures that can be imported into a document. First, Microsoft provides over a hundred selections of ***clip art***, professionally drawn pictures or images that may be used in any Office program. Clip art also comes from many other manufacturers and in various file formats. In addition, anything on a printed page can be placed on a device called a ***scanner***, where its image is converted into digits, brought into the computer, and finally reproduced electronically on the screen. Further, if the images are fairly simple, you may create your own designs in the Paint accessory in Windows or with the drawing tools on the Drawing toolbar.

Pictures in a document can be resized (scaled) or cropped. After a picture has been inserted and formatted to look the way it is supposed to, it can be moved freely just like the text around it or positioned at a certain place on the page. If a picture is fixed on a page at a certain location, any text will flow around the picture (this is called ***run-around*** text). This is an extremely effective presentation style because the text that describes the picture surrounds the picture rather than being above or below it. However, text should not flow around both sides of a picture unless the text is formatted into two columns; otherwise, the reader may become confused about how to read the text on each side of the picture.

With all of the advantages, pictures in a document have a disadvantage. Because of the memory they consume, they make the document scroll more slowly. When you scroll through a document that does not contain pictures, text in the work area scrolls smoothly. Even if you are working in Page Layout view, the delay is short. When a picture is inserted into a document, however, the computer has to work hard to keep the image updated on the screen so that it will look right. When you scroll through a document, there is a noticeable pause while the computer "refreshes" the picture that is being displayed.

To avoid this problem, once a picture looks the way you want it to, select Tools | Options | View and check the box next to *Picture Placeholders*. A box the size of the picture will be displayed in the document, but the contents of the picture will not. The document will scroll much more smoothly. Although an empty box rather than the picture is displayed, the picture is still in the document and will print correctly. To view the picture, select Print Preview or select Tools | Options | View to turn Picture Placeholders off.

Inserting Word Clip Art

Microsoft Office provides nearly 100 professionally drawn clip art images, stored in separate files in the *Clipart* folder. Do not use the command File | Open to access a clip art file; rather, use the command Insert | Picture to *import* the picture into a Word document.

The Insert | Picture dialog box, shown in Figure 10.8, closely resembles the File | Open dialog box in that file names, drives, and folders are listed. One difference is that the files listed are of several types, not just Word documents. The clip art pictures packaged with Office are primarily *metafiles*. This type of graphic may be used in every Windows software application. A few of the files are another type of file called a *bitmap*. Bitmaps may be created in Paint, a Windows accessory. If you have

FIGURE 10.8
*Insert Picture
dialog box*

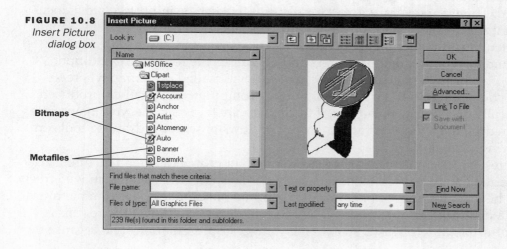

a PostScript printer, you can purchase pictures as **Encapsulated PostScript**, or **EPS**, files. The advantage of this file type is that they may be made any size and print very quickly. Scanners produce **TIFF files**, which stands for Tagged Image File Format. To see only files with a certain extension, change the selection under Files of Type.

During installation, Office creates a folder named *Clipart* where it stores the picture files. You may need to switch drives to find the folder where the *MSOffice* and *Clipart* folders are located. Once you have the correct folder on screen, you see an alphabetical list of clip art files, beginning with *1stplace*. Word makes it convenient to preview the graphics before they are actually inserted into the document. Highlight the name of the desired file, and then click the Preview button on the dialog box to display a **thumbnail** image of the picture.

GUIDED ACTIVITY 10.3

Inserting Clip Art into Text

1. Continue with the document from the previous Guided Activity.

2. Place your cursor on the last line of the document.

3. From the menu select Insert | Picture.

4. A dialog box that looks much like the one used to open documents is displayed. This box allows you to navigate through the folders and drives available to you to find graphics files. The clip art files should be stored in the *Clipart* folder. If you cannot find this folder, your teacher will instruct you.

5. Select one of the clip art files by highlighting it. If you do not see a preview of the image, click the Preview button to display a thumbnail. Scroll down in the list of files and click on another file name to preview its picture. The image in the preview box changes to display the second picture.

6. Select the file *Legal* and click OK to insert the picture into the document. You may instead double-click the file name to insert the picture directly into the document. The picture is inserted at the location of the cursor.

   Another type of graphic, bitmaps, also comes with Office. These have a different icon in the list of files and, if you display the details rather than the preview, you can see them labeled as bitmaps.

7. Press [Enter] once or twice and then insert another picture into the document. Issue the command Insert | Picture.

8. On the drop-down box, Files of Type, select Windows Bitmaps. Now only the bitmaps are displayed in the list of files.

9. Select *Auto* and click OK to insert the picture into the document.

Modifying Pictures

When pictures are first placed into a document, they become part of the text. The line spacing of the paragraph containing the picture expands to fit the picture. If the paragraph is centered, the picture within it is also centered. If text is inserted above or to the left of the picture, the picture moves down or to the right. Although the picture is inserted within the flow of the text in a document, pressing [Backspace] will *not* remove it. Rather, you must first select the picture, and then delete it.

Selecting the picture is done by clicking on it with the mouse or using the [Shift] and arrow keys. You can distinguish text in a document that is highlighted because the color of the text is different from the color of the text that is not highlighted. When a picture is highlighted, however, Word draws a nonprinting border around it and displays eight *sizing handles*, one at each corner and one in the middle of each edge of the picture, as in Figure 10.9. Besides helping you see if the picture is highlighted, these handles are used for three types of changes: sizing, cropping, and deleting.

Scaling a picture changes the size of the image. To scale a picture with the mouse, drag a sizing handle to a new location. If you drag a sizing handle that is in the middle of an edge, only that edge will be affected. Dragging a sizing handle at a corner of the picture, however, allows you to change both intersecting edges at the same time.

If you drag only one edge of the picture, you will distort the image. If you are scaling an abstract object, such distortion may be acceptable. However, if you are sizing a realistic image, such as a picture of someone's face, you probably want to keep the picture proportional. A good idea when scaling is to drag only the corner sizing handles to keep the picture proportional.

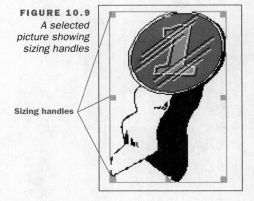

FIGURE 10.9
A selected picture showing sizing handles

Sizing handles

Pictures may also be scaled to an exact percentage from the Format | Picture dialog box. Scaling percentages smaller than 100% will decrease the image size; percentages larger than 100% will increase it.

To *crop* a picture means to remove unwanted parts of it by changing its dimensions without changing the proportions of the image. A picture is cropped when you want only a portion of the entire image to appear in the document. You may crop a picture with the mouse or use a dialog box to specify the exact dimensions to be removed.

To crop a picture with the mouse, hold [Shift] and drag the sizing handle of the edge to be cropped to increase or decrease that edge. If you drag the edge toward the picture, part of the picture will be hidden. If you drag the edge away from the picture, the area you add to the picture will be filled with white space (an empty area).

Pictures can also be cropped using the Format | Picture dialog box. While not as visual as using the mouse, it may be a more precise method. Select Format | Picture, and enter the measurements to crop from each edge of the picture.

GUIDED ACTIVITY 10.4

Scaling, Cropping, and Deleting a Picture

1. Highlight the legal picture, and eight sizing handles appear. The handles are small squares at each corner and at the middle of each edge. (Since the picture has a black edge, the handles appear white.)

2. Drag the sizing handle at the bottom-right corner down and out until the picture is about twice its original height. As you drag, the status bar displays the scaling percentage. (Double is 200%.)

   The picture stays in proportion because you sized it from a corner rather than from an edge.

3. Change to Normal view and press twice to see a larger view of the picture.

4. Select the auto picture and drag the corner sizing handle until it has approximately doubled in size.

   Bitmaps are made of tiny "bits" of color. You can see that these squares are enlarged, and the design has lost its sharpness and has become jagged, especially on the diagonal lines. Because of this, bitmaps are best used at their original size or smaller.

5. Drag the sizing handle in the middle of the right edge to the right side of the screen. This causes the picture to be stretched out of proportion horizontally. The small squares of color are each stretched into rectangles.

6. Select the legal picture and drag the sizing handle in the center of the bottom edge. As you drag, notice that the status bar reflects the change in proportion. Stretch the picture until the status bar says Scaling: 250% High. Using the edge sizing handles to size a realistic picture is generally not a good idea.

7. Select Format | Picture.

   Notice that, under Scaling, the width is around 200% but the height is about 250% of the original size, as shown in Figure 10.10. When a picture is in proportion, these values are identical.

FIGURE 10.10
Scaling shown in the Format/Picture dialog box

Picture	? X
Crop From	**Scaling**
Left: 0"	Width: 200.9%	OK
Right: 0"	Height: 250.9%	Cancel
Top: 0"	**Size**	Reset
Bottom: 0"	Width: 2.3"	Frame
	Height: 2.88"	
Original Size	
Width: 1.15"	Height: 1.15"

8. Enter 150 in both the Scaling Height and Width boxes and click on the OK button. (You need not enter the % sign.)

The picture is exactly one-and-one-half times its original height and width.

When you crop a picture with the mouse, the mouse pointer shows a new shape, and the status bar at the bottom of the screen displays the amount of the picture being removed in inches. Let's crop the black edge off the picture.

9. While holding down [Shift], drag the sizing handle on the bottom-right corner of the picture up and toward the left. As you drag, the status bar shows the measurement being cropped.

10. While holding down [Shift], drag the sizing handle in the top-left corner to crop the other sides.

The Format | Picture dialog box reflects the amount of cropping, shown in Figure 10.11 (your numbers may differ slightly). For more specific measurements, you may specify the amount of cropping by typing into the dialog box.

FIGURE 10.11
Cropping shown in the Format | Picture dialog box

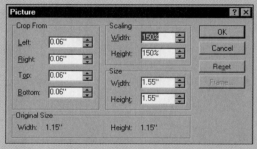

11. To restore the picture to its original uncropped and unscaled size, select Format | Picture and click on the Reset button and then OK. The size is placed back to 100% of original, and crop values are set to zero.

12. Select the auto picture, and then press [Del]. The picture is removed from the document.

Positioning Pictures

When a picture has been inserted into a document, it is treated like a single character within the text. The picture causes automatic line spacing to enlarge to accommodate the height of the picture. Text on the same line appears very small next to the picture or is placed above or below the picture. How do we get the text to flow along the side of the picture?

One way is to place the picture into a table, and then put the text into the cell next to the picture. This works well with small amounts of text such as a caption that would always be located next to the picture. To get the paragraphs in the columns to flow around the text, however, you must use another method. Or you may wish to place a picture in a certain location on a page, such as a logo or letterhead on stationery. To position pictures at a specific location on the page or to have the text flow around a picture, you must first enclose it within a special boundary called a *frame*. This may be done by selecting the picture and issuing the command Insert | Frame.

To use the frame effectively, you must work in Page Layout view. If you are working in Normal view when you insert a frame, the program prompts you to switch to Page Layout view. When the frame is applied and the view is changed to Page Layout view, the picture is surrounded by a crosshatched border and text immediately flows around it, as you can see in Figure 10.12. Whenever the mouse pointer is on the crosshatched border, it turns into a four-headed arrow.

GUIDED ACTIVITY 10.5

Positioning Pictures

1. Highlight the clip art picture. Place it into a frame by selecting Insert | Frame or by clicking on the Drawing button to display the Drawing toolbar and then clicking the Insert Frame button on the toolbar. When the program prompts you to switch to Page Layout view, choose Yes.

2. Drag the framed picture to the center of the page. Notice how text flows out of the way.

3. Use the dialog box to center the picture exactly on the page. Select Format | Frame, change the horizontal and vertical settings to Center, and click OK.

4. Change the view back to Normal view. The picture is not shown centered, although Print Preview and Page Layout view show that it will be centered when you print it.

5. Click on the Page Layout view button at the bottom of the screen, and then choose Whole Page from the Zoom Control box at the top right. Now you are able to see and edit the whole page at once in Page Layout view.

6. Drag the framed picture to the bottom-right corner of the page. Select Format | Frame and set Horizontal Position to Right Relative to Page, and then set Vertical Position to Bottom Relative to Page. Click OK. A framed picture may appear anywhere on the page, even within the margins.

7. Move the picture back within the margins, and scale it so it is approximately as wide as the right column.

8. Return your document to the normal size by selecting 100% from the Zoom Control box. Scroll to view the top of the page.

Many newspapers and newsletters use pictures or a bit of text to add contrast and attract interest to the page. A sentence or phrase pulled out of the text and set apart with a different format is called a ***pull quote***. Pictures and pull quotes (often set in a larger and contrasting font) may be placed into a frame and positioned within a column or between two columns, and the rest of the text will run around the frame.

9. Place the cursor to the left of the byline `by Thomas Bartlett.`

10. Issue the command Insert | Frame, and then drag a rectangle about 1" by 3" on top of the text in the center of the page, something like Figure 10.12.

FIGURE 10.12
A frame ready for a pull quote

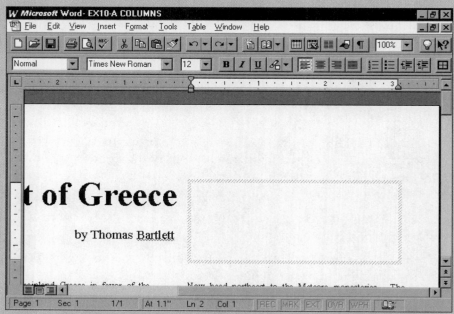

The frame appears with a crosshatched border, and the text headline and byline move out of the way. The cursor is blinking inside the frame. Enter the following sentence.

`One traveler's guide to making the most of Greece`

11. Format the text in the frame to 16-point Arial font.

12. Click on the edge of the frame and move it up or down so the bottom line is aligned with the byline.

Creating Pictures from Text

Another source for graphic images is to create a picture out of text. Word can help you create graphic images with text three ways:

- Drop caps
- Graphic fonts
- WordArt

Word can automatically format a paragraph to have the first letter or word appear as a ***drop cap*** (dropped capital) with the command Format | Drop Cap, as shown in the dialog box in Figure 10.13. To create this effect, Word changes the size of the first letter or word in a paragraph, and then sets it into a frame by itself. The framed letter or word may be positioned either within the paragraph (dropped) or out in the margin.

In another case, enlarging a single character and perhaps placing it in a frame can make an eye-catcher. The examples in Figure 10.14 demonstrate how they can be used. Couldn't a question mark in an interesting font several inches high make people curious? Certain fonts are collections of pictures. To select one of these pictures, insert the character using the Insert | Symbol program to see what pictures are available. Characters in the Wingdings font, when formatted to a large point size or substituted for a letter, might add interest to a sign or logo.

Word also can create special effects with text using the built-in program Microsoft WordArt 2.0. This program is accessed through the command Insert | Object. The screen changes to display the menus and toolbars for this new program, as shown in Figure 10.15, rather than the usual Word menus and toolbars, although you still see your Word document on screen.

FIGURE 10.13
Format|Drop Cap dialog box

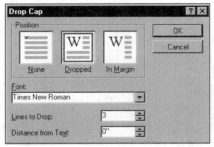

FIGURE 10.14
Two uses of text as graphic images

FIGURE 10.15
WordArt changes the toolbars and menus

Drop-down list of text shapes

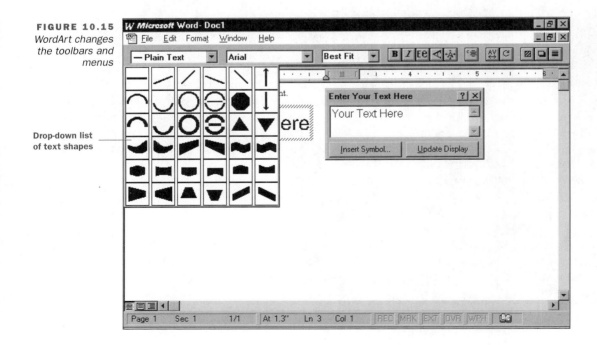

After typing your text into the small window, you may change several attributes, including the shape of the text (shown in the dropped-down box in Figure 10.15), the font, and the color. Word allows you to see the results of your work as a graphic image in a crosshatched border (a frame) within the document. To return to the usual Word screen, click anywhere in the document. WordArt images may later be edited by simply double-clicking on the image.

GUIDED ACTIVITY 10.6

Using WordArt and Drop Caps

1. Place the cursor within the first paragraph of text. Issue the command Format | Drop Cap.

2. Click on the Dropped selection. Change the font to Arial for contrast. Click OK.

   Word prompts you to change to Page Layout view if you are not already working in it. The dropped capital appears in a frame with a crosshatched border, and the rest of the paragraph flows around the frame. Because the paragraphs are indented, this looks bad. Remove the dropped capital letter by issuing the command Format | Drop Cap and clicking on None and then OK.

3. Place the cursor at the end of the document. Open the WordArt program by issuing the command Insert | Object, and select Microsoft WordArt 2.0 from the list.

4. Type in the phrase When Wanderlust Hits . . . to replace Your Text Here. Click the Update Display button to display the new words in the document.

5. Click on the arrow next to the font box in the toolbar at the top of the screen to display the drop-down list box of fonts. The fonts are listed in alphabetical order. Use the up and down arrow keys to preview the look of each font. Select the one that best communicates the message.

6. Drop down the list box containing Plain Text by clicking on the down arrow. The choices for the shape of the text are shown in Figure 10.15. Click on the second selection, an upward slanting line. Try several other selections to see their effects.

7. Click on the other buttons on the WordArt toolbar to see the effects each has on the WordArt image.

8. To exit WordArt and return to the document, click anywhere in the text of the document.

   The WordArt menus and toolbar disappear, and the usual Word screen returns. Back in the document, the WordArt image may be sized, cropped, and framed just like any other picture. Print and close the document.

Summary

Some documents and many publications require a multiple-column format. Column format is preferable to full-page width for several reasons. Pages may be laid out more readily, are easier to read, and more effectively combine text and pictures with the use of columns.

Word allows you to create documents in multiple-column format by separating the portion of the document with section breaks and by using the Format | Columns command. This dialog box allows you to specify the number of columns, the width of the columns, and the space between columns. Documents may have more than one section, each with a different number of columns. These sections are separated with section breaks. A typical problem with multiple columns is that they become uneven on the last page of the section or document. Columns can be balanced by inserting another section break at the end of the text on the page or in the section, or by adding a few words or lines to a column. This will force the columns on the last page to be approximately the same length.

Word allows you to insert pictures into documents. These pictures can be graphic images from various publishers, scanned images, or images you yourself made out of text. Scanned images and clip art are inserted with the Insert | Picture command. WordArt objects are inserted via Insert | Object, and drop caps are created with the Format | Drop Caps command.

Pictures in a document may be cropped or scaled using either the mouse or the Format | Picture command. The mouse allows you to visually crop or scale a picture and is easier to use, whereas the Format | Picture dialog box permits more precise measurements.

A picture can be framed with the Insert | Frame command so that text will flow around it. In Page Layout view, a framed picture may be dragged anywhere on the page, or it may be positioned precisely by using the Format | Frame command. This dialog box allows you to set the exact horizontal and vertical position of the frame on the page. If there is text at the location of the framed picture, the text will wrap around the picture.

EXERCISE 10.1

A Day in the Life of a College Student

1. Begin with a new document. Type three or four paragraphs about the recent activities of your club.

2. Change the margins to .5 on every side.

3. Drag on the Columns button to change to three-column format.

4. Click on the Page Layout View button to see the columns side by side. Add a section break if necessary to balance the columns. To see how the whole page looks, click on the Print Preview button, and then Close to return to the document.

5. Place the cursor at the top of the document. Enter and format the masthead of your newsletter, leaving a blank line before the article text:

```
Name of Newsletter
date published
```

6. Highlight those two lines plus the blank line and drag on the Columns button to change back to one-column format. Format the name of the newsletter as large as you can without the text wrapping to two lines. Format the date to 10 points and add borders above and below it with the Borders buttons.

7. Click on the Normal View button to see the section break that was automatically added between the different column formats.

8. Place the cursor at the end of the document and press [Enter]. Select Insert | Picture and choose an appropriate picture from the *Clipart* folder.

9. Size the file so that it is about as wide as one of the columns. Do this by dragging on the corner sizing handles.

10. With the picture selected, insert a frame using the command Insert | Frame. When prompted to switch to Page Layout view, click Yes.

11. Click the Zoom Control and change from 100% to Whole Page.

12. Place the mouse pointer over the crosshatched frame and, when it turns to a four-pointed arrow, drag the picture to the center of the center column. If the text does not flow around the picture automatically, select Format | Frame and specify Around text-wrapping.

13. On the Zoom Control menu, change back to Page Width and view the top of the first page.

14. Add a box for coming attractions. Place the cursor at the end of the document and press [Enter]. Select Insert | Frame and drag on the bottom right side of the page to insert an empty frame approximately the width of the right-hand column. This frame should be aligned with the right and bottom margins.

15. In the frame, type the text of upcoming activities and format to a contrasting font, 18-point, left-aligned.

16. Place a border around the upcoming attractions by selecting and clicking the Outside Border button.

17. Balance the columns by placing the cursor on a blank line at the end of the document, selecting Insert | Break, and clicking Continuous.

18. Save as *EX10-1 Done* and print.

EXERCISE 10.2

Crusty's Pizza

1. Open the file *EX10-2 Columns*.

2. Format the text to 16 points, and set the line spacing to 1.5 lines (the shortcut key is [Ctrl][5]).

3. Place the cursor at the top of the document. Select Insert | Picture and double-click on the file name *Party*.

4. Select all the text after the picture and before the last blank line. Drag on the Columns button to create two columns.

5. Click on the Page Layout View button to see the columns side-by-side. Click on the Normal View button to see the columns all on the left side separated by section breaks from the top and bottom portions of the document.

6. Place the cursor to the right of the party picture and press [Enter] to get a blank line.

7. Issue the command Insert | Object and select Microsoft WordArt 2.0. In the text box that appears, type Grand Opening and press [Enter]. On the next line type Crusty's Pizza.

8. Still in WordArt, click down the list of possible text shapes and click the second-to-last choice on the bottom row, called Slant Up. Click elsewhere in the document to return to the normal menus and toolbars.

9. Drag on the sizing handles around the WordArt image till the picture is about 4" across. View the whole page in Print Preview, and then click Close to return to the document.

10. Click on the party picture to get sizing handles. Select Insert | Frame, and when prompted to change to Page Layout view, click Yes.

11. Place the mouse pointer over the crosshatched frame until it turns into a four-headed arrow. Drag the picture to the right side of the page, underneath the slanted words.

12. Place the cursor to the left of the line reading Try these tasty temptations, and insert a break so that these words go to the right-hand column. To do this, select Insert | Break, choose Column Break, and click OK.

13. Create a coupon. Place the cursor on a blank line at the end of the document. Select the command Insert | Frame, and drag to make a rectangle to cover the lower portion of the page.

14. Inside the empty frame, type the following text and format it larger and centered.

Grand Opening Special
2 Large Two-Topping Pizzas for only $12.99 + Tax
Expires 10/31/97

15. Select Format | Frame and change the Height to Auto to adjust the frame to fit the text. Select Center Relative To Margin and Bottom Relative To Margin. Click OK.

16. Click on the framed coupon and place a dotted line border around it. To do this, select Format | Borders and Shading, click on the dotted line style, click Box, and click OK.

17. Save as *EX10-2 Done* and print.

EXERCISE 10.3

The Internet

1. Open the file *EX10-3 Columns*.

2. Format the text to 16 points, and make the line spacing 1.5 lines (the shortcut key is [Ctrl][5]). Change the margins to 1" on all sides.

3. Place the cursor at the top of the document. Select Insert | Picture and double-click on the file *Computer*.

4. Select all the text after the picture and before the last blank line. Drag on the Columns button to create two columns.

5. Click on the Page Layout View button to see the columns side by side. Click on the Normal View button to see the columns all on the left side separated by sections breaks from the top and bottom portions of the document.

6. Place the cursor to the right of the computer picture and press [Enter] to get a blank line.

7. Issue the command Insert | Object, and select Microsoft WordArt 2.0. In the text box that appears, type Get Wired and press [Enter]. On the next line type Classes in Online Computing.

8. Still in WordArt, click down the list of possible text shapes and click the Wave 1 choice (third choice on the fourth row). Click elsewhere in the document to return to the normal menus and toolbars.

9. Click on the computer picture and drag a corner sizing handle till the picture is scaled to about 250%. View the whole page in Print Preview, and then click Close to return to the document.

10. Click on the computer picture to get sizing handles. Select Insert | Frame and, when prompted to change to Page Layout view, click Yes.

11. Place the mouse pointer over the crosshatched frame until it turns into a four-headed arrow. Drag the picture to the right side of the WordArt.

12. Make the space between the columns smaller. To do this, drag on the column marker or select Format | Columns, specify .3" for the spacing between columns, and click OK.

13. Create a coupon. Place the cursor on a blank line at the end of the document. Select the command Insert | Frame and drag to make a rectangle to cover the lower portion of the page.

14. Inside the empty frame, type the following text and format it larger and centered.

```
Full two-hour class only $10
Monday night 7 p.m.
Municipal Library
Sign up today and get free club membership.
```

15. Click on the framed coupon and place a dotted line border around it. To do this, select Format | Borders and Shading, click on the dotted line style, and then click Box and OK.

16. Change the Zoom Control to Whole Page. Click on the coupon and use the menu command Format | Frame. Set the horizontal position to Center Relative To Margin and the vertical position to Bottom Relative To Margin, and set the Height to Auto. Click OK.

17. Save as *EX10-3 Done* and print.

EXERCISE 10.4

Thrill Seeker Tours

1. Open the document *EX10-4 Columns*.

2. Change the margins to .5 on every side.

3. Drag on the Columns button to change to three-column format.

4. Click on the Page Layout View button to see the columns side-by-side. Change the Zoom Control to Page Width, if necessary. To see how the whole page looks, click on the Print Preview button. Then click Close to return to the document.

5. Place the cursor at the top of the document. Enter and format the following lines, leaving a blank line before the article text.

```
Back Doors into Greece          format to 36 points, bold, left-aligned
by Thomas Bartlett              format to 14 points, bold, right-aligned
```

6. Highlight those two lines plus the blank line, and drag on the Columns button to change back to one-column format.

7. Click on the Normal View button to see the section break that was automatically added between the different column formats.

8. Place the cursor at the top-left corner of the document. Select the command Insert | Picture and double-click on the file name *Legal* in the *Clipart* folder.

9. Click on the picture to reveal the sizing handles. Drag the corner handles until the picture is only about twice as high as the headline.

10. Hold down the ⟨Shift⟩ key and drag the corner sizing handles to crop the black borders off the picture.

11. Place the cursor at the end of the document and press ⟨Enter⟩. Select Insert | Picture again, but this time access the file *Acroplis*. (This is a TIFF file that comes with the instructor's materials. Ask your instructor where to find the file, or use another appropriate file from the *Clipart* folder.)

12. Size the file so that it is about as wide as a single column of text. Do this by dragging on the corner sizing handles.

13. With the picture selected, insert a frame, using the command Insert | Frame. When prompted to switch to Page Layout view, click Yes.

14. Click the Zoom Control and change from 100% to Two Pages.

15. Place the mouse pointer over the crosshatched frame and, when it turns into a four-pointed arrow, drag the picture to the bottom-right side of the first page. If the text does not flow around the picture automatically, select Format | Frame and specify Around text-wrapping.

16. On the Zoom Control menu, change back to Page Width and view the top of the first page.

17. Add a pull quote to attract attention. Find an interesting, rather short sentence in the article and copy it to the Clipboard.

18. Place the cursor on the blank line below `by Thomas Bartlett`. Select Insert | Frame and drag in the center of the page to insert an empty frame approximately the width of the center column.

19. Paste the contents of the Clipboard into the frame. Format the font to a larger or bolder type, and set it off with a border.

20. Balance the columns by placing the cursor on a blank line at the end of the document, selecting Insert | Break, and clicking Continuous.

21. Print Preview the document to see the appearance of the page. If it does not all fit on the page, click the Shrink to Fit button, adjust the margins, eliminate one of the pictures, or make the font of the body text smaller.

22. Save as *EX10-4 Done* and print.

Review Questions

*1. Why is column layout preferable to full-page-width documents?

2. What is the difference between Normal view and Page Layout view in work with multiple columns?

*3. What is required if the entire document is to be placed in multiple columns?

4. What column attributes can be changed from the Format | Columns dialog box?

*5. How are the widths of columns changed?

6. Where do unbalanced columns appear? How are they remedied?

*7. What advantage does Word's graphical environment give when you are using pictures and graphics?

8. What types of graphics files are mentioned in this unit? What are the file extensions and sources for each type?

*9. What is the disadvantage of having pictures in a document? How is it overcome?

10. What are sizing handles? When do they appear? What significance does the location of a sizing handle have?

*11. What is the difference between cropping and scaling? How are cropping and scaling performed? How is each measured?

12. As a rule, what should you be careful of when sizing images that contain pictures of real things (such as people's faces)?

*13. How may pictures be positioned in any location on the page? What view must be in effect to see the picture in position?

14. What effect does a positioned picture have on text that is already on the page?

*15. What is the difference between a frame and a border on a picture?

16. What are two ways to create a graphic out of text?

*17. Multiple columns are best used to

a. Squeeze more text into the same amount of space.

b. List names in one column with the phone number next to each one.

c. Increase readability of headlines and articles.

d. Include pictures with text.

18. Page Layout view is best used for

a. Seeing framed pictures with run-around text.

b. Scrolling quickly through the document.

c. Editing the text of a newsletter or newspaper.

d. Seeing multiple columns as if they were one long narrow column.

*19. You can tell that a picture has been framed if you see

a. The crosshatched border in Page Layout view.

b. A border around the picture on the printed page.

    c. The sizing handles in Normal view.

    d. Multiple columns in the text.

20. Cropping differs from sizing in that

    a. You hold down the Shift key when dragging the sizing handles.

    b. You can only crop the edge but you can size corners or edges.

    c. You can only crop framed pictures.

    d. Cropping might make a picture look stretched out of proportion.

Key Terms

Bitmap	Frame	Run-around
Byline	Import	Scaling
Clip art	Masthead	Scanner
Crop	Metafile	Section break
Drop cap	Picture	Sizing handle
Encapsulated PostScript (EPS)	Picture Placeholders	Thumbnail
	Pull quote	TIFF file

Creating a Newsletter

Now that you have the skills to create an effective newsletter, apply your knowledge to create a one-page newsletter from scratch. You will need to write one long article, of around 500 to 600 words, and one shorter article on a related topic to be used in a sidebar. Change the margins and design the masthead. Create or paste the long article in place, specifying the column format. Insert a frame along the left or right side of the page and then write or paste the sidebar article in the frame. To add interest to the page, insert pictures, WordArt, or pull-quotes into frames on the page. Add lines between columns or at the top or bottom of the page, as you see fit. Proofread carefully, print, and save as *Application E*.

Creating a Brochure

The techniques you used in previous units will now be applied to creating a brochure. Brochures are necessary advertising or promotional literature that can be used to inform or persuade. Most tri-fold brochures are printed in landscape orientation, so you have six panels for different bits of information. Plan your approach by sketching out the contents on a sheet of blank paper folded in thirds. Label the pages in the order you will read them, and then open the sheet to see where the text for each panel must be placed, as you see in Figure F.1.

FIGURE F.1
Page layout for a tri-fold brochure

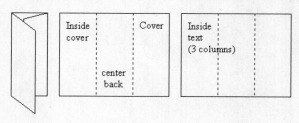

To begin creating the brochure, change the margins and page orientation. To format the panels, you can use a three-column format, three separate frames, or a three-column table, whichever seems easiest. Add pictures, Word-Art, borders and shading, and font and paragraph formatting as you see fit. Proofread carefully, print, and save as *Application F*. Copy the two pages onto the front and back sides of heavier paper and fold.

You may wish to purchase preprinted brochure paper, so that much of the brochure's design is complete. You only need to format the text to fit the design. You can purchase such paper from PaperDirect (800-A-PAPERS) and other vendors.

11

Chart and Draw

Word not only offers clip art to enhance documents. It also has the capability of adding charts to depict numbers. In addition, the Drawing toolbar contains numerous buttons that help you easily draw simple objects and edit the clip art that comes with Word.

Learning Objectives

At the completion of this unit you should know

1. why and how to create a chart using Microsoft Graph,

2. the best type of chart to use to depict data,

3. how to format and add enhancements to charts,

4. how to draw and format simple shapes,

5. techniques for modifying professionally drawn clip art images.

Important Commands

IN MICROSOFT WORD

Format | Drawing Object

Insert | Object

Insert | Picture

View | Toolbars

IN MICROSOFT GRAPH

Data | Exclude Row/Col

Format | Chart Type

Format | Column Group

Insert | Data Labels

Insert | Titles

Adding Charts to Documents

Even though your prose is eloquent and your document is formatted professionally, the time may come when the best way to make your point is to accompany the
text with a chart or graph. Often numbers arrayed in a table, even if they are nicely
formatted, require several moments to comprehend. In contrast, the eye can comprehend numbers presented in a chart with a single glance. This is the reason that Windows includes a mini-application for creating charts, Microsoft Graph 5.0.

You access Microsoft Graph in a way similar to the way you access Microsoft
WordArt. You select Insert | Object and double-click the selection for Microsoft Graph
5.0. As you can see in Figure 11.1, a sample chart is immediately inserted into the document, the menu and toolbars for Microsoft Graph replace Word's toolbars, and the
datasheet appears, a table-like window that will contain the text and numbers for the
chart.

FIGURE 11.1
Microsoft Graph

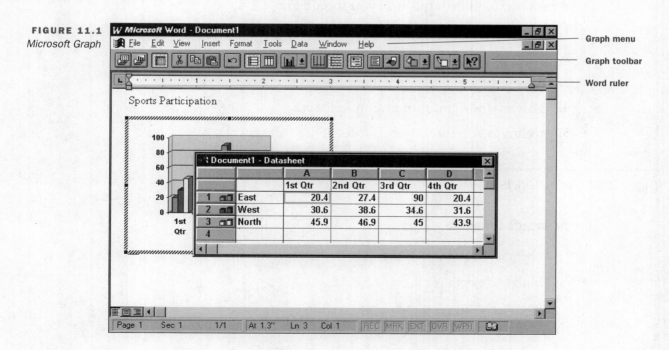

The process of creating a chart using Microsoft Graph follows these four steps:

1. Enter the information in the datasheet.

2. Select the appropriate chart type.

3. Add necessary titles, labels, and legends to add meaning.

4. Format the chart's fonts, colors, and other features.

Entering Data in the Datasheet

The datasheet, similar to a Word table or Excel worksheet, consists of columns, rows, and cells. The text and numbers in the datasheet are reflected on the chart. The top row of the datasheet contains the information that appears on the X-axis of the chart. The left column of the datasheet contains the information that typically appears in the legend, and the numbers in the other cells are the values that will be plotted on the chart itself. Figure 11.2 shows the relationship between a sample datasheet and the resulting chart.

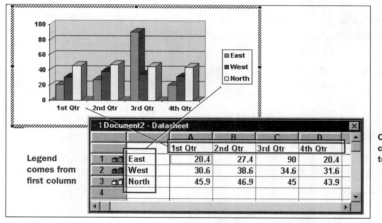

FIGURE 11.2
Sample chart and datasheet

To enter data, simply click in the cell and type new entries, replacing the sample information. To delete an entire column or row, click on the row or column heading to highlight, and then press [Del]. However, sometimes you may wish to retain the information in the datasheet but not have it displayed on the chart. Instead of deleting these columns and rows, you may simply exclude them from the chart by highlighting them and then selecting the command Data | Exclude Row/Col. When the datasheet is correct, click the View Datasheet button to remove the datasheet and view the resulting chart.

GUIDED ACTIVITY 11.1

Using the Datasheet

1. Create a new document and type the title Sports Participation. Press ⌨Enter a couple of times.

2. Select Insert | Object. From the alphabetical list, double-click Microsoft Graph 5.0.

3. Type the following data in the datasheet that appears, so that the default titles and figures are replaced. Press ⌨Tab or the arrow keys to move around the datasheet.

	1965	1975	1985	1995
Football	.5	.7	.6	.7
Baseball	3.5	3.1	2.7	2.5
Basketball	1.4	2.2	2.9	3.7
Soccer	.1	1.2	1.7	2.2

4. When the datasheet is correct, click the View Datasheet button to remove it from the screen and view the resulting chart in Microsoft Graph. Widen the chart by dragging the sizing handle on the right side of the blue crosshatched border, so that it resembles Figure 11.3.

FIGURE 11.3
Default 3-D column chart

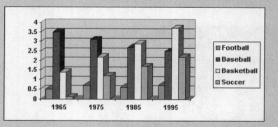

5. Although you are working in Microsoft Graph, you can see the Word document around it. Click in the title of the document to exit the Graph program and restore the normal Word menus and toolbars.

    Sometimes it's better to modify an existing chart than it is to create one from scratch. Let's make another chart using the same sports participation data.

6. Charts within a document are handled the same way as clip art. After you click on them to get sizing handles, as you see in Figure 11.4, you can copy, scale, crop, or delete charts. Click on the chart, and then copy and paste the chart on a blank line below the current chart.

7. To modify the second chart, you must first open the Graph program. To do this, double-click on the chart. A chart is *open* when you see it surrounded by the crosshatched border, and the Microsoft Graph menus and toolbars appear at the top of the screen.

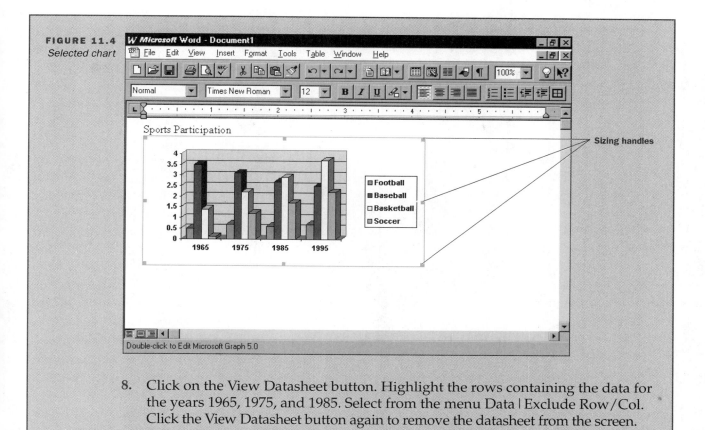

FIGURE 11.4
Selected chart

8. Click on the View Datasheet button. Highlight the rows containing the data for the years 1965, 1975, and 1985. Select from the menu Data | Exclude Row/Col. Click the View Datasheet button again to remove the datasheet from the screen.

9. Click the By Column button to see the difference in the chart. Click the By Row button to change it back again. Click back in the title to return to the Word program.

Selecting the Chart Type

By default, Microsoft Graph creates a 3-D column chart. The type of chart you use depends on your purpose. The various types of charts and their most appropriate uses are outlined in Table 11.1.

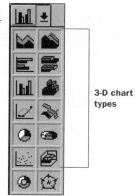

FIGURE 11.5
Drop-down list of chart types

To change the chart type, click on the arrow next to the Chart Type button to drop down buttons for the various chart types, as you see in Figure 11.5. On the left are the *2-D chart* types, and on the right are the *3-D chart* types. Usually 2-D chart types will display your data more clearly, since they do not have the distortion that comes from the perspective added to make the chart look 3-D.

You can also change the chart type by selecting Format | Chart Type from the Microsoft Graph menu. If you have the correct chart type selected and want to change other options, you can select the bottom choice from the Format

TABLE 11.1
Purposes of various chart types

BUTTON	CHART TYPE	BEST USED TO SHOW
	Area	Trend of total of several items over time
	Bar	Comparisons of size
	Column	Comparisons over time
	Line	Trends over time
	Pie	Proportions of a whole
	Scatter or XY	Whether two factors are related

The following two chart types are available only through Format|Column Group:

BUTTON	CHART TYPE	BEST USED TO SHOW
	Stacked Column	Comparison of totals of several items over time
	100% Stacked Column	Proportions over time

menu. This choice changes depending on what kind of chart you have created. In this case, it would be Format|3-D Column Group.

GUIDED ACTIVITY 11.2

Chart Types

When we examine the sports participation data in the default 3-D column chart, we can quickly see that participation in baseball and basketball is higher than the other two sports. It is difficult to see exactly what numbers the chart reveals, however, because we can't tell whether to measure the front edge or back edge of the top of the column. For this reason, it is usually best to stick with a 2-D chart instead.

1. Double-click on the first chart to edit it.

2. To change the chart type to a 2-D column chart, click on the down arrow next to the Chart Type button and select the column chart on the left side of the drop-down menu. The chart immediately changes to a 2-D chart, shown in Figure 11.6, and we can easily measure the height of the columns.

FIGURE 11.6
2-D chart

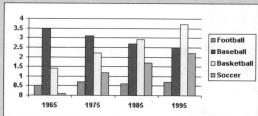

3. This chart shows the years along the X-axis, and groups the sports by each decade. What if you wanted to see the years grouped by sports instead? Click on the By Column button to see how the chart changes, and what is immediately apparent with this chart. Click on the By Row button to return to the original view.

What if we wanted to see whether the total participation in sports has changed over the years? Refer back to Table 11.1, and you see that to compare totals over time you should use a stacked column chart.

FIGURE 11.7
Format|Column Group dialog box

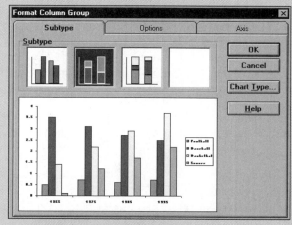

3. To change to a stacked column chart, select Format | Column Group, and on the Subtype tab, click to highlight the second choice, as you see in Figure 11.7. When you click OK, the chart changes. The stacked column chart calls attention to the fact that total sports participation has grown over the years to nearly 10 units (we have not yet defined the units). You can see a stacked column chart in Figure 11.8.

FIGURE 11.8
Stacked column chart

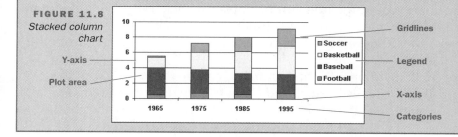

What if you wanted to see the trends in participation for each of the individual sports? Refer to Table 11.1; there you find that a line chart best displays trends over time for individual items. While the column chart can be used to show trends, the trends are more obvious on a line chart.

4. Click on the Chart Type button and select Line. The default line chart in Figure 11.9 shows a definite increase in basketball and soccer participation and a decline in baseball participation. Football participation remains steady.

FIGURE 11.9
Line chart

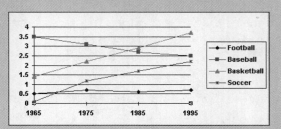

5. Click once to exit the Graph program, and then double-click on the second chart to edit it. You would like to show what proportion of total participation exists for each of the four sports. A pie chart displays proportions of a whole.

6. Change the chart type to a 2-D pie chart by clicking on the Chart Type button and selecting the Pie button. Click on the By Col button to show the proportions of each sport.

    Pie charts are unique in that they may only use a single row or column of numbers. That is why you excluded several rows of data in the previous Guided Activity.

7. For best appearance, pie slices should begin at a vertical line at the top of the chart. To modify the chart, select Format | Pie Group. Click on the Options tab and set the Angle of First Slice to 0 Degrees, and click OK. Leave the pie chart open for the next Guided Activity.

Enhancing the Chart

To make sense, you cannot merely have columns or lines on a grid. You must include identifying text, numbers, and a legend to give meaning to the chart. Microsoft knows this and by default includes a legend. Other information you would typically place on a chart would include a title, labels for each *axis* (the horizontal or vertical line on a column, bar, or line chart that represents categories or numbers), and data labels. To add these to the chart, select the appropriate item from the Insert menu.

When charts are created within a Word document, you do not need to put the title within the chart. This is because you can add it in the document itself, where you can control the formatting and placement—above, beside, or below the chart, wherever you want it.

Here's a great tip for using the title to give your chart the maximum punch. State the point of your chart directly in the title. For example, rather than titling a chart "First Quarter Sales," say "First Quarter Sales Up 25%." That way no one wonders what you are trying to demonstrate from the chart. If, in fact, you have more than one point you are trying to make concerning the data, you may need to create a separate chart for each purpose.

In contrast to titles, you must add *axis labels* within the Graph program. Some axes are self-explanatory, and need no identifier. For example, there is no need to label the categories Monday, Tuesday, Wednesday, or 1996, 1997, 1998. When you have numbers in dollar amounts, you can sometimes omit the axis label, but not always. Some dollar amounts are simplified for the chart but actually represent thousands or millions of dollars. In this case, you must label the axis Thousands or Millions to make the chart meaningful.

 Other labels such as a *legend* are also necessary. You can turn the legend off and on by clicking the Legend button. In the case of pie charts, a legend off to the side is inconvenient. Instead, you should label the pie segments themselves to make it easier to understand at a glance. To add the *data labels* to a pie chart, select Insert | Data Labels, and select either Show Label or Show Label and Percent and click OK.

 To make the actual values on the chart easy to comprehend, you can add or remove horizontal or vertical *gridlines* by clicking the appropriate buttons. Usually you will not use both sets of gridlines at the same time, because they make charts (especially line charts) too cluttered.

If the specific values being plotted on the chart are important, you can display them also as numbers placed directly on the chart. To do this, select Insert | Data Labels and click on Show Values. If this seems to be too many numbers on screen, you can specify which ones are displayed by clicking once or twice on the individual data labels until you get sizing handles, and then deleting the unnecessary ones.

GUIDED ACTIVITY 11.3

Modifying Charts

1. To label the pie segments, click the Legend button to remove the legend.

2. Select Insert | Data Labels. Click Show Label and Percent and click OK. The labels are added to the pie itself, and the size of the pie decreases to display it all in the given area, as you see in Figure 11.10. You will resize the chart in the next Guided Activity. Click on the document outside of the chart to return to the document.

FIGURE 11.10
Pie chart with data labels

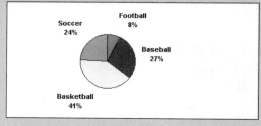

3. Double-click the line chart to open it up for editing. The line chart you just created is too cluttered because there are so many gridlines in addition to the data lines. Click on the Horizontal button to remove them.

4. Without the gridlines, it is more difficult to tell what the actual values in the chart are, but it is easy to see the trends of each of the sports. To display the specific values, add data labels. To do this, click once on the line that represents Baseball so that sizing handles appear. Select Insert | Data Labels and click Show Value and click OK.

5. We know from the title that the chart displays the number of participants, but we must label the units on the vertical axis. To do this, select Insert | Titles and select Value (Y) Axis and click OK. To the left of the vertical axis, a Y appears, surrounded by sizing handles. Type the word Millions and press Enter. We will format this to look better in the next Guided Activity.

Formatting the Chart

Formatting charts is similar to all the other formatting you have done. The first step is to select or highlight the item you wish to format. You can select the various parts of a chart two ways: click with the mouse once or twice so that sizing handles appear on the object, or click anywhere on the chart and press the arrow keys to select each element in turn.

Once the item is selected, double-click to open the formatting dialog box. This dialog box changes, depending on what is selected. Column and bar charts are formatted with the dialog box shown in Figure 11.11, which allows you to change the fill color and pattern, the border style and color, and the symbols that appear on a line chart. You may also change colors by clicking on the Fill Color and Line Color buttons on the Graph toolbar.

If you double-click on a title or labels, a different dialog box appears with several tabs, including one for formatting the font, which is quite familiar to you. You can also perform typical formatting by using the familiar buttons on the Formatting

FIGURE 11.11
*Format Data
Series dialog box*

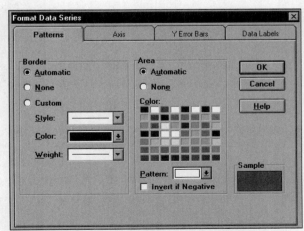

FIGURE 11.12
*Microsoft Graph
Formatting
toolbar*

toolbar. If is not displayed, select View | Toolbars, select Formatting, and click OK. The Graph Formatting toolbar is shown in Figure 11.12.

GUIDED ACTIVITY 11.4

Formatting Charts

1. If necessary, turn on the Formatting toolbar. Select View | Toolbars, click Formatting, and click OK.

2. The first thing to format is to make the axis label vertical so that it does not overlap the numbers on the chart. Double-click on the word `Millions` to access the formatting dialog box. Click on the Alignment tab to reveal the dialog box shown in Figure 11.13. Select the bottom-to-top orientation and click OK.

FIGURE 11.13
*Formatting text
alignment*

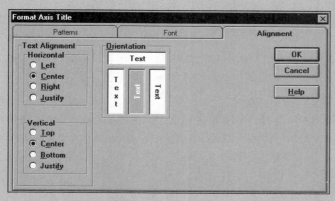

3. Click on a line to get sizing handles at each of the points. Change the color of the line by clicking on the down arrow next to the Pattern button and selecting a new color.

4. To change the line markers, double-click on the line to reveal the dialog box in Figure 11.14. Drop down the selection for Marker Style and select the open diamond. Click OK.

5. Make the background of the chart itself shaded. Click on the chart so that the sizing handles appear around the *plot area* of the chart, the part including the lines but not the labels. Select Format | Selected Plot Area. Select Automatic Border and add a light gray background shade to the Area. Click OK.

6. Click on the title to return to Word, and then click once on the pie chart to select it.

FIGURE 11.14
Formatting the line marker

Format Data Series

| Patterns | Axis | Y Error Bars | Data Labels |

Line
- ◉ Automatic
- ○ None
- ○ Custom

Style: [_____]
Color: [■■■■■■] ±
Weight: [_____]

☐ Smoothed Line

Marker
- ◉ Automatic
- ○ None
- ○ Custom

Style: ◆ ▼
Foreground:
Background:

[OK]
[Cancel]
[Help]

Sample
●

Drop-down list of marker styles

7. You can size the pie chart in Word to make it larger. Drag on the corner sizing handles so that the chart fills the width of the page.

   Sizing the chart in Word makes everything larger—the font size of the labels and the chart itself. Since this may result in a rather crude effect, it's usually better to size the individual chart elements within Microsoft Graph.

8. Click Undo. Instead, double-click the pie chart to edit it. Click on the plotting area to get a rectangular border with sizing handles. Drag the corner sizing handles to make the pie itself larger. You may also need to enlarge the blue cross-hatched area so that the labels will be visible.

9. To draw attention to a particular part of the pie chart, you can explode one of the segments, just as in Figure 11.15. Click once or twice on the Football segment, and then drag it slightly away from the pie. If you want to return it back to normal, simply drag it toward the center of the pie.

FIGURE 11.15
Pie chart with exploded segment

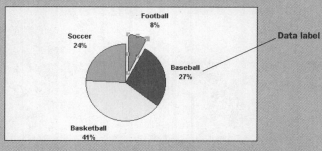

Football 8%

Soccer 24%

Baseball 27%

Data label

Basketball 41%

Draw

Usually when you add pictures to a document, you will use professionally drawn clip art. But sometimes you need to make a simple diagram combining lines, geometric shapes, and text. Microsoft Word gives you buttons to help you create basic *drawing objects*. When you click on the Drawing button on the Standard toolbar, the Drawing toolbar appears on the bottom of the screen, just above the status bar, as you see in Figure 11.16.

FIGURE 11.16
Drawing toolbar

At the same time, Word automatically changes to Page Layout view. As you know, Page Layout view shows pictures and columns just as they will appear on the printed page. Likewise, when you draw shapes on the page, you need to see exactly where they will appear in relation to the text on the page.

Unlike pictures, objects drawn on a page are actually on a different layer from the text. This means they may be placed on top of other text or pictures on the page. This is useful in case you want to draw an oval around some other text, or draw an arrow pointing to something, for instance. Drawing objects differ from pictures in that text does not wrap around them at all.

As soon as you click on the Drawing button, the Drawing toolbar appears at the bottom of the screen between the scroll bar and the status bar. At this point, objects may be added using the various drawing tools, and line and fill colors may be specified. An image may be flipped vertically or horizontally or rotated clockwise, and the parts of an image may be grouped or ungrouped to work on them together or separately.

The buttons on the left side of the Drawing toolbar show the various objects that can be drawn on a page: line, rectangle, oval, arc, freeform shape, text box, or callout. To place any of these objects on the page, click the button and drag the plus-sign mouse pointer to the correct size and shape.

If you want to draw a perfect square or circle, hold down the [Shift] key while you drag. Pressing the [Ctrl] key while you draw also has an effect on shapes. The [Ctrl] key causes the shapes to expand from the center, rather than from the corner.

Next to the five shape buttons are other buttons that let you draw a text box and a callout. A ***text box*** is a special drawing object that allows you to place text on top of other items on the page. If you want text to overlap a chart, other drawing objects, or other text, use a text box. Unlike placing text in a frame (as you did in Unit 10 when you created the pull quote), the existing text does not flow around text in a text box.

When you draw a text box on the page, it looks like a rectangle surrounded by a gray crosshatched border. It contains a cursor so that you can type information, and the text wraps within the box. If you type more than what will fit in the box, or if the box is too large, you may have to resize the text box. By default, a text box is surrounded by a thin border. You can format this by selecting Format | Drawing Object.

Text boxes and other drawing objects appear on a different layer than the text on the page. This allows you to have words or a picture in the background. Two buttons on the Drawing toolbar determine whether the text is on the top layer or the bottom layer.

One specialized use of a text box is to create a ***watermark***—pale text or graphics placed in the background of the document. For example, you can type `Confidential` or `Draft` or place a company's logo in a light shade behind the text. To create a watermark, draw a text box, insert the text or graphics, and position it on the page. If you want the watermark to appear on every page of a multipage document, you will need to insert the text box into a header or footer.

A *callout* is a specialized text box that is used to label something on the page. When you click the Callout button, you drag from the item you wish to label to where you want the callout to appear. A line is connected to a text box in which you type the label. To format the callout, click on the Format Callout button and make choices in the dialog box shown in Figure 11.17.

FIGURE 11.17
Callout Defaults
dialog box

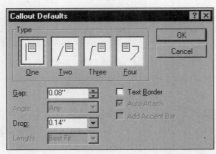

You can change the color of the *fill* and line and change the *line style* to dotted, dashed, or arrows by using the next three buttons or the Format | Drawing Object command. If you make the color and style choices first, the drawing objects will be created as you specified. If you have drawing objects you wish to change, you must click on them first to get sizing handles, and then specify the format. To select more than one object at a time, you can use the Select Drawing Objects button. This enables you to drag a dashed rectangle around the drawing objects to select several at once.

The buttons on the right half of the Drawing toolbar have to do with editing graphics that are already created. They are used to rearrange the stacking order, to group and ungroup, to flip and rotate shapes, and to align them either to a grid or to each other. You will use many of these buttons in this unit.

GUIDED ACTIVITY 11.5

Using the Drawing Tools

1. Open a new document to experiment with drawing a simple clock face. Click on the Drawing button to reveal the Drawing toolbar. The document automatically changes to Page Layout view. If the Drawing toolbar appears floating in the middle of the document, drag its title bar to move it to the bottom of the screen.

2. Click on the Rectangle button and hold down the [Shift] key while you drag a square approximately 1½ inches across. If the square is empty, click on the Fill Color button and select black as the color.

3. Click on the Ellipse button. Place the mouse pointer over the *center* of the square and hold down both the [Shift] and [Ctrl] keys while you drag a 1-inch circle

inside. When you release the mouse button, the circle won't show up because it's black on black, but it will have sizing handles around it.

4. Click on the Fill Color button and change to white.

5. Hold down the [Shift] key and click on the square so that both shapes have sizing handles. Click on the Align Drawing Objects button to reveal the dialog box shown in Figure 11.18.

FIGURE 11.18
Align dialog box

6. Select Center horizontally and Center vertically and click OK.

7. Click the Line tool, and drag a line from the center of the clock to about 11 o'clock. With the line selected, click on the Line Style button and select the style in the middle with the arrow head. If your arrow is pointing in the wrong direction, select the other arrow line style. If necessary, move the arrows into place. You can move a selected drawing object by dragging it or by pressing the arrow keys.

8. Make the line of the clock's hand thicker. To do this, double-click on the arrow to reveal the Format | Drawing Object dialog box shown in Figure 11.19. Click on the drop-down box next to Weight and change the thickness of the line to 2 pt.

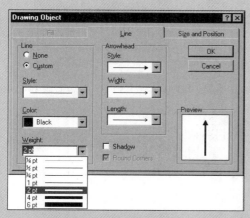

FIGURE 11.19
Format Drawing Object dialog box

9. Add another, shorter line for the hour hand extending from the center of the clock toward the 12 o'clock mark. This one should have the same format automatically applied.

10. Add a text box as a rectangular base on the clock. To do this, click the Text Box button and drag so that the text box is just a little larger than the black square. Inside type TEMPUS FUGIT (a Latin phrase meaning "time flies"). Center the text within the text box. If necessary, click on the crosshatched border to reveal the sizing handles and resize the box to fit the text. Format the fill and line as you think best.

11. Click on the Callout button. Place the mouse pointer near the Latin phrase and drag up and to the right. Type Time is running out! in the callout. Our version is shown in Figure 11.20.

FIGURE 11.20
*Results of
Guided Activity*

12. Click on the Drawing button to remove the Drawing toolbar from the screen.

GUIDED ACTIVITY 11.6

Using Text Boxes

1. Open a new document to experiment with using text boxes to place text within a decorative border. Change the margins to .5 inch on all sides.

2. Select Insert | Picture and scroll through the list of clip art and select one of the decorative borders: *Vbevbox*, *Vcontbox*, *Vprisbox*, or *Vwind*. The borders that begin with the letter V are for vertical (portrait) page layouts; the ones that begin with the letter H are for horizontal (landscape) pages.

3. Change to Page Layout view if not already in that view and click on the Zoom Control box and change to Whole Page.

4. Click on the Border clip art and drag until it is as large as the whole page.

5. Click on the Drawing button to reveal the Drawing toolbar. Click on the Text Box button and drag a large rectangle in the top-left side of the page. In the text box type Announcing . . . and format to 36 points.

6. Change the Fill Color of the text box to None and the Line Color to None by clicking on the appropriate buttons.

Draw another large text box in the center and type Hootie and the Blowfish (or the name of another performing group). Format to 72 points bold, centered. If the text box is not large enough, click on the crosshatched border to get sizing handles. Drag the sizing handles to enlarge the box.

7. Draw a third box in the lower-right area of the page and put the place, date, and ticket price for the appearance. Format this to 36 points.

8. Adjust the location of the text boxes and print.

Editing Graphics

Certain clip art images may be edited using the buttons on the Drawing toolbar. To edit a clip art image, double-click on the image. When you do this, Word changes to a special screen that includes the Drawing toolbar and the Picture toolbar, shown in Figure 11.21. The title bar changes to show that you are editing the picture within a document. You can use the buttons on the Drawing toolbar to stack, flip, group, ungroup, and align the clip art.

FIGURE 11.21
Picture toolbar

Not all clip art may be edited this way; if it is a linked or embedded object and the software that created it is available, double-clicking will open the image in the original software. However, you can edit all the clip art that comes with Word using the buttons on the Drawing toolbar.

GUIDED ACTIVITY 11.7

Editing Clip Art

1. Start a new document, and change to Normal view. Select Insert | Picture and choose the file *Sports.wmf* from the *Clipart* folder, and click OK. This clip art is also available from the Student Data Disk.

2. Click on the picture so that the sizing handles appear. Notice the message in the status bar that says `Double-click to edit.`

3. Double-click on the picture.

   Immediately, as Figure 11.22 shows, the picture is placed into a square in a document with the name Picture in Document. The document appears in Page Layout view, even if you were previously working in Normal view. The Drawing toolbar is displayed at the bottom of the screen, and a very short toolbar with only two buttons appears on top of the document, the Picture toolbar.

4. Click on the picture of the baseball bat so that sizing handles appear.

5. Click on the Fill Color button on the Drawing toolbar at the bottom of the screen. On the palette that appears, select a medium gray.

   The baseball bat is now colored like an aluminum bat, but it seems a little bland.

6. Add a black outline to the bat by clicking on the Line Color button, and selecting black.

FIGURE 11.22
Editing a picture

Boundary

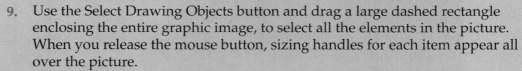

7. Elongate the baseball bat by dragging on the sizing handle on the right or left edge.

8. This picture is composed of objects in several layers. You can control in what order the layers appear. Click on the black square in the background. Click on the Bring to Front button to change the order of the picture's layers. Click on the Send to Back button to put it in the background again.

9. Use the Select Drawing Objects button and drag a large dashed rectangle enclosing the entire graphic image, to select all the elements in the picture. When you release the mouse button, sizing handles for each item appear all over the picture.

10. Click on the *Group* button to assemble these elements into a single graphic image. This prevents you from moving one out of place, but also keeps you from changing the colors or attributes of individual parts of the picture until you ungroup them.

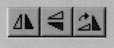

11. Suppose you want the person facing right. You can reorient the picture by clicking on the Flip Horizontal, the Flip Vertical, or the Rotate button. Experiment with these buttons until the picture looks best.

    Since you have elongated the bat, it is no longer enclosed in the *boundary* square on the edit screen. Only what is within the boundary square appears in the document after you finish editing.

12. Click the Reset Picture Boundary button on the Picture toolbar.

13. To return to the regular document and update the picture in the document to reflect the changes you made, click the Close Picture button on the Picture toolbar.

Summary

Some nice features of Word allow you to depict numbers in charts, create simple drawings or diagrams, and edit existing clip art. Microsoft Graph is accessed through the Insert I Object command, and it opens new menus, toolbars, and a datasheet in which you place the data you wish to graph. The type of chart you make depends on what you are trying to show. Line charts, for instance, show whether sales are increasing or decreasing. Pie charts, on the other hand, show how large a portion of total expenses the payroll makes up. Once a chart is selected, you can add labels, a legend, and gridlines, and you can format the various parts of the chart by double-clicking.

The Drawing toolbar, available at the click of a button, offers several buttons for drawing, formatting, and manipulating simple shapes. Objects that are drawn on the page may only be viewed in Page Layout view or Print Preview. Unlike text or pictures within frames, text does not wrap around drawing objects. They overlay the normal text found in the document because they occur in a completely different layer.

The buttons on the Drawing toolbar are also used when editing existing clip art. When you double-click on clip art, the picture is surrounded by a boundary rectangle, and the Picture toolbar appears on screen. You can group or ungroup, change the color of the line or fill, and even flip, rotate, and align the various parts of the image. When you are finished, click Close Picture to return to the normal document and see the modified picture in place.

EXERCISE 11.1

Charting

1. Open the file *EX11-1 Chart*.

2. Highlight the table of sales figures and copy to the Clipboard.

3. Select Insert I Object and double-click Microsoft Graph 5.0.

4. Click on the top-left cell and paste the sales information in the datasheet. Click on the left side of row 3 North and press [Del] to remove it.

5. Remove the datasheet by clicking on the View Datasheet button. Drag the sizing handles on the chart to make it wide enough to show the weeks clearly.

6. Click on the Chart button and change to a line chart.

7. Double-click on the vertical axis. Click on the Scale tab and change the minimum to 8000 and click OK. This changes the chart to focus on the values above $8,000.

8. Select Insert | Titles, click Category (X) Axis, and click OK. Type Week and then click on the chart.

9. Drag the top sizing handle on the blue crosshatching to make the chart taller, if necessary.

10. Click in the document to return to the normal Word toolbars and menu. Add the descriptive title 1997 Sales Exceed 1996 Sales. Center the title and chart. Preview, save, and print.

EXERCISE 11.2

Editing Clip Art

1. Start a new document and type the words All cats are gray in the dark. Press Enter several times.

2. Insert the clip art picture of the cat. To do this, select Insert | Picture, scroll through the list, and double-click on Cat.

3. Double-click the picture to edit it. Click the Drawing button if the Drawing toolbar is not visible. Click the Select Drawing Objects button and drag to select the entire cat picture. Click on the button that will flip the picture so that the cat faces right.

4. Click away to deselect the parts of the drawing, and then click to select the cat's body. Change the Fill Color to gray.

5. Use the Select Drawing Objects button again to select all the whiskers. Change the Line Color to gray.

6. Click to select the shape near kitty's legs. Change the Fill Color to black.

7. Click on the Rectangle tool and drag to cover the entire cat picture. Click on the Send to Back button so that the black goes into the background.

8. Click the Reset Picture Boundary button on the Picture (not Drawing) toolbar, and click Close Picture.

9. Select the entire document, and change the shading to black. To do this, select Format | Borders and Shading and double-click on Solid (100%).

10. Preview, save, and print.

EXERCISE 11.3

Using Text Boxes

1. Open the file EX11-3 Border.

2. Access the Drawing toolbar. If necessary, switch to Page Layout view, and drop down the Zoom Control and select Whole Page.

3. Click on the Text Box button and drag to surround the document. Set the Fill Color to None, if necessary.

4. Select Insert | Picture and select *Vwind*.

5. Drag on the corners to enlarge it to fit the page.

6. Click on the Send Behind Text button to make the text appear within the border.

7. Preview, adjust the size and position of the text box to fit within the margins, save, and print.

Review Questions

*1. Why would you use a chart rather than placing numbers in a nicely formatted table?

2. What changes on screen when you select Insert | Object and choose Microsoft Graph 5.0?

*3. What relationship does the datasheet have with the chart?

4. What labels or other kinds of text items should be added to give meaning to a chart?

*5. What is the difference between selecting a chart and opening it?

6. What happens when you double-click part of an open chart?

*7. How do you change the chart style to a line or pie chart? to a stacked column chart? to a 100% stacked column chart?

8. What is unique about the data that can be displayed in a pie chart?

*9. How do you make the Drawing toolbar appear? What are the two main uses for the buttons on it?

10. How are drawing objects and text boxes different from pictures or text in a frame?

*11. Place the following steps for creating a chart in the correct order:

A. Select the appropriate chart type.

B. Format the chart's fonts, colors, and other features.

C. Add necessary titles, labels, and legend to add meaning.

D. Enter the information in the datasheet.

a. ABCD

b. DCBA

c. ADCB

d. DACB

For the next four questions, use the following answers:

a. Column

b. Line

c. Pie

d. Stacked column

12. What kind of chart best displays the proportions of a whole?

*13. What kind of chart best displays trends over time?

14. What kind of chart best displays a comparison over time?

*15. What kind of chart allows you to compare totals of several items over time?

16. What do you call a pale picture or text that appears behind the text of a document?

a. Watermark

b. Text box

c. Callout

d. Boundary object

Key Terms

2-D chart	Data label	Legend
3-D chart	Datasheet	Line style
Axis	Drawing object	Open chart
Axis label	Fill	Plot area
Boundary	Gridline	Text box
Callout	Group	Watermark

Combining a Chart with a Document

Select File | New and use a memo template to create a memo to the Board of Directors of Thrill Seeker Tours, discussing the bimonthly sales of ski tours for March and April. In the first paragraph, thank the directors for their valuable input into decision making.

In the second paragraph, discuss the number and types of ski adventure tours that were conducted during April. Explain the reason for the declining sales. Include below this paragraph the table of figures shown below.

```
Weekly Ski Tour Sales for March-April

Week     1  2  3  4  5  6  7  8
Sales   22 25 20 22 16 17 13 12
```

Illustrate the trend by including an area chart. Create the chart in Microsoft Graph 5.0, using the numbers on the table. Format the chart with a white data area and a light gray plot area and chart background.

Exit Microsoft Graph, and in Word change to Page Layout view. Place a small text box, about one-half-inch square, in the white area of the chart. Within this text box insert the picture called *Skidown.bmp*. Position the skier where you want it by dragging the text box. The skier should appear as if he were skiing down the chart. Place the title just above the chart within the document.

In the last paragraph, urge the directors' continued support of management and advise them that they can look forward to an excellent summer vacation season. Format, proofread, and print the memo.

Placing a Watermark on a Page

Select File | New and from the templates available select the Calendar Wizard. Create a calendar for the current month. If the calendar is unavailable, use another document.

Add a watermark for Thrill Seeker Tours in the background of the page. To do this, first insert a text box to contain it. Display the Drawing toolbar, click on the Text Box button, and drag an area about 3 inches square in the center of the page.

Inside the text box, create the watermark by selecting Insert | Object to access Microsoft WordArt 2.0. Type Thrill Seeker, press Enter, and on the next line type Tours, and change the text style to Slant Up. Click the Shading button (third from right) and change the Foreground color to Silver. You want it to look very subtle, just as you see on this page.

Return to the document, and with sizing handles surrounding the WordArt, click the Send Behind Text button on the Drawing toolbar. Adjust its placement, and print.

Headers and Footers

Headers and footers appear at the top or bottom of every page of a document to give the reader pertinent information about the text on the page. Most publications have at least one or the other to help the reader keep track of the organization of the text. Examples of text found in headers and footers are page numbers, chapter titles, the addressee's name (for a letter), the date (for a policy manual), or a company's name.

Headers and footers could be added manually to the top and bottom of each page in a document, by simply typing text on the top and bottom lines. This would work for a one-page document, but not for a longer document requiring frequent editing. Typing page numbers or a company's name directly on the pages would require a great deal of work, since any modifications to the body of the document would force you to reposition the headers or footers on subsequent pages.

Word allows you to type the text for the header or footer one time, and then it automatically inserts it in the same place on every page. You can make numerous additions and deletions to the body of the document, and the word processor will take those into account and keep the headers and footers at the top or bottom of the page. This unit covers how to create and edit headers and footers for various pages.

Learning Objectives

At the completion of this unit you should know

1. what headers and footers are,

2. how to add headers and footers to different categories of pages and sections,

3. how to insert special fields into headers and footers,

4. how to edit headers and footers.

Important Commands

File | Page Setup

Insert | Break

Toggle Field Codes (shortcut menu)

View | Header and Footer

Headers and Footers

Headers are lines of text that appear at the top of every page, separate from the body of the document, to give information about the text. They may contain chapter titles, page numbers, the author's name, or any other information pertinent to the text. *Footers* function exactly like headers except that they appear at the bottom of the page. Both headers and footers are added to a document using the View | Header and Footer command.

The most common use of headers and footers is for numbering pages. You learned in Unit 8 how to insert page numbers automatically with the Insert | Page Numbers command. Page numbers created with the Insert | Page Numbers command are actually a *field code* placed in a frame within the header or footer. This field code automatically keeps track of the page numbers of every page in the document so that the word processor substitutes the actual page number for the field code.

In addition to automatic page numbers, Word also offers field codes for the system date and time. Most computers maintain the current date and time in memory. Word can look up these values and substitute them for field codes. Because field codes can be inserted anywhere in a document, including the header or footer, when you click certain buttons the date and time will be recorded in the document. This feature can be very useful if you are keeping track of different versions of a document or are working on a document with several people and need to organize each one's work.

When you are creating a document, at times you may want to see the field codes themselves rather than their results. To see a field code, point the mouse at the field and then right-click and select Toggle Field Codes from the shortcut menu. To toggle the display of every field code in the document, press the shortcut key [Alt][F9].

Inserting Headers and Footers on Every Page

A header or footer generally appears on every page of the document within the top or bottom margin. The page numbers inserted with the command Insert | Page Numbers are headers or footers that you have already created. Headers and footers consisting of other text (with or without page numbers) can be created or edited from any page by using the View | Header and Footer command.

FIGURE 12.1
*Header and
Footer toolbar*

As soon as you issue the View | Header and Footer command, the screen changes. The text of the document is dimmed, and Word displays the Header and Footer toolbar, shown in Figure 12.1.

The cursor will be positioned within the top margin area of the page in the header area that is enclosed by a nonprinting dashed rectangle and labeled either `Header` or `Odd Page Header`, as shown in Figure 12.2. A document may be set up with different headers and footers for odd and even pages. To turn this feature off, click on the Page Setup button on the Header and Footer toolbar, and clear the check box specifying Different Odd and Even.

FIGURE 12.2
*Header area
within the top
margin*

Instead of the regular default tab settings, only two tabs are set in the header or footer area of the page. If the ruler is displayed, you will see these tabs. A center tab is set at the 3" mark on the ruler and a right tab at the 6" mark. Most of the information in a header or footer is typed at the left or right margin or centered on the page, so the word processor places correct tabs at these locations, assuming that you will use them.

To jump the cursor to the footer instead of the header, click on the Switch Between Header and Footer button. To create the header or footer, type the desired text and apply formatting just as you would in a regular document. For instance, if you wish to have a black line printed at the top of every page, apply a border to a blank paragraph within the header area.

Three buttons on the Header and Footer toolbar insert field codes. The button with the number sign places a field code that automatically numbers pages. To the right of that button are the buttons for the current date and the current time. Page numbers that are inserted automatically through the Insert | Page Numbers command use the same field code as the button on the Header and Footer toolbar. The difference is this: the field code from the Insert | Page Numbers command is placed *within a frame* inside the header or footer, so they may be dragged and placed anywhere on the page. The framed page number is shown in Figure 12.3. In contrast, clicking the Page Numbers button on the Header and Footer toolbar places the field code within the header's text. To change its horizontal placement, click the Align Left, Center, or Align Right buttons or press the [Tab] key.

FIGURE 12.3
*Insert|Page
Numbers puts
the number in
a frame*

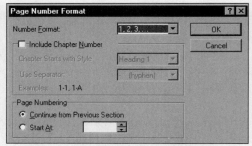

Whether you insert page numbers with the button in the Header and Footer toolbar or with the Insert | Page Numbers command, you can still change the format or the numbering scheme by clicking Format in the Insert | Page Numbers dialog box.

You specify the numbering scheme in the dialog box shown in Figure 12.4. For example, you can pick Roman numerals, which are typically used for the front matter such as the table of contents and preface. After you make changes in the page number format, click OK and then choose Close rather than OK, to avoid inserting another page number in the header and footer.

You may type as many lines of text in the header or footer as you wish, and the margin of the document will increase to hold the entire header or footer. However, if the header is more than three lines long, you may want to press [Enter] after the last line to separate it from the document body. Similarly, for long footers you may want to start the footer by pressing [Enter] to separate the footer from the last line of text on the page. As a rule, though, headers and footers should be brief. To control the vertical placement of headers and footers, specify the measurement for margins and the distance from the edge of the page in the Margins tab of the Page Setup dialog box, shown in Figure 12.5.

FIGURE 12.5
*Specifying
vertical position
of headers
and footers*

Set distance
from edge here

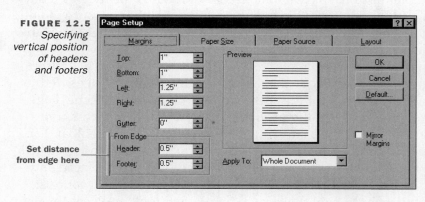

While you are editing the header or footer, you may view the main part of the document in gray or hide it completely by clicking on the Show/Hide Document Text button on the Header and Footer toolbar. When you have finished the header or footer, click the Close button to return to the main part of the document.

In Page Layout view, you can see the contents of the header and footer in gray when you view the top or bottom margin of the page. From other views, you will not see the header or footer again unless you preview the document or select the View | Header and Footer command.

GUIDED ACTIVITY 12.1

Creating and Deleting Headers

1. Start Word and create a new document. Make sure you are in Normal view.

2. Type Page One. Press [Enter]. Select Insert | Break. Page Break is already selected in the dialog box, so press [Enter]. A shortcut to insert a page break is to hold down [Ctrl] and press [Enter].

3. Type Page Two. Press [Enter]. Insert another page break.

4. Type Page Three.

   There are now three pages in your document. Each page break you inserted is represented in the work area by a horizontal dotted line across the page with the words Page Break.

5. Select View | Header and Footer. The cursor appears in a dashed rectangle in the top margin of the document and the rest of the text is grayed (dimmed).

6. If the header is labeled Odd Page Header, you will need to change settings on the Layout tab in the Page Setup dialog box.

   Click on the Page Setup button that looks like an open book. Click in the box next to Different Odd and Even to clear that option if it is selected. Make sure that Different First Page is also clear. Click OK to return to the header. It should now be labeled Header, as in Figure 12.6.

FIGURE 12.6
Header area

7. Type Chapter One.

8. Switch to the footer by clicking on the button on the left side of the Header and Footer toolbar. The cursor will be positioned within a dashed rectangle at the bottom of the page.

9. Type Section Five.

10. Click on the Close button on the toolbar to return to the main part of the document. Position the cursor on page 1. To verify the location of the cursor, read the status bar at the bottom of the window.

11. Select File | Print Preview.

    The header and the footer appear on all three pages. You may use [PgUp] and [PgDn] or use the scroll bars to see the header on each page.

12. Close the preview screen. Page Layout view also allows you to see the header within the top margin.

13. Change to Page Layout view. Each page appears separately, and the header and footer look gray (dimmed) within the top and bottom margins. Since the document is in the Page Layout view, Word shows you exactly how the page will look when it is printed.

14. Press the Next Page button at the bottom of the scroll bar to view the page numbers on page 2 and then on page 3.

To quickly edit the header and footer in Page Layout view, you may double-click the grayed header or footer.

15. Double-click the grayed header within the top margin.

Immediately the header appears in dark letters, the main document appears grayed, and the Header and Footer toolbar reappears.

16. Remove the header by deleting the text in the dashed rectangle. Click Close or double-click on the main part of the document.

Creating a Unique Header and Footer for the First Page

Often, you will not want a header or footer to appear on the first page. The top and bottom of the first page in a report or letter are usually blank. The page number and company name that may appear in the header or footer would not usually appear on the first page of a letter or report, but only on the second and subsequent pages.

Word allows you to suppress first-page headers and footers. To do this, you would specify a different header or footer for the first page and leave it blank. The different first-page header or footer is created by checking the box next to Different First Page on the Layout tab in the Page Setup dialog box.

 Now when you select View | Header and Footer, the dashed rectangle is labeled First Page Header or Header, depending on the page where the cursor was located before issuing the command. After you enter the text to appear in one header, you may use the Show Previous and Show Next buttons to move the cursor to the previous or next type of header or footer.

In the following Guided Activity you will modify your document to contain a different header and a different footer for the first page.

GUIDED ACTIVITY 12.2

Creating First-Page Headers and Footers

1. Select File | Page Setup, and choose the Layout tab. Check the box next to Different First Page, as shown in Figure 12.7. Click OK.

2. Select Print Preview. The footer that says Section Five does not appear on page 1, but only on pages 2 and 3. Selecting Different First Page creates a new,

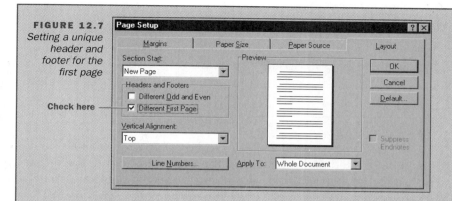

FIGURE 12.7
Setting a unique header and footer for the first page

Check here

blank header and footer for the first page. The second-page and third-page footers are still the way you left them. Only the first-page header and footer have been changed.

3. Close Print Preview. Position the cursor on the second page. Select View | Header and Footer, so that the cursor is positioned within the header box.

4. With the cursor at the left margin, click on the Date button. Type two spaces with the [Spacebar] and click on the Time button.

5. Press [Tab]. The cursor moves to the center of the screen. This is the center tab that is set by default for headers and footers. Type your name.

6. Press [Tab]. The cursor moves to the right side of the screen. This is the right tab that is set by default for headers and footers. Type Page and press [Spacebar]. Click the Page Numbers button.

   Each of these buttons places field codes in the document. You can identify field codes when you click on them because they are shaded in gray. What you see is the result of the field code, which changes each time. The actual field code is quite different.

7. With the mouse pointing at the page number in the header, click on the right mouse button to reveal the shortcut menu. Select Toggle Field Codes.

   The page number is replaced by {PAGE}. This is the field code for a page number. You may switch back and forth between displaying a field code and its results by selecting Toggle Field Codes. To toggle displaying and hiding all the field codes at once, use the shortcut key [Alt][F9].

8. To edit the First Page Header, click on the Show Previous button on the Header and Footer toolbar. Click on the Switch Between Header and Footer button to move the cursor to the footer.

9. Press [Tab] to get the cursor to the center of the footer.

10. Type Page and press [Spacebar]. With the mouse, click on the Page Number button.

    The page number appears next to the cursor.

11. Click on the Close button to return to the document, and change to Normal view. Select Print Preview to see the new footer on page 1, and the new header on the second and subsequent pages. Close Print Preview.

Creating Headers and Footers for Odd and Even Pages

When a document is to be printed on both sides of the page and bound, the headers and footers for even-numbered (left) and odd-numbered (right) pages are usually positioned so that they will be against the outside margin of the pages. This means that the headers and footers for the even-numbered pages that usually appear on the left side of the book must be left-justified, and those for the odd-numbered pages that usually appear on the right must be right-justified.

Word allows you to specify different headers and footers for odd and even pages when you check the Different Odd and Even box under Headers and Footers in the Page Setup dialog box.

In the Guided Activity below, the selections for both Different First Page and Different Odd and Even will be checked. This means that there will be three categories of headers and footers. Each category of page in the document will have its own header and footer. If the document is 20 pages long, say, all the even-numbered pages will have the same header and footer. Any modification to the header or footer on these pages will change them for all even-numbered pages. The first page has its own header and footer. Modifications to these will affect only the first page. All the odd-numbered pages after the first page will have the same header and footer. If you modify the header or footer for either of these pages, all the other pages in the same category will display the new header or footer.

GUIDED ACTIVITY 12.3

Creating Odd-Page and Even-Page Headers and Footers

1. Place the cursor on the second page. Select View | Header and Footer.

2. Click on the Page Setup button and check the box next to Different Odd and Even under Headers and Footers in the Layout tab. Click OK.

   The dashed rectangle in the header area is now labeled Even Page Header, rather than just Header and the header text you entered earlier disappears.

3. With the cursor positioned against the left margin, type Chapter One.

4. Click on the Show Next button to view the Odd Page Header.

5. Erase any text that appears in the Odd Page Header area, and press Tab twice to position the cursor against the right margin.

6. With the mouse, click on the Date button.

7. Click on the Close button or double-click on the main part of the document.

8. Change to Page Layout view and scroll through the document to see the headers.

    The header for the first page is blank. The second page header contains the words `Chapter One` against the left margin. The header on the third page contains the date against the right margin.

9. Move the cursor back to the first page.

    To get the proper effect of different headers and footers for odd and even pages, you should view two pages at once.

10. Click on Print Preview and view two pages. To do this, click on the Multiple Pages button and drag to highlight 1 x 2 pages.

    The first page is displayed on the right side of the preview screen. In bound documents page 1 and all odd-numbered pages are on the right side of the binding. The header for the first page is blank.

11. Click on the Next Page button or press `PgDn`.

    Pages 2 and 3 are displayed on the left and right sides of the preview screen, respectively. This is the way they will appear in a bound document. The header for page 2 is justified against its left margin and displays the name of the chapter. The third-page header is right-justified and contains the date.

    This document displays the three kinds of headers and footers that are available from Word. These three categories cover the majority of applications and should allow you to create a wide variety of documents.

Headers and Footers in Different Sections

Longer documents such as reports may have more than one section or chapter, each requiring a different header or footer. For example, on the even-numbered (left-hand) pages of a bound document you may have the report title next to the page number, which appears on every page of the document. On the odd-numbered (right-hand) pages, however, you may wish to have the chapter title next to the page number (as used in this book), which would change for each chapter. Word's headers and footers allow for such an arrangement. The process to set this up consists of two steps: divide the document into sections by inserting section breaks, and then specify separate headers or footers for each section by breaking the connection from the previous headers or footers.

Section breaks are used for several purposes. You learned in Unit 8 that section breaks allow you to specify different page margins or layout (portrait vs. landscape) for two parts to a document. Unit 10 taught you that section breaks are used to separate single-column layout from multiple columns, even on the same page. Unit 14 will discuss the use of master documents and subdocuments in writing long papers; subdocuments (chapters) are automatically separated by section breaks. Any time a section break occurs, a new set of headers and footers may be specified.

By default, Word assumes that the headers and footers you put in the first section of a document (that is, above the first section break) will continue throughout the document. In multisection documents the header and footer areas are labeled by section, as in Figure 12.8. When a header or footer is the same as the one in the previous section, the header or footer area displays the words `Same as Previous`, and the Same as Previous button on the Header and Footer toolbar appears pushed in.

FIGURE 12.8
Header area in another section of a document

You can break the connection and specify different headers or footers by clicking the Same as Previous button on the Header and Footer toolbar. When this button is clicked, it no longer appears pushed in, and the words `Same as Previous` disappear from the right side of the header or footer area. Word leaves the same text and field codes within the header and footer, though, assuming that you will keep some of the elements the same, such as the page number. Just as before, you can specify different headers and footers for odd and even pages. You may connect or disconnect each of the four categories individually: even headers, odd headers, even footers, and odd footers.

Let's go back to the example discussed above, where the header on the left-hand (even) page would have the report title and the header on the right-hand (odd) page would have the chapter title. In this case, the even-page header would remain connected to the previous, but the odd-page header would be disconnected and the chapter title would be edited to show the new chapter title. When you click the Show Previous and Show Next buttons, you jump from Odd Page Header -Section 2 to Even Page Header -Section 2 and on to Odd Page Header -Section 1 and Even Page Header -Section 1 and back again. This way you can edit all the headers and footers in the Header and Footer view one after the other.

If you wish to return from having separate headers and footers for each section and reconnect, simply click the Same as Previous button. The prompt in Figure 12.9 appears, warning you of the change. When you select Yes, the headers and footers from the previous section are restored to the current section.

FIGURE 12.9
Reconnecting a section's headers and footers to the previous section

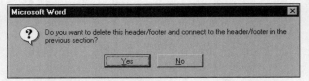

Summary

Headers and footers are lines of text that appear within the top and bottom margins of pages to give pertinent information about the text in the document, typically page numbers. They may contain any regular text and can be formatted with any of the commands on the toolbars or ruler.

Field codes may also be inserted into headers and footers. Field codes are markers in a document that cause Word to look up or calculate values. Some special field codes that can be easily and automatically inserted into headers and footers are the page number and current date and time.

The simplest headers and footers to create are those that will appear on every page in the document. However, most documents do not have the same header or footer on the first page as in the rest of the document. Word allows you to specify a set for the first page different than on the rest of the document. Likewise, the headers and footers may contain different text for even-numbered (left-hand) pages as opposed to odd-numbered (right-hand) pages. These headers and footers are used in documents that will be printed on both sides of the page and bound.

Longer documents with portions separated by section breaks automatically have one set of headers and footers, which continue throughout all the sections. If you wish to specify separate headers and footers for a section, however, you can remove the connection to the previous headers and footers and create a unique set for the new section.

EXERCISE 12.1

Headers and Footers the Same on All Pages

1. Open *EX12 Headers*.

2. Create a header that will appear on all pages of the document. To do this, you may need to go to Page Setup, Layout tab, and remove the check from Different Odd and Even and Different First Page.

3. Select View | Header and Footer. Type your name at the left side of the header and type `Thrill Seeker Tours` at the right side. Move the tab setting in the header to match the right margin.

4. Switch to the footer to create a footer for all pages. Type `Reprinted by permission of the Waco Tribune-Herald` at the left side and place the page number at the right. Format the permission information to 8.5 points but leave the page number at 10 points. Move the tab setting in the footer over to the right to match the right margin.

5. Save and print pages 1 and 2 only.

EXERCISE 12.2

Different Page Headers and Footers

1. Continue with *EX12 Headers* from the previous exercise.

2. Select File | Page Setup and on the Layout tab check the boxes for Different First Page and Different Odd and Even.

3. Create different headers for odd and even pages. Select View | Header and Footer and click Show Next to get to the Even Page Header. Place the page number on the left (outside) margin and the title `Take the Plunge` on the right (inside) margin. Click Show Next to get to the Odd Page Header. This time, delete the current header and place the title on the left (inside) margin and the page number on the right (outside). Move the tab settings in the headers to match the right margin.

4. Click the Switch Between Header and Footer button and delete the current footer text. Create different odd and even footers with the date at the outside margin and the time at the inside margin, using the Show Previous button to get from the odd page to the even page footer. Move the tab settings in the footers to match the right margin.

5. On the first page footer, place the `Reprinted by permission of the Waco Tribune-Herald` at the left side and the page number on the right. Format the permission line to 8.5 points. Click Close to return to the document.

6. Save and print the document.

EXERCISE 12.3

Different Section Headers and Footers

1. Continue with the document from Exercise 12.2.

   Place the cursor to the left of the first paragraph in the story. Insert a section break by selecting Insert | Break and clicking Continuous. Click OK.

2. Change to three columns with .2 inches of space between each column. To do this, select Format | Columns and change the number of columns to 3. Set the spacing to .2 and click OK.

3. Select View | Header and Footer and verify that the headers and footers for Section 2 are labeled Same as Previous. Close and print page 3.

4. Insert a continuous section break above `Ground Rush`. To do this, place the cursor to the left of the `G` in `Ground Rush`, select Insert | Break, and click Continuous and OK.

5. Move the cursor to the end of the document and select View | Header and Footer. Since the cursor is in Section 3 when you open the view, the header is labeled Odd Page Header -Section 3 Same as Previous.

6. Click the Same as Previous button to disconnect the section 3 header. Click OK at the prompt. Type your name on the center of the header line.

7. Print pages 4 and 5 to compare the new header and old footers.

Review Questions

*1. What are headers and footers used for?

2. How much text can be placed in a header or footer? What must be considered when creating long headers and footers?

*3. What kinds of pages can have different headers and footers? What is the purpose of each?

4. How does the screen appear after you select View | Header and Footer?

*5. What three buttons insert field codes into the document? How are the field codes viewed?

6. How do section breaks affect headers and footers?

*7. The command that allows you to place the same information at the bottom of every page is

a. View | Header and Footer.

b. Insert | Footnote.

c. File | Page Layout.

d. Insert | Footers.

8. If you don't want a header to appear on the first page of a document,

a. View the header and delete the text.

b. Select File | Page Layout and check Different First Page.

c. Select View | Header and Footer and check None on First Page

d. Insert a section break between the first and second pages and click the Same as Previous button to break the connection.

*9. The reason you might want to have separate headers and footers for odd and even pages is

a. Odd pages are on the left-hand side and even pages are on the right-hand side.

b. Chapter titles are always on one side and document titles are always on the other.

     c.   Section breaks in a document create different odd and even pages.

     d.   Binding odd and even pages together means you want the page numbers on the outside margin.

10.   Inserting the page number in a footer by clicking the button on the Header and Footer toolbar

     a.   Is the same as using the command Insert | Page Numbers.

     b.   Places the page number in a frame within the footer.

     c.   Inserts the field code {PAGE}, which is automatically updated.

     d.   Means you cannot format the page number as you can with the Insert | Page Numbers command.

Key Terms

Field code   Footer   Header

Mail Merge

Modern reality includes mass mailings of personalized copies of the same letter to hundreds (or millions) of addresses. Word's mail merge tool makes it easy for you to create one file that is representative of the form letter each person will receive and place in the form letter special markers in the places where the name and address will go. A separate file contains a list of all the names and addresses of the intended recipients. The two files can be merged and printed to create personalized letters for every person on the list.

This unit covers the creation of a main document and a data source and the use of the Tools | Mail Merge command. You will learn not only how to create personalized form letters, but also how to print mailing labels or envelopes to go with the form letters, and how to include only certain individuals from a long list of names. Another use of the mail merge tool will be to create a catalog.

Learning Objectives

At the completion of this unit you should know

1. what is required to execute a mail merge,

2. how to create a main document and the data source,

3. how to merge the two together,

4. how to select certain records for merging,

5. how to include conditional text,

6. how to create a catalog,

7. the steps in merging envelopes and mailing labels.

Important Commands

Insert | Date and Time

Toggle Field Codes (shortcut menu)

Tools | Mail Merge

View | Header and Footer

Requirements for Mail Merge

Performing a mail merge requires two files. One file, the **main document**, is the form letter that all the merged documents will resemble. The second required file is a **data source**. This document contains the information that will make each form letter unique. Each line in the data source contains all of the information required to print one copy of the main document.

The Mail Merge Helper organizes the task of mail merge into three steps:

1. Create the main document,

2. Create or locate the data source, and

3. Merge the two together.

To access the Mail Merge Helper, issue the command Tools | Mail Merge. The dialog box shown in Figure 13.1 lists the steps in setting up a mail merge. The first step is to create the main document, and it is the only option that is available since the other buttons are dimmed (grayed out). Clicking on the Create button gives the option to create form letters, envelopes, mailing labels, or a catalog. At this point you can either type a new document or use an existing document with modifications.

The next step is to create or locate the data source by clicking the Get Data button. Data may already be available in a spreadsheet such as Excel, or a database such

FIGURE 13.1
*Mail Merge
Helper*

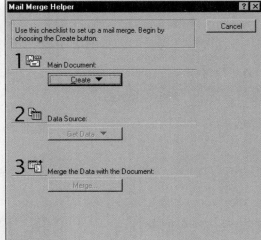

as Access, in a personal address book or contact list in Schedule+, or in another Word document. If data already exists, a dialog box resembling the File | Open dialog box allows you to specify which file contains the data so that Word can create a *link* between the data source and the main document. If this is a new set of data, you can also create the data source from scratch.

The third step is to click Merge to combine the data with the document and either create a new document on screen or send it directly to the printer.

The Data Source Document

The data source, no matter what kind of file it is, contains the information you need to customize a form letter. Like all databases, the information is organized into individual sets, called *records*, and within records the information is divided into categories called *fields*. Using the white pages of a telephone book as an example of a database, one record would be all the information for a single individual. The first name, last name, address, and telephone number would be four typical fields contained in every record.

When you create a new data source in Word, the document created is actually a table, although you will not see it as a table until later. The first row in this table, called the *header row*, contains the names of the fields that will be used to place the information in the rest of the table into the main document, much as a column heading explains the text below it. Word supplies several commonly used fields for the header row, including Title, FirstName, LastName, JobTitle, Company, Address1, Address2, City, State, PostalCode (Zip), HomePhone, and WorkPhone, as shown in Figure 13.2. These field names cannot contain spaces, either within them or at the end. From this dialog box you may remove unneeded fields, add other necessary fields, and rearrange the order of the fields in the header row. After you save the file, you may either begin typing data into it or go back to modify the main document.

FIGURE 13.2
Create Data Source dialog box

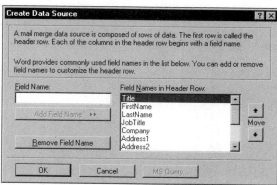

When you edit the data source, the Data Form box appears, as in Figure 13.3, allowing you to view the contents of one record at one time. The field names you added to the header row appear on the left. Type in the data, going from item to item by pressing `Tab` or `Enter`. Press `Shift` `Tab` or the arrow keys to move back up the form. When you have entered the information for one person (record), click Add New to

FIGURE 13.3
Data Form

Data Form	? ☒
Title:	OK
FirstName:	Add New
LastName:	Delete
JobTitle:	Restore
Company:	Find...
Address1:	View Source
Address2:	
City:	
State:	

Record: ⏮ ◀ 1 ▶ ⏭

begin the next. Word automatically numbers the records. You may type the records in any order, since you may easily sort the data later. To see the actual data source file rather than the data form, click on the View Source button.

Behind the data form lurks a table with the header row on the top. While the fields in the header row may be in any order, the data on the following lines—the records—must be in the same order as the fields in the header row, and each line of data must have the same number of fields (columns) as there are in the header row. Each record appears on a separate row.

Using Mail Merge activates a Database toolbar. This toolbar, shown in Figure 13.4, lets you swiftly perform several common functions, including managing fields, adding and deleting records, sorting in ascending and descending order, finding records, and jumping to either the data form or the mail merge main document.

In the following Guided Activity you will create a form letter from a magazine publisher encouraging people to subscribe by offering a large sum of money as a prize.

FIGURE 13.4
Database toolbar

GUIDED ACTIVITY 13.1

Creating a Data Source

1. Start Word.

2. Issue the command Tools | Mail Merge. When the Mail Merge Helper appears, click Create under Main Document, and select Form Letters, and then Active Window.

3. In the Mail Merge Helper under Data Source, click Get Data, and then select Create Data Source.

4. Scroll through the list of suggested field names. There are several that we can eliminate from this list for this document. Highlight JobTitle and click the Remove Field Name button. Repeat to remove Company, Address1, Address2, Country, HomePhone, and WorkPhone from the list.

The suggested field names are changed for the current document. They will be available again the next time you create a data document.

5. To add the Street field name, double-click in the text box under Field Name and type `Street`. Click Add Field Name to add it to the list.

   The new field is automatically placed at the bottom of the list. This would be awkward for typing in the names and addresses later.

6. To move the Street field so that it appears between LastName and City, click 3 times on the up arrow button above Move. The field names are finished.

7. Click OK. When a dialog box appears, save the file under the name *Addresses*.

8. When the Mail Merge Helper reappears, click on the Edit Data Source button.

9. Enter the following data into the data form, pressing `Tab` or `Enter` to proceed to the next field. Do not include the commas.

   `Mr.,John,Smith,1111 Adams Street,Mentor,OH,44060`

10. Click the Add New button when you are finished and add the next two records, clicking Add New before each.

    `Mrs.,Mary,Jones,2222 Main Avenue,Austin,TX,78746`

    `Ms.,Penelope,Peters,3333 Oak Circle,Fort Worth,TX,76106`

11. Click View Source to see the data in table form.

    The records are not in any particular order. It would be helpful to have the last names in alphabetical order.

12. Click in the LastName column, and then click the Sort Ascending button.

    To add more data records, you could go back to the data form by clicking the Data Form button, or you could type them directly into the table.

13. Click on the Add New Record button and type your name and address into the new row on the table.

    This works fine with a small table, but if there were many records, the header row would not show on the screen with the bottom row so you could not tell what field belonged with which column. This is one reason to use the data form to enter data.

14. Save the finished data source file. Click on the Mail Merge Main Document button on the right side of the toolbar to continue the mail merge process.

The Main Document

The mail merge main document contains the text all of the printed documents will have in common, plus *merge fields* in place of information that will be unique to each printout. The Mail Merge toolbar, shown in Figure 13.5, appears between the Formatting toolbar and the ruler in the main document.

FIGURE 13.5
*Mail Merge
toolbar*

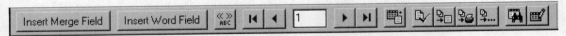

The next step for setting up mail merge is to enter the text into the main document. When you reach a place where information is needed from the data source, insert a merge field by clicking on the Insert Merge Field button on the Mail Merge toolbar. The fields listed are the very ones that are in the header row of the attached data file. After a field is selected, the field name appears in the text surrounded by chevrons, for example, «name». This indicates that this is a merge field name and not merely typed characters. Merge fields may be inserted as many times as you want and in any order. Each merge field you enter will later be replaced by information from the data source.

In the following Guided Activity, you will create a letter and merge it with the data source Address.

GUIDED ACTIVITY 13.2

Creating a Main Document

1. Continue with the mail merge main document from the previous Guided Activity. Use the File | Page Setup command to change the top margin to 2.25", typical for a letter printed on letterhead stationery.

2. The top line of the document should contain the date. Rather than typing the data, enter a field code that will cause the current date to print anytime the letter is printed. To do this, issue the command Insert | Date and Time. In the dialog box that appears, shown in Figure 13.6, select the format you wish for the date. Click in the box Update Automatically, and then click OK.

FIGURE 13.6
*Insert | Date and
Time dialog box*

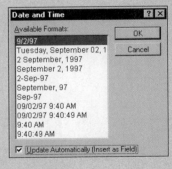

3. Place two blank lines after the date.

   The recipient's name and address usually appear after the date in a letter. This letter is going to various people. Rather than change the letter each time before printing it, customize it by placing merge fields for the name and address.

4. Click on the Insert Merge Field button. Select Title from the list of merge fields.

5. The letter will print once for each line in the data source. For each printout, this merge field will be replaced by the person's title at the beginning of each record: Mr., Mrs., and Ms.

6. Press [Spacebar]. Click on the Insert Merge Field button and select FirstName.

   Each letter will contain the recipient's first name instead of this field code. Word maintains the exact punctuation and spacing that you place between merge fields in the form letter, so you must leave a space between the Title and FirstName merge fields.

7. Press [Spacebar]. Insert the merge field for the last name.

   The first line contains the recipient's title and first and last names. The second line contains the street address.

8. Press [Enter]. Insert a merge field for Street and press [Enter].

9. Insert a merge field for City and insert a comma and a space.

10. Insert a merge field for State, leave two spaces, and insert another merge field for PostalCode. The result should look like the following:

    «City», «State» «PostalCode»

    The final line contains the city and state separated by a comma, two spaces, and the zip code. Now create the salutation.

11. Make sure the cursor is to the right of the zip field code. Press [Enter] twice.

12. Type Dear followed by a space. Insert a merge field for Title.

13. Leave a space after Title and insert a merge field for LastName, and then place a colon after it, with the following results:

    Dear «Title» «LastName»:

14. Press [Enter] twice and insert the following text and field codes. Use [Tab] to indent the names.

    You may have already won $10,000,000!!! Three of the four lucky people below have already won!!

        Robert Cranwell of Arcata, CA
        Maria Martinez of Corning, NY

```
«FirstName» «LastName» of «City», «State»
Fred Lawson of Ocala, FL

If your number is selected, all you have to do is return
the enclosed card to claim your prize!! Also, please take
this opportunity to review our wide selection of publica-
tions and include your order with the prize claim card.

Imagine the excitement when we deliver your prize money
to your doorstep in «City», «State». Return your claim
card and order today!!

Sincerely,
```

15. Press 4 times, and then type your name. Save the file as *Form Letter*.

The use of the fields in the main document is independent of the order of the fields in the data source. This has been illustrated in this Guided Activity by the fact that several of the fields were used more than once.

 If you want to view the data source, it is a simple matter to click on the Edit Data Source button on the Mail Merge toolbar. This opens the file if it is not already open, and displays the data form.

Merging the Two Documents

You can preview the merged document by clicking on the View Merged Data button on the Mail Merge toolbar. Clicking on this button replaces the merge fields with the data from the first record. You can see the merge fields and merged data in the two sample documents in Figure 13.7. Although the merged data appear just as if they were typed in place, when the cursor is on them they appear shaded, which lets you know these are merge fields.

Other buttons, shown in Figure 13.8, allow you to preview other records. Press the buttons on either side of the record number for the next or previous record, or

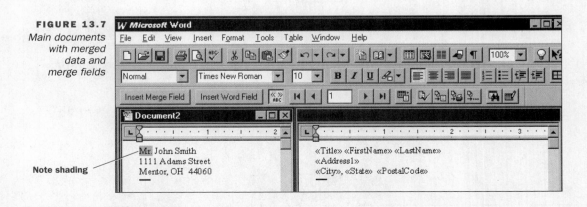

FIGURE 13.7
Main documents with merged data and merge fields

Note shading

FIGURE 13.8
*Record selection
buttons on the
Mail Merge
toolbar*

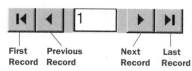

First   Previous   Next   Last
Record   Record   Record Record

type a specific record number in the box. The buttons on either end go to the first and last records. To reveal the merge fields again, click on the View Merged Data button.

If you print the main document with the merge fields displayed, Word will print a single copy of the document with the merge fields in chevrons (« »). However, if you view the merged data and then print, you will get a single copy of the main document merged with one of the records in the data source. Usually, however, you will want to print many copies of the main document, one for each record in the data source.

To merge the information in all the records of the data source with the main document, press one of the two buttons on the Mail Merge toolbar. The Merge to New Document button merges the two documents and stores the results in a single file, with each page separated by section breaks. This new file is called *Form Letters1*, rather than *Document1*, the name we are accustomed to seeing on new files. Merging to a document rather than directly to the printer allows you to check for any errors.

The Merge to Printer button merges and prints one copy of the main document for each line of data in the data source. Whether you merge to a new document or directly to the printer, the merge fields in the main document are replaced by the appropriate pieces of information from the data source.

One other way to merge the two documents is to click on the Mail Merge button. This reveals a dialog box that contains several options not available through the buttons, as shown in Figure 13.9.

The first option allows you to specify whether you wish to merge to a new document or directly to the printer (the same as clicking the buttons) or to electronic mail.

FIGURE 13.9
Merge dialog box

**This message
changes**

Another option available only in the dialog box is to merge only certain records, say records 10 to 20, rather than the entire set of data records.

In other circumstances you wish to merge only records meeting certain criteria. Asking for records matching certain criteria is called a *query*. Click the Query

FIGURE 13.10
*Query Options
dialog box*

Options button to bring up yet another dialog box, shown in Figure 13.10. Here we can specify the *filter* to be used (criteria that must be matched) for the data to be merged. An example might be to merge only those records that have the merge field State equal to TX, or those whose merge field PostalCode is less than 78700. If any criteria are specified in this dialog box, the message at the bottom of the Merge dialog box changes to Query Options have been set.

GUIDED ACTIVITY 13.3

Merging

1. Use the main document and data source created in the preceding Guided Activities. Check the main document carefully to be sure there are no errors.

   If you clicked the Print button now, a single copy of the document would be printed with the merge fields surrounded by chevrons, just as it appears on screen.

2. Click on the View Merged Data button to see the data from record 1 in place of the merge fields.

   If you clicked the Print button now, a single copy of the document with these data in place of the merge fields would be printed, just as it appears.

3. Click on the Next Record button several times to view the results of each record. Click on the First Record button to return to record 1.

4. Click on the Merge to New Document button.

   A new document appears, containing four personalized copies of the main document, separated by section breaks. Close this file and do not save it, since it can be re-created anytime by merging the form and data documents.

   You may need to print letters for a range of people in the data source instead of everyone. In this case, you do not want to send yourself a letter, so you want to eliminate record 4.

5. Click on the Mail Merge button to display the Merge dialog box and in the From box under Records to Be Merged type 1. Press [Tab] to go to the To box and type 3.

6. Select Printer under the Merge To option and click Merge. The Print dialog box appears. Click OK.

   Three documents are printed, one each for the first, second, and third persons listed in the data source. Suppose you wish to merge letters only for people who live in Ohio (OH). In a large database, it would be very time-consuming to look through the entire data source to find each record number. You can automatically merge records that match certain criteria through Query Options.

7. Click on the Mail Merge button, and then on Query Options.

8. In the Query Options dialog box that appears, click on the down arrow next to the top box under Field. Select State.

9. Click on the down arrow next to Comparison to display the comparisons available, shown in Figure 13.11. In this case, Equal To is the correct comparison.

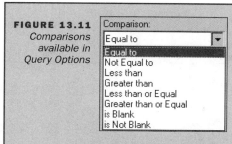

FIGURE 13.11
Comparisons available in Query Options

10. Click in the box under Compare To and type OH. Press or click OK. Click All under Records to Be Merged, and select New Document under Merge To. Click Merge to complete the merge to a new document.

   The result is a single letter to John Smith, the only record that matches the criteria. Close the *Form Letters2* file and do not save it.

Using IF Fields with Conditional Text

Form letters sometimes need to have additional text printed only when certain conditions are met. For example, people who live within your state may have to pay sales tax, whereas those from out of state may not. **IF fields** are a type of merge field that may be used to include text but only under certain conditions. Word uses this logic: examine an expression, make a comparison to another expression, and give one result if the condition is true and another if it is false.

To insert an IF field into the form letter, click the Insert Word Field button on the Mail Merge toolbar. The list provides several Word Fields, including one for If… Then…Else…. When this field is selected, the dialog box in Figure 13.12 appears.

FIGURE 13.12
Creating an IF field

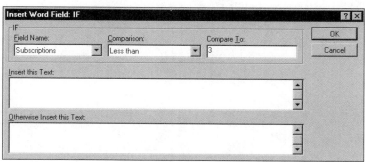

Each of the items in the IF dialog box must reflect the desired condition. Using the sales tax example, the Field Name in the IF statement must be changed to State. The choices of comparisons are the same as in Query Options. The text in the Compare To box must exactly match the data in the merge field in both spelling and capitalization for the IF statement to be true.

The final step is to type the text that we would like printed if the comparison is true or false. Type in the Insert this Text box Be sure to add 6% for sales `tax.` for when the comparison is true. Type in the Otherwise Insert This Text box `No sales tax is required.` for when the comparison is false.

Using an IF Merge Field

1. Continue with the *Form Letters2* document from Guided Activity 13.3. Click on the Edit Data Source button, and on the data form click on the View Source button to make *Addresses* the current document.

2. Click on the Manage Fields button on the Database toolbar.

    The dialog box that we used to design the original data source document appears.

3. Type in the new field name `Subscriptions` and click Add. Click OK.

4. Enter the following numbers in the right-most column of the table: 1, 2, 5, and 8, the number of subscriptions each person ordered in the past.

5. Click on the Mail Merge Main Document button on the right side of the toolbar to return to the *Form Letter* document, or use the Window menu selection.

6. The query option to select only `OH` is still in effect. Remove the query option by clicking on the Mail Merge button, clicking Query Options, and clicking Clear All. Click OK and click Close to return to the main document.

7. Place the cursor at the end of the second-to-last paragraph to add an IF statement that will urge recipients to subscribe if the number of the subscriptions in the Subscriptions field is fewer than 3.

8. Press `Spacebar` to add a space after the last sentence in the paragraph. Click Insert Word Field and select If…Then…Else….

9. Click on the down arrow next to the box for Field Name and select Subscriptions to insert the merge field.

10. Click on the down arrow next to Comparison and select Less Than. Click in the Compare To box and type 3.

11. In the Insert This Text box type `You need to subscribe to at least three magazines in order to win.` Click OK.

12. Click the Merge to New Document button and examine the resulting form letters. The new text should appear only in the first two letters. These were the two letters that had subscriptions fewer than three in the data source. Close the file without saving, and close the *Addresses* and *Form Letter* files.

Creating Catalogs of Information

Catalogs, price lists, parts lists, membership directories—these typical business documents are made up of data that are often already contained in a database of one form or another. If you had nothing better to do, you could retype such information into a document and format it professionally. Using the Mail Merge feature, however, saves you the effort of retyping, ensures accuracy of results, and allows you to specify the formatting for all the records at once.

Such documents differ from typical main documents in that information from many records appears on each page of the document, rather than just one record per page. This process requires only two modifications from the method you learned above.

First, when setting up the main document, select Catalog rather than Form Letter. Specify the data source, as usual, and insert merge fields with appropriate punctuation, spacing, and formatting for a single set of information.

Second, merge to a new document. Word automatically creates a file called *Catalog1* and places record after record of information in the document so that whole pages are filled. At this point you add a title or text that will appear once in the document, as well as column headings and headers or footers that need to appear on every page. Print the finished product by clicking on the Print button.

GUIDED ACTIVITY 13.5

Creating a Catalog

1. Start a new file. Set the left and right margins at 0.7 inches. Format the document to two columns.

2. Issue the command Tools | Mail Merge. In the Mail Merge Helper, select Create under Main Document and select the type Catalog from the drop-down list. Click Active Window.

3. Click Get Data under Data Source, highlight the file *GA13-5 Data*, and click Open.

4. In the Mail Merge Helper, select Edit Main Document.

5. In the blank main document, enter the following text, pressing Insert Merge Field at the appropriate places. Put two blank lines at the end.

   ```
   The «Mfr» sleeping bag (model «Catalog_Number») is
   «Length» inches long, «Width» inches wide. It is rated to
   «Temp_Rating» and is filled with «Fill_Weight» lbs. of
   «Fill». The sturdy cover is made of «Outer_Fabric», and
   the comfortable liner is «Inner_Fabric».

   List price                  $«List_Price»
   Your discounted price       $«Disc_Price»
   YOU SAVE                    $«Savings»
   ```

6. Underline the Discount Price merge field and dollar sign. Apply a double underline to the Savings merge field and dollar sign.

7. Place a border under the paragraph below the Savings line.

8. Highlight all the paragraphs *except* the very last blank line. Select Format | Paragraph and click on the Text Flow tab. Check the selection for Keep with Next. Click OK. Click anywhere to remove the highlighting.

   Keep with Next forces the page breaks to occur only between the catalog entries, rather than splitting one in the middle. You must leave one paragraph without this formatting, or Word will not have anywhere to break the pages. That is why you did not highlight the last blank line before selecting Format | Paragraph.

NOTE *If Keep with Next formatting has been applied to a paragraph, a small black square appears to the left of the first word whenever the Show/Hide ¶ button is pushed in.*

9. Click on the Merge to New Document button. Watch the status bar count up as each record is being merged.

10. In the *Catalog1* document that results from the merge, select View | Header and Footer. Type the following information into the Header box:

    `A great selection of sleeping bags at special prices for Co-op members only.`

11. Use Print Preview or the Page Layout view to adjust any spacing or formatting of the catalog. When all looks even, click the Print button to get a copy of the catalog pages. A sample page of the catalog appears in Figure 13.13.

12. Save the *Catalog1* document and the mail merge main document, if you wish.

FIGURE 13.13
The finished catalog

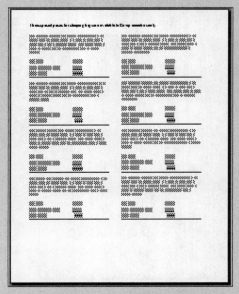

Merging Mailing Labels and Envelopes

Merged letters are often used in mass mailings (also known affectionately as "junk mail"). Not only are the letters themselves merged, but the envelopes must be directed to each address in the data records. Because bulk mailings must contain at least 200 pieces to qualify for reduced postage rates, the process of addressing the envelopes must be automated.

Some companies print the addresses on adhesive labels that are later stuck onto envelopes. Even clear labels, though less noticeable than the standard white labels, warn the recipient not to waste much time with the letter. For a more professional appearance, the addresses may be printed directly onto the envelopes. It is convenient to use Word's Mail Merge tool to create mailing labels and to address envelopes anytime you are sending mail to many recipients at once.

The process of creating mailing labels or envelopes has several variables: the size of the labels, the type of printer, and how envelopes or labels are fed into the printer. Because of these differences, only the general steps for creating labels will be given.

1. To begin the process of creating mailing labels, access the Mail Merge Helper from the button on the Mail Merge toolbar or with the command Tools | Mail Merge. Under Main Document, click Create, and then select Mailing Labels. Click Active Window.

2. Attach the new main document to the existing data source by clicking Get Data and then selecting Open Data Source and choosing the correct file. When you choose Set Up Main Document, you must select the type of labels you will be using from the Label Options dialog box that appears, shown in Figure 13.14.

FIGURE 13.14
Specifying the size and type of labels

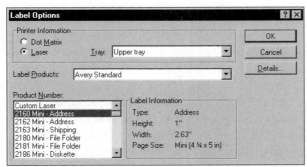

3. First, you must specify whether you wish to print the merged labels on a laser printer or a dot-matrix printer. These two kinds of printers handle the job in different ways. Laser printers only handle individual sheets. To print labels on laser printers, you must purchase adhesive labels that come in 8½"×11" sheets. Often these sheets contain two or three columns of labels, each label being an inch or two high. A dot-matrix printer, on the other hand, handles continuously fed paper best. You may purchase labels for dot-matrix printers that come in long strips, sometimes 5,000 labels long, with tractor-feed guides on each margin.

4. The next step is to specify what size labels you wish to print. There are many sizes and shapes of adhesive labels, according to their use. They come in sizes as small as file folder labels or as large as shipping labels, plus disk labels, videotape labels, and others. Even common mailing labels come in several sizes. A popular brand name of adhesive mailing labels is Avery. The product number of Avery labels is used in Word to specify the size of the labels.

5. Once the size and type of labels are specified, pressing the OK button brings up the Create Labels dialog box, shown in Figure 13.15. In the Sample Label area you will insert the merge fields in the order you wish them to appear on the mailing label, pressing the [Spacebar] between fields and [Enter] at the end of each line. If you wish to print the Postal Bar Code above the address information (assuming your printer can do so), click the appropriate button. Pressing OK returns you to the Mail Merge Helper, which displays the type of main document, the names of the two files involved, and the merge options in effect. If you were to view the mailing labels document at this point, you would see a page-sized table with cells each containing the merge fields specified in the sample label.

FIGURE 13.15
Creating the sample mailing label

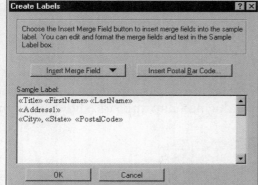

6. Before you send your merged files to the printer, it is always a good idea to print a sample page or two to make sure the addresses fit the labels. Inside the box of labels you will often find a grid sheet that you can hold up to the light along with your printout to make sure that the labels are positioned correctly. You may need to adjust the margins a little, change the height or width of the cells in the table (which is what the mailing label main document is), or change the font size so that a long address (such as South Padre Island, TX 78987-4523) does not wrap to another line.

Merging envelopes is a similar process. From the Mail Merge Helper, create a main document for Envelopes and open or create the data source. After you click Set Up Main Document, you will be asked to select the size of the envelope and you may set other envelope options. The Envelope Address dialog box is identical to the Create Labels dialog box. After you set up the main document, the process of merging envelopes and mailing labels is identical to that of merging main documents. Certain records can be selected or query options set.

Summary

Mass mailings use the same text with personalized information for many recipients. Word's Mail Merge feature is ideal for creating form letters, mailing labels, and envelopes for mass mailings. Mail Merge requires two files: a data source with the pieces of information that will be unique for each printout, and the main document with the text that will be common to all printouts.

The first line in the data source is the header row. The header row consists of merge fields that are used to associate places in the main document with information in the data source. The second and subsequent lines in the data source contain the data records that will be merged into the main document.

The main document is a normal word processing document, with two additions:

- The Mail Merge toolbar appears between the Formatting toolbar and the ruler.

- Within the document there are merge fields placed at each location that needs unique information from the data source.

The buttons on the Mail Merge toolbar perform several functions, editing the data source and viewing the data in place of the merge fields. The merged documents may be stored in a separate file for additional modification or sent to the printer through the use of the Merge to New Document or Merge to Printer button. By default, mail merge will create one copy of the merged main document for every line of data in the data source; however, you may elect to merge only information from selected records of the data source through the use of the Mail Merge button. IF statements may be used to include conditional text only when certain criteria are met.

Catalogs and price lists are good examples of another use for mail merge. The main difference between this type of main document and a form letter type is that more than one set of information appears on one page. The usual process requires you to merge to a new document and add titles and column headings after the merge process.

Word also provides an easy way to create mailing-label and envelope main documents for use in merging with name and address data. The user supplies the name of the data source, the type of label or envelope, and the format of a sample label or envelope. Merging the mailing-label document is identical to the process of merging form letters.

EXERCISE 13.1

A Day in the Life of a College Student

Objective: Send a personalized notice of an upcoming ski trip to club members and friends.

1. Open the document *EX13-1 Merge*. Select Tools | Mail Merge. Click on Create under Main Document, select Form Letters, and click Active Window.

2. Click on Get Data, and create a new data source. Remove all the fields except FirstName, LastName, and Address1. Insert a new field with the name Member. Save the data source as *EX13-1 Data*.

3. Edit the main document. At the bottom of the flyer, next to Name, insert the FirstName and LastName fields with a space between them. Put the Address1 merge field after Address. Press [Tab], if necessary, to make the name and address merge fields line up.

4. Click on the Edit Data Source button, and type in your own first name and last name.

5. To insert the entire street address as well as city, state, and zip into a single field, it is easier to work in the source document directly, rather than in the data form. Click on the View Source button.

6. The data source is a table with bold field names in the top row. Type your street address in the appropriate cell and press [Enter]. Type your city, state, and zip in the same cell. Tab to the Member cell and type yes.

7. Press [Tab] to insert a new row, and continue typing in five to ten names and addresses, some as members (put yes)and some not (put no). Save the source file again.

8. Click on the Mail Merge Main Document button to return to the flyer. Place the cursor on the line above the name.

    Members will receive a discount on the trip if they send in their deposit before November 1, but nonmembers receive no discount. We will use an IF statement to include a sentence to that effect.

9. Click Insert Word Field and select If…Then…Else….

10. In the IF dialog box under Field Name select Member. Under Comparison select Equal To. Under Compare To, type yes with the same capitalization you used in the data source. Under Insert This Text, type the following sentence:

    Register before November 1 and receive $50 off!

    Under Otherwise Insert This Text type this sentence:

    Nonmembers and friends are also welcome!

    Click OK.

11. Click on the View Merged Data button to see the data in place of the merge fields. Click through the records in the database to see the IF statement change the text.

12. Click on the Mail Merge button. In the Merge dialog box, select Merge to Printer, and specify Records to Be Merged From 1 To 3. Click Merge to print. Click OK in the Print dialog box.

EXERCISE 13.2

Crusty's Pizza

Objective: Send a letter with coupon to customers who either have received a late delivery or have proven to be good customers.

1. Create a new document and issue the command Tools | Mail Merge. Select Form Letters and Active Window.

2. Click the Get Data button and open the file *EX13-2 Data* as the data source.

3. Edit the main document and type the following text, inserting your city, state, and zip and the appropriate merge fields.

   ```
   The «Name» family
   «Address»
   Your city, state and zip
   ```

   ```
   Crusty's Pizza values you as a customer. Sometimes things
   do not go as smoothly as we would like. Because we were
   late delivering your pizza, we are sending a coupon for a
   free large pizza. Just mention this card when you place
   your order, and give it to the driver on delivery.
   ```

   ```
   Sincerely,
   ```

   ```
   The Management of Crusty's Pizza
   ```

4. Place the cursor in front of Just in the last sentence and click the Insert Word Field button. Select If...Then...Else....

5. In the drop-down list under Field Name select number_of_orders, under Comparison select Greater Than, and in Compare To, type 5. In the box for Insert This Text, type the following text:

   ```
   Because you ordered more than five times last month, you
   will receive unlimited toppings on your next order.
   ```

   In the Otherwise Insert This Text box type this:

   ```
   This free pizza may have up to two toppings.
   ```

6. Click OK to insert the IF statement.

   If you do not get the IF statement correct the first time, just delete it and start over.

7. Click the View Merged Data button to see the results. Click on the Next Record button to see the IF statement change according to the data.

   Since people who did not receive a late order should not receive this offer of a free pizza, we must set query options.

8. Select Tools | Mail Merge and click on Query Options (or else click on the Mail Merge button and click Query Options).

9. In the Field box select late_orders and in the Comparison box select Is Not Blank and click OK.

10. Merge to a new document. If all is correct, you should have four letters, two of which offer unlimited toppings, and two of which offer two toppings.

11. Create mailing labels for the envelopes and print them on plain paper rather than on real labels to see the results. Select Tools | Mail Merge, click Create under Main Document, and select Mailing Labels. Click New Main Document.

12. Click Get Data under Data Source, then Open Data Source, and again open the *EX13-2 Data* file. Click Set Up Main Document.

13. Specify if you have a laser or dot-matrix printer, and scroll through the list to find Product Number 5160 - Address labels. Click OK.

14. Set up the sample mailing label just as you did for the letter, including merge fields where appropriate, and using your own city, state, and zip.

```
The «Name» family
«Address»
Your city, state and zip
```

15. In the main mailing label document, click the Merge to Printer button to see the results.

EXERCISE 13.3

The Internet

Objective: Create name tags for people who have registered to attend the continuing education course.

1. In a new document select Tools | Mail Merge. Click on Create under Main Document and select Mailing Labels and Active Window.

2. Click on Get Data under Data Source and select Create Data Source.

3. In the Create Data Source dialog box, remove all the field names except FirstName, LastName, and Company. Click OK.

4. Save the data source as *EX13-3 Data*.

5. Click Set Up Main Document and then specify whether you will be printing to a dot-matrix or laser printer. Scroll through the list of Products Numbers and select the one labeled Name Tag. Click OK.

6. In the Sample Label box, press [Enter] twice to leave blank lines. Insert the merge fields below, and then click OK.

```
«FirstName» «LastName»
«Company»
```

7. Click Close to view the main document. You will see a table with each cell the size of a single label. Select the cells in the table and click the Center button. Format to bold and 28 points.

8. In each cell, highlight the Company merge field and format to 18 points bold.

9. Click the Edit Data Source button. Type 10 to 15 names and companies into the data form, clicking Add New each time. Click OK to return to the main document.

10. Click the View Merged Data button to see the names in place. Some names may be too long to fit on the name tag without wrapping. We will adjust that in the next steps.

11. If you are printing to real name tag labels, skip this step. If you are printing to plain paper, select Table | Select Table and apply an inside and outside border. This way we can see the individual name tags when they are printed.

12. Click the Merge to New Document button.

13. In the merged document that results, check the labels to see that all names are spelled correctly. If any names wrap to a second line, highlight them and change to a smaller point size.

14. If you are printing to plain paper, skip this step. If you are printing to real labels, print a sample page of the labels on plain paper. Hold the result up to the name tag labels to see how they fit. If margins need adjusting, do that now with the File | Page Setup command.

15. Click the Print button—if you are using real labels, load them in the printer first.

EXERCISE 13.4

Thrill Seeker Tours

Objective: Create a catalog of the nation's best roller coasters.

1. Create a new document and issue the command Tools | Mail Merge. Select Catalog for the main document and use the active window.

2. Click the Get Data button and use the file *EX13-4 Data* as the data source.

3. Edit the main document. Type the following text, inserting the merge fields as shown. Format the roller coaster name to 14 points bold.

```
«Name»
«Park»
«Location»
«Wood_steel»
Notes: «special_features»
```

4. Click the Edit Data Source button and click the arrows next to Record to look through the records in the data form for your favorite coaster. If it does not appear, add it to the database. Sort the coasters in alphabetical order.

5. Click on Add New and type in information for your favorite coasters. Click OK to return to the main document.

6. With the cursor at the end of the last line, press ⏎Enter. On the blank lines type three underscores (___) and press ⏎Enter again. This creates a bold rule across the page.

7. Highlight all the lines *except* the very last blank line. Issue the command Format I Paragraph, select the Text Flow tab, and check the box Keep with Next. Press OK to apply the format.

8. Click the Columns button and drag to change to two-column format.

9. Click the Merge to New Document button.

10. In the new catalog document, select View I Header and Footer. Type the following title, formatted bold and 22 points:

    `The Best Roller Coasters in North America`

11. Select Insert I Page Numbers, and select bottom center of page. Click OK.

12. Preview the catalog document and, if everything is correct, print.

Review Questions

*1. What is the purpose of performing a mail merge?

2. What two types of files are required to execute a mail merge?

*3. What information is found on the first line of the data source? On subsequent lines?

4. What is the difference between using Data Form and the actual data source document for entering data?

*5. What are the two differences between a main document and a normal document?

6. How do you insert a merge field into a document and how does it appear?

*7. How can you view data in the document in place of the merge fields?

8. How does Word associate merge fields in a main document with the right piece of information in the data source?

*9. What is the difference between using File I Print and using Tools I Mail Merge when printing a main document?

10. What are two ways to merge documents?

*11. What two ways can you use to select only certain lines of data from the data source to merge, rather than every line?

12. Why would you merge documents to a file rather than to the printer?

*13. What is an IF merge field used for?

14. Where can you change the data source once your main document is set up?

*15. What is the difference between the ways dot-matrix and laser printers handle mailing labels?

16. One type of document for which you would use a Catalog type of main document would be

   a. Mailing labels.

   b. Envelopes.

   c. Price lists.

   d. Name tags.

*17. The two types of files required to do a mail merge are

   a. A header document and a main file.

   b. A data source and a main document.

   c. A form letter and a data record.

   d. A header source and a main data file.

18. If you wish to mail merge only to people who live in Texas, you must

   a. Set query options.

   b. Insert an IF statement.

   c. Specify the record numbers.

   d. Reveal the merged data and print one at a time.

*19. The file containing the data should be

   a. A Word table.

   b. An Excel spreadsheet.

   c. An Access table.

   d. All of the above.

Key Terms

Data source	IF field	Query
Field	Link	Record
Filter	Main document	
Header row	Merge field	

Using Mail Merge to Apply for Jobs

People searching for jobs send out many letters and résumés. In this application, you will create a form letter using the Mail Merge feature in Word.

Create a data source with the following merge fields:

```
Title, FirstName, LastName, JobTitle, Company, Address1,
City, State, PostalCode, PositionWanted, Contact
```

Save the data source, and then enter five names in it. Use either real or fictitious names. For the `PositionWanted` merge field, enter the position at the company for which you are applying. For the `Contact`, enter a name only if you know someone inside the company. Some data records should have a blank entry in this field.

Create an application letter based on the data source above, using standard business letter format. The first paragraph in the body of the letter should, in your own words, state that you are applying for a specific job, the `PositionWanted` merge field. Put up front your best qualifications for that job. Type a sentence that mentions the name of someone you already know in the organization—`Contact`—who has encouraged you to apply.

Since `Contact` is blank for some of the records, include an IF statement that causes the sentence to print only if the data in the `Contact` merge field is not blank. The easiest way to do this is to highlight the sentence in the document, cut it, and then click Insert Word Field and paste it in the If . . .Then box.

In the second and third paragraphs, target the job you want. Use items highlighted from your résumé about your education, work experience, and activities that give evidence of how you can benefit that company in that position. Somewhere in the second or third paragraph mention the enclosed résumé.

In the last paragraph mention the name of the organization and ask specifically for an interview. If you find that you use certain words repetitively, use the thesaurus to search for suitable synonyms. Proofread carefully, as absolutely no errors are tolerated when you are applying for a job. Save the main document. Check the merged data in the letter for extra spaces or errors, and print the merged letters.

Working with Long Documents

14

Into the life of every student comes the dreaded assignment of a term paper or report. Word not only is useful for giving a professional appearance to such a long document, but also includes several features that provide real help in preparing it.

Most authors use an outline of some sort when creating a document that requires any kind of organization. An outline helps you keep a document moving in the right direction as you write it and ensures that no topics are repeated or left out. A long document requires an outline to facilitate covering ideas in order and supporting main points thoroughly. Word's outline feature not only provides an easy way to organize and plan your document, but is actually another, structural view of the same document.

Once you have determined what the major headings in your outline will be, you can divide the long document into several subdocuments in Master Document view. Each chapter or subdocument can be worked on independently by different users, and then viewed as a single file in the master document. A master document allows you to create automatic cross references, tables of contents, and indexes that involve all the chapters.

As you type the document, Word allows you to insert footnotes and cross references. Footnotes offer documentation for references made to text from another source. Generally, when you refer to another author's material you are required to give that author credit for the material you used. A footnote reference mark is used in the document body next to the material being referenced that leads to the footnote. The footnote can appear immediately below the text, at the end of the page, or at the end of the chapter or document (called endnotes).

At the end of the process of creating a long document, it generally takes a great deal of time and effort to create the table of contents and the index. Each requires the author to go through a document, find headings and subheadings and topics or terms that need to be indexed, write down their page numbers, and compile a list of them all. As a document changes, the order and contents of the table of contents will change. The pages where items in the index will appear also change as text is added to and deleted from a document. Word includes features to create these with a minimal amount of effort by the author. This allows you more time to be creative with your writing rather than slavishly spending time alphabetizing and numbering.

The power of these features is that they are dynamic. Changes to the document are reflected in the outline, and vice versa. Whenever text is moved, any footnotes affected are automatically rearranged and renumbered. Changes in page numbering within the document are updated in the table of contents and the index with one keystroke. This unit covers Word's procedures for creating an outline, footnotes, a table of contents, and an index, as well as how to use Master Document view.

Learning Objectives

At the completion of this unit you should know

1. how to create and reorder an outline,

2. how to use Master Document view to create subdocuments,

3. how to create, delete, edit, and move footnotes,

4. how to create the table of contents,

5. how to mark items for the index and how to create the index.

Important Commands

Format | Style

Insert | Footnote

Insert | Index and Tables

View | Footnotes

View | Master Document

View | Outline

Outlines

Writing a term paper is a long process, but not a difficult one, especially if you use an *outline* in planning your writing. Word allows you to take the concept of an outline one step further. The outline that you create to organize your ideas is in fact another view of the same document. Outlines help you do these four tasks easily:

- Organize the material

- Write sections of text

- Rearrange large portions of text
- Format the headings consistently.

To create an outline, you organize the material into major topics. The major topics are then divided into subtopics, and so on. The level of detail depends on you. Each section of a document has a *heading* as its title. The most general headings might include the chapter names, while the most specific would be subheadings that are titles of a section containing only one or two paragraphs. The outline is a list of these sections in the order they will appear in your document.

Besides keeping the sequential order of the topics in outline form, Word allows you to actually write the document within the outline. Once the outline is completed, you enter the text for each section under the heading for that topic. A single file contains both outline and document. When you need to view the entire document, select Page Layout view or Normal view to make additions or modifications. To view only the outline, select Outline view to see just the headings in the document. Depending on the detail desired, you may display only major topic headings or any level of subheadings.

Headings, and the material under them, can easily be rearranged or promoted or demoted to another level by clicking on buttons in the Outline toolbar. In Outline view, you may specify the *level number* of headings you wish to see, from an exclusive presentation of level 1 headings to a comprehensive look at all headings and the text under them.

Another important feature of the outline in Word is that it also helps you maintain consistent heading format attributes. All headings on the same level will be formatted the same way through the use of styles. Modifying the style changes the format for all the headings at that level.

Creating an Outline

Begin typing an outline in an empty document. Enter the heading for each topic in the document on a separate line. It is not necessary to apply any formatting to the text at this point. When the headings are all entered, select View | Outline or click on the Outline View button at the bottom of the screen to change to the Outline view.

In Outline view, the screen changes several ways. First, the Outline toolbar shown in Figure 14.1 replaces the ruler at the top of the work area. It contains buttons that allow you to promote or demote headings to different levels.

FIGURE 14.1
Outline toolbar

FIGURE 14.2
Text in
Outline view

□	Heading One
□	Heading Two
□	Heading Three

Word assumes that all the headings you entered are normal text. This is indicated by the small open square to the left of each line of text, as in Figure 14.2. Text can be changed to a heading by *promoting* it (moving the text to the left in the outline). Headings can be promoted to higher headings, or *demoted* to subheadings or to body text (to the right in the outline).

To promote a line from text to a level 1 heading, click in or highlight the line and then click on the Promote button (the left arrow) on the Outline toolbar. Another way to do the same thing is to drag it to the left. The open plus sign next to Heading One, as illustrated in Figure 14.3, indicates that this line is now a heading rather than a line of text. It also tells you that the heading has information under it: either subheadings or text.

FIGURE 14.3
Text promoted to a heading

⊕ Heading One
  ▫ Heading Two
  ▫ Heading Three

To demote a heading or make it a lower level, click on the Demote button on the Outline toolbar. You can also demote a heading by dragging it to the right. The symbol next to the line does not change, but the heading moves to the right to indicate that it is now at a lower level in the outline. The lines under that heading also move to the right because Word assumes that they are subtopics under that heading. A heading can be demoted to text rather than to another heading level by clicking on the Demote to Body Text button with the double right arrow.

When all headings in the outline are at the correct level, you may choose how much detail to display in the Outline view. The level 1 headings are the titles of the major sections or chapters in the document. They are the ones on the left margin in the outline. To display only the level 1 headings, click on the Show Heading 1 button on the Outline toolbar. Any subheadings and text in the document are *collapsed* so that they no longer show in Outline view. Clicking on the 2 button displays level 1 and level 2 headings, while all others are hidden. Each number button displays headings at or above that level. The All button *expands* to display all headings and text.

How do I write an outline for a term paper?

1. *Make a list of key words and phrases on the subject.*

2. *Arrange the list to separate ideas into main topics and subtopics.*

3. *Let the preliminary outline guide your research. Revise as necessary to fit the research.*

4. *Develop the working outline into one of these logical structures:*

   - *Chronological (give the order in which events happened)*

   - *Comparison-contrast (show similarities and differences between two aspects)*

   - *Problem-solution (state a problem, give background, analyze possible solutions)*

   - *Spatial (discuss items according to location or geography)*

   - *Topical (break down topics and analyze them one by one)*

Source: *Why Use an Outline*, Opening Doors, Indianapolis, IN.

You may also expand or collapse a single heading in the outline. Click in the heading to be affected and click on the Collapse button with the minus sign to hide its subheadings one level at a time. Clicking on the Expand button with the plus sign expands the selected portion of the outline by displaying hidden subheadings under the selected line. Another easy way to expand or collapse a heading is to double-click on the plus symbol next to it.

GUIDED ACTIVITY 14.1

Creating an Outline

1. Start Word. Create a new document.

2. Enter the following text.

    ```
    Section One
    Introduction
    Purpose
    Goals
    Section Two
    Short-Term Goals
    Weeks One Through Five
    Weeks Six Through Ten
    Long-Term Goals
    Year One
    Year Two
    ```

3. Select View | Outline or click on the Outline View button.

    Word assumes that each line in the document is a line of text rather than a heading, as shown in Figure 14.4. Promote the first line in the document, Section One, to a level 1 heading.

FIGURE 14.4
Text in Outline view

```
□  Section One
□  Introduction
□  Purpose
□  Goals
□  Section Two
□  Short-Term Goals
□  Weeks One Through Five
□  Weeks Six Through Ten
□  Long-Term Goals
□  Year One
□  Year Two
```

4. Position the mouse pointer to the left of Section One and click once. Click on the Promote button (with the left arrow) on the Outline toolbar to promote the line to a heading.

    Section One is now a heading rather than text, as in Figure 14.5. The rest of the lines in the document are still just text. Make the next three lines in the document subheadings under Section One.

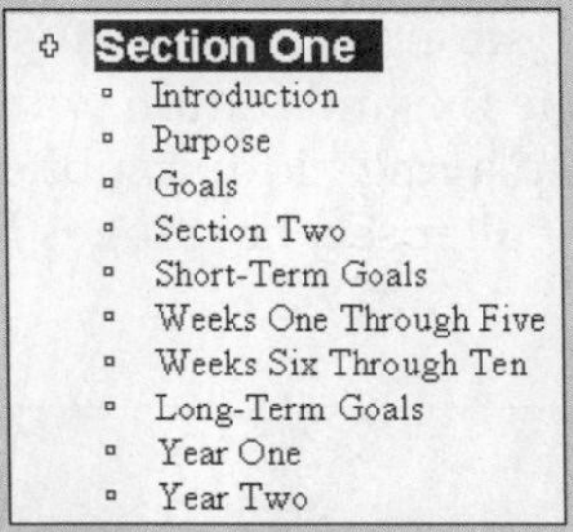

FIGURE 14.5
*Section One
promoted to a
level 1 heading*

```
◇  Section One
   ▫  Introduction
   ▫  Purpose
   ▫  Goals
   ▫  Section Two
   ▫  Short-Term Goals
   ▫  Weeks One Through Five
   ▫  Weeks Six Through Ten
   ▫  Long-Term Goals
   ▫  Year One
   ▫  Year Two
```

5. Highlight the `Introduction`, `Purpose`, and `Goals` lines in the document. Click on the Demote button (with the right arrow) on the Outline toolbar. Use the Demote button to make it a subheading from the previous heading.

   Figure 14.6 shows that `Section One` is a level 1 heading. `Introduction`, `Purpose`, and `Goals` are level 2 headings under `Section One`. The open minus signs next to `Introduction` and `Purpose` indicate that there are no subheadings or text under these titles.

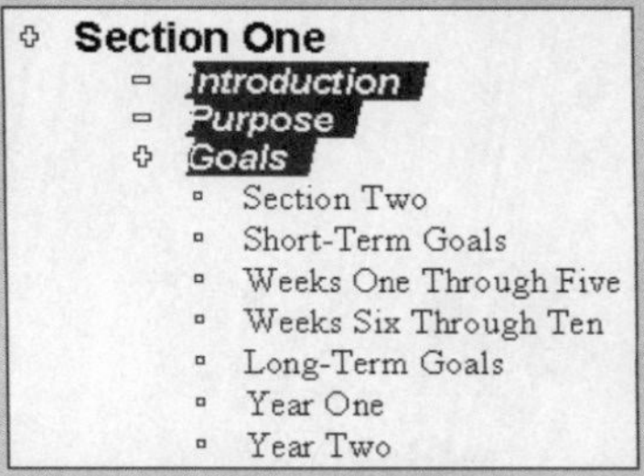

FIGURE 14.6
*Level 2
headings under
Section One*

```
◇  Section One
   ▭  Introduction
   ▭  Purpose
   ◇  Goals
      ▫  Section Two
      ▫  Short-Term Goals
      ▫  Weeks One Through Five
      ▫  Weeks Six Through Ten
      ▫  Long-Term Goals
      ▫  Year One
      ▫  Year Two
```

   `Section Two` should also be a level 1 heading. `Short-Term Goals` and `Long-Term Goals` will be level 2 headings, while the other lines will be level 3 headings.

6. Drag the symbol next to `Section Two` to the left to promote Section Two to a level 1 heading.

7. Drag the symbol next to `Short-Term Goals` to the right to make it a level 2 heading.

8. Highlight `Weeks One Through Five` and `Weeks Six Through Ten`. Click on the Demote button to make them level 3 headings.

9. Make `Long-Term Goals` a level 2 heading by dragging its symbol even with that of `Short-Term Goals`. Highlight the two lines under it and click on the Demote button to make them level 3 headings.

   The headings should line up like those in Figure 14.7.

   Now that your outline is created, you may choose the level of detail displayed in the Outline view.

10. Click on the Show Heading 1 button on the Outline toolbar.

FIGURE 14.7

Level 1, level 2, and level 3 headings

⬦ **Section One**
  ▫ *Introduction*
  ▫ *Purpose*
  ▫ *Goals*
⬦ **Section Two**
  ⬦ *Short-Term Goals*
    ▫ Weeks One Through Five
    ▫ Weeks Six Through Ten
  ⬦ *Long-Term Goals*
    ▫ Year One
    ▫ Year Two

The outline has been collapsed to display only level 1 headings. Both headings have subheadings under them, as indicated by the symbols to their left and the faint underlines beneath them, as in Figure 14.8.

FIGURE 14.8

Outline collapsed to show only level 1 headings

⬦ **Section One**
⬦ **Section Two**

11. Click on the Show Heading 2 button on the Outline toolbar.

    The outline expands to include the level 1 and level 2 headings, as shown in Figure 14.9. You may also expand just a portion of the outline rather than the entire outline.

FIGURE 14.9

Outline expanded to show both level 1 and 2 headings

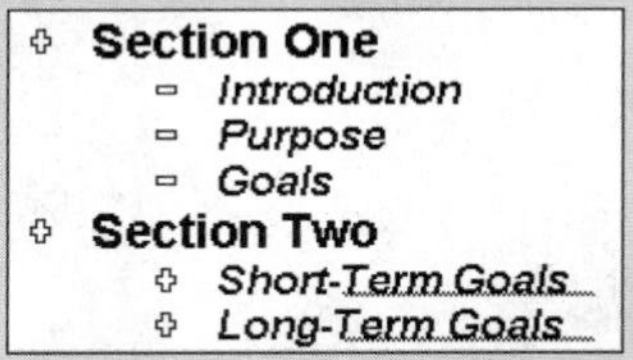

⬦ **Section One**
  ▫ *Introduction*
  ▫ *Purpose*
  ▫ *Goals*
⬦ **Section Two**
  ⬦ *Short-Term Goals*
  ⬦ *Long-Term Goals*

12. Highlight the line containing `Long-Term Goals`. Click on the Expand button that resembles a plus sign on the Outline toolbar.

    The level 3 headings under `Long-Term Goals` appear, but the ones under `Short-Term Goals` are still hidden, as shown in Figure 14.10. Only the area highlighted is affected when you click on the Expand or Collapse button.

FIGURE 14.10

Expanding only one heading

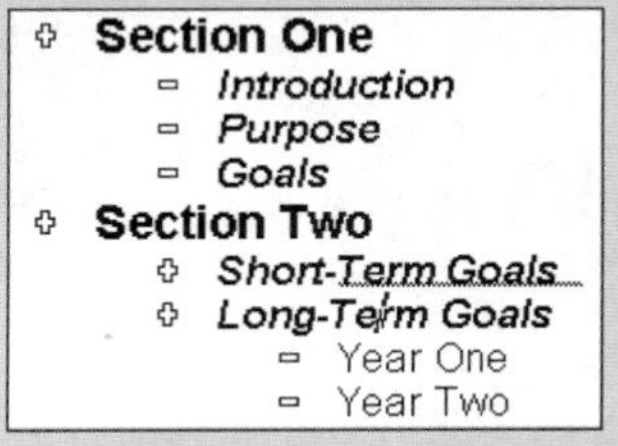

⬦ **Section One**
  ▫ *Introduction*
  ▫ *Purpose*
  ▫ *Goals*
⬦ **Section Two**
  ⬦ *Short-Term Goals*
  ⬦ *Long-Term Goals*
    ▫ Year One
    ▫ Year Two

Modifying and Adding Text to an Outline

Once the outline is created, you may add text under each topic heading. This is done by returning to Normal view or Page Layout view, positioning the cursor at the end of the heading after which you wish to add text, pressing [Enter] to start a new paragraph, and typing the text. In revising the text, you may move sections of the outline around by collapsing or expanding heading levels or selecting the portion to be moved and clicking on the up arrow or down arrow on the Outline toolbar. All the subheadings and text under the highlighted heading will be moved along with it.

This is an incredibly easy and efficient way to reorganize a document, when you have a brainstorm and need to add a few new sections, or place some sections in a more logical order. By simply moving the title of a section, you also move all the text under that heading to the new location. You can examine the structure of your paper to make sure you have adequate examples, statistics, analysis, or discussion to support your statements.

Do I need to revise my outline?

If the answer to any of the following questions is no, make revisions. You may find you need to do more research in a certain area.

- *Is my overall thesis supported?*

- *Are each of the main points supported with examples?*

- *Do the ideas have a logical flow?*

- *Does background information precede analysis or opinion?*

- *Do explanations come before consequences?*

- *Do arguments and reasons come before conclusions?*

- *Are conclusions sound?*

- *Are spelling and grammar correct?*

- *Is the outline parallel—are the headings in noun form (as in Modification of the Structure), gerund form (as in Modifying the Structure), in infinitive phrases (as in To Modify the Structure), or full sentences (Modifying the Structure Is a Snap)?*

Source: *Why Use an Outline*, Opening Doors, Indianapolis, IN.

GUIDED ACTIVITY 14.2

Adding Text and Moving Headings

1. Exit the Outline view by clicking on the Normal View button or the Page Layout View button.

   All the headings should return to the left margin but will retain the format attributes of their respective levels.

2. Position the cursor at the end of the line containing `Weeks One Through Five`. Press `Enter` to start a new paragraph. Word assumes that you want the next paragraph after this heading to be Normal style. Enter the following text:

   `Our first priority is to determine the demand for the product in its current state.`

3. Move the cursor to the end of the line containing `Weeks Six Through Ten`. Press `Enter` and type the following text:

   `The second step is to find ways to modify the product to increase its marketability.`

   Any amount of text can be added under outline headings. Using an outline is an excellent way to write a document because it helps organize your thoughts and can be easily revised as you think more about your project. When the text has been entered, you can change back to the Outline view and rearrange the document by moving the headings.

4. Select View | Outline or click on the Outline View button. Double-click the symbol next to `Short-Term Goals` to expand the subheadings. The new text you entered is included in the outline.

5. Click the Show First Line Only button to compress the text somewhat, as shown in Figure 14.11. Only the outline headings have an open minus sign or an open plus sign next to each of them. Body text has a small square next to each paragraph.

6. Click on the Show Heading 3 button on the Outline toolbar.

FIGURE 14.11
Outline showing added text

```
⊹  Section Two
     ⊹   Short-Term Goals
           ⊹   Weeks One Through Five
                   □    Our first priority is to determine the demand for the product in its …
           ⊹   Weeks Six Through Ten
                   □    The second step is to find ways to modify the product to increase …
     ⊹   Long-Term Goals
           □   Year One
           □   Year Two
```

Since you chose to see only level 3 headings and higher, the body text is no longer displayed.

When you move a heading to a different location in a document, all sub-headings and text under it also move.

7. Position the pointer over the open plus sign next to `Weeks Six Through Ten`.

When positioned correctly, the mouse pointer should change shape from a normal pointer to a four-headed arrow.

8. Drag the open plus sign upward. When the horizontal line is between `Short-Term Goals` and `Weeks One Through Five,` release the mouse button.

A horizontal line with an arrowhead will appear as you drag the mark up, as shown in Figure 14.12.

FIGURE 14.12
*Rearranging
the outline*

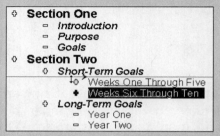

`Weeks Six Through Ten` has now moved above `Weeks One Through Five` in the outline.

9. Click on the All button on the Outline toolbar.

Moving the collapsed heading in the outline also moves anything under the heading, as shown in Figure 14.13. Here, the body text under `Weeks Six Through Ten` moved with it. Using this method, you can move a large portion of a document by simply dragging its title in the Outline view. You may drag the headings directly with the mouse or click the Move Up and Move Down arrow buttons on the Outline toolbar to move a heading in the outline. You may move any level heading by using these methods.

FIGURE 14.13
*Moved heading
rearranges text*

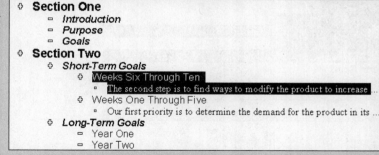

Formatting Outline Headings

It is important that all the headings on the same level be formatted the same way. The reader keeps track of major topics in a document by the format of its headings. Word maintains a set of format attributes for each level. Every heading in a level will automatically have these attributes applied to it. The set of attributes for each level is stored in a style. As you learned in an earlier unit, a style is a set of format attributes that are collected under a single name on the toolbar or in the Format | Style dialog box. The name of the style for each heading is the word Heading followed by the number of the level. For example, all level 1 headings are formatted to the style Heading 1. You may view and modify the attributes for Heading 1 by selecting Format | Style, as shown in Figure 14.14.

FIGURE 14.14
Format | Style dialog box

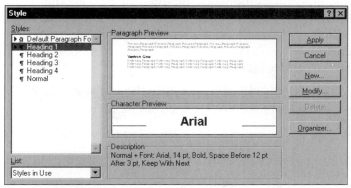

All the attributes for the style are given in the Description box. Highlight the name of the style to be modified, and click on the Modify button.

From the Modify Style dialog box, shown in Figure 14.15, by clicking on the Format button you may change the format of the font; the paragraph; the tabs, frame, or border; or any other attribute. The dialog boxes that appear are the same ones that

FIGURE 14.15
Modify Style dialog box

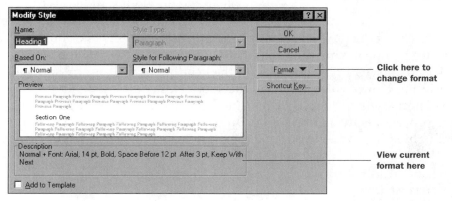

Click here to change format

View current format here

appear if you select Format | Font, Format | Paragraph, Format | Tabs, Format | Frame, and Format | Borders and Shading. The difference, though, is that changing the format of the style (rather than formatting the individual paragraphs) changes every heading at that level throughout the document at one time.

Every heading of the same level whose style is being modified will reflect the format attributes you select here. This will ensure that all headings of the same level will be formatted the same way. The reader will be able to follow the organization of the document more easily and with greater comprehension because of the consistent headings.

Using Master Document View

Outlines work well for organizing a long document, rearranging blocks of text, and keeping the formatting consistent. But for very large projects, Word provides a handy addition to Outline view called *Master Document view*. Master Document view works by dividing a very long document, called a *master document* into *subdocuments*. This has several advantages:

- It enables more than one person to work on different sections at the same time but also to view them together as a single document.

- It allows page numbering and cross references to flow continuously.

- It simplifies creating a comprehensive table of contents and index.

Techniques for creating and working with master documents are similar to techniques you have already used. Once an outline has been created, select View | Master Document to switch from Outline view to Master Document view. At a glance you can see the additional buttons on the Outline toolbar, shown in Figure 14.16, which compose the Master Document toolbar.

FIGURE 14.16
Master Document toolbar

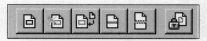

Subdocuments are created from the headings on a given level. For example, you could have subdocuments for Section 1 and Section 2 in the example in the previous Guided Activity, or create a subdocument for each of the level 2 headings. You can create subdocuments one at a time by clicking the plus or minus sign to highlight a heading and clicking the Create Subdocument button. As you can see in Figure 14.17, this places a pale box around the heading as well as any subheadings and text beneath it. You can also create all the subdocuments at once. To do this, highlight all the material you wish to subdivide and then click the Create Subdocument button. This process results in one subdocument for each heading at the same level as the top highlighted line. When you save the master document, the subdocuments are auto-

FIGURE 14.17
A subdocument within a master document

⊞
 ✧ **Section One**
    ▫ *Introduction*
    ▫ *Purpose*
    ✧ *Goals*
        ▫

matically saved and named according to the first few characters in their respective headings.

Once created, subdocuments may be edited and manipulated as separate documents or within the master document. This allows more than one person to work on separate sections of a big document at the same time. When the master document is reopened, the text flows from one subdocument to another, separated only by a section break.

GUIDED ACTIVITY 14.3

Sampling Master Document View

1. Continue with the outline from the previous Guided Activity. Make sure all the text is visible by clicking the All button on the toolbar. Select from the menu the command View | Master Document.

   Immediately, the buttons of the Master Document toolbar appear to the right of the Outline toolbar.

2. Place the cursor in the heading `Section One` and click the Create Subdocument button.

   Immediately the heading is surrounded by a pale box. This box will not be printed and only appears in this view.

3. It makes no sense to include only the heading and not the subheadings beneath it, so click the Remove Subdocument button.

4. Highlight `Section One` and all its subheadings. Click the Create Subdocument button.

   Now the pale box appears around the entire text of Section One.

5. Highlight the subheadings and text below `Section Two`, beginning with `Short-Term Goals`. Click the Create Subdocument button.

   The result is two subdocuments made up of each level 2 heading as shown in Figure 14.18. The level 1 heading `Section Two` remains a part of the master document, but is not part of any subdocument.

6. Select File | Save As and save the master document as *GA14 Report*.

   Not only is the master document saved, but all of the subdocuments are saved at the same time, each one named according to the first characters in their heading.

7. To examine the Short-Term Goals subdocument, double-click on the subdocument icon that appears next to the subdocument heading in the master document.

   The subdocument appears in its own document window with the file name *Short* on the title bar.

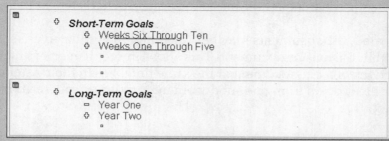

8. Using cut-and-paste or drag-and-drop, highlight the `Weeks Six Through Ten` text heading and the paragraph that follows and move it below the Weeks One Through Five material.

9. Switch back to the master document by selecting the file *GA14 Report* from the Window menu.

   The order of the Section Two subheadings in the master document has not changed, although you changed them in the subdocument. The master document is updated only when the subdocument has been saved.

10. Return to the *Short* subdocument with the Window command. Save and close the subdocument.

    The master document has now been updated to show the headings in the correct order.

11. Switch back to Normal view by clicking on the Normal View button or by selecting View | Normal. The master document contains each of the subdocuments separated by section breaks. From Normal view you can print the entire document at once without having to open separate documents. Using a master document, you can also format the headers and footers and number pages consecutively without fussing with several documents. Furthermore, you can only create cross-references among several documents when you use a master document.

Footnotes

As you type in the information for your report (either in a document, a master document, or a subdocument), whenever you refer to an outside source, the reference must be documented to avoid plagiarism. Some report manuals (such as MLA) allow you to place the reference within parentheses directly following the information. If that is the case for your school, skip this section.

Other manuals, such as *The Chicago Manual of Style* (affectionately known as Turabian, after the woman who devised the scheme so painful to students), instead require references to occur at the bottom of the page, as footnotes, or the end of the document, as endnotes. *Footnotes* or *endnotes* must be inserted whenever you use an idea, information, or a quotation from another author. This is done by inserting a single-character *footnote reference mark* immediately after the text being cited. The footnote reference mark leads the reader to the footnote, which explains in detail the publication or source from which the text or idea was taken.

It would be difficult to take care of footnotes and footnote reference marks manually. Because the footnote appears at the bottom of the page, if any text on the page is added or deleted, the footnote would have to be moved to make sure that it remains at the end of the page. Additionally, if the text being referenced is moved, the footnote must be repositioned on the new page. Finally, if the footnote itself is edited so that it fits on a different number of lines, the entire page must be changed so that the footnote still fits at the bottom.

Instead of forcing you to manually create footnotes, Word allows you to insert a footnote reference mark anywhere in the body of your document. After the mark is inserted, you type the footnote into the *Footnote pane* at the bottom of the work area if you are working in Normal view or, if you are working in Page Layout view, directly into the footnote at the bottom of the page. The footnote remains attached to the footnote reference mark and will automatically appear at the bottom of the page wherever the footnote reference mark appears.

If any text on the page is added or deleted or if the size of the footnote is changed by editing, Word will adjust the document body to leave enough room for the footnote to fit above the bottom margin. Additionally, if you move the text containing the footnote reference mark to another page, the word processor will automatically move its linked footnote to the bottom of the page where the reference occurs, and if necessary will renumber all footnotes correctly. The footnote feature alleviates many problems that writers usually have with footnotes.

Creating Footnotes

Footnote reference marks are inserted immediately after the text that is being referenced from another source. The footnote reference mark is usually a number, but you may choose to replace it with any character.

To insert a footnote reference mark, select Insert | Footnote to reveal the dialog box shown in Figure 14.19. This dialog box allows you to specify whether the reference will be a footnote shown at the bottom of the page or an endnote printed at the end of the document (acceptable form in many scholarly and professional publications). In addition, you can specify the numbering scheme you would like to use in the footnotes. Normally, footnotes are numbered consecutively with Arabic numerals. Some documents may use ABCs or symbols (such as * † ‡ or §). If you use an automatic numbering scheme, Word will keep track of the numbering without your having to type a specific footnote number. You may enter a symbol in the Custom Mark box to use to refer your readers to a footnote; however, Word does not automatically renumber custom marks.

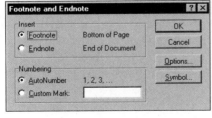

FIGURE 14.19
Insert | Footnote dialog box

When you have made your selection of footnote or endnote and specified the footnote reference mark, click on the OK button. In Normal view the Footnote pane

FIGURE 14.20
Footnote pane

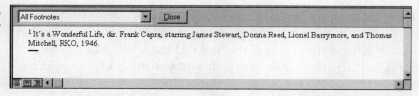

appears at the bottom of the screen, as in Figure 14.20. In Page Layout view, the footnote appears at the bottom of the page just above the bottom margin, separated from the text with a 2" line. Type in the text of the footnote. Word places a superscript number at the location of the footnote reference mark and the same number at the beginning of the footnote at the bottom of the page. You do not need to keep up with these numbers, because the word processor will increment them for you with each footnote you add. Additionally, if you move a footnote from one location to another, all the footnotes affected by the move will be automatically renumbered.

In Normal view, the window has been split into two panes. The Footnote pane has its own scroll bar, as does the work area. To change the size of the Footnote pane, drag the pane's top border. To close the Footnote pane, click on the Close button in the pane.

Rather than issuing the Insert | Footnote command and specifying the information for subsequent footnotes or endnotes, it is often easier for you to use the shortcut key, Ctrl Alt F. Using the shortcut key inserts the next higher number for the footnote reference mark.

GUIDED ACTIVITY 14.4

Inserting Footnote Reference Marks

1. Use the document from the previous Guided Activities. If Page Layout view is selected, change to Normal view.

2. Place the cursor at the end of the sentence that begins with `Our first priority`. Type the following text: `According to a recent market survey, 46 percent of households with an annual income of over $40,000 use a product like ours regularly.`

3. Select Insert | Footnote. By default, Footnote and AutoNumber are selected. Click on the OK button in the dialog box.

    The Footnote pane appears at the bottom of the screen. It contains a superscripted 1 (1) followed by the cursor. Another superscripted 1 appears above in the body text, wherever the cursor was located before executing the command.

4. Type `This is the first footnote.`

    While this is not an acceptable footnote style, it will be helpful for learning how footnote reference marks work.

5. Close the Footnote pane.

6. Select File | Print Preview. You can see the footnote at the bottom of the page. Click Close.

7. Type `Only 15 percent of households with an annual income between $26,000 and $39,999 use our product regularly.`

8. Use the shortcut key to insert a second footnote. Hold down the [Ctrl] and [Alt] keys and press [F]. A superscripted 2 (2) appears at the end of the sentence you just typed, and also in the Footnote pane. Type `This is the second footnote.` The result should resemble Figure 14.21. Click Close to close the Footnote pane.

FIGURE 14.21
The document and two footnotes in Normal view

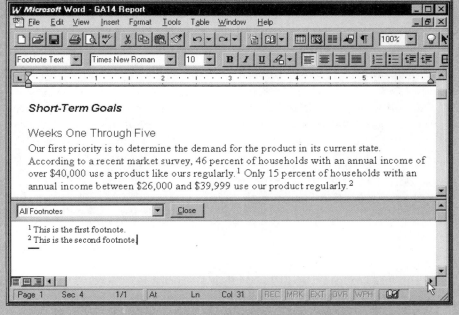

Editing Footnotes

To modify the contents of footnotes or endnotes in Normal view, you need to open the Footnote pane. To do this, either double-click on the footnote reference mark within the document or use the View | Footnotes command. This command acts just like Insert | Footnote by opening the Footnote pane, except that it does not insert a new footnote reference mark in the document body. You may edit or format the text in the Footnote pane and close the pane in the same way you did above.

Footnotes are deleted by highlighting the footnote reference mark in the document body and pressing [Del]. This removes from the document both the footnote reference mark and the entire text of the footnote. Deleting the text from the Footnote pane does *not*, however, delete the footnote reference mark or the space left for it at the bottom of the page or end of the section. Of course, if you delete a footnote by mistake, you can recover it by immediately clicking the Undo button.

GUIDED ACTIVITY 14.5

Editing and Deleting Footnotes

1. Select View | Footnotes.

    The cursor appears in the Footnote pane at the bottom of the work area.

2. Change the first footnote text to read `This is the modification to the first footnote.`

3. Close the Footnote pane. Select Page Layout view to see the footnote in place.

    The footnote has changed to reflect the modification you made. You now decide the footnote is unnecessary and wish to remove it. However, if you just delete the text of the footnote, the reference mark would still appear within the text.

4. Position the cursor to the right of the superscripted 1 in the document body. Press `Backspace`.

    The computer may beep to indicate an error. While footnote reference marks may appear as single characters, they are actually hidden markers in the text. Footnote reference marks must be highlighted before pressing `Backspace` or `Del`.

5. Highlight the superscripted 1 and press `Del`. Scroll down to the bottom of the page to see that the footnote reference mark and footnote text have been removed from the document.

Moving Footnotes

When a segment of text that contains a footnote reference mark is moved, Word does two things. First, if the footnote reference mark is moved to another page, its associated footnote moves to the bottom of that page. Second, if the order of the footnotes in the document is changed, the word processor automatically rearranges and renumbers the footnotes.

To move a footnote reference mark, highlight it and use cut-and-paste or the drag-and-drop technique, just as you would move any other text. Usually, however, the footnote reference mark is moved along with a block of text, not by itself. (Some instructors may ask you to move all marks to the end of a sentence.)

GUIDED ACTIVITY 14.6

Moving Footnotes

1. Click on the Undo button to restore the deleted footnote.

2. Position the cursor at the end of the paragraph after the second footnote. Press `Enter`. Type `This is another reference to an outside source.`

3. Press [Ctrl][Alt][F], or select Insert | Footnote and click OK.

    In Page Layout view, the cursor jumps to the bottom of the page, rather than to the Footnote pane. The other footnotes are just above. The new footnote will be added next to the superscripted 3.

4. Type `This is footnote number three.`

5. Highlight the sentence in the document containing the first footnote reference mark. An easy way to select an entire sentence is to hold down the [Ctrl] key and click on the sentence. Select Edit | Cut or click on the Cut button.

    Scroll down in the document to see that the remaining footnote reference marks change from superscripted 2 and 3 to 1 and 2.

6. Move the cursor to the end of the sentence containing the last footnote. Press [Enter]. Select Edit | Paste or click the Paste button.

    The original first footnote reference mark is now the third. It changes to a 3.

7. Use the mouse or the cursor to view the bottom of the page, shown in Figure 14.22.

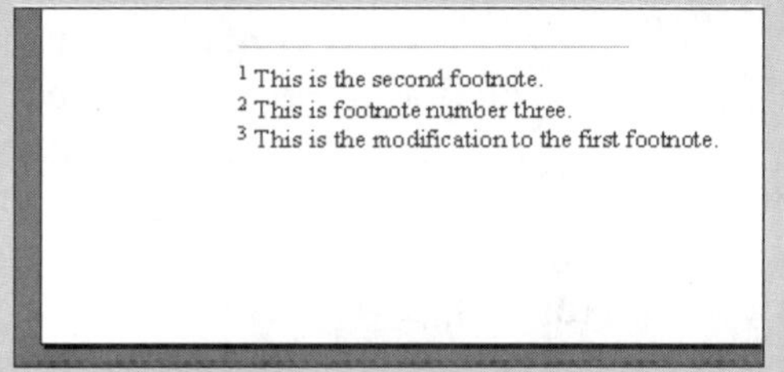

FIGURE 14.22

The rearranged footnotes in Page Layout view

> [1] This is the second footnote.
> [2] This is footnote number three.
> [3] This is the modification to the first footnote.

The footnotes have changed places to reflect the new locations of their associated footnote reference marks.

8. Highlight the sentence containing footnote 1 and remove it with Edit | Cut.

    The second footnote reference mark changes to 1 because it is now the first one in the document.

9. Position the cursor after footnote 2 and press [Ctrl][Enter].

    This inserts a page break. The cursor appears at the top of the second page, as evidenced by the status bar.

10. Select Edit | Paste.

    The cut sentence appears at the top of the second page. Its footnote reference mark has changed to a superscripted 3 to reflect its location in the document with respect to the other footnote reference marks.

11. Page through the document in Page Layout view or Print Preview. Each footnote appears on the same page as its associated footnote reference mark.

Adding an Index

The process of creating an *index* is usually quite tedious, though in Word it is extremely simple. While the author still has to decide which entries will be placed in the index, Word does the tedious work of gathering the entries, compiling them into alphabetical lists, and keeping up with current page numbers. If the document body is later revised so that text is added, deleted, or moved, the index may be easily updated to reflect the changes.

To create the index, you go through the document and place an *index entry* specifying the location and text that should appear in the index. First, highlight the text that should appear in the index, and then press the shortcut key combination Alt Shift X. (The menu selection in this case—Insert | Index and Tables, select the Index tab, and then click Mark Entry—is too tedious to use.) The highlighted text appears in the dialog box, shown in Figure 14.23, so that you can fix capitalization, if necessary. Click Mark to insert the index entry into the document once, or click Mark All to automatically mark the first occurrence of the word in every paragraph. You can continue to display the dialog box on screen as you highlight and mark repeatedly throughout your document. Each time you click Mark, a field code is inserted into the document, as shown in Figure 14.24. Word automatically displays these index entry field codes.

FIGURE 14.23
Mark Index Entry dialog box

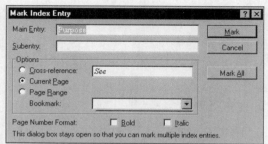

FIGURE 14.24
Index entry field code

Purpose{ XE "Purpose" }

FIGURE 14.25
Index tab

Once the index entries are placed in the document, position the cursor at the desired location of the index. Select Insert | Index and Tables and click on the Index tab, shown in Figure 14.25, and then click OK. Word searches through the document, collecting each index entry field code. The fields are compiled into an index and listed alphabetically at the location of the cursor along with the page numbers where each appears. If you selected bold or italic in the Mark Index Entry dialog box as you marked, that attribute is applied to those entries in the index.

The resulting index is a single field code. This means that you may not edit or format individual words or characters in the index. It may only be modified as a whole. If the document containing index entries is later revised, the index must be updated. To update the index, highlight it entirely and press F9. Any modifications made to the entries in the document will be reflected in the index.

GUIDED ACTIVITY 14.7

Creating an Index

1. Highlight `Purpose` on the first page. Press [Alt][Shift][X]. Click in the box next to Bold in the dialog box since this is a heading, and click on the Mark button. Click Close.

   The highlighted text appears in the index entry field code.

2. With the cursor at the end of that line, press [Enter]. Type `This is the first index entry that is not a heading.`

3. Highlight `first index entry` and press [Alt][Shift][X]. Click on the Mark button. Do not click Close; leave the dialog box on the screen.

4. Highlight `Introduction` and press [Alt][Shift][X]. Check next to Bold, and then click Mark to create a bold index entry for the highlighted text. Click Close, so that you can add more text.

5. Press [Enter] twice. Type `This is the second index entry field code that is not a heading.`

6. Create an index entry by highlighting `second index entry` and pressing [Alt][Shift][X]. Click Mark, but do not close the dialog box.

7. On the Short-Term Goals line, highlight `Goals` and press [Alt][Shift][X]. In the Subentry box, type `Short Term` and click Mark. Repeat for Long-Term Goals, entering `Long Term` next to Subentry and clicking Mark. Click Close to exit the dialog box.

8. Position the cursor at the end of the document and press [Ctrl][Enter] to insert a page break. Type `Index` and apply the Heading 1 style, by clicking on the down arrow next to the Style box showing Normal, and selecting Heading 1. Move the cursor to the end of the line, and press [Enter] again.

9. Select Insert | Index and Tables. Preview several of the formats. The Run-In choice places the subentries in a single paragraph along with the main entry. Choose Classic and Indented. Click OK.

   The index is created from each of the index entry field codes you inserted into the document. Notice that the page numbers for the heading entries are bold.

   If any other entries are marked after you compile the index, you must update the index before it will reflect the changes.

10. Position the cursor at the end of the line containing `Year One`. Press [Enter]. Type `This is the third index entry field code that is not a heading.` Create an index entry for `third index entry`.

11. Highlight the index and press [F9] to update it.

    The updated index now includes the latest index entry you added to the document.

If you move an index entry to another page, the index will reflect the change when you update the index. When moving text that may be in the index, you must be sure to move the index entry along with the text.

Most field codes, such as those for the table of contents or index, are not shown until you select Toggle Field Codes from the shortcut menu or press [Alt][F9]. Index entry field codes are an exception, since they are formatted as hidden text and do not appear with the gray shading within the document.

12. Highlight the entire line containing Purpose, including the index entry, and click the Cut button. Move the cursor to the end of the document and press [Ctrl][Enter] to insert a page break. Paste the Purpose line on the top of the third page.

13. Click in the index to highlight it and press [F9].

Purpose has changed to page 3 in the index.

Creating a Table of Contents

Both an index and a table of contents are helpful in finding a particular subject or term in a large document. The *table of contents* is a listing, in order of appearance, of the major sections of the book. It usually includes chapter titles, headings, and sub-headings, along with the page numbers where each appears.

Besides helping you create documents in a logical order, Outline view (as well as Master Document view) allows you to create tables of contents. Each heading in an outline, along with its corresponding page number, can automatically be included in a table of contents. To create a table of contents from outline headings, select Insert | Index and Tables, and select the Table of Contents tab, as shown in Figure 14.26.

Specify which format you wish the table of contents to have, and preview the effect in the Preview box. When you click OK, every heading in the document above the given level will be included in the table of contents.

FIGURE 14.26
Table of Contents tab

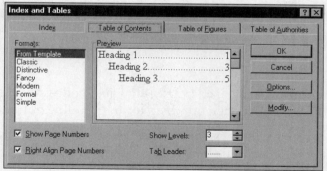

GUIDED ACTIVITY 14.8

Creating a Table of Contents

1. Return to Normal view. Move the cursor to the top of the document.

2. Press `Enter` to leave a blank line above `Section One`. Press `Ctrl` `Enter` to insert a page break.

3. Repeat step 2 after positioning the cursor at the beginning of the line containing `Section Two`.

   The cursor should now be on page 3.

4. Move the cursor to page 1. Select Insert I Index and Tables, click the Table of Contents tab, and preview several formats. Select the one you like best. If the one you choose does not include dot leaders extending from the heading to the page number, select a leader from the Tab Leader drop-down list. Click OK. Note that the page number for each heading is in the same style and size as the heading.

A table of contents is inserted on the first page of the document. Level 1 headings are against the left margin. Headings of other levels may be indented for each level number. The page number where each topic appears is automatically inserted at the right margin.

The entire table is the result of a single field code. When you click in the table of contents, the entire table becomes shaded. To view the field code for the table of contents, select Toggle Field Codes from the shortcut menu, or press `Alt` `F9`. A list of all the shortcut keys for working with long documents is found in Table 14.1.

The table of contents or its field code may be highlighted and moved or deleted, but it cannot be deleted with the `Backspace` or `Del` keys unless the field code is highlighted. To delete a table of contents (and its field code), highlight the entire table so that it turns an even darker shade of gray and press `Del`.

TABLE 14.1
Long document shortcut keys

SHORTCUT KEY	FUNCTION
`Ctrl` `Alt` `F`	Insert a footnote now
`Ctrl` `Alt` `E`	Insert an endnote now
`Alt` `Shift` `X`	Insert an index entry
`F9`	Update a field
`Alt` `F9`	Toggle Field Codes

Summary

Word allows you to create an outline of the headings and subheadings for each topic in a document. By clicking buttons on the Outline toolbar, headings can be moved, promoted, or demoted to higher or lower levels.

After creating an outline you may enter text under each heading in the outline. This is a useful feature because it provides a guide to maintain the organization of the document. After text has been entered, it may be moved to another location in the document by moving its heading in the Outline view.

It is important for all headings of the same level to be formatted the same way. Word maintains a style for each heading level. The format attributes of styles are changed, using the command Format | Style. When a style is changed, all the headings of that level reflect the change.

Master Document view is a handy approach to breaking a long document into component chapters. Whether you create one subdocument at a time or highlight the whole outline and create all the subdocuments at once, once you save the master document the subdocuments are automatically saved at the same time. This allows you to work on an individual chapter, or even allows for more than one person to work on different chapters at the same time. You can then use Master Document view to see all the individual chapters in a single long document. The advantage in using a single master document rather than handling separate documents is that headers, footers, cross-references, tables of contents, and an index are easily made all at one time.

Footnotes are added as documentation for references to outside sources. Word handles footnotes by allowing you to insert footnote reference marks into the text. Footnotes are added by using the Insert | Footnote command. This inserts a footnote reference mark at the location of the cursor and opens the Footnote pane. The footnote text is typed into the pane. To edit footnotes, select View | Footnotes, or double-click the footnote reference. This also opens the Footnote pane but does not insert a footnote reference mark into the text. To delete a footnote, highlight its associated mark in the document body and press [Del]. The word processor prints the associated footnote at the bottom of the page containing the mark, or as an endnote after the last paragraph of the document.

Creating an index is also simple. Entries for the index are added to the document with the shortcut key [Alt][Shift][X]. Once the entries have been entered, the index is created by selecting Insert | Index and Tables. If there are any additions, deletions, or text movements in the document that affect the order of entries in the index, you can update the index to reflect changes in the document by pressing [F9] with the index highlighted.

Word allows you to quickly create a table of contents for any document. The table of contents is created with the command Insert | Index and Tables. Word searches the document for outline headings and places each one in the table of contents along with the page number where it appears. Like the index, the table of contents can be updated to reflect any changes to the document by highlighting the table of contents and pressing [F9].

EXERCISE 14.1

Outline View

1. Open the file *EX14 Report*. Switch to Outline view by selecting View | Outline or clicking on the Outline View button.

2. Promote the items in all caps to level 1 headings. Either drag each heading to the left or click the Promote button.

3. Change all the bolded items to level 2 headings.

4. Demote all the remaining lines except the title to level 3 headings. Print the outline.

5. Display only level 1 headings. Print.

6. Expand the Rock Climbing section only so that all the level 2 and level 3 headings appear. Print.

7. Move the Whitewater section below the Snowboarding section. Print the result.

8. Change to Normal view and examine the heading styles. The bolding that was on the outline before you changed it to headings has affected the format. Highlight the entire document and press [Ctrl] [Spacebar] to return the format to the appropriate style.

9. Change the Heading 1 style so that it is centered rather than left-aligned. To do this, select Format | Style, select Heading 1, and click Modify. Click on the Format button and from the drop-down list select Paragraph. Change the alignment to Centered. Click OK twice and close. Print page 2 only.

EXERCISE 14.2

Master Document View

1. Continue with the outline from the previous exercise. Write a paragraph of body text under the Tour Features heading for any tour you like.

2. Select View | Master Document. Highlight the entire heading of the Skydiving tour and create a subdocument. Click All to see what text in the outline has been included in the subdocument. If you did it correctly, the subdocument will contain all the level 2 and level 3 headings within the pale box. Return to Normal view and print only page 1 of the document.

3. Return to Outline view. Remove the subdocument. Highlight all the text beginning with Skydiving. Click the Create Subdocument button, and you should get four subdocuments, one for each tour.

4. Select File | Save As to save the master document as *Master Document*. The subdocuments are automatically saved at the same time.

EXERCISE 14.3

Footnotes

1. Continue with the subdocument created in Exercise 14.2. Double-click the sub-document icon of your favorite tour to open the subdocument. Add a paragraph of text under the Destinations and schedule heading.

2. Cite a specific fact or expert's opinion about the tour destination (or make one up). For example, you could mention that it was rated #1 by *Backpacker* magazine.

3. At the end of the sentence, insert a footnote. In the footnote, give the reference for the information, including author, source, publication information, and page numbers (make it up, if necessary). Print the page with the footnote.

4. Add another sentence with a footnote. Print the page.

5. Move the second sentence with a footnote above the first sentence with a footnote. Print the page.

6. Delete the second footnote. Print the page. Save and close the document and return to the master document.

EXERCISE 14.4

Index

1. Continue with the document created in the previous exercises.

2. Insert an index entry for each level 1 and level 3 heading. To do this, highlight the heading and press the shortcut key, [Alt][Shift][X]. Click Mark and, with the dialog box still open on the screen, repeat the highlighting and marking process. You can simplify the process by clicking Mark All for the level 3 headings. Also insert an index entry for key words, such as destination cities, in the body text paragraphs you wrote in the previous exercises.

3. Move the cursor to the end of the document and insert a page break. On the new page, compile the index. To do this, select Insert | Index and Tables, and on the Index tab click Indented and Modern, 1 column. Click OK.

4. Type the word Index above the index. Format it to the style Heading 1.

   Print the index page only.

5. Rearrange the document so that Skydiving is last. Update the index. To do this, click in the gray index area and press [F9]. Print the index page with the updated page numbers.

EXERCISE 14.5

Table of Contents

1. Continue with the document created in the previous exercises. Position the cursor at the top of the document. Create a table of contents using the outline headings. To do this, select Insert | Index and Tables. On the Table of Contents tab select From Template, set Show Levels at 3, and make the Tab Leader dots. Check Right Align Page Numbers and click OK.

2. Put the heading `Table of Contents` on the top line only.

3. Because the first line of the document, Thrill Seeker Tours Upcoming Adventures, is not a heading, it shows up on the same page as the table of contents. Put a page break between the table of contents and this line. Print the table of contents.

4. The table of contents is too long to fit on a single page. Change the table of contents so that only the level 1 and level 2 headings are included. To do this, place the cursor anywhere within the grayed table of contents area and select Insert | Index and Tables. This time change Show Levels to 2 and click OK. When the prompt appears asking if you want to replace the table of contents, click OK. Print the table of contents only.

5. Move the Whitewater information to the top of the document. Update the table of contents. To do this, click in the grayed area and press `F9`. When the prompt appears, select Update Entire Table and click OK. Print the revised table of contents.

6. Save the master document and close.

Review Questions

*1. What is the purpose of Outline view?

2. What is different on the Word screen when Outline view is selected?

*3. How is a heading changed to a subheading or line of text in an outline?

4. In Outline view, how can you tell if a heading has other headings or text under it if they are not displayed?

*5. What is the name of the style for level 2 headings?

6. How are the format attributes for a style changed?

*7. What is the advantage to rearranging headings in Outline view compared to the other views?

8. What changes on screen when subdocuments are created? How does the master document appear?

*9. What happens when a master document is saved?

10. When several headings, subheadings, and text are highlighted and the Create Subdocument button is clicked, what determines how the subdocuments are divided?

*11. What are footnotes used for? How do footnotes differ from footers?

12. How are footnotes edited? How is this different from inserting a footnote?

*13. What is a footnote reference mark? How can it be deleted? What else is deleted when a footnote reference mark is deleted?

14. What happens when a footnote reference mark is moved to a different page?

*15. How is an index entry field code created? What is the shortcut key?

16. How is an index created from the index entry field codes? In what order do the index entries appear?

*17. What determines the text that appears in each index entry?

18. How is the index updated when index entries are added, deleted, or moved in the document?

*19. How is an entire table of contents or index deleted?

20. How is the table of contents created from an outline?

*21. What does the table of contents actually consist of?

22. How can a table of contents be updated when entries are added to or deleted from it?

*23. To expand a single heading in an outline

    a. Select View | Outline.

    b. Click the All button.

    c. Drag the plus symbol at the left side of the heading.

    d. Double-click the symbol at the left side of the heading.

24. As soon as you create a subdocument,

    a. It is automatically saved.

    b. The table of contents and index are updated.

    c. A box and an icon appear in Master Document view.

    d. The Master Document toolbar appears.

*25. When you are NOT in Master Document view, subdocuments

    a. May only be edited as separate documents.

    b. Have section breaks between them.

    c.   Appear as field codes within the master document.

    d.   All the above.

26.   When you select the command Insert | Footnote in Normal view

    a.   A superscripted number or symbol appears in the document body.

    b.   The Footnote pane opens automatically.

    c.   The footnote is automatically numbered.

    d.   All the above.

Key Terms

Collapse	Footnote reference mark	Master Document view
Demote	Heading	Outline
Endnote	Index	Promote
Expand	Index entry	Subdocument
Footnote	Level number	Table of contents
Footnote pane	Master document	

Macros and Customizing

Many tasks in word processing are repetitive, requiring the user to press the same sequence of keys or make identical menu choices over and over again. As computers become increasingly powerful, more of the repetitive tasks are performed by equally powerful software.

Word allows you to record sequences of keystrokes that you perform often into a structure called a *macro*. These macros can then be executed by pressing a shortcut key, by selecting a command that you place on the Word menus, or by clicking on a toolbar button. These macros are written in an extremely powerful programming language, but you do not need to know programming to create them. To build the macro, you simply execute the key sequence as you normally do while the word processor records your actions to create the program.

Word gives the user complete control over the menus, toolbars, and shortcut keys. Making changes to how commands are accessed is not difficult to do. This unit covers the procedures in Word to create and manipulate macros, as well as those that customize the menus, keyboard, and toolbars.

Learning Objectives

At the completion of this unit you should know

1. how to record a macro,

2. how to run a macro,

3. how to customize the toolbars, menus, and keyboard.

Important Commands

File | Save All

Tools | Macro

Tools | Customize

View | Toolbars

Recording Macros

Many tasks that you perform in a word processor happen over and over again. You can let Word do most of the work in these repetitive tasks by recording the series of actions required to perform the command.

As an example, consider the actions required to insert a picture into a document, format it to double its size, insert it into a frame, and position it on the bottom-right corner of the page. You would use four commands: Insert | Picture, Format | Picture, Insert | Frame, and Format | Frame. If this were a procedure you used often, it would become tedious. Instead of performing this set of keystrokes every time yourself, make Word do the work—accurately and speedily—by storing the sequence of commands in a macro.

FIGURE 15.1
Record Macro dialog box

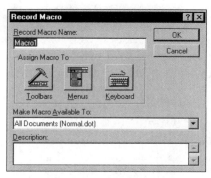

Before you record the macro, it is a good idea to practice the steps to be recorded to avoid making mistakes and having to record the macro again. If the sequence of actions is quite long, you may wish to write them down before beginning. You can begin the task of recording a macro by selecting the command Tools | Macro and clicking the Record button or by double-clicking REC (for Record) on the status bar at the bottom of the screen.

The dialog box that appears, shown in Figure 15.1, asks you to enter a name and an optional description for the macro. You may also assign the macro to the menus, the toolbars (or any one of them individually), or the keyboard. After you click on OK, any key that you press or mouse movement you record will be added to the macro. The mouse has a pointer with an image of a cassette tape attached, to remind you that you are recording, and the Macro Record toolbar appears on screen, allowing you to pause or stop recording at the touch of a button. Execute the sequence of keystrokes or movements with the mouse as you normally would. The only actions you are not able to perform are highlighting text or moving the insertion point with the mouse. When the sequence is complete, click on the Stop button on the Macro Record toolbar, or double-click again on REC on the status bar. The macro is now stored with the name you entered before starting to record.

In the following Guided Activity, you will automate several tasks you usually perform before you print a letter on letterhead stationery. Of course, if you planned ahead, you could open a template that had all the settings stored as the default, but too often you find yourself typing a letter first and thinking about formatting procedures later. Rather than execute these commands repeatedly, the Guided Activity will help you create a macro to perform these functions.

GUIDED ACTIVITY 15.1

Recording a Macro

1. Start Word. Create a new document.

2. Enter the following text:

    `Macros make the computer do the repetitive work, leaving me to be creative.`

    Now practice the keystrokes or mouse movements you will be using before recording the macro.

3. Select File | Page Setup. Select the Margins tab, and change the top margin to 2.25". Select the Paper Source tab, and change the paper tray to Manual Feed for both the first and subsequent pages, and then click OK. (If you are using a printer that does not have manual feed as a choice, skip that step.) Because you often need to examine the finished letter before you print to make sure it is neither too high nor too low on the page, select File | Print Preview. Click Close.

4. Click Undo to change the settings back. Now record the steps in the macro.

5. Select Tools | Macro and click Record or double-click on REC on the status bar. Enter the name of the macro—Letterhead. In the Description box, enter a phrase that describes what the macro does. For now, do not assign the macro to the toolbars, menus, or keyboard. Click on the OK button.

    If you later assign this macro to a menu or a toolbar, the name you give the macro will appear on the menu or on the ToolTips next to the mouse when you point to the button on the toolbar. Whatever you type as a description (if any) will appear in the status bar when you select it from the toolbar or menu.

6. Select File | Page Setup. Select the Margins tab, and change the top margin to 2.25". Select the Paper Source tab, and change the paper tray to Manual Feed for both the first and other pages, and then click OK.

7. Select File | Print Preview.

8. These are all the steps you needed to record, so stop the macro recorder by clicking on the Stop button on the Macro Record toolbar, or by double-clicking REC on the status bar.

    Your macro is saved under the name *Letterhead*. Exit the preview screen by selecting Close.

Executing and Editing Macros

The recorded macro may be executed, edited, or deleted by using the command Tools | Macro, as shown in Figure 15.2.

FIGURE 15.2
*Tools | Macro
dialog box*

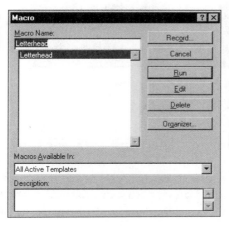

To run the macro, select the macro name and click Run, or double-click its name. The macro will execute exactly as you recorded it. If there are any problems executing the macro, a dialog box will appear with the number of the line containing the error. (Make note of it.)

Clicking the Edit button will open a screen displaying the actual programming lines in your macro and the settings in dialog boxes. Macros are recorded in a powerful programming language called *WordBasic*. Programming in WordBasic requires a certain amount of knowledge of that language. If you want to (and know how), you can change the macro by adding or deleting program lines at this point. Even if you are unable to write a macro using WordBasic, you should be able to tell if there are obvious mistakes in the macro. Choose File | Close to exit the macro editing screen and return to the document.

GUIDED ACTIVITY 15.2

Executing a Macro

1. Click on Undo to change the settings back to normal. Click on the Print Preview button to verify that the top margin is set at 1". Close preview.

2. Select Tools | Macro.

   The dialog box appears. The list of macros may not be exactly like the one shown in Figure 15.2, since different macros may have been recorded in your copy of Word.

3. Double-click on Letterhead, or highlight Letterhead and click Run. Word should automatically change the page setup and display the preview screen. Click Close to return to the document.

   You can also use the Tools | Macro command to view the programming of the macro.

4. Select Tools | Macro. From the dialog box, highlight the macro name Letterhead, and then click Edit. The screen will begin with the following information:

```
Sub MAIN

FilePageSetup .Tab = "2", .PaperSize = "1", .TopMargin =
"2.25"
```

and will end with this:

```
FilePrintPreview
End Sub
```

Although the language is confusing, you can see that `FilePageSetup` and `FilePrintPreview` echo the selections you made in recording the macro.

5.   Select File | Close to exit the macro program and return to the document.

Customizing the Toolbars

The toolbars in Microsoft Word are completely customizable. You can display any or all of nine toolbars on screen at a time. These toolbars may be displayed at their default position at the top of the screen, or dragged onto the screen, or *docked on* (stuck against) any side of the screen. You can further customize each toolbar by arranging the buttons in any order, or even drag (move) buttons from one toolbar to another. Word allows you to create a brand new toolbar customized with your favorite buttons. For instant access, macros that you create and other commands may be assigned to a button on a toolbar, and you can even design your own button face.

Rearranging Toolbars

You know how to turn on and off the toolbars with the View | Toolbars command. By checking the selections in the Toolbars dialog box, shown in Figure 15.3, you dis-

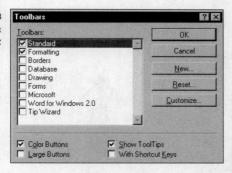

FIGURE 15.3
Toolbars dialog box

play one or more of the toolbars on screen in their default position on the screen. The toolbar shortcut menu with the same commands is available by clicking on the *right* mouse button whenever your mouse is pointing at a toolbar.

The Standard toolbar and Formatting toolbar are normally shown below the menu bar and above the ruler. If you wish to move a toolbar, place the mouse pointer over the shaded area behind the buttons and drag it. If you drag a toolbar on top of the work area, it appears as a window floating on screen, with a title bar and a close button, as shown in Figure 15.4. Just as with any window, dragging the border will change its size, dragging the title bar moves it, and clicking on the close button removes it from the screen. If you drag it to the left or right side of the screen, the toolbar is docked in place with the buttons arranged vertically, often allowing more lines of text to fit in the work area. You may also dock a toolbar at the top or bottom of the screen.

Just as the location of the toolbars is not fixed, neither are the locations of buttons on the toolbars. You can move buttons around on one toolbar, or drag them between

FIGURE 15.4
Floating toolbar

toolbars. The trick to moving buttons is that you must hold down the [Alt] key while dragging. That is because if you attempted to click on a button in order to drag it without holding down [Alt], you would cause the button to perform its function. To copy (not move) a button, hold down *both* [Ctrl] and [Alt] and drag the button to the new location, either on the same toolbar or a different one. Alternatively, you could create a new toolbar and drag all your favorite buttons to one location. That would allow you to display only one toolbar at a time, saving space on the screen for your document.

The changes to the toolbars are automatically saved to the Normal template when you exit Word or choose the command File | Save All. Anytime you wish to reset the toolbars to their default appearance, click the Reset button in the View | Toolbars dialog box.

GUIDED ACTIVITY 15.3

Rearranging Toolbars

1. Select View | Toolbars, and place a check in every square to display all the toolbars on screen at one time. Click OK.

   The screen is cluttered with toolbars! Toolbars appear above the ruler, floating, and at the bottom of the screen below the horizontal scroll bar, depending on where they were last displayed.

2. Click once on the close button on every floating toolbar to remove them one by one from the screen.

3. Point the mouse at the shaded area behind the buttons of any toolbar and click the *right* mouse button. The shortcut menu reveals a list of the toolbars with a check next to the ones displayed. Click Borders to remove the Borders toolbar from the screen.

   As you know, you could also remove it from the screen by clicking the Borders button on the right side of the Formatting toolbar.

4. You may also see near the top of the screen the Database toolbar used in creating the data document in mail merge. Point the mouse at the shaded area between the buttons and drag the toolbar down onto the screen.

   The buttons are arranged in two columns of five buttons each.

5. Resize the floating Database toolbar by dragging on its side border. As you drag, the outline of the box jumps to appropriate sizes to accommodate the buttons.

6. Drag the Database toolbar over to the right or left border. When you release the mouse button, the toolbar is docked in its new location. When it is correctly docked, the title bar will disappear.

7. Select View | Toolbars and click to remove the checks next to all the toolbars except three, those for Standard, Formatting, and Word for Windows 2.0. Click OK, and one or more toolbars disappear while three remain on screen.

The Word for Windows 2.0 toolbar is for people who have used the older version of Word and want to see the buttons in their familiar location. Many of the buttons on this toolbar are found in other places on the Microsoft Word for Windows 95 screen. One button, however, is not—the Envelope button. This button automatically accesses the command Tools | Envelopes and Labels and selects the Envelopes tab, a very handy button to have in an office.

8. Hold down the [Alt] key and drag the Envelope button to the Standard toolbar to the space between the Save and the Print buttons. As you drag, the mouse pointer shows a gray silhouette of a button.

The button is moved from one toolbar to another. To make room on the toolbar, you may wish to delete a button. The AutoFormat button is less commonly used and its command is easily accessed form the Format menu.

9. Remove the AutoFormat button by holding down the [Alt] key and dragging it off the toolbar.

10. Remove the Word for Windows 2.0 toolbar from the screen with the View | Toolbars command.

11. Either save the changes by selecting File | Save All, or reset the toolbars back to their default. To do this, select View | Toolbars, highlight the changed toolbar, and click the Reset button. Repeat for each toolbar that was changed, and then click OK.

Assigning Macros and Other Commands to a Toolbar

When a macro is very short, it may be more trouble to run a macro from the Macro | Run dialog box than to actually perform the steps the macro covers. The solution is to place a macro on the toolbars as a customized button to let you execute it with a click of the mouse. You may create a toolbar button for every Word command, and for fonts, styles, and AutoText entries as well.

The Toolbars tab of the Tools | Customize dialog box brings up the same dialog box as the View | Toolbars, Customize button, as shown in Figure 15.5. This dialog box shows every button listed for each menu selection—File, Edit,

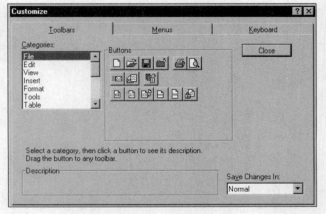

FIGURE 15.6
*Dialog box of
button choices*

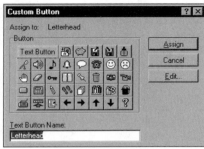

View, and so on. For instance, when you click on File, you see a display of the buttons for New, Open, Save, Print, and many more. To examine the function for each button, click on it and read the description.

As you scroll through the list of categories, you will see near the bottom of the list the selection for Macros. When you highlight Macros, a list of all the macros created appears in a box. Click on the *Letterhead* macro, and the description you gave it appears in the dialog box. When you drag the macro name to the toolbar, a new dialog box appears, giving you several choices for a button face, as in Figure 15.6. You may select one and click the Assign button, or click Edit to create your own button face.

GUIDED ACTIVITY 15.4

Creating a Toolbar and Buttons

1. Select View | Toolbars, and click on the New button. In the dialog box that appears, type the name of the toolbar—say, your first name—and click OK.

   As soon as you click OK, a square toolbar appears on the Word screen. This toolbar has no buttons yet.

2. Scroll down the list under Categories and select Macros. You will see the *Letterhead* macro that you created in Guided Activity 15.1.

3. Drag the macro name Letterhead over to the new, empty toolbar. As soon as you do so, the Custom Button dialog box appears.

   None of these buttons represents a sheet of letterhead graphically, so we'll design one that does.

4. Highlight any button and click Edit. Immediately, the Button Editor appears, as shown in Figure 15.7.

5. Click the Clear button to erase the face of the button. Use the various colors to modify the appearance of the button face to match Figure 15.7 or any way you like. When the preview looks the way you want it, click OK, and then click Close.

6. To add a button with text on its face rather than a picture involves a similar process. Select Tools | Customize and the Toolbars tab. Scroll through the categories and select Macros. Click on Letterhead and drag to the new toolbar. Select Text Button, and click Assign. The macro name appears on the face of the button. Click Close.

7. Test the buttons on the toolbar by clicking on the Letterhead buttons you added. Word automatically runs the macro, making settings in page setup, and displaying the preview screen.

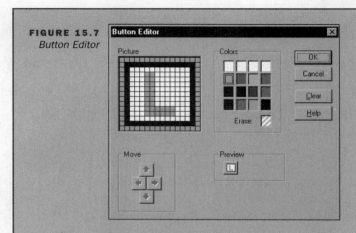

FIGURE 15.7
Button Editor

Add a button on your new toolbar that will automatically apply a hanging indent.

8. Issue the command Tools | Customize and select the Toolbars tab. Scroll through the categories and select All Commands. In the list of commands that appears, scroll down until you see HangingIndent. Drag the command to the new toolbar. From the Custom Button dialog box, select the button of your choice and click Assign.

You now have three buttons on your custom toolbar.

9. Test the new button by typing a two-line paragraph and clicking on it.

Customizing the Keyboard

The third way to execute a macro is to use a shortcut key. You may assign the macro to a shortcut key through the use of the Keyboard tab under Tools | Customize, shown in Figure 15.8. This option also displays the shortcut keys for commands that are defined by Word. These may also be customized through the settings in this dialog box.

Just as when customizing the toolbars, you must first select the category Macros, and then highlight the macro name. After you click in the Press New Shortcut Key box, you may press a key or a combination of keys you wish to perform this function. If your selection is already assigned to another command, the description will appear under Currently Assigned To. If you wish to reassign it, click Assign, or try another key combination

FIGURE 15.8
Keyboard tab under Tools | Customize

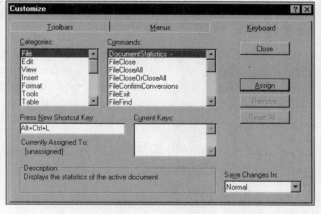

to find one not currently assigned to another command. Click Close to register the change and exit the dialog box.

GUIDED ACTIVITY 15.5

Customizing the Keyboard

1. Select Tools | Customize, and click on the Keyboard tab.

2. Select Macros from the Category list, and highlight Letterhead.

3. Click in the list box labeled Press New Shortcut Key.

4. Hold down the [Ctrl] and [Shift] keys and press [L] for Letterhead.

   This key combination is already assigned. Press [Backspace] to clear the box.

5. Hold down the [Alt] and [Ctrl] keys and press [L].

   This key combination is unassigned currently, so it is a good choice.

6. Click on the Assign button, and then click Close.

7. Test your new shortcut key by holding down the [Alt] and [Ctrl] keys and pressing [L]. Click Close to exit the preview screen. You might want to keep a handwritten list of your shortcuts for ready reference.

Customizing Menus

A fourth way to run a macro is to place it on a menu to access it that way, rather than cluttering your screen with buttons you only occasionally use. The Menus tab in the Tools | Customize dialog box, shown in Figure 15.9, allows you to assign your macro to a menu, and to customize the menus displayed by adding or deleting commands.

First, pick Macros from Categories, just as you did when customizing the toolbars and keyboard, and select the macro to be assigned from the Macros list. At this point you may specify the menu to place it on and the location on the menu, whether at the top, or the bottom, or (Auto) for Word to place it. The text you enter for the menu command will be the actual text that will appear on the menu, so check your spelling and capitalization. The ampersand (&) is used before whatever letter you wish to have underlined on the menu selection.

FIGURE 15.9
Menus tab in the Tools | Customize dialog box

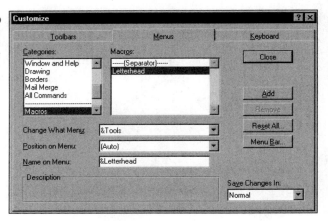

GUIDED ACTIVITY 15.6

Customizing a Menu

1. Select Tools | Customize and select the Menus tab. Scroll through the list of categories and click on Macros to display the list of macros.

2. Select Letterhead from the Macros list box.

   You will add this to the Window menu, since it is relatively short.

3. Select &Window from the Change What Menu list. Leave the Position on Menu setting (Auto). Under Name on Menu, you will see &Letterhead.

   Word assumes that you want to give the menu command the same name as your macro. An ampersand (&) is placed before the letter that will be underlined. You may recall that the underlined letters are used when accessing menu selections from the keyboard with the [Alt] key.

4. Click on the Add button to assign the macro to the Window menu. Click Close to exit the dialog box.

5. Click on the Window menu to see the results, which should resemble Figure 15.10.

FIGURE 15.10
The modified menu

The macro has been assigned to the Window menu, at the end of the current commands, under the name Letterhead. The L is underlined to indicate that L is the key you would press to access this menu selection with the keyboard. The shortcut key, which you customized the keyboard to use, is also listed on the menu.

6. Select Window | Letterhead to execute your macro. Click Close to Exit the preview screen.

   Since macros and customizing are automatically saved in the Normal template when you exit Word, you may wish to reset them to the default before you finish your work. If you are working in a computer lab, you will need to remove these effects. If you wish to retain the macro and customizing on your own machine, skip the following steps.

CAUTION   *These commands cannot be undone, so you will be prompted to decide if you are absolutely sure you wish to delete.*

7. To remove the custom buttons from the toolbars, hold down the [Alt] key and drag the buttons off the toolbar.

8. To remove the custom toolbar from the list of toolbars, select View | Toolbars, highlight the custom toolbar's name, and click Delete. At the prompt, click Yes to delete the toolbar, and then click Close.

9. To put the menus and shortcut key assignments back to the default settings, select Tools | Customize. Click on the Menus tab and click Reset All. Click Yes at the prompt. Click on the Keyboard tab and click Reset All. Click Yes at the prompt and then click Close.

10. To delete the macros, select Tools | Macro. Highlight the Letterhead macro name and click Delete, and then answer Yes to the prompt asking whether you want to delete the macro. Click Close.

Summary

Word allows you to store sequences of keystrokes and mouse movements in short programs called macros. Macros allow you to automate the many repetitive tasks that are encountered in word processing. More of the tedious work can be delegated to the word processor, freeing you for more creative tasks. Macros are created by the invisible hand of a programming language called WordBasic.

Macros are recorded by using the Tools | Macro command and clicking Record; all keystrokes and commands from that point forward will be recorded until you click on the Stop button on the Macro Record toolbar. You may also start and stop recording by double-clicking REC on the status bar.

You may execute a macro in four ways:

■ Select Tools | Macro, highlight the macro name, and click Run.

■ Click on a macro button you created.

■ Use the assigned shortcut key for the macro.

■ Select your macro from a customized menu.

A macro is assigned to a toolbar, a shortcut key, and a menu by selecting Tools | Customize. After selecting which of the three you wish to assign it to, you must then specify the name of the macro, and also specify to which toolbar, menu, or key combination you wish to assign it. If you assign a macro to a button, you may design your own button face or select from several different designs.

Toolbars may be rearranged to suit the user's needs. You may move toolbars to any edge of the screen (called docking), or leave them floating on the work area. Buttons may be moved from one place to another by holding down the [Alt] key and dragging them, or copied by holding down [Ctrl] and [Alt] while dragging. Turn the toolbars on and off by selecting View | Toolbars, or by using the shortcut menu.

The customizing changes you make to Word, such as recording macros and changing the toolbars, menus, and shortcut key assignments, are automatically saved to the Normal template when you exit Word, but can be deleted or reset to the default.

EXERCISE 15.1

Creating a Macro

Objective: Create a macro called *Header* that adds your name and your course to a header that will print on the top-right side of every page. Practice the following steps before recording, and then repeat them with the macro recorder running.

1. Double-click the REC area on the status bar to turn on the recorder (skip this step if you are only practicing the steps). Name the macro *Header*.

2. Select File | Page Setup and click the Layout tab. Remove the check from the box next to Different Odd and Even, if necessary. Click OK.

3. Select View | Header and Footer. In the header area, type your name and class information and format right-aligned. Click Close.

4. Click the Stop button on the Macro Record toolbar.

5. Print the macro. To do this, select Tools | Macro, highlight the name of the macro, click the Edit button, and select File | Print. When printing is complete, select File | Close to exit the macro editing screen.

EXERCISE 15.2

Customizing a Menu

Objective: Assign the macros you created in Exercise 15.1 to the Window menu.

1. Select Tools | Customize and click on the Menus tab.

2. Scroll down the Categories and select Macros. Click on the Header macro. Specify to change the &Window menu, and click Add and Close.

3. Select the Window menu to make it drop down and display its contents, and press PrtSc to copy a picture of your screen to the Clipboard.

4. Open a new document, and select Edit | Paste to display the picture of the screen showing the customized Window menu. Print the document.

EXERCISE 15.3

Customizing a Toolbar

Objective: Create a new toolbar and place a button on it for double-spaced formatting.

1. Select View I Toolbars.

2. Click New and name the toolbar with your name.

3. The Customize dialog box appears showing the Toolbars tab. Click on the Format category.

4. Click on the button for double-spacing. Drag it to the new customized toolbar. (If necessary, move the Customize window out of the way by dragging its title bar.) Click Close.

5. Copy (do not move) five of your favorite buttons to it. Dock the new toolbar on one side of the screen.

6. Assign the macro from Exercise 15.1 to a button on your custom toolbar. Create a new, unique button face for it.

7. Press [PrtSc]. Open a new document and select Edit I Paste to insert the picture of the screen with your customized toolbar. Print the document and do not save.

Review Questions

*1. What is the basic purpose of macros?

2. How are macros created? What preparations should you make before recording a macro?

*3. Give four ways to run a macro.

4. How are toolbars moved around on screen?

*5. How are toolbars turned on to be displayed? How are docked toolbars removed from display? How are floating toolbars removed from display?

6. How are buttons moved from one location to another? How are buttons copied?

*7. What happens when you exit Word after creating a macro or customizing the menu or toolbar?

8. What should you do if you want to remove the changes you made to the menus, toolbars, or keyboard?

*9. Macros are best used for

a. Complicated text formatting.

b. Repetitive typing of the same text over and over.

    c.   Repeated use of the same sequence of commands.

    d.   Customizing a template.

10.   To begin recording a macro,

    a.   Practice all the steps first so you do not record a mistake.

    b.   Double-click on the REC portion of the status bar.

    c.   Select Tools | Macro and click Record.

    d.   All of the above.

*11.   To make a previously recorded macro run,

    a.   Double-click the REC area on the status bar.

    b.   Double-click the Run button on the toolbar.

    c.   Select Tools | Macro, highlight the name, and click Run.

    d.   None of the above.

12.   Customizing Microsoft Word can be done by

    a.   Adding a command to a menu.

    b.   Rearranging the buttons on the toolbar.

    c.   Docking the toolbars on the sides of the screen.

    d.   All of the above.

Key Terms

| Docked | Macro | WordBasic |

0-1. Windows is like a desktop because you put your work on it. Some things are kept handy for easy use, such as the taskbar, Start button, Recycle Bin, and My Computer. You can have several items on your desktop at once, or put them away.

0-3. With a mouse you can point, click, right-click, double-click, and drag.

0-5. To start Windows, turn on the computer. If requested, type in your username and password to log in.

0-7. ToolTips are words that appear when the mouse pointer is on a button on the toolbar. ToolTips tell you what the button name or function is.

0-9. 1 = Title bar, 2 = Minimize button, 3 = Maximize button, 4 = Close button, 5 = Menu bar, 6 = Scroll bar, 7 = Border, 8 = Desktop, 9 = Taskbar.

0-11. d.

0-13. Four advantages to using Windows 95 are these. Windows has a graphical user interface that makes it easy to learn and to use. It allows several programs to run at once, which is called multitasking. Its Clipboard allows text, pictures, and numbers to be shared among different documents and programs. Windows makes difficult things easy to do, such as run utilities and create shortcuts to keep programs and files handy on the desktop.

0-15. The triangles on the Start menu mean that another menu will appear to the right when this item is selected. This most often occurs when the selection on the menu is a folder.

0-17. The Clipboard is a temporary storage place provided by Windows that holds information that has been cut or copied. When the Paste command is issued, the material that has been placed on the Clipboard will be deposited wherever the cursor is located.

0-19. To swap the mouse buttons so that the mouse works better in the left hand, click on the Start button, highlight Settings, and select Control Panel. In the Control Panel, double-click the Mouse icon. On the Buttons tab, click the option for Left-handed.

0-21. b.

1-1. All Windows applications have a title bar, three buttons on the right (minimize, maximize, and close), and scroll bars. Several other features are included in Microsoft Word: a menu bar, toolbars, a ruler, and a status bar.

1-3. The Alt key is the most important to remember when using the keyboard to execute commands. This key allows you to access menus in the menu bar and commands in dialog boxes without using the mouse.

1-5. b.

1-7. c.

2-1. The three general procedures in word processing are entering and editing text, formatting, and using advanced procedures.

2-3. The ↑ and ↓ arrow keys move the cursor up or down one line. The ← and → arrow keys move the cursor left or right one character. The PgUp and PgDn keys move the cursor up or down one screen in a document. The Home key moves the cursor to the beginning of the current line, whereas the End key moves it to the end of the line. Any of these keys may be used in conjunction with the Ctrl key to increase the distance the cursor moves.

2-5. The Shift key is used to highlight or select text.

2-7. The insert mode adds typed text at the position of the cursor; the text to the right of the cursor is shifted farther to the right to make room for the new text. The overtype mode replaces the character to the right of the cursor with the next character typed.

2-9. The File | Save As command is executed in this case. Since the document has not been saved, it is still called *Document1*. Word for Windows will request a file name for the document before saving it.

2-11. d.

2-13. b.

3-1. Documents are stored on disks so that they can be retrieved, edited, and printed at a later time. Documents that are not stored on disk are erased when Word for Windows is exited or when the computer is turned off.

3-3.   Heat, cold, smoke, dust, fingerprints, condensation, and magnetic fields all damage disks.

3-5.   Windows 95 allows file names to be up to 255 characters long including spaces, but may not contain any of eight special characters. In DOS, file names must be eight characters or fewer and may contain no spaces or special characters. DOS also requires an extension of three characters or fewer on the file name.

3-7.   If you close a file that has not been saved, Word warns you and gives you one last chance to save it. If you want to save it, Word reveals the Save As dialog box so that you can name the file.

3-9.   Edit | Cut removes highlighted text from the document and places it on the Clipboard, a temporary storage place provided by Windows. Edit | Copy copies the highlighted text to the Clipboard, leaving the original in place. Edit | Paste places the contents of the Clipboard into the document at the location of the cursor.

3-11.   Many commands may be performed by selecting them from the menu bar, by selecting them from the shortcut menu, by clicking on buttons on the toolbars, or by pressing shortcut keys.

3-13.   d.

3-15.   a.

4-1.   The icon appears in the status bar when you begin typing; wavy red lines appear under misspelled words; and Automatic Spell Checking is checked on the Spelling tab in the Tools | Options dialog box.

4-3.   AutoCorrect changes common misspellings, fixes certain capitalization errors, and converts awkward fractions and symbols to professional-looking ones.

4-5.   It may take several seconds for Word for Windows to display a list of suggestions for misspelled words. If you wish to make corrections yourself without looking at suggestions, click Options in the Spelling dialog box, turn off the Always Suggest option, and click OK.

4-7.   AutoCorrect works only after you type a word and then press the `Spacebar`.

4-9.   The thesaurus may be used to find a synonym of a word to get the exact shade of meaning you need. If a word has several meanings, it provides synonyms for each meaning.

4-11.   d.

4-13.   b.

5-1.   Many printers can be connected to a computer. Three popular types are dot-matrix, laser, and multifunction inkjet printers.

5-3.   Clicking the Print button prints a single copy of the entire document to the default printer. Selecting the menu command brings up a dialog box that allows you to specify the number of copies, the destination printer, and which pages will be printed.

5-5.   Double-clicking on the Printer icon on the status bar takes you directly to the Printers dialog box for you to manage the printing process.

5-7.   Check that you have selected the proper command, that the correct printer is selected, that the printer is turned on and is online, that paper is in it, that the cables are plugged in tightly, and that the network is operational.

5-9.   As of the writing of this book the answer is b. By the time you read this, the answer may have changed to d (or something else not yet invented!).

5-11.   d.

6-1.   Character (or font), paragraph, and document are the three levels of formatting.

6-3.   Text that already exists is formatted by highlighting it and selecting the desired format attribute. To format text as it is being typed, position the cursor at the desired location of the new text. Select the format attribute to be applied. As you enter text, it will appear with the format attribute selected. When you finish typing the text, turn off the format attribute.

6-5.   Word includes often-used commands on the toolbars, while those that are seldom used are only available from dialog boxes.

6-7.   The default font for Word is Times New Roman in a 10-point size. To change the default font, issue the command Format I Font, specify the desired font, and click on the Default button.

6-9.   Word contains special characters such as em dash, en dash, and copyright and trademark symbols. They are accessed from the Insert I Symbols dialog box.

6-11.   a.

6-13.   c.

7-1.   Paragraph format commands will affect the paragraph where the cursor is located and any other paragraphs that are completely or partially highlighted.

7-3.   Left alignment aligns text against the left margin. As the default setting, left alignment is used most often for regular text. Right alignment aligns text against the right margin. It is generally used for short lines of text. Justification aligns text against both margins. It is used in letters or newspapers that have a very formal appearance. Center alignment centers text between the left and right margins. It is most often used for titles and headings.

7-5.   A tab is a mark on the ruler used to quickly align text in columns. The four types of tabs work much like the four types of paragraph alignments: text typed after a left tab will have the left edge of the text directly under the tab. Text typed after a right tab will have its right edge directly under the tab. Text typed after a center tab will be centered directly under the tab. Decimal tabs are used to align columns of numbers with their decimal places directly under the tab. Tab leaders are repeated characters that appear between the position of the cursor before the `Tab` key was pressed and the location of the next tab on the ruler. Tab leaders may be dots, dashes, or underlines.

7-7.   These commands are used to keep page breaks from occurring at incorrect places in the document. Keep Lines Together will avoid having a page break in a specific paragraph; the paragraph will always appear complete on one page. Keep with Next will avoid having two paragraphs split by a page break; the two paragraphs will always appear together on the same page.

7-9.   When you click the Borders button on the Formatting toolbar, the Borders toolbar appears on screen. From this toolbar you may set borders on the top, bottom, left, or right side of a paragraph. You may also specify the line style of the border. In addition, you may specify the intensity of the shading behind a segment of text.

7-11.   Styles are Word's method for saving a certain format for characters or paragraphs. Once defined, they save time by applying complex formatting with only one step. To define a style, format an existing paragraph to the desired style, and then give the style a name in the Style box on the Formatting toolbar and press Enter.

7-13.   b.

7-15.   a.

8-1.   The File | Page Setup commands affect the entire document or sections of the document, not just highlighted text or the paragraph where the cursor is located.

8-3.   When setting the paper size in the File | Page Setup dialog box, you must select a paper size supported by the printer selected. The default paper size for most printers is 8½"×11".

8-5.   Margins are the space between the edges of a page and the text printed on it. Indents are the amount of space between the margin and the text. Indents are added to the margins. For example, if the margins are increased, the indentation will still be added to the larger margin size.

8-7.   A gutter is additional space at the edge of a page for document binding. In a document printed on only one side of the page, the gutter appears on the left. In a document printed on both sides of the page, which is the case when Mirror Margins is selected, the gutter always appears on the inside margin of the page.

8-9.   Page Layout view shows the vertical ruler on the left side of the screen. New buttons appear at the bottom of the scroll bar that allow you to jump to the previous page or next page. The document appears as pages on a shaded desktop, with the margins and page numbers visible. Under Zoom Control, there is an option to view Two Pages that is not available in Normal view.

8-11.   a.

9-1.   Tables are best suited for information that can be displayed two-dimensionally, in rows and columns.

9-3.   Tables are created from scratch with the command Table | Insert Table or by clicking the Table button on the toolbar. You must supply the number of rows and columns for the new table. All the new columns are the same width, so the entire table fits exactly between the left and right margins if you use the button, or you may specify column width exactly if you use Table | Insert Table.

9-5.   Text that is too wide to fit in a table cell will wrap to new lines in the same cell. All the cells on that row of the table will change in height to accommodate the extra lines.

9-7.   To insert a new row at the bottom of a table, position the cursor in the last cell of the table and press Tab.

9-9.   To add a row or column to the middle of the table, highlight the row or column you want to follow the new one and press the Table button. The new row is added above the highlighted row; the new column is added to the left of the high-lighted column. To move a row or column, highlight the row or column and drag.

9-11. Cells in a table are merged by highlighting them and selecting Table | Merge Cells. Cells are merged when they contain information that is valid for two or more columns. Before cells can be merged, they must be highlighted and must not be previously merged.

9-13. Cell borders are printed lines used to make cells stand out in a printed table. Cell borders are turned on with the Format | Borders and Shading command or by using the buttons on the Borders toolbar. Gridlines are nonprinting lines that appear on a table by default. Gridlines are turned off and on with the Table | Gridlines command. AutoFormat formats fonts, column widths, borders, shading, and color.

9-15. Tabs may be used to align text in columns within the cells of a table. The decimal tab is most often used to align numbers within a table column. To align text at a tab setting within a table cell (except a decimal tab), you must press Ctrl Tab.

9-17. b.

9-19. d.

10-1. Columns of text allow the reader to scan information more quickly. It is also easier to lay out a page with pictures and advertisements in a multiple-column format.

10-3. Section breaks must be inserted before and after the portion of the document that will be in column format. Section breaks are inserted automatically if text is first highlighted and then the number of columns is chosen.

10-5. Column widths are changed either by dragging the column markers on the ruler or by setting column widths and the space between the columns with For-mat | Columns. Column widths are also affected by changing the margins with File | Page Setup.

10-7. Word for Windows allows you to see pictures and graphics on the screen the way they will appear on paper.

10-9. Displaying pictures in a document slows the speed at which the document will scroll. This may be avoided by selecting Tools | Options | View and checking the box next to Picture Placeholders.

10-11. Cropping trims off a portion of a picture or adds white space to the sides of a picture. Cropping reduces the overall size of the picture you can see, but the size of the part of the graphic image that remains in view does not change. To crop, hold down the [Shift] key while dragging the sizing handles. Scaling enlarges or reduces the graphic image itself. By dragging the corner handles, you will keep the size proportional as you change the overall size. By dragging the handles on the edges, in contrast, you will distort proportions and stretch or compress the graphic.

10-13. Pictures may be positioned in any location on the page by placing them within a frame. You may specify the exact position with the Format | Frame command, or, if you change to Page Layout view, you may use the mouse to drag pictures into position on the page.

10-15. Frames allow you to position the picture anywhere on the page but do not appear when you print. Borders print a box around the picture.

10-17. c.

10-19. a.

11-1. A chart lets you see at a glance the relative size of the numbers.

11-3. The datasheet contains the information for the chart. The categories on the top row appear on the horizontal axis of the chart. The items in the left column become the items in the legend. The numbers become the values that are plotted on the chart.

11-5. If a chart is selected, it has sizing handles on it. It may be copied, deleted, sized, and cropped, just like a picture in a document. If you want to modify a chart, you must double-click on it. Then the chart appears surrounded by a blue cross-hatched border, and the Word menu and toolbars are replaced with the Microsoft Graph menu and toolbars.

11-7. To change the chart style to a line or pie chart, click on the Chart Type button and select one of the chart types from the drop-down list. If you want to change a column chart to a stacked column chart or 100% stacked column chart, you must select from the menu Format | Column Group and specify the subtype.

11-9. The Drawing toolbar appears whenever you click on the Drawing button on the Standard toolbar. It also appears automatically whenever you double-click clip art to edit it. The buttons on the Drawing toolbar are used for placing drawing objects on a page and for editing clip art.

11-11. d.

11-13. b.

11-15. d.

12-1. Headers and footers are used to place information at the top and bottom of all pages in a document.

12-3. Headers and footers can be created for the first page, odd pages, and even pages. The first page of a document often does not have a header or footer. If a document is printed on both sides of the page, odd and even pages will need different headers and footers to avoid having information close to the binding.

12-5. The buttons on the Header and Footer toolbar allow you to insert a field code for the date, time, or page number in the header or footer. To view field codes, press [Alt][F9] or point the mouse at the shaded field code, right-click, and select Toggle Field Codes from the shortcut menu.

12-7. a.

12-9. d.

13-1. Mail merge allows you to merge information from a data document into variables in a form document.

13-3. The first line of a data source, called the header row, contains the names of the merge fields. The subsequent lines in the data source document, called data records, contain information to be placed in the form document during merging.

13-5. A main document contains the Mail Merge toolbar between the Formatting toolbar and the ruler. It also contains merge fields surrounded by chevrons throughout the document; during the merge, these will be replaced by information from the data document. Normal documents do not contain these.

13-7. To see the actual data from the data source in place of the merge fields in chevrons, click the View Merged Data button.

13-9. File | Print will print one copy of the main document, including merge field codes. Tools | Mail Merge will print one copy of the form document for each line of information in the data document.

13-11. In the Mail Merge dialog box, enter values in the From and To boxes under Records to Be Merged to print one copy of the form document for selected records of information from the data document. You may also set Query Options to filter out only records that meet specified criteria.

13-13. An IF merge field is used to include a segment of text only when certain criteria are true for a record, and to include a different segment of text when the criteria are false.

13-15. Dot-matrix printers handle long, continuously fed strips of labels with tractor-feed guides on each margin. Laser printers require individual sheets of labels, usually two or three columns to a page.

13-17 b.

13-19 d.

14-1.　The Outline view allows you to integrate your outline into the document that you are creating. This helps you keep the ideas in the document organized and in order, and also makes it easy to see if you are lacking supporting evidence for a main point.

14-3.　A heading may be demoted to a subheading by clicking the Demote button or dragging it to the right. A heading is changed to text by positioning the cursor on the heading and clicking the Demote to Body Text button with the double right arrow on the Outline toolbar.

14-5.　The style for level 2 headings is `Heading 2`.

14-7.　When you use Outline view to move headings in a collapsed outline, all the sub-headings and text beneath them are moved as well. This makes it easy to quickly rearrange and reorganize large amounts of text all on one screen, rather than scrolling through page after page in other views of a long document.

14-9.　When a master document is saved, all the subdocuments are saved first. Each subdocument is saved as an individual file, with the first few characters of the heading used as the file name. The master document is saved last, so links to all the subdocuments are retained.

14-11.　Footnotes are used to give reference information for any material that is used from another author's information. Footnotes are connected to the text by footnote reference mark. Footnotes appear above the bottom margin on the page where the reference mark is located, whereas footers appear within the bottom margin on every page.

14-13.　A footnote reference mark is a superscripted number, letter, or symbol that is dynamically linked to the footnote text. You must first highlight the reference mark before you can delete it. Whenever a footnote reference mark is deleted, the accompanying footnote is also deleted from the document.

14-15.　An index entry field code is created by highlighting the material, pressing the shortcut key [Alt][Shift][X], and clicking Mark.

14-17.　The text for the entry is entered into the Mark Index Entry dialog box. Whatever is highlighted before pressing [Alt][Shift][X] will automatically become the entry.

14-19.　The entire table of contents or index must be highlighted before pressing the [Del] key.

14-21.　The table of contents is actually a single field code in the document.

14-23.　d.

14-25.　a.

15-1.　Macros store sequences of keystrokes or mouse movements that are used repeatedly in a document. These sequences may be reproduced with a single keystroke or click of the mouse, saving the user time.

15-3. a. Select Tools | Macro, pick the name of the macro from the list, and click on Run.

b. Press the shortcut key that you assigned to the macro.

c. Click the customized button on the toolbar.

d. Select the macro name from a customized menu.

15-5. Turn on toolbars to display them by selecting View | Toolbars and checking the boxes next to the toolbar names. You may also use the shortcut menu to select a toolbar name and display it. Docked toolbars are removed by using the same methods as displaying them. Floating toolbars are also removed from screen by clicking on the close button in their upper-right corner.

15-7. When you exit, Word for Windows automatically saves any changes you have made to the Normal template.

15-9. c.

15-11. c.

Using Word with Other Applications

One of the main advantages of using Microsoft Office and other Windows-based software is the ability it gives you to exchange information with other applications with very little trouble. When copied, information is stored on the Clipboard. From the Clipboard it may then be pasted into any other Windows application. Another technique is to drag and drop highlighted information between two open applications. To do this, drag highlighted material down onto a taskbar button and continue to hold the mouse button down until the next application opens on screen.

Microsoft Word for Windows 95 comes with several mini-applications that may be used within a document. The mini-applications include Equation, Graph (which you learned in Unit 11), Organization Chart, and WordArt (which you used in Unit 10). All of these mini-applications are accessed in Word through the command Insert | Object.

Inserting objects from the mini-applications or from any other application is called *object linking and embedding*, sometimes called *OLE* (pronounced *olé*). Both linking and embedding allow you to include information created in other applications. Linking and embedding differ, however, in the way the information is handled.

Embedding causes the actual information, or *object*, to be inserted in the document. This object is simply a snapshot of the original information and does not change if the source information is later altered. Because the object is placed directly into the document, the document increases greatly in size and uses up much more space on the disk. When you double-click on an embedded object in a document, the original application is activated to allow you to edit, but does not open the original source file.

Linking, on the other hand, sets up a connection between the source and what is displayed in the document. This link causes the information to be dynamic, so that whenever the source changes, the object in the document reflects the change automatically. Since the object is stored in another file, and only the link (the location of the source file) and a picture are stored in the Word document, the size of the document does not increase very much. When you double-click to edit a linked object, the original application *and* source file open automatically.

Word allows for the easy exchange of linked and embedded data between many applications. Because Microsoft Office combines Word with Excel, Access, and PowerPoint, these three applications will be discussed in this appendix.

Using Word with Excel

Although you may place numeric or financial information into a Word table and do simple calculations in Word, you will find Excel or another spreadsheet program to be generally the better application to use for complex calculations. You can bring part of an Excel worksheet into Word in three ways:

- Edit I Paste (or the Paste button) results in text in a Word table.
- Drag-and-drop results in an embedded object.
- Edit I Paste Special gives a choice for either Paste (embedded) or Paste Link.

If Excel is already running, you may use Edit I Copy and Edit I Paste to bring numbers into Word as a table. Using Copy and Paste in this way is neither linking nor embedding, since any formulas in the spreadsheet are converted into numbers, and the resulting table becomes just part of the text in a document. In contrast, the command Edit I Paste Special allows you to select the option to Paste (and embed) or Paste Link. If Excel is not running, both linking and embedding are accomplished through the Insert I Object command.

Embedding an Excel Worksheet or Chart

You can embed an Excel worksheet in either of two ways: by creating a new worksheet or by opening an existing one. Both are accomplished with the command Insert I Object. The dialog box contains two tabs: Create New and Create from File. The Insert Microsoft Excel Worksheet button on the Standard toolbar, as shown in Figure B.1, may be used in place of the Insert I Object command to create a new worksheet.

After you specify the desired size of the worksheet by dragging on the grid, the computer automatically activates Excel. A sample worksheet surrounded by a cross-hatched border appears, and the Word menus and toolbars are replaced with those from Excel, as in Figure B.2, although your document is still on the screen.

FIGURE B.1
Inserting a new Excel worksheet

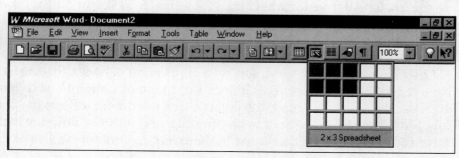

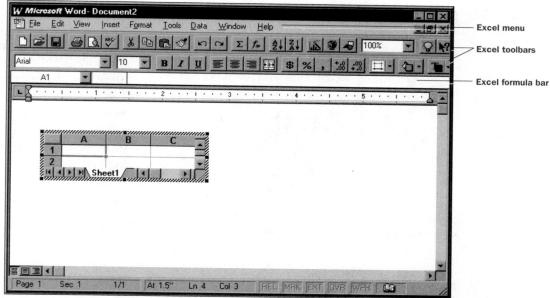

At this point, you have access to all of Excel's functions, formulas, and tools to build a worksheet. You cannot save the worksheet as a separate file, but that would be unnecessary, since this worksheet will be embedded or saved entirely within the Word document. To activate Word's menus and toolbars again, simply click anywhere in the document outside the worksheet area.

Within the document, the worksheet appears with gray gridlines. When you click on the worksheet, sizing handles appear, just as on a picture, and the status bar prompts you to double-click to edit the worksheet. Double-clicking on the worksheet reactivates Excel, replaces the menu bar and toolbars again, and allows you to edit without closing the document or Word. This powerful feature is termed *in-place activation*.

You may view the field code that is riding behind this worksheet by selecting Tools | Options, selecting the View tab, clicking Field Codes, and then OK (the shortcut key to toggle View Field Codes is [Alt][F9]). The field code for the embedded worksheet is { EMBED Excel.Sheet.5 }. Deleting, sizing, moving, and framing are performed by using the same techniques you use for pictures.

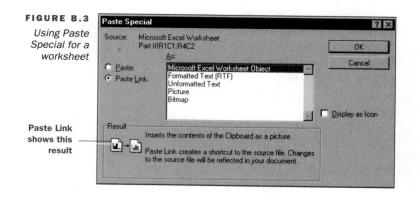

If you wish to copy all or a portion of an existing worksheet or a chart into Word, open it in Excel, use Edit | Copy, then switch to Word and use the command Edit | Paste Special, as shown in Figures B.3 and B.4. The contents of the dialog box change, depending on what is contained on the Clipboard. In either case, what is inserted into the document will only reflect changes made to the

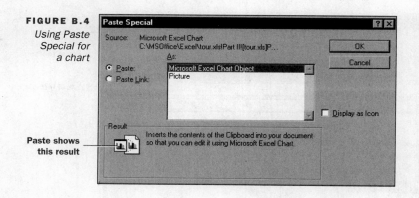

Paste shows
this result

Excel worksheet or chart if you click the option for Paste Link. Charts and worksheets may be edited within the Word document using the Excel menus and toolbars, without having to return to the Excel window.

Clicking the check box next to Display as Icon allows you to include information that may only be used as reference. Including an icon in the file conserves space on screen, but when the reader double-clicks it, the linked or embedded worksheet or chart is displayed. When you check this box, you have the option of changing the icon that will represent the object.

Even if Excel is not currently running, you may use the command Insert | Object to insert an existing Excel worksheet or chart. The Create from File tab in the Insert | Object dialog box allows you to specify the name and location of the file. The main difference is that you will be able to access only an entire worksheet, not just a highlighted portion. You may crop and scale the inserted object to display only the desired portion of the worksheet.

Linking Word to Excel

Linking may be a better choice than embedding if the amount of data is very large, since the data is stored in the source file rather than within the Word document. Linking is also better than embedding if you want the numbers to be dynamic rather than simply a snapshot of the worksheet at a certain time. Like embedded worksheets and charts, double-clicking linked objects activates Excel and allows for editing. The difference in editing linked charts and worksheets is that Excel opens the original source worksheet, allowing you to make changes that affect the document.

You cannot tell the difference between a linked chart and an embedded chart merely by their appearance. When you press [Alt][F9], however, the field code shown for a linked chart contains within dark braces the key word LINK, as well as the name and location of the source file, for example, { LINK Excel.Sheet.5 "D:\\Office\\Budget.xls" "Part I![Budget.xls]Part I Chart 2" \a \p }. Because the linked chart in the document is connected to the source in Excel, any changes that occur in the original worksheet are reflected automatically in the document. The embedded chart remains unchanged.

Embedding may be a better choice than linking in some circumstances. For example, if the source document is located where it may not always be accessible, such as on a network server, a linked chart or worksheet will appear only if the source is available. Embedded charts or worksheets are always available. If a source file is moved or renamed after a portion of the file has been linked to a document, an error message appears when you try to edit it. The links must be managed or updated manually with the Edit | Links command, shown in Figure B.5.

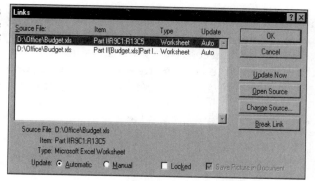

Word may also shift information into Excel. Portions of a document may be copied to, embedded in, or linked with a worksheet. The document may be inserted as text in a cell, inserted as a document object, or placed into a text box.

Using Word with Access and Schedule+

A database is often used to contain information that can be categorized. Word tables may be used as a small database, as we saw in Unit 13. For very large amounts of data, however, Microsoft Access or another database application is more appropriate.

You may use an Access query or table as the basis for a mail merge data document. To do this, use the Mail Merge Helper to connect the main document to the data source. Clicking the Get Data button allows you to specify a file. When you select an Access file, you may either insert the database into a Word table if it is not too large, or insert only field codes rather than the actual data. In either case, you can run a query to limit the data to those fields and records that meet specified criteria, rather than using the entire database.

Addresses from a contact list in Schedule+ can be accessed through the Insert Address button on the Standard toolbar. These addresses may be inserted into letters or envelopes.

Using Word with PowerPoint

Word's table feature, which you used in Unit 9, is integrated into PowerPoint for aligning text in rows and columns. By clicking the Insert Microsoft Word Table button on the PowerPoint Standard toolbar, Word is activated inside the PowerPoint presentation. The resulting table is saved as an embedded object.

PowerPoint and Word work together seamlessly to create presentations from a document outline, or to create an outline from a presentation without repetitive typing. Any Level 1 headings in a Word outline are turned into titles on PowerPoint slides, with subheadings becoming the text on the slides. You may use the simple copy and paste technique to move text between Word and PowerPoint's Outline view. Additionally, you may use the Report It button in PowerPoint to automatically convert the outline of a PowerPoint presentation to a Word outline.

Not only can you share text between Word and PowerPoint, you can also share clip art. PowerPoint comes with beautiful, full-color graphic images that are a wonderful addition to the images that come with Word. You can select the clip art images in PowerPoint and use copy and paste to move them into Word documents. These images are organized in a mini-application called ClipArt Gallery. If PowerPoint is installed, you can also access the ClipArt Gallery in Word through the Insert | Object command. If you want to edit the images, however, you must use PowerPoint to convert them to drawing objects before bringing them into Word.

Index

A

Access, 383, 301
Accessories, 17
Active
    document, 84
    window, 9, 13–14
Add New Record button, 303
Align dialog box, 275
Align Drawing Objects button, 275
Align Left button, 46
Alignment
    paragraph, 165–166
    tab, 168–169
[Alt] key, 47
Answer Wizard, 49, 136, 194
Apple System 7, 3, 15
Area chart, 266
Arrow keys, 55
Ascending sort, 223
Attribute, 143
AutoCorrect, 110–112, 115, 157
AutoFit, 216, 220
Automatic Save, 97–98
Automatic Spell Checking, 55, 62, 73–110
Avery labels, 314
Axis, 268

B

[Backspace] key, 42, 55, 66, 90
Backup files, 98–101
Balance columns, 239, 241
Bar chart, 266
Bar code, postal, 314
Bitmap files, 242, 245

Bold button, 44, 149
Border, 42, 177–180, 220–122, 273, 287
    window, 10
Borders button, 177
Borders toolbar, 177
Boundary, 278
Breaks, section, 293
Bring to Front button, 278
Bullet, 179
Button, 4, 39
    choices, 361
    copying, 359
    custom, 360–362
    Editor, 361–362
    moving, 359
    taskbar, 11
    See also individual button names
By Column button, 267
By Row button, 267
Byline, 240

C

Calculator, 17, 19–20, 222
Callout, 274
    button, 274, 276
    dialog box, 274
Capitals, 151
    all, 151
    drop, 248–250
    small, 151
    Toggle Case, 153
Caption, 176
Cascade, window, 13
Catalog, 300, 311–312
Categories, 263, 267, 301

CD-ROM, 80
Cell, 209, 212, 216, 224
    Excel worksheet, 383
    height, 219
    marks, 209
Center
    alignment, 165
    button, 43, 211
    tab, 287
    table, 219
Character, 143–151
    based user interface, 3–4
    nonprinting, 181
    spacing, 152
    special, 155–157
Chart, 262–272
    axes, 268
    axis labels, 268
    data labels, 269, 272
    default, 264
    formatting, 270–272
    gridlines, 269
    legend, 268
    marker style, 271–272
    menu, 262
    open, 264
    pie, 268
    plot area, 271
    purposes, 266
    steps in creating, 263
    title, 268
    Type button, 265
    types, 265, 266–268
Check box, 23, 24
Chevrons, 304
Circle, 273
Click, 4
Clip art, 241
    editing, 277–279

Clipboard, 19, 20, 21, 92, 241, 381
Close button, 11, 15, 39, 87, 288
Collapse, 328
Color
    font, 151
    highlight, 157
    scheme, 27
Column(s), 233–241
    button, 235
    chart, 266
    insert, 212, 214
    line between, 236
    marker, 215, 216,
            235–236, 238
    width, 235
        default, 209
        tables, 215–217
        unequal, 236
COM1:, 128
Command button, 22, 23
Commands, 39
Commands and Settings button,
    55, 90
Compact disc, 79
Condense, font, 152
Conditional text, 309
Contents, 49
Context-sensitive, 50
Ctrl key, 59, 64–65, 83, 94, 273
Control Panel, 22–27
Copy, 19–21, 91–94, 241
    buttons, 359
    formatting, 155, 181
Create Subdocument button, 337
Criteria, 307
Crop, 244, 246
Cross reference, 325
Crosshatched border
    chart, 264
    frame, 247, 250
    text box, 273
Cursor, 3, 19, 41, 55, 60, 62, 273
Customize
    AutoCorrect, 109–110
    desktop, 25
    keyboard, 362–363
    menu, 363–365
    mouse, 22
    toolbar, 358–362
Cut, 19, 20, 91–94, 241

D

Data
    form, 301–302
    label, 269, 272
    source document, 300,
        301–303
Data | Exclude Row/Col, 263
Database toolbar, 302, 310
Datasheet, 262, 263–265
Date, 286, 287
Decimal tab, 169, 218
Decrease Indent button, 173
Default
    column width, tables, 209
    font, 145
    margins, 190
    tab, 169, 172
Delete, 66
Demote, 327–328
Descender, 149
Descending sort, 223
Desktop, 6
    customizing, 25–30
Detail button, 89, 90
Dialog box, 19, 40, 50
Dictionary, 108
Different first page header, 290
Different odd and even header,
    287, 292
Direct formatting, 143
Disk, 78
    backup, 98–101
    drive, 80
    floppy, 79
    formatting, 80, 81
    hard, 79
    high-density, 79
    low-density, 79
    system, 81
Docked, 358
Document, 84
    active, 84
    formatting, 190–197
    open, 84
    views, 195–201
DOS, 3, 21
Dot-matrix printer, 127, 313
Double-click, 4, 8–9, 23
Drag, 4, 5

Drag and drop, 21, 94, 212, 215,
    225, 380
Draw, 272–279
Drawing
    button, 272–273
    object, 272–273
    toolbar, 241, 273, 277
Drop caps, 248–250
Drop-down list, 24, 26
Drop-down menu, 40, 47

E

Edit | Clear, 67
Edit | Copy, 93, 94, 380
Edit | Cut, 93–94
Edit | Paste, 93, 94, 213, 380
Edit | Paste Cells, 213
Edit | Paste Special, 380–382
Edit pictures, 277–279
Edit | Replace, 120
Edit | Select All, 43, 65, 169
Edit text, 46–47, 61–63, 176
Edit | Undo, 63, 67
Ellipse button, 274
Ellipses, 19, 40, 97
Embedding, 277, 379, 382
Emoticon, 157
Encapsulated PostScript files, 243
End key, 59
Endnote, 338
Enter character. See Paragraph
            symbol
Enter key, 42, 55, 57
Envelopes
    button, 360
    merging, 300, 313–314
EPS files, 243
Esc key, 40
Excel, 89, 300, 380–383
Expand
    font, 152
    outline, 328
Explode, pie slice, 272
Explorer, 29, 88, 99
Exit, 30
Extension, 68

F

F1 key, 48
F9 key, 344
Alt F9 key, 286, 347
Field, 301, 302
    code, 286, 287, 347
    index entry code, 344
File, 16
    backup, 98–101
    menu, 89
    name, 68
    recently used, 90
    search for, 92–93
File | Close, 48, 87–88
File | Copy Disk, 99, 101
File | Format, 81
File | New, 83–87
File | Open, 88–91
File | Page Setup, 190, 192, 194, 200, 239, 304
File | Print, 128, 131, 136
File | Print Preview, 48, 132
File | Properties, 130
File | Save, 67–69
File | Save All, 359
File | Save As, 97, 99
File | Send To, 99
Fill, 274
Fill Color button, 275
Filter, 307
Flip buttons, 278
Floating toolbar, 358
Floppy disk, 68, 79
Folder, 16, 90
    new, 29
Font, 143–147
    color, 151
    default, 145
    hidden, 151
    nonproportional, 144
    proportional, 144
    sans serif, 144
    serif, 144
    size, 44
    strikethrough, 151
    TrueType, 145
Footer, 273, 285–295, 311
    first page, 290
    long text in, 288
    multiple sections, 293
    odd and even pages, 292
    pane, 338, 339
    placement of, 288
Footnote, 325, 338–343
    creating 338
    deleting, 341
    editing, 341–342
    moving, 342
    reference mark, 325, 338, 342
Form letters, 300. See also Mail merge
Format
    characters, 143–154
    disks, 80
    headings, 327, 335
    reveal, 181
Format | Borders and Shading, 220
Format | Bullets and Numbering, 178
Format Callout button, 274
Format | Change Case, 152–153
Format | Chart Type, 265
Format | Column Group, 266, 267
Format | Columns, 236, 239
Format | Drawing Object, 275
Format | Drop Cap, 249–250
Format | Font, 147–148, 151–152, 211, 336
Format | Frame, 247, 336
Format Painter button, 155
Format | Paragraph, 172, 176, 217, 336
Format | Picture, 244, 246
Format | Pie Group, 268
Format | Style, 182–183, 335
Format | Style Gallery, 183
Format | Tabs, 171, 336
Formatting, 42–44
    charts, 270–272
    copying, 181
    direct, 143
    documents, 190–197
    Graph toolbar, 271
    indirect, 143
    paragraph, 164–181
    toolbar, 43, 143, 146, 157, 164, 182
Frame, 247, 250, 273

Full Screen
    button, 198
    view, 198

G

Games, 17, 29
Getting Help. See Help
Global move, 60
Grammar checker, 116–118
Graph, 262–272. See also Chart
Graphical user interface, 2, 3
Gridline, 209, 215, 216, 220, 267, 269, 381
Group button, 278
Gutter, 190

H

Handles, sizing. See Sizing handles
Hanging indent, 173
Hard disk, 79
Hard page break, 176
Header, 194–197, 273, 285–295, 311
    and Footer toolbar, 287
    area, 287, 289
    different odd and even, 287, 292
    first page, 290
    long text in, 288
    multiple sections, 293
    odd and even pages, 287, 292
    placement of, 288
    row, 301, 302
    same as previous, 294
Heading, outline, 346
Help, 48–51
    Answer Wizard, 49
    button, 48, 181
    Contents, 49
    context-sensitive, 50
    dialog box, 50
    Index, 49
Hidden font, 151
High-density, 79
Highlight, 5, 43, 143
    button, 157

Highlighter, 157
Home key, 59
Hourglass, 5

I

I-beam, 56, 133
Icon, shortcut, 28–30
IF fields, 309
Import, 242
Increase Indent button, 173
Indentation, 172–175, 218
    markers, 172, 238
Index, 49, 325, 344–346
Indirect formatting, 143
Inkjet printer, 127
In-place activation, 381
Insert Address button, 383
Insert | Break, 176, 241
Insert | Data Labels, 270
Insert | Date and Time, 304
Insert | Footnote, 339
Insert | Frame, 247
Insert | Index and Tables, 344, 346
Ins key, 62
Insert Microsoft Excel Worksheet
    button, 380
Insert mode, 62
Insert | Object, 249, 250, 262,
    380–383
Insert | Page Numbers, 194–195,
    286, 287, 288
Insert | Picture, 45, 241
Insert | Symbol, 155–156, 249
Italic button, 44, 149
Italics, 149

J

Junk mail. *See* Mail merge
Justified alignment, 165

K

Keep with Next, 176, 312
Kerning, 152

L

Labels, mailing, 314
Landscape orientation, 193
Laser printer, 127, 313
Leader, 171
Leading, 166
Left alignment, 165, 217
Left-handed, mouse, 23
Legend, 263, 267, 269
Level number, 327
Line, 274
    between columns, 236
    button, 275
    chart, 266, 268
    spacing, 166–168, 246
    style, 274
Line Style button, 275
Linking, 277, 301, 379, 382
List box, 24
List button, 89, 90
Low-density disk, 79
LPT1:, 128

M

Macro, 354
    assign to button, 360–362
    assign to menu, 363
    assign to shortcut key,
        362–363
    recording, 355–356
    running, 357, 365
Macro Record toolbar, 356
Magnifier, 133
Mail merge, 299–315
    button, 307
    data source document, 300,
        301–303
    Helper, 300
    main document, 300,
        304–306
    printing, 307, 311

required files, 300
    steps in, 300
    toolbar, 304
Mail Merge Main Document
    button, 303
Mailing labels, 300
    merging, 313–314
Main document, 300
Manage Fields button, 310
Margins, 190–192, 195–196, 198,
    209, 237, 288
    default, 190
    mirror, 191
Markers
    indent, 172
    line chart, 271–272
Masthead, 239
Master document, 294, 325, 336
    advantages of, 336
    toolbar, 336
    view, 336–338, 346
Maximize, 10, 12
    button, 39
Menu, 4, 7–8, 262, 355, 381
    bar, 10, 39, 381
    customize, 363–365
    drop–down, 40, 47
    selections, 19, 363
    WordArt, 249
Merge fields, 304
Merge to New Document button,
    307
Merge to Printer button, 307
Merging
    certain records, 307–308
    envelopes, 313–314
    mailing labels, 313–314
    See also Mail merge
Metafiles, 242
Minimize, 10, 12
    button, 39
Mirror margins, 191, 194, 198
Mouse, 4–5, 17
    customizing, 22
    left–handed, 23
    pointer, 4, 11, 23, 50, 55, 65,
        96, 132, 212, 217,
        246, 355
    movements, 60

Move,
   buttons, 359
   data, 19–21
   See also Drag and drop
Movement keys, 60
Multifunction printer, 128
Multitasking, 2, 15
Multiple Pages button, 133–134
My Briefcase, 6
My Computer, 6, 29, 81, 88, 92,
      99, 101

N

Network, 128
Network Neighborhood, 6
Newsletter Wizard, 233
Next Page button, 133, 196
NLQ, 127
Nonprinting characters, 181
Nonproportional font, 144
Normal template, 359
Normal view, 195, 199, 235, 240,
      245, 247, 277, 338
Normal View button, 41, 195
Numbering
   button, 178
   footnotes, 339
   pages, 194, 286, 287, 326
   paragraphs, 178–181
NumLock key, 62

O

Odd page header, 287
Object linking and embedding,
      379
Office, 379
   shortcut bar, 86, 88, 89
OLE, 379
100% stacked column chart, 266
One Page button, 133–134
Open
   button, 88
   chart, 264
   dialog box, 90
   document, 84
   list box, 23, 24

recently used files, 90
Operating system, 3
Option button, 22, 23
Orientation
   page, 193
   text, 271
OS/2, 3
Outline, 326–336, 383
   advantages of, 326–327
   collapse, 328
   creating, 327–331
   demote, 327–328
   expand, 328
   format headings, 335
   heading levels, 333–334
   headings, 327, 346
   how to write, 328
   level number, 327
   modifying, 332–334
   promote, 327–328
   toolbar, 327, 336
   View button, 195, 327
   view, 327, 346
Overtype mode, 62
OVR, 62

P

Page break, 312
   before a paragraph, 176
   hard, 176
   soft, 175
PgDn key, 58
Page Layout view, 195, 199, 235,
      236, 238, 250, 273
   button, 195
   footnotes in, 343
   header and footer in, 288, 289
Page numbering, 194, 286, 287,
      326, 346
   formatting, 288
Page Setup button, 287
Page Setup dialog box, 288
PgUp key, 58
Paper
   orientation, 192–193
   size, 192
   source, 194

Paragraph, 246
   alignment, 165
   centered, 165
   indentation, 172–177
   justified, 165
   left-aligned, 165
   right-aligned, 165
   symbol, 181
Parallel port, 128
Paste, 21, 241
   button, 380
   link, 381
Path, 92
Pattern button, 271
Pattern, desktop, 25–26
Peripheral device, 128
Picture, 44–45, 233, 241–250
   editing, 277–279
   from text, 248–250
   modifying, 244–246
   toolbar, 277–278
Pie chart, 266, 268
   arranging slices, 268
   explode slice, 272
Pixel, 27
Placeholders, 242
   positioning, 246
   scaling, 244–245
   sizing, 244–245
Plot area, 267, 271
Point
   amount of line spacing, 166
   size of font, 143–147
   with mouse, 4
Pointer, mouse, 23, 355
Port, 128, 130
   parallel, 128
   serial, 128
Portrait orientation, 193
Positioning pictures, 246
Postal bar code, 314
PowerPoint, 89, 383
Preview
   button (Open dialog box), 89,
      90, 91, 243
   fonts, 148
   toolbar, 133
   See also Print Preview
Previous Page button, 133, 196

Price list, 311
Print
    button, 134, 136
    envelopes, 137
    merge documents, 307
    queue, 135–136
Print Preview, 46, 48, 132–134,
        160, 242
    button, 46, 197
    toolbar, 195
Printer, 127–128, 135, 194, 313
    dot-matrix, 127, 313
    inkjet, 127
    laser, 127, 313
    multifunction, 127
    port, 128, 130
    types, 127
    window, 129–130, 135
Printing, 134–137
    troubleshooting, 136
Programming, 354
Proofread, 57, 58, 115
Promote, 327–328
Properties, 22
    display, 25
    button, 89, 90
Proportional font, 144
Pull quote, 247, 273

Q

Query, 307, 309
Quotation marks, 110

R

RAM, 67
Readability, 146, 153, 168, 173,
        184, 234
    fonts, 146
    tables, 221
    paragraph, 168
    statistics, 118
Recently used files, 90
REC, 355
Record, 301
    numbers, 302
    selection buttons, 306–307

Recording macros, 355–356
Rectangle button, 274
Recycle Bin, 6, 28, 29
Redo button, 66
Remove Subdocument button,
        337
Replace, 63
Reset Picture Boundary button,
        278
Reset toolbars, 359
Restore, 10, 12
Reveal format, 181
Reverse text, 177, 221
Right alignment, 165
Right tab, 287
Right-click, 4, 5, 29
Row height, 219–220
Rule. See Border
Ruler, 39, 40, 42, 164, 169,
        196–197, 198–199, 238
    measurements, 175, 196–197
    vertical, 195–196
Run-around text, 241

S

Same as Previous, 294
Sample label, 314
Sans serif font, 144
Save
    automatic, 97–98
    button, 68
    document, 67–69, 87
    master document, 336
Scaling, 244–245
Scanner, 241
Scatter chart, 266
Schedule+, 301
Screen saver, 26
Scroll bars, 11, 60
Scroll box, 60
Scrolling, 60, 242
Search
    for files, 92–93
    for text, 120
Search and Replace, 120–121
Section, 239
    break, 239, 293, 337

Select, 7
    All, 43
    text, 43, 63–66
Select Drawing Object button, 274
Send to Back button, 278
Serial port, 128
Serif font, 144
Shading, 177–178, 220, 221
Shapes. See Drawing objects;
        WordArt
Sharing data, 18–21
Shift key, 63–64, 217, 244, 273
Shortcut
    bar, Office, 86, 89
    desktop, 28–30
    icon, 28–30
    key, 83, 94, 143, 150, 154, 165,
        167, 173, 174, 340,
        344, 347, 362–363
    menu, 5, 8, 13, 14–15, 92,
        93–94, 99, 100, 143,
        164, 216, 224, 286
Show Previous button, 291
Show/Hide ¶ button, 57, 181,
        209, 239, 312
Show/Hide Document Text
        button, 288
Shrink to Fit button, 134
Shut Down, 16, 30
Sizing
    handles, 244, 265, 271, 272,
        277
    pictures, 244–245
Small capitals, 151
Soft page break, 175
Sorting, 222
Sort Ascending button, 303
Spacebar, 110
Spacing
    character, 152
    line, 166–168
Special characters, 155–156
Spelling checker, 107, 112–115, 117
    limitations, 115
    suggestions, 114
Spin box, 26, 27
Square, 273
Stacked column chart, 266, 267
Standard toolbar, 380, 383

Start
    button, 15, 17, 22, 91, 222
    menu, 15–16, 28, 99, 129, 222
Statistics, 121
Status bar, 39, 109, 133, 135, 355
Strikethrough, 151
Style, 182, 335
Subdocument, 294, 325, 336
Subscript, 151–152
Suggestions, 114
Superscript, 151–152
Switch Between Header and
        Footer button, 287
Symbol, font, 148, 179
System disk, 81

T

Tab, 168–172, 218, 287
    center, 169, 287
    decimal, 169
    dialog box, 22, 23
    inserting, 169
    leader, 171
    left, 169
    right, 169
Tab Alignment button, 169, 170,
        218
[Tab] key, 168–171, 210, 218, 301
Table, 193, 207, 233, 246, 301, 314,
        380, 383
    button, 208, 214
    centering, 219
    column width, 215–217
    creating, 208–209
    Wizard, 208
Table | Cell Height and Width,
        216, 219
Table of contents, 325, 346–347
Table | Delete, 211, 212, 213
Table | Formula, 222
Table | Gridlines, 209
Table | Insert, 208, 211
Table | Merge Cells, 224
Table | Select, 212
Table | Sort, 223
Table | Split Cells, 224

Table | Table AutoFormat, 220
Taskbar, 6, 9, 16–17
    buttons, 11, 12–13
Template, 84
Text
    as pictures, 248–250
    box, 273–274, 276–277
    flow, 175–177, 246–247, 312
    moving, 332
    orientation, 271
    run-around, 241
    search for files with, 92–93
Thesaurus, 118–119
3.5-inch disk, 79
3-D chart types, 265
Thumbnail, 243
TIFF files, 243
Tile, window, 13
Time, 286, 287
Tip Wizard, 51
Tip Wizard button, 51
Title bar, 9, 39, 68
Title, chart, 268
Toggle, 167
    case, 153
    field codes, 224, 286, 347
Toolbar, 39, 195, 262, 355, 381
    Borders, 177
    custom, 358–362
    Database, 302
    docked, 358
    Drawing, 241, 273, 277
    floating, 358
    Formatting, 43, 146, 164, 178
    Graph, 270–271
    Header and Footer, 287
    Macro Record, 356
    Mail Merge, 304
    Master Document, 336
    moving, 358, 365
    Outline, 327, 336
    Picture, 277–278
    Preview, 133
    resetting, 359
    Standard, 383
    Tip Wizard, 51
    Word for Windows 2.0, 360
    WordArt, 249

Tools | AutoCorrect, 111, 157
Tools | Customize, 360

Tools | Envelopes and Labels, 137
Tools | Grammar, 117
Tools | Macro, 355, 357
Tools | Mail Merge, 299
Tools | Options, 98, 108, 114,
        116–117, 195, 242
Tools | Spelling, 112
Tools | Thesaurus, 119
Tools | Word Count, 121
ToolTips, 7, 43
Triangles. *See* Indentation
        markers
TrueType font, 145
Truncate, 68
2-D chart types, 265

U

Underline, 149
Underline button, 149
Undo button, 63, 66
UNIX, 3
Up One Level button, 89, 91
User interface, 3

V

View, 40, 195–199
    Master Document, 336–338
    Normal, 41, 199, 235, 240, 247
    Page Layout, 235, 236, 238,
        250
    field codes, 381
    Full Screen, 198
    Zoom, 199
View Datasheet button, 263
View Merged Data button, 306
View Source button, 302, 310
View | Footnotes, 341
View | Header and Footer, 286
View | Outline, 327
View | Toolbars, 271

W

Wallpaper, 25–26
Watermark, 273
Wavy red underline. *See*
         Automatic Spell
         Checking
White space, 171, 244
Widow/Orphan, 176
Window, 8, 9–11, 58
    active, 9, 13–14
    border, 10
    cascade, 13
    closing, 11
    elements, 9–11
    maximize, 10, 12

menu, 84–85
minimize, 10, 12
moving, 9
open, 15
properties, 22
restore, 10, 12
sizing, 10
tile, 13
Window | Arrange All, 84, 96
Windows 3.1, 3, 15, 21
Windows 95, 2–31
    advantages of, 2
Windows NT, 3
Wingdings font, 156, 179, 249
Wizard, 84, 85–86, 208, 233
Word Count, 121

Word documents, 89, 91
    screen, 39
    wrap, 55, 210, 216
Word for Windows 2.0 toolbar,
         360
WordArt, 248–250
WordBasic, 357
WordPad, 17, 20
Work area, 41
Write-protect, 80
WYSIWYG, 145, 147

Z

Zoom Control box, 198, 247

Quick Reference

Selected Shortcut Keys

COMMANDS

Ctrl N	File	New
Ctrl O	File	Open
Ctrl S	File	Save
Ctrl P	File	Print
Ctrl Z	Edit	Undo
Ctrl Y	Edit	Repeat
Ctrl X	Edit	Cut
Ctrl C	Edit	Copy
Ctrl V	Edit	Paste
Ctrl A	Edit	Select All

Ctrl F	Edit	Find
Ctrl H	Edit	Replace
Ctrl G	Edit	Go To
F1	Help
F4	Edit	Repeat
F5	Edit	Go To
F7	Tools	Spelling
F9	Update fields
Alt Shift X	Insert index entry

FORMATS

Ctrl B	Bold
Ctrl I	Italic
Ctrl U	Underline
Ctrl L	Left-align
Ctrl E	Center-align
Ctrl R	Right-align
Ctrl J	Justify
Ctrl 1 *	Single-space
Ctrl 2 *	Double-space
Ctrl 5 *	Space-and-a-half
Ctrl 0 *	Add/Remove blank line space preceding
Ctrl M	Increase left indent
Ctrl Shift M	Decrease left indent
Ctrl T	Increase hanging indent
Ctrl Shift T	Decrease hanging indent

Ctrl Spacebar	Remove font formats
Ctrl Q	Remove paragraph formats
Ctrl Shift F	Change font
Ctrl Shift P	Change point size
Ctrl Shift >	Increase font to next size larger
Ctrl Shift <	Decrease font to next size smaller
Ctrl]	Increase font size by 1 point
Ctrl [	Decrease font size by 1 point
Ctrl Shift A	All capitals
Ctrl Shift W	Underline words
Ctrl Shift D	Double-underline
Ctrl Shift H	Hidden text
Ctrl Shift K	Small capitals
Ctrl =	Subscript
Ctrl Shift =	Superscript

* Use keyboard number, not keypad number.

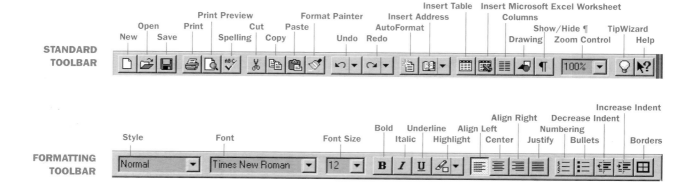

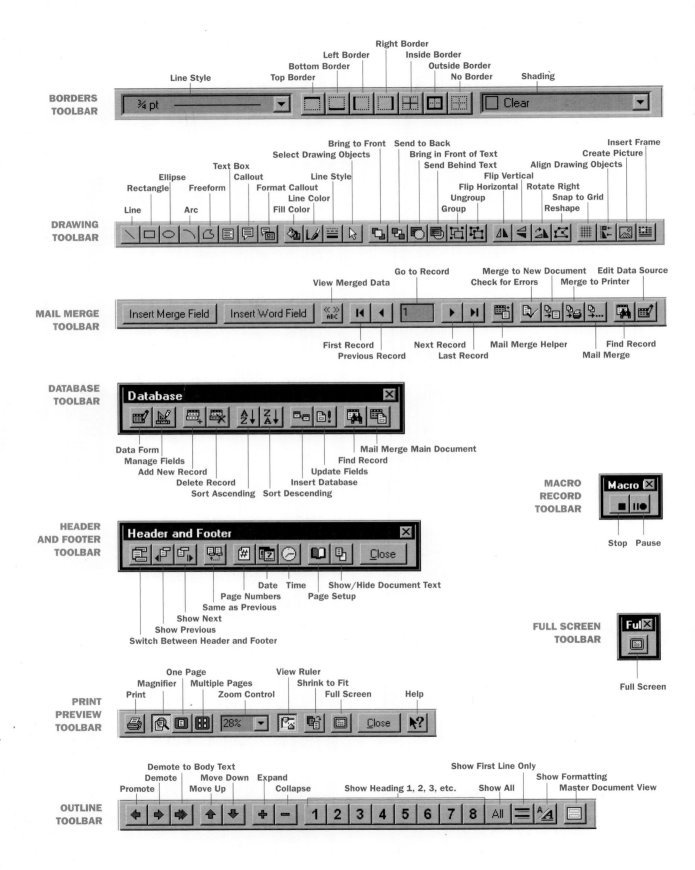

BORDERS TOOLBAR

Line Style · Top Border · Bottom Border · Left Border · Right Border · Inside Border · Outside Border · No Border · Shading

DRAWING TOOLBAR

Line · Rectangle · Ellipse · Arc · Freeform · Text Box · Callout · Format Callout · Fill Color · Line Color · Line Style · Select Drawing Objects · Bring to Front · Send to Back · Bring in Front of Text · Send Behind Text · Group · Ungroup · Flip Horizontal · Flip Vertical · Rotate Right · Reshape · Snap to Grid · Align Drawing Objects · Insert Frame · Create Picture

MAIL MERGE TOOLBAR

Insert Merge Field · Insert Word Field · View Merged Data · First Record · Previous Record · Go to Record · Next Record · Last Record · Check for Errors · Merge to New Document · Mail Merge Helper · Merge to Printer · Mail Merge · Find Record · Edit Data Source

DATABASE TOOLBAR

Database

Data Form · Manage Fields · Add New Record · Delete Record · Sort Ascending · Sort Descending · Insert Database · Update Fields · Find Record · Mail Merge Main Document

MACRO RECORD TOOLBAR

Macro · Stop · Pause

HEADER AND FOOTER TOOLBAR

Header and Footer · Close

Switch Between Header and Footer · Show Previous · Show Next · Same as Previous · Page Numbers · Date · Time · Page Setup · Show/Hide Document Text

FULL SCREEN TOOLBAR

Full · Full Screen

PRINT PREVIEW TOOLBAR

Print · Magnifier · One Page · Multiple Pages · Zoom Control · 28% · View Ruler · Shrink to Fit · Full Screen · Close · Help

OUTLINE TOOLBAR

Promote · Demote · Demote to Body Text · Move Up · Move Down · Expand · Collapse · Show Heading 1, 2, 3, etc. · 1 2 3 4 5 6 7 8 · All · Show All · Show First Line Only · Show Formatting · Master Document View